Lecture Notes in Computer

Edited by G. Goos, J. Hartmanis, an

Springer
Berlin
Heidelberg
New York
Barcelona
Hong Kong
London
Milan
Paris
Tokyo

Akinori Yonezawa   Satoshi Matsuoka (Eds.)

Metalevel Architectures and Separation of Crosscutting Concerns

Third International Conference, REFLECTION 2001
Kyoto, Japan, September 25-28, 2001
Proceedings

Springer

Series Editors

Gerhard Goos, Karlsruhe University, Germany
Juris Hartmanis, Cornell University, NY, USA
Jan van Leeuwen, Utrecht University, The Netherlands

Volume Editors

Akinori Yonezawa
University of Tokyo, Faculty of Information Science and Technology
Department of Computer Science
7-3-1 Hongo, Bunkyo-ku, Tokyo 113-0033, Japan
E-mail: yonezawa@is.s.u-tokyo.ac.jp
Satoshi Matsuoka
Tokyo Institute of Technology, Global Scientific Information and Computing Center
Department of Mathematical and Computing Sciences
2-12-1 Oo-okayama, Meguro-ku, Tokyo 152-8552, Japan
E-mail: matsu@acm.org, matsu@is.titech.ac.jp

Cataloging-in-Publication Data applied for

Die Deutsche Bibliothek - CIP-Einheitsaufnahme

Metalevel architectures and separation of crosscutting concerns : third
international conference ; reflection 2001 ; Kyoto, Japan, September 25 -
28, 2001, proceedings / Akinori Yonezawa ; Satoshi Matsuoka (ed.). - Berlin ;
Heidelberg ; New York ; Barcelona ; Hong Kong ; London ; Milan ; Paris ;
Tokyo : Springer, 2001
   (Lecture notes in computer science ; Vol. 2192)
   ISBN 3-540-42618-3

CR Subject Classification (1998): D.3, D.4, D.2, C.2.4, F.3, D.1

ISSN 0302-9743
ISBN 3-540-42618-3 Springer-Verlag Berlin Heidelberg New York

Springer-Verlag Berlin Heidelberg New York
a member of BertelsmannSpringer Science+Business Media GmbH

http://www.springer.de

' Springer-Verlag Berlin Heidelberg 2001
Printed in Germany

Typesetting: Camera-ready by author, data conversion by Steingr ber Satztechnik GmbH, Heidelberg
Printed on acid-free paper   SPIN: 10840614   06/3142   5 4 3 2 1 0

Preface

This volume constitutes the proceedings of REFLECTION 2001, the Third International Conference on Metalevel Architectures and Separation of Crosscutting Concerns, which was held in Kyoto, September 25-28, 2001.

Metalevel architectures and reflection have drawn the attention of researchers and practitioners throughout computer science. Reflective and metalevel techniques are being used to address real-world problems in such areas as: programming languages, operating systems, databases, distributed computing, expert systems and web computing.

Separation of concerns has been a guiding principle of software engineering for nearly 30 years, but its known benefits are seldom fully achieved in practice. This is primarily because traditional mechanisms are not powerful enough to handle many kinds of concerns that occur in practice. Over the last 10 years, to overcome the limitations of traditional frameworks, many researchers, including several from the reflection community, have proposed new approaches.

For the first time, papers on advanced approaches to separation of concerns were explicitly solicited. Following the success of previous conferences such as IMSA'92 in Tokyo, Reflection'96 in San Francisco, and Reflection'99 in Saint Malo, we hope that the conference provided an excellent forum for researchers with a broad range of interests in metalevel architectures, reflective techniques, and separation of concerns in general.

Given such a background in paper solicitation, 44 papers were submitted from throughout the world. There was a good mixture of papers on reflection, papers on SOC issues, and those at the crossroads of the two. Through a strict review process including a program committee meeting (of nearly 20 attendees) held in Paris in early May, 11 long papers and 7 short papers were accepted. In order to spur discussion in a technically tight community, the program committee also elected to solicit posters, of which 8 were accepted and whose abstracts are being presented in the proceedings as well.

Kyoto is well-known as an ancient capital in Japan, with numerous historical landmarks. We hope that the concentrated four-day efforts there also played a decisive role in establishing a good intermixture of the reflection and SOC communities, which will lead to the construcion of more effective software frameworks.

We would like to acknowledge the efforts of the organizing committee, the program committee, and especially Hirotaka Ogawa who carried out more than several administrative tasks including the maintenance of the conference web site and the overview of the electriconic paper submission system. We would also like to thank the technical contributors to the conference without whom the conference would not have happened.

July 2001   Akinori Yonezawa
                                                                   Satoshi Matsuoka

Organization

REFLECTION 2001 was organized by the following committees under the auspices of AITO (Association Internationale pour les Technologies Objets).

Organizing Committee

Conference Chair: Satoshi Matsuoka (TITECH)
Program Chair: Akinori Yonezawa (U. Tokyo)
Coordinator, America: Gregor Kiczales (U. British Columbia)
Coordinator, Asia: Shigeru Chiba (TITECH)
Coordinators, Europe: Pierre Cointe (École des Mines de Nantes),
                      Jacques Malenfant (IRISA & U. de Bretagne sud)
Local Arrangements: Hirotaka Ogawa (TITECH)

Program Committee

Mehmet Aksit (U. Twente)
Gordon Blair (Lancaster U.)
Gilad Bracha (Sun Microsystems)
Jean-Pierre Briot (LIP6)
Vinny Cahill (Trinity College)
Roy Campbell (UIUC)
Walter Cazzola (U. Genova)
Jean-Charles Fabre (Laas)
Shigeru Chiba (TITECH)
Pierre Cointe (École des Mines de Nantes)
Charles Consel (U. Bordeaux)
Dan Friedman (Indiana U.)
Andrew Grimshaw (U. Virginia)
William Griswold (UCSD)
Yuuji Ichisugi (ETL)
Yutaka Ishikawa (RWCP)
Gregor Kiczales (U. British Columbia)
Karl Lieberherr (Northeastern U.)
Jacques Malenfant (IRISA & U. de Bretagne sud)
Hidehiko Masuhara (U. Tokyo)
Mira Mezini (Darmstadt U. Tech)
Harold Ossher (IBM T.J. Watson)
Robert Stroud (U. Newcastle)
Carolyn Talcott (Stanford U.)
Akinori Yonezawa, Chair (U. Tokyo)

Sponsoring Institutions

 Association Internationale pour les Technolo-
gies Objets (AITO)

 Japan Society for Software Science and Tech-
nology (JSSST)

Cooperating Institutions

 ACM SIGSOFT

Information Processing Society of Japan
(IPSJ) SIGSE

Table of Contents

Testing and Verification of Reflective and SOC Systems

Foundations of Reflection and Separations of Concerns

Software Methodologies for Separation of Concerns

Poster Session

JAC: A Flexible Solution for Aspect-Oriented Programming in Java

Renaud Pawlak[1], Lionel Seinturier[2], Laurence Duchien[1], and Gérard Florin[1]

[1] CNAM, Lab. CEDRIC, 292 rue Saint-Martin, F-75141 Paris cedex 03, France
{pawlak, duchien, florin}@cnam.fr
[2] Univ. Paris 6, Lab. LIP6, 4 place Jussieu, F-75252 Paris cedex 05, France
Lionel.Seinturier@lip6.fr

Abstract. This paper presents JAC (Java Aspect Components), a framework for aspect-oriented programming in Java. Unlike languages such as AspectJ which are mostly class-based, JAC is object-based and does not require any language extensions to Java. It uses the Javassist class load-time MOP. An aspect program in JAC is a set of aspect objects that can be dynamically deployed and undeployed on top of running application objects. Aspect objects may define three kinds of aspect methods: wrapping methods (that wrap application methods and provide the ability to run code before and after the wrapped methods), role methods (that add new functionalities to application objects), and exception handlers. The aspects composition issue is handled through a well-defined wrapping controller that specifies for each wrapped object at wrap-time, runtime or both, the execution order of aspect objects.

1 Introduction

Separation of concerns in software engineering has always been a very natural means to handle complexity of software developments [15]. However, modularizing concerns can be a very tricky task for the programmer and rise some issues such as performance, crosscutting, or redesigning when the software is used in a context that is quite different from the overseen one. By handling crosscutting within the language or system, the recent approach of Aspect-Oriented Programming (AOP) [9] seems to be a very promising way for helping developers to handle separation of concerns and to overcome the drawbacks of traditional design approaches.

However, if AOP introduces a new programming paradigm that complements existing ones, it is clear that it brings a new bunch of difficult problems. The composition of an aspect to an application (the aspect is said to be woven) is one of them. Several approaches exist: AspectJ [8] which is a general language for AOP, the composition filter object model [1] where aspects are defined as filters applied upon application objects, aspectual components [10] that define patterns of interaction with roles and connectors to map these roles to application objects, subject-oriented programming [6][13] which decomposes an application into subjects and provides composition rules to recompose them, domain specific

A. Yonezawa and S. Matsuoka (Eds.): REFLECTION 2001, LNCS 2192, pp. 1–24, 2001.

languages to define crosscutting concerns based on patterns of events [5]. We review some of them in the related works section of this paper.

Nevertheless, when several aspects have to be composed to an application, a given aspect not only crosscuts the application, but may also crosscut others aspects. Indeed, aspects may not be orthogonal to each others. We call this issue the *inter-aspects composition* aspect. Some solutions exist, e.g. precedence rules in AspectJ [8] or composed connectors in aspectual components [10] (see section 5 for a discussion of these features), but as far as we know, this is still an open issue for the AOP community. Most of the time aspect programmers still have to invent some *ad hoc* means to handle it. This problem deeply affects the potential power of AOP by making aspects less re-usable that they should be and dramatically limits the simplicity of using a set of aspects.

In this paper, we present a framework called JAC (for Java Aspect Components) [7] that is a proposal to cleanly deal with *inter-aspects composition* within an aspect-oriented application, making by this way aspects more reusable. JAC is the continuation of A-TOS [17], a previous work developed in Tcl. The paper is structured as follows. First, we point out that one of the main problem in AOP is to be able to easily compose several aspects coming from different sources, during the development process, and while the application is running. In section 3, we present JAC and the way we deal with the *inter-aspects composition* issue at weave-time and at runtime. Section 4 discusses JAC performances. We compare JAC with other related works in section 5. Finally, section 6 concludes this paper and presents our future works.

2   Important Issues in AOP

When programming aspects with an aspect-oriented language, framework, or system (AOS) the main problems programmers have to face is to handle the consistent composition of aspects. In a general development process, aspects can be programmed by different programmers and can conflict if nothing is done to avoid it. We call this problem the *inter-aspects composition* issue [16]. This issue can occur at weave-time but also at runtime and can be split in several sub-problems of different natures. The following list shortly depicts some of the most currently encountered. Most of them remain open issues that are discussed in the AOP community. We don't assume an AOS to handle them automatically. We rather think that a neatly designed AOS should provide solutions (e.g. API, language constructs, ...) to support programmers in addressing them.

2.1   Weave-Time Issues

The weave-time issues occur when the weaver weaves the aspects (or a particular aspect) into the base program. Depending on the AOS, weaving can be at compile-time or at runtime (when an aspect is dynamically added or removed from the application). We name the weave-time issues *WIn* to be able to refer them later.

Checking for aspect compatibility with the application (WI1): assuming that we know that our application should never contain a given aspect, the underlying AOS should be able to check its type (assuming the aspect programmer provides a formal or semi-formal type system) and refuse to weave it. For instance, if the base program already implements an authentication policy (by choice or because you add some aspect to an existing application), then you should add a composition constraint that prevents an authentication aspect to be woven.

Checking for inter-aspect compatibility (WI2): if we know that two aspects are incompatible (e.g. some redundancy and fault tolerance algorithms) the program can refuse to weave one aspect if the other is already woven.

Checking for inter-aspect dependence (WI3): if an aspect is woven and needs another aspect (e.g. a binding aspect may need a naming aspect), the AOS should be able to automatically weave the needed one (or report an error).

Checking for aspect redundancy (WI4): if we know that two aspects implement the same concern in two different ways (e.g. two different authentication algorithms or two different persistence implementations), then the program can refuse to weave one of both aspects or unweave the previous one to replace it by the new one.

Ordering the aspects at weave-time (WI5): regarding a join point (a location in the base program where a set of aspects can intercess their behaviors), some aspects must always be called before others (e.g. authentication) and some must always be called after others (e.g. persistence). The AOS should place the different aspects so that they are correctly ordered and so that the aspect programmer does not care anymore about the others.

2.2   A Solution for Weave-Time Issues

For all the above described issues, the AOS must be able to define some checking and/or ordering rules. This code can be seen as an aspect that rules how aspects behave regarding each others at weave-time. In several works, this aspect has been called a composition aspect. At weave-time, the weaver will refer the composition aspect to decide how to weave an aspect to an application program.

2.3   Runtime Issues

By runtime issues, we mean the issues that may occur when the aspect is already woven, and that can arise when the execution of a join-point that is intercessed by the aspect occurs. In some cases, the set of advices that is defined in the aspects for a given join-point may change regarding the context. Since it depends on the execution context, the weave-time composition aspect can hardly deal with the runtime issues. Using a few examples, we will show that the AOS can take advantage of using a runtime composition aspect to deal with these issues. We name the runtime issues *RIn* to be able to refer them later.

Checking for intra-aspect consistency (RI1): Some aspects need to perform context-dependent tests to remain semantically consistent. Let take the example of a counting aspect, that counts the number of calls to a given method. The following pseudo code is inspired from the AspectJ [8] syntax. It increments the *counter* variable before each execution of method *A.m1*.

```
aspect CountingAspect {
    private int counter;
    joinpoint jp1 = ( class A, method m1 );
    before jp1 advice1 {
        counter++;
    }
}
```

Now imagine that method *m2* calls *m1* 10 times. The aspect programmer (that is aware of the base program code) can optimize the application by adding another *before* advice for method *m2*.

```
aspect WrongOptimizedCountingAspect {
    private int counter;
    joinpoint jp1 = ( class A, method m1 );
    joinpoint jp2 = ( class A, method m2 );
    before ( jp1 ) advice1 {
        counter++;
    }
    before ( jp2 ) advice2 {
        counter += 10;
    }
}
```

However, this aspect is wrong because, if the user of class *A* calls method *m2*, then the counter will be incremented by 20 (first by 10 by *advice2*, and next 10 times by 1 by *advice1*) instead of 10. Thus, the aspect code needs to perform a contextual test to skip the first *before* advice when the second has already been applied (this is informally expressed in the following pseudo code by the advice2.alreadyApplied() method call that returns true if *advice2* has already been applied).

```
aspect OptimizedCountingAspect {
    private int counter;
    joinpoint jp1 = ( class A, method m1 );
```

```
joinpoint jp2 = ( class A, method m2 );
before ( jp1 ) advice1 {
    if ( advice2.alreadyApplied() ) { skip }
    counter++;
}
before ( jp2 ) advice2 {
    counter += 10;
}
}
```

These kinds of aspects has been pointed out in [2]. Brichau and al. call them *"jumping aspect"* since *the join points seems to be jumping around the code depending on the context in which a component is used.* This aspect code supposes that the aspect system is able to memorize the aspect advices that have been already applied (note that AspectJ [8] can support this feature with *CFlows*). The *skip* operation means that the current advice is skipped. We will see later on that this solution is not totally satisfying.

Skipping an aspect (RI2): depending on the state of the application (and of the context), some aspects may be skipped for optimization matters. This can be a generic optimization, e.g. a persistence aspect may be called only one time out of ten so that the objects states are saved less often; or an authentication aspect may be skipped if we know that the client has already been authenticated. It can also be a more application semantics dependent optimization. For example, the GUI aspect could be skipped if we know that the action performed on the base object will not affect its graphical representation.

The following pseudo code skips a persistence aspect advice when the load of the system goes over a given threshold.

```
after ( jp ) advice1 {
    if ( System.getLoad() > THRESHOLD ) { skip }
    // serialize and write...
}
```

Choosing an aspect (RI3): we previously talked about checking for aspect redundancy. On the other hand the application programmer could deliberately weave several aspects that implement the same concern so that, depending on the program context, the AOS could use the aspect that seems to be the most efficient. For instance, we can choose a different image compression algorithm whether the client is locally or remotely connected or whether s/he asked for a real-time QoS.

Similarly to previous examples a simple means to deal with this issue is to apply some contextual tests.

```
aspect CompressionAspect {
```

```
before ( jp ) advice1 {
    if ( Network.getLoad() > THRESHOLD ) {
        // low quality compress...
    } else {
        // high quality compress...
    }
}
}
```

Ordering the aspects at runtime (RI4): in some cases (that most of the time depend on the application semantics) the aspect ordering is not known at weave-time. In these cases, the AOS should be able to re-order the aspects for a given join point and a given context within the runtime system. Let us take the example of a logging aspect that can switch from a verbose mode to a very verbose one. In the verbose mode, the log traces only the successfully authenticated access to an object, and in the very verbose mode, the log traces also the non authenticated access tries. A simple way to implement the verbose mode is to apply the authentication aspect *before* the logging aspect, whilst the very verbose mode implies that the authentication aspect is applied *after*. Moreover, the application programmer may want to be in verbose mode for a set of trusted client hosts and in very verbose mode for all the other hosts. As a consequence, the aspect ordering depends on some runtime contextual information and the AOS should provide features to help the programmer to deal with this in a clean way.

Inter-aspect dependence at runtime (RI5): assuming that we can skip an aspect at runtime, the WI3 issue is also applicable at runtime. For instance, if we skip a tracing aspect, all the aspects that depend on it must also be skipped.

2.4   Discussion

As one can see in figure 1, the aspect composition issue is a critical point in Aspect-Oriented Programming. In most of the existing languages or systems that more or less support aspect-orientation, handling these issues is mostly part of the aspect programmer task (like shown in the previous examples). This is a very important limitation to AOP since the composition issue is a *crosscutting* concern in the sense that some code should be added in the whole set of aspects to deal with it, especially when the composition problem can not be entirely solved at weave-time but must also be handled at runtime.

   To illustrate this, let us take again the counting aspect depicted in section 2.3. The applied optimization (incrementing the counter by 10 when $m2$ is called) skips the default increment. However, for other base programs, such optimization can be applied for several other kinds of join-points. Thus the skipping test is difficult to generalize and the aspect can hardly be reused as this. Moreover, another aspect could use the same kind of contextual test (for instance, a security

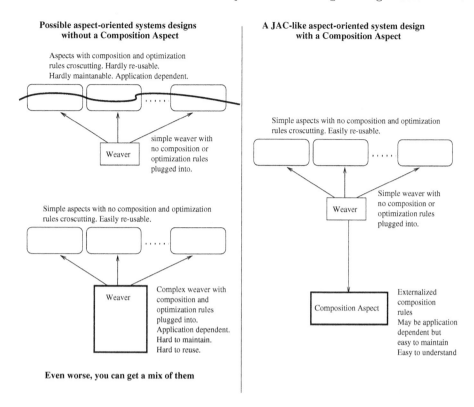

Fig. 1. With or without a Composition Aspect ?

aspect that also needs to count the calls to *m1*). The same problem occurs for the other examples when the aspects check the system or network loads to know if they have to be applied. Regarding this, it becomes clear that the contextual tests crosscut the aspects and make them hardly maintainable and reusable. In addition, since the same contextual tests may appear in a set of aspects for the same join-point, they can finally lead to performance issues.

For us, the only way to solve the runtime issues is to externalize the contextual tests into a well-modularized *inter-aspect composition* aspect. If we can do this, the AOS can apply a global contextual test for each join point and handles all the contextual tests at once. As shown in figure 1, the aspects remain free from runtime issues pollution and are more efficient and easier to maintain in comparison with other approaches without contextual part and aspect composition. Regarding our examples, it appears that we can classify the runtime issues into two categories: the issues that involve only one aspect (RI1, RI2, and RI3), and the ones that involve several aspects (RI4, RI5).

In the next section, we present our framework called JAC (for Java Aspect Components). With JAC, programmers develop applications in an aspect-oriented fashion and have support for the composition issue so that they are able to solve most of the previously described issues. Indeed, JAC programmers can cleanly describe how the composition of the aspects will be handled by the application within a well-bounded part of the program called a wrapping controller.

3   The JAC Framework

3.1   An Overview

JAC is a Java framework that provides support for dynamic aspect-oriented applications. By dynamic, we mean that an aspect can be woven and unwoven at runtime. An aspect-oriented program in JAC is entirely written in regular Java and is composed of four main parts. Figure 2 illustrates this architecture.

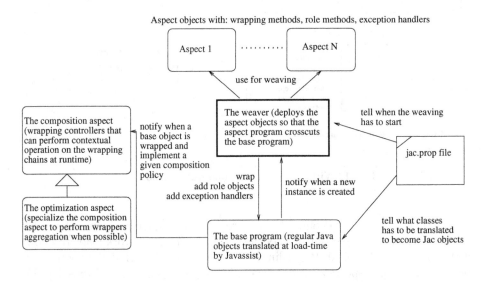

Fig. 2. JAC applications architecture.

The base program: A JAC base program is composed of a set of Java objects that implement the core functionalities of the application. These objects run on a regular JVM.

The aspect programs: A concern that refines or modifies the base program behavior is implemented in an aspect program that can be woven to the base program. An aspect program is implemented by a set of aspect objects (also called dynamic wrappers) that can hold three kinds of aspect methods *wrapping methods*, *role methods*, and/or *exception handlers*. Contrary to AspectJ [8] that mixes join-points definitions and advice definitions within the same aspect code, we separate the core functionalities of the aspects within independent aspect objects that can be compared to pure advice sets. The join points are defined by the weaver and the link between a join-point and a pure advice is done at weave-time. This choice makes the advices more reusable and, for instance, several aspects can reuse the same advice (for instance, a counting advice can be reused for a security or for a debugging aspect). This design choice is similar to the one made by aspectual components [10]. Compared to this approach, a JAC aspect program corresponds to an aspectual component, and a JAC aspect object corresponds to a participant.

- **Wrapping methods**: A wrapping method can wrap any method of any base object and seamlessly executes some code *before* and *after* this method (they are thus equivalent to the *before, after,* and *around* advices of AspectJ and to the *replace* keyword of aspectual components). A base method can be wrapped by as much wrapping methods as needed and a wrapping method can be added and removed at runtime (contrary to regular wrappers, JAC wrappers do not change the base object reference when wrapping it and implement the wrapping by using an internal and dedicated MOP).
- **Role methods**: A role method can be attached to one or many base objects at runtime and extend the base object interface (similarly to the *introduce* statement in AspectJ and to the participant methods of aspectual components). A role method can be invoked by calling the *invokeRoleMethod* on a base object.
- **Exception handlers**: An exception handler is a method that is notified when an exception is raised within (or from) the base object method it is attached to. For instance, this is very useful when the invoked object is wrapped by a wrapping method that raises an exception that is not defined by the base object.

The weaver: The weaver is responsible for deploying the aspect objects on the appropriate base objects so that a set of functionalities crosscut the base program and implement a new concern. The weaving code implicitly defines pointcuts and links the advices (wrapping methods, role methods and exception handlers) to them. Since the composition rules are externalized within the composition aspect, the weaver does not take this issue into account. The weaving process is configured by a property file that says where and when aspect objects are to be deployed. This file is described in more details in section 3.4.

The composition aspect: This part defines rules about how the different aspects of the program are composed at weave-time (to solve WI1, ..., WI5) or at runtime (to solve RI1, RI2, RI3). The composition aspect provides an *WrappingController* interface that is a MOP dedicated to aspect composition and that is implicitly upcalled by the system each time some composition issue can occur. For performance issue, the composition MOP is not activated by default (since it is sometimes not needed). It is the weaver that is responsible to activate the composition MOP for a given base object.

Table 1 compares the JAC programming model with the AspectJ and the aspectual components ones. Contrary to these two examples, the JAC model externalizes the run-time composition rules so that the aspects are more reusable. Only AspectJ integrates its pointcut definition within the aspect entities Thus, reusing aspects implies the definition of abstract aspect classes.

Features	JAC	AspectJ	Aspectual Components
Aspect definitions	aspect programs	aspect classes	aspectual components
Aspect entities	aspect objects	aspect classes	participants
Aspect entities members	OO model members, wrapping methods, role methods, exception handlers	OO model members, pointcuts, advices (before / after / around / introduce)	OO model members, replace
Pointcut definitions locations	weavers	aspect classes	connectors
Weave-time composition	wrapping controllers (before/afterWrap)	precedence rules	composite connectors
Runtime composition	wrapping controllers (getNextWrapper)	aspect classes (CFlows)	

Table 1. Comparison of JAC, AspectJ, and aspectual components programming models.

Next section more precisely describes the objects that compose a JAC application and how they are used. Section 3.3 describes the JAC base and aspect objects, section 3.4 gives an overview of how to program weavers, and section 3.5 deals with wrapping controllers.

3.2   JAC Objects Internal Structure

Base objects are regular Java objects, but, to be able to dynamically add a wrapper, attach a role object, or attach an exception handler to the base object, the objects run with JAC need to be transformed to provide some new capabilities. This translation is done at class load-time with the Javassist [4] tool. Since Javassist works on the bytecode and during load-time, the source code is not needed and the class files of the program are never changed on disk. Programmers can still use them to build regular Java applications.

Figure 3 zooms on a JAC object that has been translated by the JAC class loader and that initially offers two methods *m1* and *m2*. To each initial method

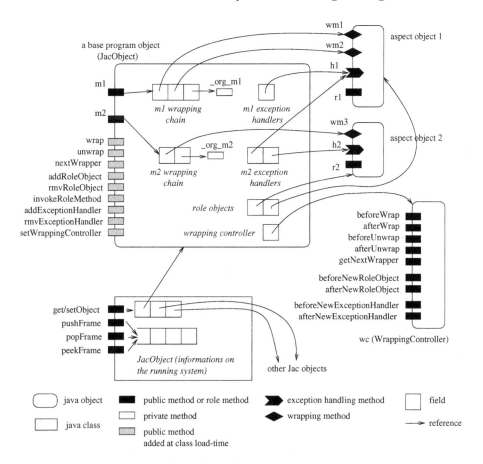

Fig. 3. A JAC object overview.

is attached a wrapping chain (a vector of references to wrapping methods), and
a set of references to exception handling methods that are called if the kind of
exception they catch is raised by the method. Some global information is also
added during the translation: a field that contains a reference to the wrapping
controller (that is upcalled to handle the composition, as it will be explained
later), and a vector that contains references towards the role objects attached
to the JAC object. These data are manipulated by the weaver that uses the
JAC Object Manipulation interface that is also added at load-time and that
furnishes methods to manipulate wrappers (*wrap*, *unwrap*, *nextWrapper*), role
objects (*addRoleObject*, *rmvRoleObject*, *invokeRoleMethod*), exception handlers
(*addExceptionHandler*, *rmvExceptionHandler*).

In the example of figure 3, the configuration applied by the weaver (at run-
time) is the following: *m1* is wrapped by {*aspect object 1, wm1*} and {*aspect
object 1, wm2*}, it is attached to one exception handling method {*aspect ob-*

ject 1, h1} while *m2* is wrapped by {*aspect object 2, wm3*} and is attached to {*aspect object 1, h1*} and {*aspect object 2, h2*}.

3.3   How to program Aspect Objects

We now explain how to program aspect objects with JAC. In a first step for clarity sake, we will not externalize the composition code. It will be done in section 3.5.

A case study base program

To reason about aspects, let us take the example of a simple agenda application. In this application, the agenda class is defined as follows:

```
public class Agenda {
    /** The agenda ID (must be unique) */
    public String id;
    /** The appointment list */
    public Vector appointments = new Vector();
    /** The repository for the agendas */
    public static AgendaRepository repository;
    /** Creates a new agenda and registers it into the repository */
    public Agenda ( String id, AgendaRepository repository ) {...}
    /** Make an appointment with other users */
    public void makeAppointment(
            String agenda_id, String date,
            String object, String[] with ) {
        // resolve the agendas of the with array with the repository
        // call the makeAppointment method on all these agendas
    }
    /** Print the appointments */
    public void printAppointments () {
        System.out.println ( "** Appointment list for " + id + ":" )
        for (int i = 0; i < appointments.size(); i++) {
            printAppointment( i );
        }
    }
    /** Print an appointment */
    public void printAppointment ( int i ) {
        System.out.println( i + 1 + ". " + appointments.get(i) );
    }
}
```

It is easy to figure out that the agenda repository class implements some methods to register and to resolve agenda with a string ID. We also assume that an AgendaClient class that calls Agenda instances is defined.

The counting aspect

This aspect illustrates the RI1 issue of section 2.3. The idea is to be able to count the number of times the *printAppointments* by the printing methods of the method is called. As depicted in section 2.3, a simple but not optimized way is to create a wrapper that simply increments a counter.

```
public class CountingWrapper {
  int counter;
  public Object incr(Wrappee wrappee,String meth,Object[] args) {
    // before code ...
    counter++;
    Object ret = wrappee.nextWrapper( meth, args );
    // after code ...
    return ret;
  }
}
```

In this example, *incr* is the wrapping method. The three mentioned parameters are mandatory for each JAC wrapping method. Their values are automatically set. The first parameter is a reference to the wrappee (i.e. the application object), the second one is the name of the wrapped method, and the third contains the arguments transmitted by the client that invoked this wrappee. The `wrappee.nextWrapper(method,args)` method call belongs to the JAC API, and allows either to run the code of the next wrapper in the wrapping chain, or to run the code of the wrappee. Notice, that, at this stage, you do not specify that the *incr* method will wrap the *printAppointment* method. This will be defined later in the weaver. For this reason, our aspect objects can be regarded as pure advices that can be reused for several aspects.

As depicted in section 2.3, this wrapper can be optimized to avoid several calls (one for each agenda) to the *incr* wrapping method when the *printAppointments* method is called. The following aspect defines two wrapping methods: *incr* for *printAppointment* like methods, and *multiIncr* for *printAppointments* like methods. *incr* takes advantage of the JAC API (call to *JAC.peekFrame* method) and checks whether the client calling method is *printAppointments*. If so, nothing is done as the update of *counter* is handled elsewhere. If not, *printAppointment* has been directly called and *counter* needs to be incremented. *multiIncr* increases the value of *counter* depending of the number of agendas in the application object (we use the Java reflection API to introspect the wrappee fields). The *field* and *callingMethod* fields connect this aspect to a base program.

```
public class CountingWrapper {
  int counter;

  // The following fields allow the wrapper to be generic and
  // customizable regarding the base program class it has to count
  String field, callingMethod;
```

```
public CountingWrapper( String field, String callingMethod ) {
    this.field = field;
    this.callingMethod = callingMethod;
}
public CountingWrapper() {
    field = "appointments";
    callingMethod = "printAppointments";
}

public Object incr(Wrappee wrappee,String meth,Object[] args) {
    // we increment the counter only
    // if the calling method is "printAppointments".
    if( ! ( JacObject.peekFrame(1)[0] == wrappee &&
            JacObject.peekFrame(1)[1] == method ) )
        counter++;
    return wrappee.nextWrapper( meth, args );
}

public Object multiIncr
    (Wrappee wrappee,String meth,Object[] args) {
    counter +=
    wrappee.getClass().getDeclaredField(field).get(wrappee);
    return wrappee.nextWrapper( meth, args );
}
}
```

The authentication aspect

A simple means to implement an authentication aspect is to wrap the *A-gendaClient* instances with a client-side wrapper that adds the agenda ID in the context and to wrap the agendas with a server-side authentication wrapper that will read the context to check if the client accesses the right agenda. Notice that the server-side authentication wrapper throws an exception in the case the authentication fails. This is a good example to illustrate the use of (1) exception handlers (defined here at the client-side), and (2) contexts. Contexts in JAC are hashtables that map attribute names to values. They are thread dependant and allow us to propagate data along a call graph. The JAC API provides methods to get the current context (method *getContext*), and to add (method *addAttribute*) and get (method *getAttribute*) attributes.

The following class defines a wrapping method *addAuthInfos* and a exception handler *catchAuthenticationException* for *AgendaClient* instances

```
public class ClientAuthenticationWrapper {
    public Object addAuthInfos
        (Wrappee wrappee,String meth,Object[] args) {
        JacObject.getContext().addAttribute( "clname", args[0] );
```

```
        return wrappee.nextWrapper( method, args );
    }

    public void catchAuthenticationException(
        AuthenticationException e ) {
      System.out.println ( e.printStackTrace() );
    }
}
```

At the server-side, another RI1 issue type occurs. Indeed, since the *Agenda* class also calls the *makeAppointment* method to notify the other agendas that a common appointment has been taken, it implies that the server-side authentication wrapper must be skipped if the *makeAppointment* is called by an agenda. Once this has been done by the *checkAuthInfos* wrapping method we check whether the *clName* attribute is present in the context transmitted by the *Agenda* client and if so, if the client is authorized to access this agenda. If not, we throw an exception that will be catch by the exception handler defined previously.

```
public class ServerAuthenticationWrapper {
    public Object checkAuthInfos
        (Wrappee wrappee,String meth,Object[] args)
        throws AuthenticationException {
      if ( ! ( JacObject.peekFrame(1)[0] instanceof Agenda ) ) {
        Object clientName =
          JacObject.getContext().getAttribute("clname");
        if ( clientName == null ||
            ! clientName.equals(wrappee.getFieldValue("id")) ) {
          throw new AuthenticationException(
              clientName+" is not authorized to access "+meth);
      }
      return wrappee.nextWrapper( method, args );
    }
}
```

3.4   Weavers

The weaver is the part of a JAC program that weaves the aspects to the base program, i.e. deploys the aspect objects on the base objects. For example, the following weaver weaves the counting and the authentication aspects to a base program that contains several instances of the *Agenda* and *AgendaClient* classes (the involved base and aspect objects have been explained in the previous section). The JAC introspection API allows us to get all objects that are instances of a given class (calls to *JacObject.getObjects*). We then call the *wrap* method, that are part of the JAC Object Manipulation interface and is automatically added by Javassist, to define the needed wrapping links.

```
public class AgendaWeaver extends Weaver {
  // Some information to parameterize the join-points
  String calledMethod = "printAppointment";
  String callingMethod = "printAppointments";
  String field = "appointments";
  String authenticatedMethods = {
   "makeAppointment", "printAppointment", "printAppointments" };
  String clientMethods = { "makeAppointment" };

  public void weave() {
    Object[] agendas = JacObject.getObjects(Agenda.class);
    Object[] clients = JacObject.getObjects(AgendaClient.class);

    // create a server authentication wrapper
    ServerAuthenticationWrapper saw =
      new ServerAuthenticationWrapper();
    // create a server authentication wrapper
    ClientAuthenticationWrapper caw =
      new ClientAuthenticationWrapper();

    // wrap the agendas to add authentication and counting
    for ( int i=0 ; i < agendas.length ; i++ ) {
      // create one counting wrapper per agenda
      CountingWrapper cw =
        new CountingWrapper( calledMethod, callingMethod, field );
      agendas[i].wrap( cw, "incr", calledMethod );
      agendas[i].wrap( cw, "countWithField", callingMethod );
      agendas[i].wrap( saw, "checkAuthInfos", authenticatedMethods );
    }

    // wrap the clients to add authentication
    for ( int i=0 ; i < clients.length ; i++ ) {
      agendas[i].wrap( caw, "addAuthInfos", clientMethods
    }
  }
}
```

Each weaver is also associated with a property file that is parsed when the program is launched. Its main role is to configure the weaver. A typical property file for a JAC program looks like the following:

```
# Define classes that are to be adapted by Javassist
jac.toAdapt: Agenda AgendaClient
# Define the weaver for this application
jac.weaver: AgendaWeaver
# Define when the weaver have to be called
jac.startWeavingPlace: AgendaClient any 0 0
```

With this property file, the weaving starts when the first method call is performed on any instance of the base program class, i.e. the *AgendaClient* class (*any* means that it can be any method, the first 0 indicates that we want it to start at the first call, and the second 0 indicates that there is no precondition on the number of instances of the *AgendaClient* class). For a finer tuning of the weaving moment, and depending on the base program, we can be more precise, like weaving when the *printAll* method is called for the second time and when the number of instances is a least 5.

```
jac.startWeavingPlace: AgendaClient printAll 1 5
```

3.5   The Composition Aspect

Weave-time issues

In the weaver previously described, one can notice that the weaver programmer does not have to deal with aspect composition issues at weave-time since it is implemented in the composition aspect. This composition aspect is implemented by a specific entity called a wrapping controller and that provides a MOP to control the way the wrapping of the base objects will be done by the weaver.

At weave-time, i.e. when the weaver is upcalled, the composition consistency and rules can be defined by subclassing the *WrappingController* class and overloading the *beforeWrap* method. This method returns a rank that represents the default place of the wrapper within the current wrapping chain and that allows the composition aspect to implement precedence rules (issue WI5). Since the rank -1 implies that the wrapper will not wrap the base object, the composition aspect can also implement exclusion rules (issues WI1, WI2).

Taking our example, the implementation of a rule that forces the authentication aspect to be, by default, called before any other aspect follows. It also check that the authentication wrapper is applied only once to the same base object.

```
public class MyWrappingController extends WrappingController {
  public int beforeWrap (
                Wrappee wrappee, String wrappee_method_name,
                Wrapper wrapper,
                Object[] wrappers, Object[] wrapping_methods
                int default_rank ) {
    if ( wrappers.length > 0 && wrappers[0].getClass() ==
                        ServerAuthenticationWrapper.class ) {
      // refuse to wrap authentication twice !
      if ( wrapper.getClass() ==
                        ServerAuthenticationWrapper.class) {
        return -1;
      }
```

```
    // put the new wrapper after the authentication wrapper
    return 1;
  }
  return default_rank;
 }
}
```

Run-time issues

By default, the wrappers are called in the order they are placed within the wrapping chain. However, ordering or choosing the right wrapper at the right time is a crucial issue since a wrapper inversion can drastically change the final wrapped object semantics [16]. In real-world applications, it is not rare that the application of a set of wrappers on the base object changes, depending on the calling context. For example, for performance reasons, the authentication wrapper may not be applied if the user is already authenticated.

Some samples in section 3.3 shown how to solve this issues thanks to some contextual tests within the wrappers. However, to produce better maintainable code, the aspect programmer can also externalize these tests so that they do not crosscut and pollute the aspect codes anymore. This externalization can be achieved within the wrapping controller by defining the *getNextWrapper* method that is called each time the next wrapper has to be called and that returns the next wrapper to be called.

The sequence diagram shown in figure 4 focuses on the objects interactions within the JAC system when a method is called. This protocol allows the wrapping controller to entirely control the way wrappers are applied at runtime. The figure shows the (simplified) case of a method *m* that is called on a base object *o* and that is wrapped by two wrapping methods (*wm1* and *wm2*). One can see that the wrapping controller is called when the wrapping method has finished its *before* work and calls the next wrapper. Thus, the wrapping controller can choose the next wrapper (in this example, it chooses to call *wm1* before *wm2*).

The following wrapping controller externalizes the counting wrapper optimization rule described in section 3.3.

```
public class MyWrappingController extends WrappingController {
  String calledMethod = "printAppointment";
  String callingMethod = "printAppointments";
  public int getNextWrapper (
                Wrappee wrappee, String wrappee_method_name,
                Object[] wrappers, Object[] methods, int rank ) {
    // check if the calling method is "print"
    if ( wrappee_method_name == calledMethod &&
         JacObject.peekFrame(1)[0] == wrappee &&
         JacObject.peekFrame(1)[1] == callingMethod &&
         wrappers[rank] instanceof CountingWrapper ) )
      // skip the wrapper!
```

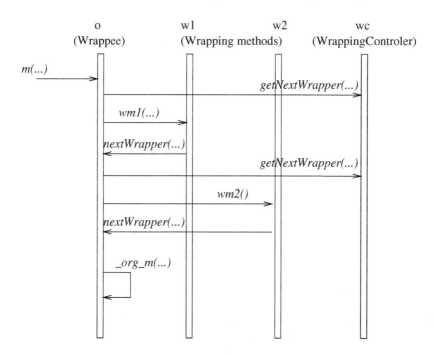

Fig. 4. The wrapping control mechanism.

```
        return rank + 1;
    else
        return rank;
    }
}
```

By using the wrapping controller, we let the aspect code free from any pollution and the composition policy can be centralized within a well-bounded code that is called the composition aspect.

4 Performance Issues

This section studies the cost of running an aspect-oriented program with JAC. As illustrated in figure 4, we need one regular invocation to the wrapping controller before choosing each wrapper and two invocations per wrapping method (one to call it, and one when the *nextWrapper* method is called by the wrapper).

The following trace is the output of a benchmark program that creates an object and calls 100 times an empty method on it. It runs under JVM2 and Linux with a Pentium 300 MHz processor. The program performs nothing, objects are regular Java objects, they are not translated by Javassist, and there is no weaving by JAC. We just run it to get the amount of time taken by the JVM to do this job.

```
>>> start time: 981972594672 ms
>>> end of class loading: +639 ms [duration: 639 ms]
>>> end of benchmark: +1242 ms [duration: 588 ms]
```

To test the overload due to the wrapping mechanism, we implement an empty aspect that wraps the base object with 10 empty wrappers and adds a wrapping controller that is upcalled but does not change the wrappers ordering. Note that 10 wrappers is quite a huge number and we don't expect such a case to be encountered (1, 2 or 3 aspects seems to be a more adequate case for the near future). The same program running with JAC produces the following trace.

```
>>> start time: 981973419075 ms
>>> end of class loading/translating: +1484 ms [duration: 1484 ms]
>>> end of weaving: +1586 ms [duration: 102 ms]
>>> end of benchmark: +6249 ms [duration: 4663 ms]
```

The overhead of the dynamic application of 10 wrappers (even empty) when the base method is called 100 time is huge: 4663 ms against 588 ms. This is no surprise as we replaced calls to 1 base object with calls that go through 10 wrapper objects and 1 base object. This roughly gives us an overhead of 4 ms per base call per wrapper. The first duration gives the time needed to load the classes and adapt them with Javassist. Compared to the previous case where the classes where loaded with the standard classloader of the JVM, the duration is multiplied by 2.4. To reduce it, JAC proposes a starting option that writes the result of the class translation in a temporary directory so that, at the next start of the application, the class will not be translated anymore (unless we explicitly require it). When the translated classes are stored, the result is almost the same than when no translation occurs (655 ms against 639 ms).

```
>>> start time: 981973903301 ms
>>> end of class loading/translating: +655 ms [duration: 655 ms]
>>> end of weaving: +755 ms [duration: 100 ms]
```

This gives us a simple mean to optimize class translation. The second overhead already mentioned (4663 ms against 588 when 10 wrappers are inserted before 100 calls to 1 base object) can only be overcome if fewer wrappers are used. We are in the process of working on a mechanism that we call *wrapper aggregation* that dynamically aggregates the whole wrapping chain and the wrappee into one unique object. Each method of this aggregation is constructing by inlining the bytecode of wrapping methods and of the wrapped method (note that it also aggregates the states of the wrappers and of the base object; this mechanism induces some state consistency issues between the aggregations and the regular objects but we will not enter into details here). By this way, we can expect the cost of running a application weaved by 10 aspects to be greatly improved.

5   Related Works

In [3], Büchi and Weck designed a mechanism called generic wrappers. Generic wrappers are type safe and support modular reasoning. Their focus is oriented towards the definition of reusable and composable components implemented by different vendors. Type soundness is one of their main concerns. Multiple wrappers for a single wrappee can be defined in their approach. Nevertheless, their system does not dynamically manage the execution order of wrappers in a wrapping chain as our wrapping control does.

The composition filter object model [1] (CFOM) is an extension to the conventional object model where input and output filters can be defined to handle sending and receiving of messages. This model is implemented for several languages, including Smalltalk, C++ and Java. The latter implementation is an extension to the regular Java syntax where keywords are added to declare, for instance, filters attached to classes. The goals of this model and ours are rather similar: to handle separation of concerns at a meta level. Nevertheless, JAC does not require any language extension (i.e. wrappers and wrappees are written in regular Java).

AspectJ [8] is a powerful language that provides support for the implementation of crosscutting concerns through pointcuts (collections of principle points in the execution of a program), and advices (method-like structures attached to pointcuts). Precedence rules are defined when more than one advice apply at a join point. In many features (e.g. pointcuts definition) AspectJ has a rich and vast semantics. Nevertheless, we argue that in many cases that we have studied, simple schemes such as the wrapping technique proposed by JAC are sufficient to implement a broad range of solutions dealing with separation of concerns.

Aspectual components [10] and their direct predecessors adaptative plug and play components [11][12] define patterns of interaction, called participant graphs (PG), that implement aspects for applications. PGs contain participants roles (e.g. publishers and subscribers in a publish/subscribe interaction model) that, (1) expect features about the classes upon which they will be mapped, (2) may reimplement features, and (3) provide some local features. PGs are then mapped onto class graphs with entities called connectors, that define the way aspects and classes are composed. Aspectual components can be composed by connecting part of the expected interface of one component to part of the provided interface of another. Nevertheless, it seems that by doing so, the definition of the composition crosscuts the definition of the aspects, loosing by this way the expected benefits of AOP. The approach taken in JAC consists in modularizing this crosscuting concern (i.e. inter-aspects composition) in the so-called wrapping controller (see section 3.5).

Subject oriented programming [6][13] (SOP) and its direct successor the Hyper/J tool [18], provide the ability to handle different subjective perspectives, called subjects, on the problem to model. Subjects can be composed using correspondence rules (specifying the correspondences between classes, methods, fields of different subjects), combination rules (giving the way two subjects can be glued together, and correspondence-and-combination rules that mix both approaches. Prototype implementations of SOP for C++ and Smalltalk exist, and a more recent version for Java called Hyper/J is available. This latter tool implements the notion of hyperspace [14] that *permits the explicit identification of any concerns of importance.*

We rather think that JAC covers a field that, up to our knowledge, is not fully and cleanly addressed by any of these solutions: dynamic ordering of aspect programs and context-sensitive optimizations within the composition aspect. JAC is widely inspired from the Lasagne abstract model [19] that defines some concepts to achieve dynamic and context-sensitive selection of collaboration refinements depending on the client of the application (but that is less flexible since it does not allows runtime reordering of the wrapping chain).

6   Conclusion and Future Works

Separation of concerns is one of the major requirements for modern applications. Flexibility and dynamic evolution are also needed most of the time. In this paper, we present the JAC framework that meets both needs by using the notion of wrapping controller to implement a composition aspect. To fix the ideas, figure 2 summed up how all the JAC parts interoperate when building an aspect-oriented application. JAC takes advantage of the Javassist [4] load-time MOP to transparently implement the needed glue between aspect and application programs.

It is to notice that, contrary to AspectJ [8] that focuses on the pointcuts expression with a new language, we mainly focus on the definition of a generic architecture for AOP. We believe that we have reached many of the desirable properties needed by aspect-oriented system and languages and that our framework can be later on coupled with a more high-level language in order to facilitate the programmer task. The following list summarizes the main features provided by JAC.

- The base program is written in regular Java, can be launched independently from the aspects, and the source code is not needed for the weaving.
- Aspect programming does not require any syntactical extension. Aspect objects with JAC contains methods that can be either wrapping methods (that provides the ability to run *before*, *after*, and *around* code), role methods (that introduce new features in application objects), or exception handlers. Compared to AspectJ they can be seen as pure advice entities. Aspect objects in JAC remain free from any deployment or composition issues that are completely handled by the weaver and the wrapping controller. In our sense, this makes aspect programs more generic and more reusable.
- The weaver is a regular Java program that uses introspection features so that any kind of crosscutting schemes can be implemented. The weaver is responsible for deploying aspect objects onto application objects. So it defines the way aspects are composed with applications. Several wrapping methods can wrap a given application method creating by this way, wrapping chains. Several role methods and exception handlers can also be attached to a

given application object. Furthermore, the weaver is notified when a new instance of a base class is created so that the aspect can be extended in the mean time of the base program extension. Assuming some transactional features, aspects could also be smoothly added and removed at runtime, without stopping the application. The weaving mechanism is object-based and is well-fitted to distributed programming since the modification of a given instance do not necessary affect the other class instances (thus allowing heterogenous environments).

– The wrapping controller is a regular Java program that externalizes aspect composition. It allows context-sensitive modifications of the wrapping chains. This composition aspect should be programmed by a programmer that knows about the whole set of aspects that can be woven to the application. The main advantages of this feature are to greatly simplify the programming of the weaver (that just handles the deployment of aspect objects) and of aspect objects (that just perform core functionalities). This last property allows the aspect programmer to produce much more generic and reusable aspect code than it would be if s/he had to deal with the aspect composition issue.

The JAC framework is used by the "Ecole Centrale de Lille" Laboratory to implement the software part of the CarVia application that consists in controlling electronic devices via the power-line network. JAC is currently under evaluation by Alcatel Research to implement a security aspect within a network management platform. JAC has also been used to implement the Lasagne abstract model [19] and a distributed agenda management application. These concrete projects tend to prove that the JAC framework allows the programmer to produce high quality and easily maintainable code. During the development process of these applications, the benefits of AOP are fully used and the concerns are developed independently from each other.

In the future, we will focus on the aggregation optimization so that JAC can be as efficient as less dynamic aspect-oriented frameworks. We will also study the composition aspect to find out some recurrent patterns and useful abstractions so that we can propose a more high-level programming interface to deal with this issue. The purpose of this work is to make the composition process as automatic as possible.

References

1. Bergmans, L., and Aksit, M. Software Architectures and Component Technology: The State of the Art in Research and Practice. Kluwer Academic Publishers, 2000, ch. Constructing Reusable Components with Multiple Concerns Using Composition Filters.
2. Brichau, J., Meuter, W. D., and Volder, K. D. Jumping aspects. Presented at the ECOOP 2000 workshop on Aspects and Dimensions of Concerns, June 2000. http://trese.cs.utwente.nl/Workshops/adc2000/.
3. Buchi, M., and Weck, W. Generic wrappers. In Proceedings of the 14th European Conference on Object-Oriented Programming (ECOOP'00) (June 2000), vol. 1850 of Lecture Notes in Computer Science, Springer, pp. 201–225.

4. Chiba, S. Load-time structural reflection in java. In Proceedings of the 14th European Conference on Object-Oriented Programming (ECOOP'00) (June 2000), vol. 1850 of Lecture Notes in Computer Science, Springer, pp. 313–336.

5. Douence, R., Motelet, O., and Sudholt, M. A formal definition of crosscut. In Proceedings of the International Conference on Reflection and Crosscutting Concerns (Sept. 2001).

6. Harrison, W., and Ossher, H. Subject-oriented programming (A critique of pure objects). In Proceedings of OOPSLA'93 (Oct. 1993), vol. 28 of SIGPLAN Notices, ACM Press, pp. 411–428.

7. JAC. The JAC project home page. http://www.aopsys.com/jac/.

8. Kiczales, G., Hilsdale, E., Hugunin, J., Kersten, M., Palm, J., and Griswold, W. An overview of AspectJ. In Proceedings of the 15th European Conference on Object-Oriented Programming (ECOOP'01) (2001).

9. Kiczales, G., Lamping, J., Mendhekar, A., Maeda, C., Lopes, C., Loingtier, J., and Irwin, J. Aspect-oriented programming. In Proceedings of the 11th European Conference on Object-Oriented Programming (ECOOP'97) (June 1997), vol. 1241 of Lecture Notes in Computer Science, Springer, pp. 220–242.

10. Lieberherr, K., Lorenz, D., and Mezini, M. Programming with aspectual components. Tech. Rep. NU-CCS-99-01, Northeastern University's College of Computer Science, Apr. 1999.

11. Mezini, M., and Lieberherr, K. Adaptative plug-and-play components for evolutionary software development. In Proceedings of OOPSLA'98 (1998), vol. 33 of SIGPLAN Notices, ACM Press, pp. 96–116.

12. Mezini, M., Seiter, L., and Lieberherr, K. Component integration with pluggable composite adapters. In Software Architectures and Component Technology: The State of the Art in Research and Practice (2000), L. Bergmans and M. Aksit, Eds., Kluwer Academic Publishers.

13. Ossher, H., Kaplan, K., Harrison, W., Matz, A., and Kruskal, V. Subject-oriented composition rules. In Proceedings of OOPSLA'95 (1995), vol. 30 of SIGPLAN Notices, ACM Press, pp. 235–250.

14. Ossher, H., and Tarr, P. Multi-dimensional separation of concerns and the hyperspace approach. In Software Architectures and Component Technology: The State of the Art in Research and Practice (2000), Kluwer Academic Publishers.

15. Parnas, D. On the criteria to be used in decomposing systems into modules. Communications of the ACM 15, 12 (1972), 1053–1058.

16. Pawlak, R., Duchien, L., and Florin, G. An automatic aspect weaver with a reflective programming language. In Proceedings of Reflection'99 (July 1999).

17. Pawlak, R., Duchien, L., Florin, G., Martelli, L., and Seinturier, L. Distributed separation of concerns with Aspect Components. In Proceedings of TOOLS Europe 2000 (June 2000).

18. Tarr, P., Ossher, H., Harrison, W., and Sutton, S. N degrees of separation: Multidimensional separation of concerns. In Proceedings of the International Conference on Software Engineering (ICSE'99) (1999), pp. 107–119.

19. Truyen, E., Vanhaute, B., Joosen, W., Verbaeten, P., Joergensen, and Bo, N. Dynamic and selective combination of extensions in component-based applications. In Proceedings of ICSE'01 (2001).

Reflex – Towards an Open Reflective Extension of Java

Éric Tanter[2], Noury M.N. Bouraqadi-Saâdani[1], and Jacques Noyé[1]

[1] École des Mines de Nantes
La Chantrerie - 4, rue Alfred Kastler
B.P. 20722
F-44307 Nantes Cedex 3
France
{Noury.Bouraqadi, Jacques.Noye}@emn.fr
[2] University of Chile
Faculty of Physics and Mathematics
Computer Science Department
Av. Blanco Encalada 2120, Casilla 2777
Santiago, Chile
etanter@dcc.uchile.cl

Abstract. Since version 1.1 of the Java Development Kit, the Java reflective facilities have been successively extended. However, they still prove to be limited. A number of systems (e.g. MetaXa, Guaraná, Kava, Javassist) have addressed this limitation by providing reflective extensions of Java with richer MetaObject Protocols (MOPs). All these extensions provide a particular, monolithic, infrastructure that reflects the commitment of the designer to particular trade-offs between efficiency, portability, expressiveness and flexibility. Unfortunately, these trade-offs are not satisfactory for all applications, since different applications may have different needs. This calls for breaking down the building of a reflective extension into different components that can be specialized in order to fit specific needs. We qualify such a reflective extension as *open*. In this paper, we present Reflex, a prototype *open reflective extension of Java*. Reflex can be seen both as a reflective extension of Java and as a first step towards a framework for building such extensions.

1   Introduction

Our initial objective was to apply a reflective extension of Java to enhance mobile agent systems with regards to the way the resources attached to a mobile agent are handled upon migration (see [23]). Using a reflective extension in such an application domain implied several strong requirements such as portability and the ability to attach a metaobject to only some specific instances of a given class.

When looking around for appropriate reflective extensions, we could not find one that would fit our needs. We therefore started implementing our own simple extension based on Javassist [5]. In this extension [23], a reflective object was attached to a unique metaobject which understood a single MOP (MetaObject

A. Yonezawa and S. Matsuoka (Eds.): REFLECTION 2001, LNCS 2192, pp. 25–43, 2001.

Protocol) method for trapping method invocations. That is, the metaobject was activated on each invocation of a public method of its reflective object through *hooks* introduced via code transformation. These hooks were looking as follows:

> *metaobj*.`trapMethodcall`(*args*);

Later on, we discovered that, in some cases, it was necessary to give control to metaobjects when their base object was being serialized. However this feature was not offered by our simple reflective extension. The code transformation process was extended in order to add to each reflective class a method of the Java serialization API, `writeReplace`, automatically invoked when serialization occurs. This method was made to give control to the metaobject via the following invocation:

> *metaobj*.`trapSerialize`(*args*);

This means that the MOP was extended with a new method. The annoying part of this was that the previously developed metaobjects were not compatible with the new MOP, since they did not implement the new method. It was all the more annoying as this extended MOP was only required for some particular objects and metaobjects.

In fact, the issue we encountered there is a recurrent one. On the one hand, there are *high-level* reflective extensions providing hardwired choices about MOP definition and hook introduction, as well as about some important trade-offs such as performance vs. portability. What happens then if these choices are not compatible with the application requirements? On the other hand, there are *low-level* byte-code manipulation APIs allowing the definition of a custom-built reflective extension, at some non-negligible development cost. There is no middle ground, no reflective extension that would both limit the number of hardwired choices and allow seamless customization and extension in order to suit the requirements of a particular application or class of applications.

This paper suggests that providing such a reflective extension, which we arguably qualify as *open*, is a worthwhile task. It presents Reflex, a prototype *open reflective extension of Java*. Reflex can be seen both as a reflective extension of Java and as a first step towards a framework for building such extensions. This introduces, besides the classical roles of metaobject programmer and end-user, a new role in the development of a reflective application: the *architect of the metalevel*, who is responsible for defining, based on the framework as well as a number of existing building blocks, a fully-defined reflective extension.

The main ideas on which Reflex is based are the definition of a generic MOP and the reification of the code transformation process as an extensible entity.

The idea of a *generic MOP* replaces the idea of a global, all-encompassing, MOP since needs in this regard are unpredictable. It is of course possible to offer a large MOP, but it will never cover all possible needs. In general, a MOP method is devoted to handle a particular type of *event* occurring at the base level, like method invocation, serialization, creation... Even if these types of event could be completely identified, the way each type of event has to be dealt with cannot be predicted. For instance, in the case of method invocation, there is a possibly infinite set of ways to deal with it: one could like to handle accessor methods in a particular way (therefore requiring a method like `trapAccessor`), or to handle methods distinctly, depending on some *method categories* (hence requiring methods like `trapMethodCategoryA,...`). This is why Reflex is based on a generic and minimal MOP consisting of a single method, called `perform` due to its similarity with the *perform* method of Smalltalk. This method takes as its first argument a string describing the event. Metaobject invocations, and therefore hooks, look as follows:

   $metaobj$.`perform`($event$, $args$);

To put the generic MOP into practice, these hooks must be inserted where needed. The corresponding code transformation is reified as an extensible entity, which we call a *class builder*, in order to set up the appropriate hooks within a given class, using *subclassing* when the class cannot be modified.

The following section, Sect. 2, comes back on the requirements that should be met by an open reflective extension. Section 3 describes Reflex, a first step towards such an extension, details its main concepts, the generic MOP and class builders, its architecture, and shows how it meets the above-mentioned requirements. Section 4 provides some examples that illustrate the use of Reflex. Section 5 discusses related work, Sect. 6 future work and Sect. 7 concludes.

2   Requirements

This section reviews the basic requirements in terms of portability, expressiveness, and efficiency which led to the design of Reflex. Apart from the fact that portability is not compromised over, great care is taken not to discard any option too early.

2.1   Portability

A major benefit of Java is its *portability*. Source code is compiled into byte-code which is independent from the underlying platform (operating system and hardware). Only the virtual machine (VM), which executes the byte-code, is platform dependent. Thus, it is possible to write and compile an application once, and then run it on very different platforms. If necessary, efficiency can be improved through just-in-time or optimizing compilers taking byte-code as input.

In our opinion, this major benefit should not be lost when considering a reflective extension. It would be somehow contradictory to provide an extension which would include portability restrictions! We have previously mentioned that the initial target application of Reflex, mobile agents, requires portability. We expect many applications of a reflective extension of Java to share such a requirement.

This discards the idea of relying on a specific virtual machine or just-in-time compiler, as considered by systems such as Guaraná [18] or MetaXa [13], as well as extending the VM with native, and therefore platform-dependent, code through the Java Native Interface (JNI), as in Iguana/J [19][1]. This also means that the hooks intercepting base level events should be introduced through code transformation (either byte-code or source-code transformation). Moreover, in order to be 100% Java compliant this transformation should be restricted to application code. Java core classes should be kept untouched.

2.2   Expressiveness of the MOP

Let us first consider how the link between the base and the meta-level is handled. In the following, we shall refer to this link as the *metalink*. For the sake of generality, we shall assume that the metalink is instance-based (rather than type-based), has cardinality n-n (that is, a metaobject can be associated to several objects and, conversely, an object to several metaobjects), and is dynamic, making it possible to dynamically adapt the behavior of a base object. Let us note that, obviously, a type-based link can easily be built on top of an instance-based one by associating the same metaobject to all the objects of the same type.

A second important issue is the definition of the base events. A quick review of the literature on the applications of reflection (see, for instance, [3,20,17]) shows that a simple MOP providing only control of method invocation covers the needs of a large range of applications. However, application developers may need metaobjects that control other events than method invocation (e.g. object creation), or may need to handle these events in an adapted manner (e.g. for performance enhancements, or to introduce method categories). We have previously mentioned our need to control object serialization.

This means that the architect of the metalevel should be able to define new kinds of events together with the corresponding hooks. This includes the definition of the hooks, the definition of the code transformation responsible for their introduction and the time when this code transformation takes place. Note that, in a given application, the set of events of interest may vary, at least from one type of object to the other, if not from one object to the other. In the latter case, the introduction of different hooks should nevertheless keep the objects *type-compatible*. Actually, the set of events of interest could even vary along the lifetime of an object. We shall assume here that all the potential interesting events are known when the hooks are introduced. However, we do not assume any specific time (compile time, load time or object creation time) for hook introduction. This means that a standard, *non-reflective*, object (an object which is not hooked to the metalevel) may be turned into a *reflective* one.

Finally, expressiveness also covers metaobject composition, i.e. assembling the metaobjects attached to a given base-level object. Let us note that this goes

---

[1] The case for rejecting this possibility is actually weaker and would require a more thorough discussion.

beyond the provision for a metalink of cardinality n-n as soon as the different metaobjects associated to a given base object interact. A *composition policy* describes the strategy according to which metaobjects are assembled. As there is no universal composition policy, an open reflective extension should make it possible to support different composition policies and allow the definition of new policies. For the sake of reusability, composing metaobjects designed to handle different sets of events should be possible.

2.3   Efficiency

The use of reflection introduces two different kinds of overhead. There is one kind of overhead which is due to the introduction of reflection, more precisely the introduction of hooks in base-level code. There is another kind of overhead which is due to the execution of the hooks. Paying these costs for any class and object would be an overkill. There is therefore a basic rule which says that these costs should only be paid for classes and objects that require it. This has a number of implications:

- Reflective and non-reflective objects may live together within an application. The execution of the standard objects should not be affected by the presence of the reflective objects. Note that, with respect to the previous discussion on portability, this requirement is difficult to guarantee when modifying the standard Java compilation and run-time support.
- It should be possible to apply reflection on an instance basis. Care must be taken to keep the reflective and non-reflective instances of a given base class type-compatible.
- Even if the interesting hooks are known at object creation time, it makes sense to delay their introduction so that a non-reflective object which is bound to become a reflective one is not slowed down until really needed. Conversely, if the hooks are not needed any longer, it would be nice to be able to transform the reflective object back into a non-reflective one. Type-compatibility should again be ensured. The decision of delaying hook introduction may depend on the respective overheads of executing the hooks (with a useless indirection via a dummy metaobject immediately transferring the control back to the base object) and introducing the hooks after object creation time.
- It should be possible to choose to perform hook introduction at compile time (dealing with source code or byte-code) so that the cost of hook introduction is not incurred at load or run time (if it matters), or even to merge the base level and the metalevel as is done in the so-called compile-time MOPs [6], when both levels and their links are known at compile time. Much more aggressive optimization techniques could actually be envisionned, based on run-time code generation [10] and partial evaluation [14,2], but being able to seamlessly combine well-known compile-time and run-time reflection techniques would already be quite a progress.

3   The Reflex Framework

Reflex can be seen both as a framework for building reflective extensions of Java, fulfilling the requirements presented in Sect. 2, and as an actual reflective extension. Indeed, the framework has itself been specialized, leading to a working extension, which provides a first validation of the framework, as well as some building blocks which could be reused in new extensions. This includes hook introduction for the generic MOP (see Sect. 3.1 and 3.2) as well as specialized MOPs (e.g. the one presented in Sect. 4), and a specific composition scheme (see Sect. 3.4 and 4). Additionally, the `Reflex` package, available for download (with all source code) at the Reflex website [24], comes along with several sample metaobjects and programs.

This section focuses on the APIs and abstractions provided to the architect of the metalevel. The upper part of Fig. 1 shows the main elements of the Reflex framework. We shall come back to the lower part of the figure, showing an actual specialization, in the next section. These elements are:

- `ReflexMetaobject`: an interface defining the basic services provided by a metaobject,
- `ReflexClassBuilder`: an interface defining the basic protocol for hook introduction,
- `Reflex`: a class that allows triggering code transformation (statically or dynamically) and attaching metaobjects to base-level objects, and
- `ReflexObject`: an interface that defines the protocol to access the metaobjects linked to a given object. Class builders are responsible for making *reflective classes*, i.e. classes defining reflective objects, implement this interface.

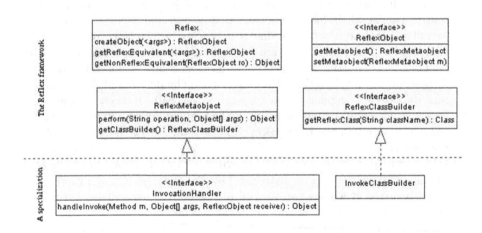

Fig. 1. The Reflex framework and one specialization

3.1   The Generic MOP

Figure 1 shows that, by default, a metaobject implements the interface
`ReflexMetaobject`. The `Reflex` package includes a default implementation of
such a metaobject. The interface `ReflexMetaobject` defines two methods. The
method `getClassBuilder` returns the class builder implementing hook introduction (see below) as required by this metaobject. A hook is an invocation of
`perform` with two arguments: the event type and an array of additional parameters depending on the events.

As an example, let us consider hooks for method invocations. In a more "traditional" MOP, trapping a method invocation would be done using the following
hook:

$$metaobj.\texttt{handleInvoke}(method,\ args,\ receiver);$$

While, with Reflex, trapping the same method invocation can be done using the
following *generic* hook:

$$metaobj.\texttt{perform}(\texttt{"handleInvoke"},\ invokeArgs);$$

This hook could result, for instance, in the invocation of a method
`handleInvoke` of the metaobject. The argument *invokeArgs* describes the base-
level invocation trapped by the hook: method, arguments, and receiver.

Such a MOP makes it apparent that a metaobject *interprets* base-level events.
It is very flexible in that new event types can be introduced without redefining
the MOP (including generic class builders), which also means that metaobjects
defined in such a context are quite easy to reuse even in the presence of new
events. We shall also see in Sect. 3.4 that it may also help when implementing a
composition policy.

There are however some drawbacks associated to this flexibility. First, the
use of a generic hook has some cost (an additional indirection with a dispatch
on the event type and some argument packing and unpacking) which may turn
out to be prohibitive. Second, the choice of a uniform metaobject type may be
counterproductive in a context where many *intended* types of metaobjects are
manipulated, with the risk of preventing early type mismatch detection.

This could indeed be a serious problem if Reflex were a closed reflective
extension, which it is not. The architect of the metalevel may choose to extend
the MOP, as will be illustrated in the next section.

3.2   Class Builders

Class builders are responsible for hook introduction. A class of class builders
implements the `ReflexClassBuilder` interface (see Fig. 1), i.e. a class builder is
able to take as input a standard class and return a *reflective* class. This reflective
class can then be instantiated in order to get reflective objects which are type-
compatible with instances of the initial class.

Therefore, a class builder corresponds to the set of events attached to the
input class. It operationally defines these events as a program transformation

introducing the proper hooks at the proper places in the code. Depending on the class builder, this code may be either source code or byte-code and the transformation may happen in place (the input class is destructively turned into a reflective class) or not. In the latter case, *subclassing* should be used in order to get type compatibility between instances of the input class and the output class. Different class builders corresponding to different events can then produce different compatible reflective classes that can coexist in a running system. Class builders can therefore be built according to the precise requirements (performance, dynamic adaptability, events of interest. . .) of the target applications. They play an essential role with respect to the flexibility of the framework.

A number of classes have been implemented with the Javassist API [5] (they operate on byte-code) in order to help defining class builders. The class `SubclassCreator` makes it possible to generate a subclass of the original class. A number of transformations can then be performed on this subclass using classes such as `MetalinkInserter` (metalink insertion), `MethodcallHookInserter` (method wrapping), `MethodCopier` (copying compiled methods). . . These classes are used by the generic class builder provided in the `Reflex` package, which allows metaobjects to trap, through the generic MOP, invocations of public methods. Defining a new class builder is a matter of extending this predefined builder (e.g. by subclassing) or defining a new one (for instance avoiding generating a subclass).

Any reflective class, created via a class builder, implements the `ReflexObject` interface, which defines the `getMetaobject` and `setMetaobject` methods for respectively retrieving and setting the metaobject attached to a base reflective object. This means that, in this preliminary version of the framework, the metalink has cardinality n-1, i.e. a base object is directly linked to a single metaobject (it may indirectly be linked to several metaobjects via the composition scheme). This is bound to change in the near future (see Sect. 6.1).

Note that there is another classical way of introducing hooks: using object wrappers. This is the technique used in Dalang [26] and the dynamic proxy classes offered by JDK1.3 [15]. Such a scheme suffers from a number of well-identified problems [26], in particular from the identity problem and the lack of type compatibility between a standard, non-reflective, object and its wrapper, making it reflective. These problems can be circumvented either by merging the object and its wrapper, as in the successor of Dalang, Kava [26], or by making the wrapper inherit from the wrapped object, as in the MOP used by ProActive [4]. In the former case, the issue is then to combine reflective and non-reflective instances of the same class. [26] mentions the introduction of hooks on the sender's side, without more details. In the latter case, there is the cost of an additional object.

The idea of relying on inheritance in order to control invocations is not new [9,11]. As for Java reflective extensions, the idea has already been used by Reflective Java [27]. However, Reflective Java does not provide any creation protocol (see below), which requires, when programming at the base level, to know the reflective classes attached to a base class and to manipulate these classes explicitly.

3.3   Creating Reflective Objects

The `Reflex` class (see Fig. 1) defines the *creation protocol*, i.e. static methods dedicated to creating reflective objects as well as turning non-reflective objects into reflective objects (and vice versa).

The `createObject` methods are used to create a reflective object from scratch. These methods should be used instead of `new` statements by the application programmer when a reflective version is needed[2]. The `createObject` method exists in different overloaded versions. The first argument is always the name of the class to be instantiated (with the idea that, behind the scene, a reflective version of it is going to be used). One version of the `createObject` method takes a second argument which is the metaobject to attach to the created reflective object. As previously seen, the metaobject gives access to the class builder to use to create the appropriate reflective class in case this class has not been constructed yet. Another version takes as second argument the class builder. The metaobject is then a default metaobject which does not modify the behavior of the object.

The `getReflexEquivalent` methods are used to build a reflective instance from an existing, non-reflective, one. As, in Java, there is no way to dynamically change the class of an object, this reflective instance is a shallow copy[3] of the non-reflective instance. The `getReflexEquivalent` method exists as well in different overloaded versions. The only difference with the `createObject` methods is that the first argument is an object (the one to get a reflective equivalent of) instead of a string representing the name of a class.

A dual `getNonReflexEquivalent` method makes it possible to produce, again through cloning, a non-reflective object from a reflective one.

3.4   Composition Framework

Reflex does not enforce the use of a particular composition scheme, nor does it enforce the use of a composition scheme at all. However, to simplify the creation of such composition schemes, the Reflex framework includes a generic composition framework.

This framework simply makes explicit the distinction between three types of metaobjects, composers, extensions, and interpreters:

– A *composer* acts as a *facade* [12] of the set of composed metaobjects. It defines the composition policy and is in charge of managing the construction and evolution of the composition set.

---

[2] Obviously, this is not needed if the original class has been directly modified, may it be at compile time or load time.

[3] The values of the object fields are not copied recursively.

- An *interpreter* defines a complete meaningful interpretation of base-level events (e.g. method invocation). A remote call metaobject is an example of an interpreter.
- An *extension* simply extends the interpretation of such events with some extra behavior. A trace metaobject is an example of an extension.

The generic composition framework therefore consists of three empty interfaces, `Composer`, `Interpreter`, and `Extension`, deriving from the root interface `ReflexMetaobject`. Section 4 describes a concrete composition scheme deriving from this framework.

A composer should be as generic as possible, hence it should make as few assumptions as possible on the types of the metaobjects it will compose. Therefore, since metaobjects in the composition set will not be retrievable directly through the metalink, and may offer public methods for configuration that may be invoked from the base level, the composer has to offer a *communication channel* between the base level and the composed metaobjects.

This communication channel is based on the method `perform`. In a set of collaborative metaobjects, when a metaobject receives a message, it checks if it knows how to handle it. If so, it performs the associated operation, otherwise it ignores it. It is up to the specific composition scheme to guarantee that the message will be handled by the appropriate metaobjects. Messages can be sent in order to invoke a particular method on a specific metaobject, or to perform a kind of *broadcast* within the composition set. This mechanism is illustrated in Sect. 4.3.

4   Reflex in Practice

In this section we successively illustrate the use of Reflex for an architect of the metalevel through a MOP extension, for a metaobject programmer through the development of a metaobject, and for an application programmer through the creation and manipulation of a reflective object. We end by showing how the generic hook of Reflex can be used to control a new kind of event and support heterogeneity of metaobjects.

4.1   Perspective of the Architect of the Metalevel

Defining the MOP. The Reflex framework can be specialized in order to fit application requirements. The architect specializing the framework can introduce a new MOP, with a default implementation, define which hooks will be introduced and how. The lower part of Fig. 1 shows a specialization of the Reflex framework that we developed for applications for which trapping method invocations is a major feature. This specialization consists of definitions of:

- an extended MOP (interface `InvocationHandler`) that defines a method for handling method invocations, `handleInvoke`,

– a specific class builder (class `InvokeClassBuilder`) that introduces hooks, through subclassing, for trapping invocations of public methods via `handleInvoke`.

The hypothesis here is that performance is an issue with metaobjects performing, on average, very little work, which means that the cost of jumping to the metalevel should be minimized.

Defining a composition scheme. The architect of the metalevel can then design and implement a composition scheme. We already extended Reflex with such a scheme, inspired by Mulet et al. [16]. In this scheme (see Fig. 2), each *extension* metaobject performs its tasks and then transfers control to the next metaobject in the cooperation chain. The chain composer ensures that there is always one and only one interpreter placed at the end of the chain. Therefore, extensions in this scheme are directly linked to another metaobject (which can be another extension or an interpreter) and explicitly cooperate with it.

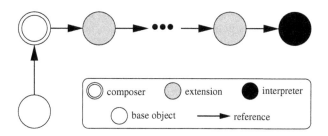

Fig. 2. Composition chain

4.2   Perspective of the Metaobject Programmer

Now that the metalevel architecture has been set up, the metaobject programmer can start implementing metaobjects. These metaobjects conform to the MOP defined by the architect of the metalevel, and possibly make use of a composition framework. We illustrate here the development of a configurable trace metaobject for the MOP defined by the `InvocationHandler` interface, using the composition framework presented above.

The `Trace` class is declared as implementing the base interface for extensions in the chain composition scheme. The role of such a metaobject is to trace, on a given output, the method invocations that occur on a set of base objects. This trace is selective: it applies to some methods only. To this end, the trace metaobject aggregates a hash set containing the names of the methods to trace. This hash set and the target print stream on which the trace is performed can be given at instantiation time or later, and can be updated dynamically. The simplified (without exception handling) implementation of the `handleInvoke` method is as follows (`out` is the target print stream object, and `toTrace` is the hash set containing the names of the methods to trace):

```
public Object handleInvoke(Method m, Object[] args,
                           ReflexObject receiver){

    if(toTrace.contains(methodname))                              (1)
        out.println("call: '' + m.getName + '' with: '' + args ); (2)

    return this.getComposed().handleInvoke(m,
                                           receiver,
                                           args);                 (3)
}
```

First, the trace metaobject[4] checks if the hash set contains the name of the invoked method (1). If it does, a trace is produced, giving the name of the method and its arguments (2). The invocation is then forwarded to the next metaobject in the chain (3). Depending on the exact use of such a metaobject, there may be situations where a trace is generated for a fraction of the invocation, in which case, on average, the metaobject does not do much and performance becomes an issue. It makes sense to use a specific MOP.

Since the trace metaobject is a configurable one, different public services for setting it up are offered. These services include setting the methods to trace (`setMethodsToTrace(HashSet)`, `addMethodToTrace(String)`...) and the print stream on which to perform the trace (`setOutput(PrintStream)`). All these public methods can seamlessly be invoked by the base level at any time, by using the `perform` method, as illustrated later on.

4.3   Perspective of the Application Programmer

Once the library of metaobjects up and ready, the application programmer can introduce metaobjects in his application. His role is basically that of identifying which objects should be reflective, and which metaobjects should be attached to each of these objects (even if this is actually hidden behind code transformation tools and wizards). Let us illustrate the creation of a reflective vector to which a trace metaobject is attached.

The first step is to create and set up the metaobject to be attached to the base object:

```
ChainComposer composer = new ChainComposer();                     (1)
Trace trace = new Trace();                                        (2)
composer.addExtension(trace);                                     (3)
```

---

[4] For a more realistic implementation of a trace metaobject, we refer the reader to the samples included in the `Reflex` package.

First, the composer is instantiated (1). Since no interpreter is specified in the constructor, the composer automatically instantiates a default interpreter, with default semantics.

Then the trace metaobject is created (2). Finally, the trace metaobject, which is an extension metaobject, is inserted into the composition chain managed by `composer` (3).

Once this is done, the reflective object can be instantiated, using the services of the `Reflex` class:

```
Vector v = (Vector) Reflex.createObject("java.util.Vector",
                                        composer);
```

The `createObject` arguments indicate that a reflective instance of `java.util.Vector` should be created, with the metaobject `composer` attached to the instance. When this statement is executed, the `createObject` method queries the composer for the class builder to use, and then delegates to the class builder the task of retrieving the reflective `Vector` subclass. At this point, if the reflective subclass has already been created, it is loaded if needed. Otherwise, it is created and loaded dynamically. The `createObject` method instantiates the reflective class, and attaches the metaobject to the created instance. Finally, it returns the reflective object.

Now, `v` is a reference of (declared) type `Vector` that points to a reflective object, instance of a reflective subclass of the `Vector` class. Let us suppose that, later on, the print stream used to perform the trace has to be updated. This must be done via an invocation of the `setOutput` method on the trace metaob-ject. Unfortunately, the metaobject is not directly accessible from the base-level object since the metalink only gives access to the composer. The composer be-ing generic, it does not understand `setOutput`. This problem is circumvented by invoking the `perform` method on the composer. The first argument of the invocation is the ''setOutput" string. The composer will forward this event to metaobjects of the composition chain. Eventually, the event will reach the trace metaobject, and will be processed:

```
PrintStream file = new PrintStream(
                        new FileOutputStream("trace.log")); (1)
Reflex.sendEvent("setOutput", v, file);                    (2)
```

First, a print stream object is created on the desired output file (1). Then, a ''setOutput" event is sent, together with its argument (2). This `sendEvent` method is a static method of the `Reflex` class. It is a useful shortcut which casts `v` to `ReflexObject`, retrieves a reference to the metaobject associated to it, and packs the arguments into an array of objects in order to be able to invoke the `perform` method.

4.4   Handling Heterogeneous Metaobjects

In this section, we illustrate how the generic hook of Reflex can be used to control a new kind of event and support heterogeneity of metaobjects.

In the context of mobile agents, an agent is normally seen as a closed entity which encapsulates all its data. Therefore, upon migration, all the objects that an agent references are passed by copy with the agent. However, this policy is not always desirable: some objects should be passed by reference, for instance if they belong to some other agents or if they are huge and should be accessed lazily. This is feasible in Java using Remote Method Invocation (RMI) [22]. However, RMI is very demanding on the class to be passed by reference. It first has to implement the `Remote` interface, and, moreover, it has to be a subclass of `UnicastRemoteObject`. We would like a more flexible system allowing any object to be passed by reference, without any constraint on its class. Upon migration of the agent, passing the object by reference means passing a proxy to the object rather than the object itself. This can be done by making the object reflective and linking the appropriate metaobject. Such a metaobject is informed when serialization occurs and can specify an alternative object for serialization (the proxy). Once passed, the proxy is controlled by a metaobject which performs all method invocations remotely through the network.

We therefore need to give the control of serialization to metaobjects. The Java serialization API [21] offers a method, `writeReplace`, which can be used to specify an alternative object for serialization. Therefore, reflective objects should implement this method and a hook has to be inserted so that when this method is invoked automatically by the serialization process, the metalevel is informed and has the possibility of specifying an alternative object (such as a proxy).

We have implemented a new class of class builders, `SerializeClassBuilder`, which extends `InvokeClassBuilder`. The `SerializeClassBuilder` seamlessly adds a `writeReplace` method to each generated class using a `MethodCopier` object. This method, defined below, plays the role of a generic hook:

```
private Object writeReplace() throws ObjectStreamException {

    ReflexMetaobject mo = this.getMetaobject();                    (1)
    Object replace = mo.perform("handleSerialize",
                                null);                             (2)
    if(replace == null)                                           (3)
      return this;                                                (4)
    else
      return replace;                                             (5)
}
```

When serialization on the base object occurs, this method is invoked. It first retrieves the metaobject associated to the base object (1), and sends to this metaobject a ''handleSerialize" event (2). If the result is null (3), i.e. no metaobject understood the event, then the default policy applies (4). Otherwise, the alternative object is returned (5).

If a metaobject wants to be informed when serialization occurs, it simply has to implement the `handleSerialize` method. Heterogeneous metaobjects can now cooperate, some understanding the `handleSerialize` method, some not. All existing metaobjects can be used seamlessly along with metaobjects newly developed for handling serialization.

5   Related Work

The work on MetaJ [8] shares with ours the objective of making it possible to tailor reflective extensions to the specific constraints of its target applications. However, it only deals with meta-circular interpreters. On the one hand, this makes it possible to adopt a semantics-based approach, and therefore to be very systematic and deal with formal correctness. On the other hand, the gap with practical considerations such as performance is far from being bridged.

On the opposite, all the practical Java reflective extensions [28,26,4,13,25,18] provide a fixed MOP with some universal decisions made on the trade-offs between portability, expressiveness, and performance. The only point on which Reflex does not offer any freedom is portability, on the basis that this decision is actually set by the very definition of Java.

In spite of its fixed MOP, the case of Iguana/J [19] is peculiar. Indeed, its MOP seems to cover all the elementary execution events, for which metaobjects have already been designed. Iguana/J introduces then the idea of combining these metaobjects through protocol declarations, protocols which can then be, again declaratively, associated to base classes. This is a very elegant and flexible way of structuring customized metalevels from elementary building blocks with the protocols themselves providing higher-level building blocks. The implementation is based on the Java Native Interface and should therefore be still reasonably portable with an efficient capture of the basic events (but more implementation work). However, some points would require some clarifications. In particular, it seems that base classes are associated with protocols, which precludes the possibility of sharing metaobjects. Also, hook introduction is said to be performed by the native library! Finally, the model does not consider the possibility of performing hook introduction at the source code level or combining compile- and run-time MOPs. In Reflex, the introduction of class builders makes it much easier to combine these different approaches.

As for composing metaobjects, with the exception of MetaXa [13] and Guaraná[18], the other Java reflective extensions do not offer any help. In MetaXa, the composition scheme is fixed. The VM systematically organizes the metaobjects in a chain of metaobjects, following the order of introduction of these metaobjects. Guaraná is more open in that it offers metaobjects similar to the composers introduced in the specialization of Reflex as well as an extensible communication protocol similar to the propagation of events realized through the use of `perform`.

6   Future Work

In its current state, Reflex still suffers from some limitations to claim to be a full-fledged open reflective extension of Java. We have already started working on these limitations.

6.1   Metalink Cardinality

The current release of Reflex only supports a metalink cardinality 1-n, meaning that a base object can only be linked to one metaobject, and a metaobjet can control several base objects. Though a composition framework can be used to allow different metaobjects to participate in the control of a base object, a more mature open reflective extension should support a metalink cardinality n-n. A preliminary design is available but has not been implemented yet.

Supporting such a cardinality may enhance performance since, for a given object, different hooks can then directly give control to the relevant metaobject (or set of metaobjects). Metaobjects that are not interested by the corresponding event are not affected any longer.

6.2   Allowing More Optimizations

Some applications do not require the flexibility provided by features such as the ability to dynamically change the set of metaobjects attached to a base object. In such a case, hooks should not be introduced, instead base and meta levels should be merged, like in compile-time MOP such as OpenJava [25].

Also, allowing the coexistence of non-reflective and reflective instances (possibly with different sets of controlled events) is a motivation for not directly modifying a base class and generating implicit subclasses. However, some applications do not require such a feature, e.g. when all instances of a class have to be reflective with the same set of controlled events. In this case, it is better to directly introduce hooks in the base class than to generate subclasses. This direct introduction of hooks into the base class should possibly be made at load time in order not to modify the standard version of the base class.

Conceptually, Reflex allows for such optimizations through the use of particular class builders. Some class builders could operate by merging the base and meta levels at compile time, some by introducing hooks statically in a class (or source) file, some others by introducing hooks in a base class at load time. However no such class builder has been implemented yet.

6.3   Class Builders and Dynamic Adaptability

A base-level object can be controlled by several metaobjects, either through the use of a composition framework in order to share a metalink, or through a metalink cardinality n-n. Each of these metaobjects is designed to react to a particular kind of events, requiring the necessary hooks to be introduced in the class of the base-level object. As a consequence, the base-level object has to be an instance of a class that includes the union of all the hooks needed by the metaobjects used to control it.

Two issues derive from this statement. The first one relates to the specification of the required hooks and how they are mixed together in order to obtain the adequate class to instantiate. As of now, a metaobject has to be able to specify which class builder should be used. The composer then needs rules determining which available class builder meets the needs of all the composed metaobjects. We plan to make this specification finer-grained by allowing metaobjects to specify their needs in terms of basic transformations, and having a generic class builder able to compose all these transformations. This is on-going work.

The second issue concerns the dynamic evolution of the set of metaobjects that control a base-level object. Conceptually, when adding a metaobject that requires hooks that are not present in the class of the base-level object, a new reflective class must be generated, with all the hooks. The instantiation link of the base-level object has then to be changed in order to make it an instance of the newly generated class. However, changing the instantiation link is not possible in Java, nor is it possible to really *replace* an existing object by a new one. The only implementable solution we envision at this time is that of obtaining a shallow copy, instance of the new class, similarly to what is done when "converting" a non-reflective object to a reflective one. However, this solution is not satisfactory for obvious identity problems. The possibility of class reload, offered by the upcoming JDK 1.4 [1], may help solve this issue.

6.4   Performance

One of the goals of Reflex is to minimize performance loss by providing the minimum reflective system needed for a particular application. In order to validate the gain, we plan to carry performance tests between Reflex and other non-customizable reflective extensions. We also plan to compare the use of the generic MOP of Reflex to that of a specialized MOP, and to study how the implementation of the base components of Reflex could be optimized.

7   Conclusion

This paper has presented Reflex, a prototype *open* reflective extension of Java. As such, Reflex is a specializable framework and a toolkit that can be used to build or adapt reflective extensions that meet particular needs. It fills the gap between low-level byte-code manipulation APIs allowing the definition of custom-built reflective extensions and high-level non-specializable reflective extensions through two main concepts: a generic MOP and class builders.

As of now, a working specialization of Reflex has been implemented and applied to mobile object systems. We plan to pursue the validation of Reflex with new applications, testing different composition schemes, and work on the limitations to Reflex openness.

The **Reflex** package (binaries, source, examples and documentation) can be obtained from the web at the following URL:

`http://www.dcc.uchile.cl/~etanter/Reflex`

Acknowledgements

This research is supported in part by the EU-funded IST Project 1999-14191 EasyComp.

References

1. V. Aggarwal. The magic of Merlin – how the new JDK 1.4 levitates its functionality. *Java World*, March 2001.
2. M. Braux and J. Noyé. Towards partially evaluating reflection in Java. In *ACM SIGPLAN Workshop on Partial Evaluation and Semantics-Based Program Manipulation*, Boston, MA, USA, January 2000. ACM Press. ACM SIGPLAN Notices, 34(11).
3. J.-P. Briot, R. Guerraoui, and K.-P. Löhr. Concurrency and distribution in object oriented programming. *ACM Computer Surveys*, 30(3), September 1998.
4. D. Caromel, W. Klauser, and J. Vayssiere. Towards seamless computing and meta-computing in Java. In *Concurrency Practice and Experience*, volume 10. Wiley & Sons, September 1998.
5. S. Chiba. Load-time structural reflection in Java. In E. Bertino, editor, *ECOOP 2000 - Object-Oriented Programming - 14th European Conference*, number 1850 in Lecture Notes in Computer Science, pages 313–336, Sophia Antipolis and Cannes, France, June 2000. Springer-Verlag.
6. S. Chiba and M. Tatsubori. Yet another java.lang.class. In *ECOOP'98 Workshop on Reflective Object-Oriented Programming and Systems*, Brussels, Belgium, July 1998.
7. P. Cointe, editor. *Proceedings of Reflection '99*, volume 1616 of *Lecture Notes in Computer Science*, Saint-Malo, France, 1999. Springer-Verlag.
8. R. Douence and M. Südholt. A generic reification technique for object-oriented reflective languages. *Higher-Order and Symbolic Computation*, 14(1), 2001.
9. S. Ducasse. Evaluating message passing control techniques in Smalltalk. *Journal of Objet-Oriented Programming*, June:39–50, 1999.
10. *Proceedings of the ACM SIGPLAN Workshop on Dynamic and Adaptive Compilation and Optimization (Dynamo'00)*, Boston, MA, USA, January 2000. ACM Press. ACM SIGPLAN Notices, 35(7).
11. B. Foote and R.E. Johnson. Reflective facilities in Smalltalk-80. In N. Meyrowitz, editor, *OOPSLA'89, Conference Proceedings*, pages 327–335, New Orleans, Louisiana, USA, October 1989. ACM SIGPLAN Notices, 24(10).
12. E. Gamma, R. Helm, R. Johnson, and J. Vlissides. *Design Patterns : Elements of Reusable Object-Oriented Software*. Addison-Wesley, 1994.
13. M. Golm and J. Kleinöder. Jumping to the meta level, behavioral reflection can be fast and flexible. In Cointe [7], pages 22–39.
14. N.D. Jones, C.K. Gomard, and P. Sestoft. *Partial Evaluation and Automatic Program Generation*. International Series in Computer Science. Prentice Hall, 1993.

15. SUN Microsystems. Dynamic proxy classes.
    `http://java.sun.com/j2se/1.3/docs/guide/reflection/proxy.html`, 1999.
16. P. Mulet, J. Malenfant, and P. Cointe. Towards a methodology for explicit composition of metaobjects. In *Proceedings of OOPSLA'95*, pages 316–330. ACM Press, October 1995.
17. H. Okamura and Y. Ishikawa. Object location control using meta-level programming. In *Proceedings of ECOOP'94*, pages 299–319, 1994.
18. A. Oliva and L. E. Buzato. Composition of meta-objects in Guarana. In *Proceedings of the 5th USENIX Conference on Object-Oriented Technologies & Systems (COOTS'99)*, San Diego, California, USA, May 1999.
19. B. Redmond and V. Cahill. Iguana/J: Towards a dynamic and efficient reflective architecture for Java. ECOOP 2000 Workshop on Reflection and Metalevel Architectures, June 2000.
20. R.J. Stroud and Z. Wu. Using metaobject protocols to satisfy non-functional requirements. In C. Zimmermann, editor, *Advances in Object-Oriented Metalevel Architectures and Reflection*, pages 31–52. CRC Press, 1996.
21. SUN Microsystems. *Object Serialization*, 1998.
    `http://java.sun.com/products/jdk/1.2/docs/guide/serialization/`.
22. Java Remote Method Invocation specification. Technical report, SUN Microsystems, 1999. `http://java.sun.com.products/jdk/1.2/docs/guide/rmi/`.
23. E. Tanter. Reflex, a reflective system for Java — application to flexible resource management in Java mobile object systems. Master's thesis, Universidad de Chile, Chile – Vrije Universiteit Brussel, Belgium, 2000.
24. E. Tanter. *Reflex Website*, 2001. `http://www.dcc.uchile.cl/~etanter/Reflex`.
25. M. Tatsubori. An extension mechanism for the Java language. Master's thesis, University of Tsukuba, Japan, 1999.
26. I. Welch and R. Stroud. From Dalang to Kava — the evolution of a reflective Java extension. In Cointe [7], pages 2–21.
27. Z. Wu. Reflective Java and a reflective-component-based transaction architecture. In J.-C. Fabre and S. Chiba, editors, *Proceedings of the ACM OOPSLA'98 Workshop on Reflective Programming in Java and C++*, October 1998.
28. Z. Wu and S. Schwiderski. Reflective Java: Making Java even more flexible. APM 1936.02, APM Limited, Castle Park, Cambridge, UK, February 1997.

System Checkpointing
Using Reflection and Program Analysis

John Whaley

Computer Systems Laboratory
Stanford University
Stanford, CA 94305
jwhaley@alum.mit.edu

Abstract. This paper describes a technique for checkpointing a running system by a combination of reflective introspection and program analysis. By using an extension to Java's Reflection API which allows activation frames and other aspects of execution state to be reflectively inspected and modified, we can halt at and restart from arbitrary points in the execution. We apply this checkpointing technique to an area that is not typically associated with reflection — optimization of memory footprint and startup time. We have successfully used this technique in the joeq virtual machine to reduce the heap size and the application startup time significantly.

1 Introduction

The Java programming language has gained a significant following due to a number of reasons, including its clean, object-oriented design and automatic storage management. It is a very popular choice for server-side applications; however, on the client side, Java has yet to make significant headway against more established languages like C and C++.

There are currently two major problems that must be overcome before Java can become prevalent on the client side. The first is application startup time [5]. Applications using the Swing GUI interface can take on the order of minutes to start up. This is due to a number of factors, including large amounts of inefficient initialization code in the class libraries and the fact that (in most virtual machines) the code is recompiled from class files on every execution.

The second major stumbling block in the adoption of Java on the client side is memory footprint. Even simple GUI applications can regularly consume 20 megabytes or more of memory [8]. What is more, in most systems this memory is not shared among applications, which means that 20 megabytes *per running instance* are consumed. Again, this is due to a number of factors, including the liberalism of virtual machine garbage collectors in allocating memory and the dynamic and object-oriented nature of the Java language. Because of dynamic features such as reflection and dynamic class loading, the system cannot perform whole-program analysis to eliminate the (as-of-yet) unused fields, methods, and other runtime data structures.

A. Yonezawa and S. Matsuoka (Eds.): REFLECTION 2001, LNCS 2192, pp. 44–51, 2001.

To attack these problems, we developed a general technique of checkpointing the state of the system using reflection. Checkpointing is the act of saving the state of a running system such that it can be recreated later in time. Checkpointing has many applications, including system recovery, debugging, bootstrapping, and process migration. We use checkpointing for a different purpose. By running the system up to a certain point and then checkpointing it, we can use the checkpointed version to avoid startup time costs; in essence, application startup time becomes bounded only by disk latency. Furthermore, we can perform analysis during the checkpointing process to optimize the system, reducing the memory footprint by eliminating unnecessary code, objects, fields, classes, and runtime data structures.

Using reflection makes our technique very flexible. Because we use reflection, we can precisely control the checkpointing process, deciding what data to ignore and what data needs to be reinitialized on virtual machine startup. Furthermore, the technique is entirely virtual machine and architecture independent; we actually use this technique to bootstrap the joeq virtual machine across platforms [14].

The remainder of the paper is organized as follows. Section 2 outlines the checkpointing technique and associated algorithms. Section 3 presents data on the effectiveness of the technique in reducing code and heap size and improving startup time in our implementation in the joeq virtual machine [14]. Section 4 discusses related work, and we conclude in Section 5.

2   Technique

Our basic checkpointing technique is as follows:

1. Start the virtual machine and let it execute until a desired point. Suspend all threads.
2. Determine the root set. If necessary, inspect the activation records (stack traces) of the threads.
3. Given the root set, determine the necessary parts of the system (code and data) and any code necessary to reconstruct the necessary state.
4. Serialize the necessary code and data to a file, in the standard format for the virtual machine.
5. On subsequent executions, simply map the file to memory and execute the reconstruction code to continue execution from the given point.

Our current implementation uses a very simple flow-insensitive, context-insensitive type-based pointer analysis to determine the necessary code and data. Namely, any field that is accessed, any method that is called, and any class that is instantiated is considered to reach all program points. Section 2.1 describes the algorithm in more detail.

After the necessary code and data are determined, we serialize the code and data in the standard format for the virtual machine. We also include relocations for every code and data reference, so that the code and data segments can be relocated between executions. Section 2.3 gives details on this process.

2.1   Algorithm Description

```
doAlgorithm() {
  method_worklist = buildRootSet();
  while (!method_worklist.isEmpty()) {
    Method m; InstructionIndex a;
    (m, a) = method_worklist.pull();
    analyzeReachableCode(m, a);
  }
}
```

Fig. 1. The checkpointing algorithm

Pseudocode for the algorithm can be found in Figure 1. The algorithm first initializes a worklist of <*Method, InstructionIndex*> pairs using the root set, and then analyzes each of the methods in the worklist. There are two techniques to obtain the root set. The first technique, which is portable, is to have it specified by the programmer, *e.g.* the main method or event loop of a program. The second technique, which requires some virtual machine extensions, is to build the root set using the stack traces of the running threads.

```
addObject(Object o) {
  if (table.contains(o)) return;
  HeapAddress a = allocateSpace(getObjectSize(o));
  table.add(o, new Pair(o, a));
  addType(o.getClass());
  forall (Field f = o.getClass().fields()) {
    if (f.isReferenceType() && isNecessaryField(f)) addObject(f.get(o));
  }
}
```

Fig. 2. Pseudocode for adding an object

Figure 2 contains the pseudocode for marking an object as necessary. To keep track of the necessary objects, we use a hash table keyed on the identity hash code of the objects. This hash table maps from the object to a pair: <*object, address*>. *object* is a reference back to the object; *address* refers to the address of the object in the output image.

When an object that has never been encountered before is added, we reserve space for it in the output image, generate an <*object, address*> pair for it, and register the pair in the hash table. We also mark the object's type as instantiated. Then, for each reference field of the object that has been marked as necessary, we add the object referenced by that field.

Figure 3 contains pseudocode for analyzing the reachable code from a given starting point. We traverse the instructions using a worklist algorithm. For each

```
analyzeReachableCode(Method m, InstructionIndex a) {
  Worklist w = new Worklist(); w.add(a);
  while (!w.isEmpty()) {
    Instruction i = w.pull();
    forall (Field f = i.getAccessedFields()) addField(f);
    forall (Class c = i.getInstantiatedTypes()) addType(c);
    forall (Method m2 = i.getTargetMethods()) addMethodToWorklist(m2, 0);
    forall (Instruction j = i.successors()) w.add(j);
  }
}
```

Fig. 3. Pseudocode for analyzing the reachable code from a given starting point

instruction, any field that can be accessed is added to the list of necessary fields. Likewise, if an instruction can instantiate an object, we add the type to the set of instantiated types. For call instructions, we add all target methods to the method worklist. Finally, we add the indices of all possible successor instructions in the current method to the worklist.

```
addType(Class c) {
  if (classes.contains(c)) return; classes.add(c);
  addObject(c);
  forall (Method m = visited_methods) {
    if (c.overrides(m)) addMethodToWorklist(c.getMethod(m), 0);
  }
}
```

Fig. 4. Pseudocode for marking a type as instantiated

Figure 4 gives the pseudocode for marking a type as instantiated. When a new type is encountered, we add the Class object, which ensures that the vtable and other run time structures will be correctly allocated in the image. We then add the implementations of any necessary overridden method to the worklist.

Figure 5 lists the pseudocode for adding a field as necessary. When adding a new reference (non-primitive) instance field to the necessary set, we need to add any objects that are reachable via that field on already visited objects, so we iterate through the set of necessary objects that contain the newly added field and use reflection to get their values. In the case of reference static fields, we always add their values.

2.2   Generating Startup Code

Some objects contain values that are specific to the particular execution instance, or require some code to be executed on startup. For example, memory needs to be reallocated and file handles need to be reopened. Therefore, the algorithm also

```
addField(Field f) {
  if (fields.contains(f)) return; fields.add(f);
  if (f.isReferenceType()) {
    if (f.isInstanceField()) {
      forall (Object o = necessaryObjects()) {
        if (o.getClass().containsField(f)) addObject(f.get(o));
      }
    } else addObject(f.get(null));
  }
}
```

Fig. 5. Pseudocode for marking a field as necessary

calculates the code to be executed during virtual machine startup to reinitialize the execution-specific data values.

Execution-specific data values are determined in one of two ways. The first way is by using the type of the object. Certain fields in objects always refer to data that is execution instance specific and therefore must be reinitialized on virtual machine startup. When reflectively inspecting these fields, we keep track of their instances so that we can generate the correct reinitialization code. In some cases, it is not possible to reconstruct the state using only the object fields. In such cases, we run the application using instrumented versions of the initialization routines which cache the incoming parameters. To perform reinitialization, we simply call those routines again with the same parameters. Some data values that are execution-specific cannot be determined solely by their type. For example, system properties are stored as Strings in a Vector object, so we cannot determine simply from their type that they should be reinitialized at run time. We explicitly enumerate such values along with the code necessary to reinitialize them.

In some cases, special application knowledge is necessary for correct checkpointing. If code has executed that was dependent on some value that may change between executions, we may run into problems. In such cases, the programmer must manually specify the application data to be reinitialized along with the code necessary to perform the reinitialization. However, in many applications such code is not necessary [9].

2.3   Serializing the Code and Data

After we have determined the set of necessary objects, methods, fields, and classes, we serialize them to a file using the standard object format for the virtual machine. We iterate through all of the entries in the hash table by starting address, using reflection to examine each of their fields and writing the object at the specified address. For each non-null object reference that we encounter, we also store relocation information so that it can be successfully relocated. Likewise, we generate code for all of the necessary methods, adding relocations where necessary.

	Fields Before	Fields After	Objects Before	Objects After	Heap Size Before	Heap Size After	Code Size Before	Code Size After
joeq	3840	2590	474231	326539	16690524	11029044	939981	774637
javac	5674	3882	587061	432073	20752496	14829948	1310719	1138206
SwingSet	13496	11491	1040864	687935	38333768	24642388	2157767	1745599
Forte	19348	15698	3832894	1812932	64398534	38304308	3639503	3048391

Fig. 6. Savings in heap memory

	Original Startup time	Checkpoint Startup time
joeq	27.2 s	1.7 s
javac	35.7 s	1.9 s
SwingSet	140.7 s	3.6 s
Forte	241.6 s	5.9 s

Fig. 7. Savings in startup time

3   Results

This section presents some experimental results from our implementation in the joeq virtual machine [14]. In the results, joeq refers to the "application" of the virtual machine itself. javac refers to Sun's javac compiler. SwingSet is the example Swing application contained in the standard Java distribution. Forte is the Forte for Java integrated development environment. Applications were executed to the start of their main methods and checkpointed at that point.

Table 6 shows the reduction in heap and code size after our technique. As we can see from this data, our technique is very effective in reducing object counts and heap size, up to a 39% reduction. It also significantly reduces code size, up to 19%.

Table 7 shows the reduction in startup time due to our technique. The times given in the table are wall-clock times until the entry point of the application. We rebooted between runs to avoid caching effects. The first column is the time it takes to start up the application normally. The second column gives the time it takes to start up the application from the checkpointed file. All timings were taken when executing on the joeq virtual machine. We were able to attain huge savings on application startup time with our technique. The checkpoint version was, in essence, bounded by disk time. Later executions (once the checkpoint file was in the disk cache) only took a fraction of a second.

4   Related Work

The technique described in this paper of system checkpointing using execution-state reflection has similarities to many prior techniques. In this section, we compare and contrast our technique to related work.

Our overall checkpointing technique is similar to a proposal called Orthogonal Persistence for the Java platform (OPJ) [2]. Orthogonal persistence is an approach to making application objects persist between program executions. To assist in recreating state, similar to our technique OPJ uses *restart callbacks*, which allow the programmer to specify code that will be executed on restart. The major difference between our technique and OPJ is that because OPJ is only concerned with persisting individual objects, it requires more support from the application program. It does not perform any kind of program analysis; it simply uses reachability. Furthermore, OPJ requires the use of a special virtual machine, whereas our technique can use the built-in Java Reflection API.

Our technique is similar to the technique used by the Jalapeño virtual machine to bootstrap itself [1]. However, the Jalapeño technique does not include any support for the serialization of execution state, nor does it support reinitializing state at run time. Also, it does not include any sort of program analysis to determine the extent of the checkpointing.

There has been other work on checkpointing in the context of migrating applications [10], using extra processors for fault tolerance [12], post-mortem and replay debugging, elimination of boundary condition errors [13], etc. Our work is very similar to user-level transparent checkpointing techniques [11]. Such techniques usually work by compiling the application program with a special checkpointing library. Our technique, on the other hand, relies on program analysis and therefore can optimize the result for size and speed. Our system also shares many of the same restrictions as user-level checkpointers; for example, programs should not cache certain types of data [9].

Other researchers have attacked Java's large memory usage and long startup times in other ways. Systems like Echidna [4], rheise os [6], and others [3] allow multiple "processes" to run inside a single virtual machine. This allows the virtual machine startup time and the memory consumption for the base virtual machine to be amortized across each process.

The analysis technique of using the program state to optimize code has similarities to the well-known technique of partial evaluation [7]. The analysis as described here is very simple and only makes minimal use of the available information. Much more extensive use of the data to perform true partial evaluation optimizations is possible.

5   Conclusion

Checkpointing has many useful applications, such as system recovery, debugging, bootstrapping, and process migration. This paper introduces a new use for checkpointing — improving startup time and memory footprint. Our checkpointing technique uses a combination of reflection and program analysis to determine the necessary parts of the program, and serializes only those parts. By using reflection, our technique is very general and powerful. We can easily and precisely adjust what data we checkpoint and automatically generate reinitialization code for data that must be reinitialized on every execution.

We implemented this technique in the joeq virtual machine and presented performance results that show that even with a very simple flow-insensitive and context-insensitive program analysis, this technique can be very effective in reducing application startup time and memory footprint.

There are many further opportunities for taking advantage of the extra information about the program that is available at checkpoint time. For example, by using partial evaluation, we can optimize the application based on values that are not known at compile time, but known at the checkpoint time. A higher level example is to examine the elements of a hash table and use them to derive a perfect hash function. Such techniques will improve not only startup time and heap size, but also overall execution time.

This research was supported in part by a fellowship from the National Science Foundation.

References

1. B. Alpern. Jalapeño virtual machine. *IBM Systems Journal*, 39(1):211–238, 2000.
2. M. P. Atkinson, L. Daynes, M. J. Jordan, T. Printezis, and S. Spence. An orthogonally persistent Java. *ACM SIGMOD Record*, 25(4):68–75, Dec. 1996.
3. G. Czajkowski. Application isolation in the Java virtual machine. In *Proceedings of OOPSLA-00*, pp. 354–366, Oct. 15–19 2000.
4. L. Gorrie. Echidna http://www.javagroup.org/echidna, 1998.
5. E. Gun, S. Arthur, J. Gregory, and B. Bershad. A practical approach for improving startup latency in Java applications, In Proceedings of the Workshop on Compiler Support for Systems Software, Atlanta, Georgia, May 1999.
6. R. Heise. rheise.os. http://www.progsoc.uts.edu.au/r̃heise/projects/rheise.os
7. N. Jones, C. Gomard, and P. Sestoft. Partial evaluation and automatic program generation. Prentice Hall. 1993.
8. Tornado Labs. Java 3D benchmark results. http://www.tornadolabs.com/News/BenchJ3d_Results/benchj3d_results.html, 2000.
9. M. Litzkow and M. Livny. Making workstations a friendly environment for batch jobs. In Proc. 3rd Wks. on Work. Oper. Sys., April 1992.
10. M. Litzkow, T. Tannenbaum, J. Basney, and M. Livny. Checkpoint and migration of unix processes in the Condor distributed processing system, 1997.
11. J. S. Plank. An overview of checkpointing in uniprocessor and distributed systems, focusing on implementation and performance. Tech Report UT-CS-97-372, 1997.
12. J. S. Plank, Y. Kim, and J. J. Dongarra. Algorithm-based diskless checkpointing for fault-tolerant matrix operations. In *FTCS-25: 25th International Symposium on Fault Tolerant Computing Digest of Papers*, pp. 351–360, 1995.
13. Y. M. Wang, Y. Huang, and W. K. Fuchs. Progressive retry for software error recovery in distributed systems. In *Proc. 23rd Int. Conf. on Fault-Tolerant Computing (FTCS-23)*, pp. 138–144, Toulouse, France, 1993.
14. J. Whaley. joeq virtual machine. http://joeq.sourceforge.net, 2001.

Experiments with JavaPod, a Platform Designed for the Adaptation of Non-functional Properties

Eric Bruneton[1,*] and Michel Riveill[2]

[1] SIRAC Project, INRIA,
655 av. de l'Europe, 38334 Montbonnot Saint-Ismier Cedex, France
[2] Ecole Supérieure en Sciences Informatiques,
930 route des Colles, 06903 Sophia Antipolis, France

Abstract. In order to be able to adapt the non-functional properties of distributed applications, we designed and implemented the JavaPod platform. Then, in order to evaluate this platform, we used it to reimplement Baghera, a "real-world", distributed application for computer-aided learning of elementary geometry.
After a brief description of Baghera and of our platform, this article presents how we implemented and associated with Baghera components several non-functional properties. These experiments show that our platform can be extended with new non-functional properties, and that these properties can be composed and associated with applications at deployment time, without changing the application's code. Finally this article shows that the new composition mechanism used in JavaPod is more adapted than existing ones to compose non-functional properties.

1 Introduction

Middleware platforms like CORBA allow programmers to add non-functional properties (e.g. transactions, persistence, etc.) to distributed applications, but the code that implements these properties, through calls to specific services, is intertwined with the application's code. Enterprise Java Beans (EJB) allow a more modular design, by a clean separation of the functional and non-functional aspects through a simple form of a reflective mechanism. While promising, this approach lacks extensibility, as the allowed set of non-functional properties is wired in the EJB container mechanism.

In an attempt to overcome these limitations, we designed and implemented a middleware platform, called JavaPod [1,2], that was intended (*a*) to allow the separation of functional and non-functional code, (*b*) to allow the definition and composition of several non-functional properties, and (*c*) to be modular and extensible. In order to evaluate the basic mechanisms and costs of the JavaPod platform, we implemented extensions [3] providing three non-functional properties: mobility, replication, and persistence.

---

* in collaboration with France Telecom, 38-40 Rue Gal Leclerc, 92794 Issy Moulineaux.

A. Yonezawa and S. Matsuoka (Eds.): REFLECTION 2001, LNCS 2192, pp. 52–72, 2001.
© Springer-Verlag Berlin Heidelberg 2001

While this experiment showed that these properties could indeed be conveniently supplied, it did not assess the usefulness of the extension mechanism for the actual applications that JavaPod was designed to support. We therefore selected a "real-world" distributed application, Baghera, as a test bed for this assessment. Baghera is a computer-aided learning assistant, whose behavior regarding persistence, protection, and disconnected mode needs to be adapted to widely different execution environments. This article presents this case study and the lessons we learned from it.

The next two sections present the architecture and implementation of the JavaPod platform. Section 4 presents the Baghera application and its non-functional requirements. Section 5 explains how we implemented Baghera's non-functional properties, and section 6 gives the results we obtained. Finally section 7 compares JavaPod to other platforms and section 8 concludes this article.

2 The JavaPod Platform Architecture

This section briefly presents the JavaPod platform, which was used to implement the Baghera application. It presents the programming model of this platform, its high-level and low-level architecture, and finally some implementation details.

2.1 Programming Model

The programming model of the JavaPod platform (i.e. the concepts offered to programmers to build their applications) is a very general model inspired from ODP [4,5]. According to our model, applications are made of *components*, linked together through *connectors* (see Fig. 1):

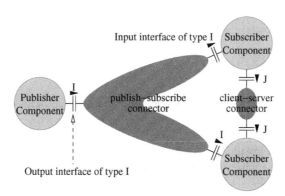

Fig. 1. The concepts of our programming model

- a *component* encapsulates data and code, like an object. However, unlike an object, a component can have multiple access points, called facets in the CORBA component model [6], and that we call *interfaces*[1].
- an interface has a type, which is a list of method signatures, and a direction: an *input* interface is used to call methods inside a component, while an *output* interface is used to call methods outside a component, i.e. on a connector.
- a *connector* is a special component that links together two or more interfaces, not necessarily of the same type. The role of a connector is to allow communication between "normal" components. A connector can represent any type of interaction: client-server, publish-subscribe, group communications, broadcast...

2.2   High-Level Architecture

In order to execute distributed applications programmed according to the above model, we propose to use a middleware platform architecture based on the following elements, inspired from the Enterprise Java Beans (EJB) [7] model[2] (see Fig. 2):

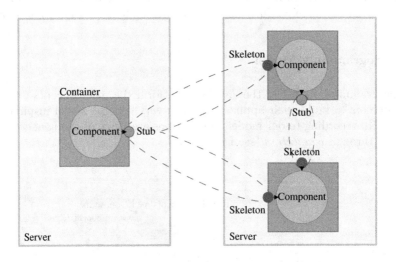

Fig. 2. High-level architecture of the JavaPod platform

- a *container* encapsulates a component, and intercepts all the interactions of this component with its environment. This interception is done, principally, thanks to interposition objects, called `EJBObject`s in the EJB model, and

---

[1] Here, as in ODP, an "interface" does not designate a type, but "a place at which independent systems meet and act on or communicate with each other".

[2] Because the EJB platform partially fulfills one of our goals, namely the separation of the functional and non-functional code.

that we call *skeletons* (because they can play the roles of CORBA skeletons and of `EJBObjects` - or CORBA interceptors). When a container intercepts a remote method call directed to its component, it can authenticate the caller, load the component from disk, launch a transaction... before effectively calling the method on the component. The container can therefore manage the non-functional properties of its encapsulated component.

- a *stub* (resp. a *skeleton*) corresponds to an output (resp. input) interface. As suggested in Fig. 2 and 4, a stub (or a skeleton) is at the interface between a container and a connector, and belongs to both. As we said above, our stubs and skeletons can play the roles of CORBA stubs and skeletons, as well as the roles of CORBA interceptors. However, they do not necessarily play these roles (the marshaling and interception functions of a client-server connector's skeleton would be meaningless for a stream connector's skeleton). Stubs and skeletons are also called *gates*.
- a *server* is an execution environment for containers. It provides communication protocols and *system services* (such as a persistency service, a transaction manager...) that are shared between containers. It can also provide management services, such as monitoring, deployment...

2.3   Composition Mechanism

In order to be able to separate and compose non-functional properties, a composition mechanism is required to build stubs, skeletons and containers in a modular way. The composition mechanism we propose in order to do this allows objects to be *dynamically* composed into *composite* objects, and was designed to *simulate* class inheritance. Indeed, intuitively, the semantics of a composite object $[c_1, \ldots, c_n]$, where c_i is an instance of class C_i, is the same as the semantics of an instance of class C_n extends $(C_{n-1}$ extends $\ldots (C_2$ extends $C_1))$. More formally, composite objects are defined as follows (a more precise definition can be found in [3]):

- first of all, the members of a composite object are ordered in a list. The first member (i.e. c_1, the head of the list) is called an *extensible object*, and the others are called *extensions*. The extensible object can not be removed or replaced, but extensions can be *dynamically* added, removed and replaced.
- a call to a method m on a composite object is executed by the *last* member of the composite in which m is defined. In extensions, a special form of method call is available, noted `dsuper.m`. A call to `dsuper.m` in an extension e is executed by the last member in which m is defined, and that is strictly *before* e in the extension list.

The composite object example of Fig. 3 illustrates these definitions. The extensible object is a minimal bank account object. It is extended by a first extension that manages fidelity points. This extension *overrides* the `withdraw` method, and *adds* three new methods. It is itself overridden by two other extensions: one that modifies the management of fidelity points, and another that checks the amount of withdrawals. When a client calls the `withdraw` method on

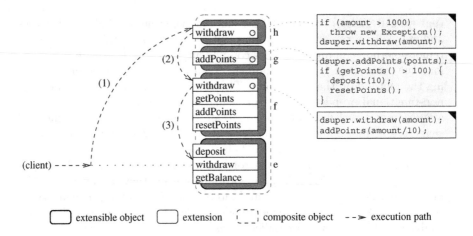

Fig. 3. A composite object

e, the call is executed as if e were an instance of H extends (G extends (F extends E)): the call is *transparently* redirected to h and then, through explicit calls to dsuper, to f and e.

This example shows that our mechanism simulates class inheritance, but in a more flexible way. For example, the bank account's behavior can be changed *dynamically*, by adding and removing extensions at runtime. Moreover, the 6 possible ways to compose the 3 extensions of Fig. 3 do not need to be explicitly defined, as would be the case with class inheritance. In other words, there is no combinatorial explosion. Finally, our composition mechanism applies to objects instead of classes, which allows different instances of the same class to have different extensions.

As mentioned at the beginning of this section, we propose to build stubs, skeletons and containers, and also servers, as composite objects. The resulting platform architecture is depicted in Fig. 4.

3   Implementation of the JavaPod Platform

The JavaPod platform is implemented in ejava [3], a Java extension we have defined in order to facilitate the use of composite objects. It is made of a small kernel (~ 1500 lines), which only provides a framework, and of several extensions layers (~ 11000 lines), which provide all the functionalities of the platform (communication protocols, system services...).

3.1   The JavaPod Kernel

The JavaPod kernel defines four basic classes named Server, Container, Stub and Skeleton, which correspond to the concepts presented in Sect. 2.2.

The Server class is almost empty. Its main method is the createContainer method, to create a container for a component. The Container class contains

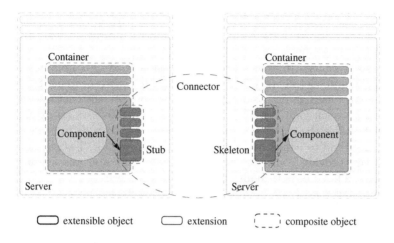

Fig. 4. Summary of the JavaPod platform architecture

methods to manage the container's stubs and skeletons. The `Stub` and `Skeleton` classes contain an `invoke (Method m, Object[] args)` method, whose role is to return the result of a call to `m(args[0],...,args[n])`. In the `Stub` class, this method does nothing, since its precise semantics depends on the connector to which the stub belongs. It must therefore be overridden by stub extensions. In the `Skeleton` class, this method invokes the given method on the application component, by using the Java Reflection API.

Finally, the JavaPod kernel includes a generic stub compiler which, given a Java interface `I`, generates a `Stub`'s sub-class implementing `I` (`I`'s methods are implemented by a call to the `invoke` method, with appropriate arguments).

3.2   The JavaPod Extensions

The JavaPod extensions provide communication protocols, various connector categories (client-server, stream and "shared memory"), several system services (providing mobility, persistence, protection, replication...) and management services (to configure and deploy components). This section presents some of these extensions.

Client-server connectors are implemented by three "layers" of extensions called `stp` (server transport protocol), `gtp` (gate transport protocol) and `rpc` (remote procedure call)[3]. The first two layers implement communication protocols to send messages between servers and gates. They are not specific to client-server connectors, and are also used to implement stream and "shared memory" connectors. Each layer is specified by an interface which can be implemented in various ways.

The default `stp` layer is based on TCP/IP sockets and the Java Serialization mechanism. It implements an extension which must be added to each JavaPod

---

[3] The `rpc` layer corresponds to the layers called `csp` and `ie` in [3].

server. This extension provides the `getSTPAddress`, `stpSend` and `stpRecv` methods, to get the address of the local server, to send a message to another server, and to handle incoming messages (cf. Fig. 5).

The `gtp` layer uses in each server an extension to store a mapping between container IDs and containers, which can be consulted with the `gtpGetContainer` method. It also uses an extension per container to store the container's ID and a mapping between gate IDs and gates[4]. Finally, it also uses an extension per gate, which stores the gate's ID, and which provides methods to send messages to other gates and to handle incoming messages (cf. Fig. 5). Two versions of the `gtp` layer are provided: one for "normal" components and another for mobile components. They are both built on top of the `stp` layer.

The `rpc` layer uses two complementary gate extensions, for the client and server sides (cf. Fig. 5). On the client side the `rpc` extension overrides the stub's `invoke` method in the following manner: it constructs an object describing the original method call and sends it to the server with the `gtp` layer. The server side `rpc` extension overrides the `gtpRecv` method and executes the requested method calls by calling the skeleton's `invoke` method.

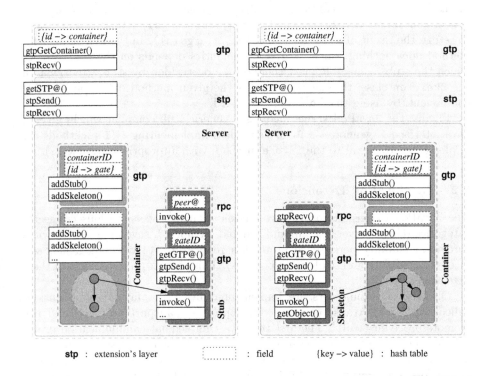

Fig. 5. Summary of client-server connectors (several extensions are not shown)

---

[4] This extension overrides the container's `addStub` and `addSkeleton` methods (among others) to be notified when new gates are created - in order to update its mapping between gate IDs and gates.

The JavaPod platform also provides some extensions to configure and deploy components. These extensions work as follows:

- a container extension uses Java's introspection capabilities to manage component *ports*, which are named access points (the ports provided and required by a component are defined by using design patterns. For example, a T get$X$InputPort () method defines a port X of type T).
- another container extension is used to associate a *configuration* to each component. A configuration describes the extensions to be used to create new stubs and skeletons. It therefore describes the connector categories that must be used with a component, as well as the non-functional properties of this component. For example, a configuration can indicate that interfaces of type I, J and K must be accessed through simple client-server connectors, protected client-server connectors, and stream connectors respectively.
- finally, a server extension uses configuration and deployment scripts, such as the one shown in Fig. 7, to deploy components.

3.3 An Example

This section presents how the traditional HelloWorld application can be implemented with JavaPod, how it can be deployed, and how it works.

The HelloWorld application can be implemented in Java (ejava is only used in the JavaPod *platform*) as shown in Fig. 6: the programmer just needs to specify an interface, to implement the client and server components in Component subclasses, and to define their ports with three simple methods.

```
public interface Hello extends JavaPodInterface {
  void hello (String msg) throws JavaPodException;
}
public class ServerImpl extends Component implements Hello {
  public Hello getHelloInputPort () { return this; }
  public void hello (String msg) { System.out.println(msg); }
}
public class ClientImpl extends Component implements Runnable {
  private Hello server;
  public Hello getHelloOutputPort () { return server; }
  public void setHelloOutputPort (Hello server) { this.server = server; }
  public void run () {
    try { server.hello("Hello World!"); }
    catch (Exception e) { System.out.println(e.toString()); }
  }
}
```

Fig. 6. A simple HelloWorld application. The JavaPodInterface, JavaPodException and Component classes, defined in the JavaPod kernel, are similar to the Remote, RemoteException and RemoteServer classes in Java RMI

This application can be deployed in a basic configuration, i.e. without any non-functional properties, by using the script depicted in Fig. 7. It can also be deployed with a protected and/or mobile server component, by using slightly more complex scripts, but *without modifying* the components source code.

```
GATE = { skel javapod.JavaPodInterface
  { root
      javapodx.protocol.gtp.basic.BasicGTPGatex
      javapodx.connector.rpc.basic.BasicImportExportGatex
      javapodx.connector.rpc.basic.BasicServerGatex
  } { stub javapod.JavaPodInterface
      javapodx.protocol.gtp.basic.BasicGTPGatex
      javapodx.connector.rpc.basic.BasicImportExportGatex
      {javapodx.connector.rpc.basic.BasicClientGatex "getGTPAddress"}
  }
}
CONTAINER = {
  javapodx.management.admin.basic.BasicAdminContainerx
  javapodx.management.binding.basic.BasicPortManagerContainerx
  {javapodx.management.config.basic.BasicConfigurationContainerx $GATE}
  javapodx.protocol.gtp.basic.BasicGTPContainerx
}
SERVER = {
  {javapodx.management.admin.basic.BasicAdminServerx $CONTAINER}
  {javapodx.protocol.stp.basic.BasicSTPServerx $PORT}
  javapodx.protocol.gtp.basic.BasicGTPServerx
}
ERR := init($SERVER,$NULL)
#ifdef DEPLOY_SERVER
  S   := $THIS->createComponent(ServerImpl,$CONTAINER,$NULL)
  REF := $S->createPort(INPUT,Hello,$NULL,$NULL)
  ERR := bindReference($REF,"server.ref")
#endif
#ifdef DEPLOY_CLIENT
  C   := $THIS->createComponent(ClientImpl,$CONTAINER,$NULL)
  REF := lookupReference("server.ref")
  ERR := $C->createPort(OUTPUT,Hello,$REF,$NULL)
  ERR := $C->run()
#endif
```

Fig. 7. A script to configure and deploy a client-server application. The first part defines the extensions to be used to build the gates, the containers, and the JavaPod servers. The second part describes how to deploy and connect the two components

Once deployed, the components are organized as shown in Fig. 5. A remote method call then proceeds as follows:

– the client calls the `hello` method on `server`, a local object representing an interface of the remote component, i.e. a stub.

- the stub's `hello` method, generated by the JavaPod stub compiler, *reifies* the initial call, and passes it to the stub's `invoke` method (i.e. it calls `invoke(HELLO,new Object[] {"Hello World!"})`).
- the `invoke` method is executed by the stub's `rpc` extension: it encapsulates the reified call in a message M, and sends this message to the server by calling the stub's `gtpSend` method.
- the `gtpSend` method adds a header to the given message, and sends the result N by using TCP sockets.
- on the server side, the message M is extracted from N and is dispatched to its destination skeleton by using the `gtpGetContainer` method, provided by the `gtp` server extension.
- the message M is passed to the skeleton's `gtpRecv` method. This method is executed by the skeleton's `rpc` extension: it extracts the reified method call contained in M and passes it to the skeleton's `invoke` method.
- the `invoke` method *reflects* the reified method call, i.e. it calls `hello("Hello World!")` on the server component.

4   The Baghera Application

As explained in the introduction of this article, we decided to implement a "real-world" application with the JavaPod platform in order to evaluate if it really could achieve its goals. We chose for this the Baghera application.

This application is inspired from the BAGHERA research project [8], whose goal is to build a distributed application for computer-aided learning, in the field of elementary geometry. More precisely, the main goal is to use artificial intelligence techniques, such as multi-agent systems, to automate the learning process as much as possible, and to adapt it automatically to each student's level. In order to concentrate on distributed systems problems, we defined a simplified version of the application which is being built by the BAGHERA project members. In particular, we removed all artificial intelligence aspects. This simplified application, called Baghera, is presented below.

4.1   Presentation

The Baghera application (see Fig. 8) is organized around a *virtual school* concept. A virtual school has students, grouped into classes according to their level. A virtual school also has professors, who are assigned to a class, propose exercises to their students, and correct their solutions. Finally, the virtual school administrator manages the list of students and professors, and the distribution of students into classes.

Each student has an *electronic case*, which contains the geometry exercises solved by this student, as well as the exercises that still need to be solved. It also contains the messages exchanged with other students and professors. Similarly, each professor has a *mailbox*, which contains the messages exchanged with his or her students and with other professors. There is also an *exercise repository*.

It contains a list of geometry exercises (together with their solution) which can be used by professors to propose exercises to their students.

Each student uses the application through a graphical user interface (GUI) which displays the content of its electronic case, and allows him or her to propose a solution for an exercise, and to send messages to other users. Similarly, each professor uses the application through a GUI which displays the list of his or her students and, for each student, the content of its electronic case. This GUI allows professors to add exercises in an electronic case or in the exercise repository, to correct a solution proposed by a student, and to send messages to other users. Finally, the administrator uses a GUI which allows him to add and remove students and professors, and to modify the assignment of students to classes.

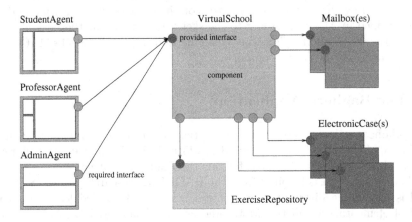

Fig. 8. Architecture of the Baghera application

4.2   Non-functional Requirements

The goals of the JavaPod platform are mainly to separate and to compose non-functional properties. To evaluate our platform, we therefore needed an application that required several non-functional properties. This is the case of Baghera, which may require, for example, the three following properties:[5]

- the VirtualSchool, Mailbox, ElectronicCase and ExerciseRepository components need to be persistent: their data must not be lost between two uses of the application by a student, a professor or an administrator. One way to ensure this is to keep a copy of these components on stable storage. However, the stable storage to be used may depend on the environment: with few students, each component can be stored in its own file; with many students, a relational or object database is probably more efficient.

---

[5] This set of non-functional properties is of course not exhaustive (for example, the Baghera application may also require synchronization aspects). However, we limited ourselves to this set in this case study.

– by default, the previous persistent components are not protected. For example, it would be possible for a student to use the exercise repository to get the solution of an exercise. However, this requires programming skills, because the GUI used by students does not allow access to the solutions. If students are believed not to have these skills, and if professors can be trusted, then it is acceptable not to protect the persistent components. In the opposite case it is necessary to protect them, for example to ensure that only professors can get the solution of an exercise from the repository.

– the application can be used in a real school, in which case it can be deployed on hosts that are always connected to the school's local area network (LAN). But the application can also be used, as in the BAGHERA project, by students that must stay at an hospital. These students will probably not have a permanent connection to the school's LAN. In this case, the application must be adapted so that students can still work while disconnected. For example, they should be able to propose solutions for their exercises, and to "send" messages. Upon reconnection, these solutions and messages should automatically be integrated to the persistent components.

5   Implementation of Baghera with JavaPod

The functional code of the Baghera application presents no difficulty and will not be presented here. It is much more interesting to present how the three non-functional properties (persistence, protection and disconnected mode) were implemented and associated with the functional code.

5.1   Persistence

Since we were not primarily concerned with performance (our goal here was to experiment with the separation and composition of non-functional properties), we systematically chose the easiest way to implement non-functional properties. For persistence, we therefore chose the following approach: a persistent component is serialized into a file, as well as its container and all its stubs and skeletons. This is done after each remote execution, by this component, of a method that may have changed its state.

To this end, the programmer must indicate, separately from the functional code, the methods that may change the component's state. This information is used at deployment time, and stored in an extension of the component's container. Another extension is used to override the skeleton's `invoke` method: this allows intercepting incoming remote method calls, and serializing, if necessary (i.e. as indicated by the previous container extension), the component and its container after the execution of each of these calls. Finally, a server extension is used to automatically load the persistent components that have not yet been loaded into memory: the `getGTPContainer` method that returns a component from its identifier (see Sect. 3) is overridden by this extension so that, in case of failure of the original method, the requested component is loaded from disk.

5.2   Protection

We chose to implement protection by using *access control lists* (ACLs): a list of authorized users is associated with each method that needs to be protected. Each component has an associated identity, transmitted at each remote method invocation, and used at the server side to check if the calling component has the permission to call this method. An authenticator component is used to store the identity and password of each user of the application. It is used to ensure that the identity transmitted with each remote method call is not usurped.

To protect a component, the programmer must define, separately from the functional code, the authorized users for each method of the component. This information is used at deployment time, and stored in an extension of the component's container. Another extension is used to override the skeleton's `invoke` method: this allows this extension to intercept incoming remote method calls, and to check that these calls are authorized before effectively executing them. To transmit the caller's identity with each remote method invocation message, a stub's extension is used to override the `gtpSend` method (see Sect. 3), and a symmetric skeleton's extension is used to override the `gtpRecv` method. These two methods respectively add and extract the caller's identity to or from each message. Finally, two other extensions, overriding the same methods and placed before the previous extensions, are used to cipher and uncipher each message, so that the identity (and password) added by the previous extensions to each message can not be intercepted on the network.

5.3   Disconnected Mode

In order to be able to use a component while in disconnected mode, a complete or partial copy of this component must be made upon disconnection. It is then possible to work with this copy while disconnected. Upon reconnection, this copy must be merged with the original component, knowing that they may both have evolved since the copy was made.

Two problems must be solved to implement this solution: what should be copied upon disconnection? how should be merged the copy and the original component? Unfortunately, there seems to be no generic response. In other words, the semantics of these operations strongly depends on the application semantics. For example, in the baghera application, when a student wants to disconnect, the VirtualSchool component and the student's ElectronicCase component are copied completely, but the other components are not copied or only partially: only the exercises (and not their solutions) that appear in the student's electronic case are copied from the ExerciseRepository, and the electronic cases and mailboxes of other users are not copied. When a student reconnects, the messages he or she has written during disconnection are really sent, and the exercises he or she has solved are added to the original student's ElectronicCase component. The VirtualSchool and ExerciseRepository component are not merged, since students, connected or not, cannot modify these components.

Because of this lack of genericity we were only able to separate in extensions the mechanisms to send, upon disconnection and reconnection, disconnect and reconnect messages to each appropriate component, and to transmit, install and uninstall these copies. The clone and merge operations were not separated from the functional code: they must be programmed in *upcalls* in the functional code of components. It was not possible to define or to configure these operations separately, as was the case with persistence and protection.

6   Results

This section gives the results of our experiments. More precisely, the first three subsections explain, for each of our goals (separation of functional and non-functional code, composition of non-functional properties, and modularity and extensibility), to what extent we were able to achieve it, in the particular case of the Baghera application.

6.1   Separation of Functional and Non-functional Code

This goal is achieved for persistence and protection, but only partially for the disconnected mode. It is probably possible to improve this separation by requiring the application to give more information to the middleware about the representation and semantics of its data. However, unless this information can be given separately from the functional code, this does not allow for a complete separation.

The separation of functional and non-functional code is therefore difficult to achieve for properties that are not very "generic", as could have been expected. However, we also found that this separation is never really complete, even for very generic properties: even when the functional and non-functional code seem completely separated, *implicit* links may remain between them.

– the "granularity" of application components depends on their non-functional properties. For example, it would have been possible to group the VirtualSchool, ExerciseRepository, ElectronicCase, and Mailbox components into a single big component: functionally, this makes no difference. However, such a strategy would be very inefficient because of the persistency: the whole component would need to be serialized, even for very small modifications.
– the "granularity" of component interfaces depends on the protection policy. For example, to prevent students from getting the solution of an exercise from the ExerciseRepository, while allowing them to get the text of these exercises, we use two methods in the interface of this component: one to get the text of an exercise, the other to get its solution. This way, two different ACLs can be associated with these methods. But the protection policy is the only reason to use two methods instead of one.

6.2   Composition of Non-functional Properties

This section defines and illustrates the concept of *independent* non-functional properties, and presents our solution for the composition of the non-functional properties of the Baghera application.

The algorithm used to protect a component is the same for persistent and transient components. Similarly, the algorithm used for persistence is the same for protected and unprotected components. Protection and persistence are therefore said to be *independent*. On the contrary, protection and disconnected mode are not independent, because the algorithm used to protect a component can not be the same in connected and in disconnected mode. For example, the access check used in connected mode to prevent students from getting the solution of an exercise would be ineffective in disconnected mode (because, to protect a component's local copy, this access check would have to be performed by a local, untrusted client's host). The only solution here is to send to clients, in disconnected mode, a partial and *unprotected* copy of the ExerciseRepository component, containing only the text of the exercises.

Composing independent non-functional properties, such as persistence and protection, or persistence and disconnected mode, is easy with our platform. It is indeed sufficient to compose the extensions related to the two non-functional properties, in the right order (manually specified), and to associate them with stubs, skeletons, etc. But it is more difficult to compose non-functional properties that are not independent. For example, to compose protection and disconnected mode, we had to modify the disconnection algorithm, so as to send to clients, during the disconnection process, unprotected copies of protected components (by default, a component's copy has the same non-functional properties as the original component, because the disconnection algorithm makes a complete copy of the component's container). Fortunately, we were able to modify the disconnection algorithm by using *additional* extensions: it was not necessary to change the existing extensions related to disconnected mode.

In order to facilitate the composition of non-functional properties, the system services providing these properties should be implemented by using components and connectors. Thus, non-functional properties designed for applications can be applied to system services as well. For example, we implemented the authenticator service in a component (see Sect. 5.2), so that it can easily be made persistent. Likewise, the disconnection and reconnection protocols were implemented on top of standard client-server connectors, so that these protocols can easily be protected against illegal use.

6.3   Modularity and Extensibility

Modularity was easily achieved: it was not difficult to program separately the extensions related to persistence, protection, and disconnected mode. Moreover, these "modules" can be removed when unused. They can also be replaced by other versions. For example, we implemented a protection mechanism based on hidden software capabilities instead of access control lists.

Extensibility is sometimes possible, but not always. For example, we wanted to prevent users from sending messages with false emitter names. This required to extend the protection model, so that it can use the method arguments, and not only the method name, to decide if a call can be accepted or not. This was easily done by implementing an application specific[6] extension overriding the skeleton's `invoke` method. Likewise, in order to improve performance, we were able to add application specific extensions to cache, on the client side, the results of frequently called remote methods (although these extensions were absolutely not foreseen).

But, in some cases, it was necessary to modify existing code in order to add new functionalities to the platform. For example, it was necessary to change the component identifiers used to implement basic client-server connectors (see Sect. 3) when we introduced persistency. Indeed, these identifiers needed to remain valid across several executions of the server, but they were initially valid only during the lifetime of a server. In other cases, it was necessary to reorganize some code to isolate a portion of it in an extensible method, so that it could be easily overridden.

The extensions' granularity is very important: if extensions are too coarse-grained, then the platform's modularity and extensibility may be reduced. On the other hand, if extensions are too fine-grained, the performances may decrease. In our experiments with Baghera, we found that the granularity of JavaPod's extensions was "well adapted".

6.4 Performance

This section just gives an overview of the performance of our platform: a detailed performance analysis would be out of the scope of this article. Depending on the Java Virtual Machine, an empty method call is five to fifteen times slower on a composite object than on a normal Java object. Despite this overhead, an empty remote method call is only 1.5 times slower with JavaPod than with Java RMI. Moreover, this overhead is mainly due to our unoptimized remote method call algorithm. In other words, the overhead due to our composition mechanism alone is negligible when compared to the duration of remote method calls.

7 Related Work

This section compares our object composition mechanism to other related mechanisms. It also compares our middleware platform architecture to other modular and extensible middleware platforms.

7.1 Composition Mechanisms

Our composition mechanism can be compared to mixin-based inheritance [9]. Indeed, extensible objects and extensions are similar to normal and mixin classes respectively, and the semantics of a composite object is similar to the semantics of a class composed of several mixin classes (this is not a coincidence, but derives from the fact that our mechanism was designed to simulate class inheritance). There is however a significant difference bewteen the two: mixin-based

---

[6] Because this extension uses application specific data structures.

inheritance applies to *classes* while our mechanism applies to *instances*, and can therefore be used dynamically.

Our object composition mechanism can also be compared to *delegation*, i.e. to the mechanism used in languages such as SELF [10] to handle messages that are not supported by the receiver object. A composite object can indeed be accurately simulated in SELF by linking its members through *mutable* `parent*` slots (cf. Fig. 9). But this requires to put the extensible object at the tail of this linked list, and to put an empty "sentinel" object at the head (so that references to this composite object, which must be references to its head, need not be changed when its composition is modified). Another difference is that our mechanism has been integrated into a strongly typed language (i.e. Java), while SELF is not statically typed. Therefore, unlike SELF "composite objects", our composite objects can be used in conjunction with "normal", unextensible but statically typed objects, which helps to reduce the number of runtime errors.

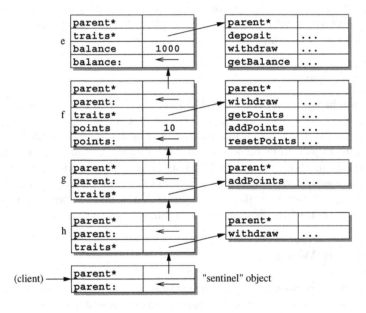

Fig. 9. Simulation of the composite object of Fig. 3 with SELF

Our composite objects can also be simulated with the Composition Filters (CF) object model [11], in the same way as with SELF. Indeed the CF model supports delegation, it provides a pseudo-variable `server` similar to the `self` keyword in SELF... Moreover the CF model is strongly typed, and therefore does not have SELF's typing problems.[7] But the CF model is much more powerful than what is needed to simulate composite objects. In particular most of the

---

[7] But this strong typing is perhaps a problem, even with the `Any` type, to simulate composite objects: even if the interface of an object can change at runtime, it seems

default filters and most of the rules to compose them are not required. Therefore, it would probably be inefficient to use the CF object model just to simulate composite objects.

Finally our object composition mechanism can be compared to the Decorator pattern [12], which also uses some form of delegation. An extension can indeed be implemented as a wrapper of an extensible object or of another extension. But this solution has many well known drawbacks:

- a wrapper must implement all the methods provided by the wrappee, even if it just needs to override one of them. This is not really a problem for the programmer (such a wrapper can be implemented as a subclass of a default, "null" wrapper), but for performances (this mechanism introduces unnecessary indirections).
- the wrappee and its wrappers have different identities which are not equivalent. A composite object must therefore be referenced through a "sentinel" wrapper (which introduces yet another indirection), so that references to this composite object need not be changed when its composition is modified.
- a wrapper can not transparently intercept the calls made by the wrappee on itself (i.e. the wrappee must use the previous sentinel wrapper instead of this to make a self call).

Moreover, and perhaps most importantly, the Decorator pattern can not simulate an extension that adds new methods to an extensible object. It must therefore be used in conjunction with other patterns (such as the Extension Object [13] or the Role Object [14] patterns), which greatly complicates the model: in the general case, a composite object must be implemented as a directed acyclic graph of "wrappers", instead of as an ordered list of extensions. This is for example the case in the Lasagne model [15]. However, in this model, the wrapper graphs remain implicit: the wrapper chain through which each message flows is indeed dynamically selected. This simplifies the configuration and adaptation of these graphs, and allows wrappers to be dynamically selected and composed, depending on composition policies and context-sensitive information.

7.2 Middleware Platforms

Our middleware platform architecture is related to several other research platforms, whose goals were either the separation of functional and non-functional code, or the platform's modularity and extensibility. Among these platforms we can cite:

- the Tj platform [16]. This platform uses the CodA language, i.e. a meta-space based approach, to implement mobility, replication, and various marshaling rules at the meta-level.
- the platform proposed by Singhai et al. [17]. This platform also uses a meta-space based approach (for example a stub has two meta-spaces named

---

that all its possible interfaces must be known statically, which is not the case for our composite objects. But we are not sure of this.

invoker and marshaler) and was used to implement real-time constraints, load balancing and fault tolerance at the meta-level.

- the Flexinet platform [18]. This ORB does not use meta-spaces but decomposes stubs and skeletons in an ordered list of "meta-objects" which can implement communication protocols as well as non-functional properties. It has been used to implement mobility at the meta-level [19].
- the OpenORB platform [20,21,22]. This platform, which also uses a meta-space based approach, was mainly designed to allow applications to inspect and to adapt the platform to their own needs. But it can also probably[8] be used to separate and compose non-functional properties at the meta-level.

Compared to these platforms, the main advantages and disadvantages of our architecture are the following:

+ like OpenORB, our architecture was designed to allow any type of interactions between components. On the contrary the Flexinet platform and the platform proposed by Singhai et al. are restricted to client-server interactions (the Tj platform can probably support other types of interaction, but the examples given in [16] are all based on client-server interactions).
+ our architecture has a component concept, which allows non-functional properties to be applied to groups of objects (when a component moves or is serialized, all the object it contains are moved or serialized simultaneously). On the contrary the Tj platform associates meta-objects with individual objects. Likewise, Singhai et al. and the Flexinet platform concentrate on bindings, and do not propose a component concept (it is however possible to add a "cluster" concept on top of Flexinet [19]).
+ our architecture makes a good tradeoff between extensibility and performance. Tj is extremely extensible but probably slow (there are no quantitative results, but the use of CodA, based on SmallTalk, probably slows down the platform and its applications). On the contrary the very limited form of reflection used by Singhai et al. makes their platform efficient but also poorly extensible.
- our architecture has not been tested with a real-world middleware platform, but only with the JavaPod prototype. Therefore, it is not sure that our architecture still "works" with a real-world platform. On the contrary the Flexinet platform is not a "toy" platform. In particular, it is fully resource controlled, and uses pools for resources such as buffers and threads.
- like all the previous platforms, OpenORB excepted, our prototype is language specific. It is however perfectly possible, in theory, to implement our architecture and our composition mechanism so as to support extensible objects and extensions programmed in any language.

---

[8] The authors do not give many details about the ability of their platform to separate and compose of non-functional properties at the meta-level. This does not seem to be their main goal.

8   Conclusion

The non-functional properties of distributed applications need to be adapted to the environments in which applications are deployed. In order to be able to do this adaptation easily, we designed and implemented the JavaPod platform, an extensible middleware platform based on a new object composition mechanism [2,3]. Then, as described in this article, and in order to evaluate our platform, we tried to implement a "real-world" application with it, and we tried to adapt its non-functional properties.

The results of these experiments are that, globally, our middleware platform architecture can actually be used to achieve our goals. We were indeed able to separate completely the non-functional code related to persistence and protection, to compose persistence, protection and disconnected mode, and to add unforeseen extensions to the middleware platform. Moreover, we think that our composition model is more adapted for our needs than other composition techniques such as mixin based inheritance or the Decorator design pattern. There are however some limitations. Some non-functional properties are not very "generic", and therefore not easy to separate from the functional code. Composing non-functional properties can require additional code to cope with the interdependencies of non "orthogonal" properties. Finally, it is sometimes necessary to modify existing code when extending the platform. However, these limitations seem more intrinsic than linked to our architecture. They seem to arise from (irreducible?) semantic interdependencies between the functional and non-functional code, and between the system services.

In addition to these limitations, a lot of open issues remain to be solved. For example we do not know if our architecture, which was only tested with the JavaPod prototype (where all low-level mechanisms such as buffer management, thread scheduling, or communication protocols are overly simplified), still applies to an "industrial" platform. It would also be interesting to study the problems that we voluntarily set aside, such as the dynamic and automatic adaptation of the platform (we limited ourselves to a static adaptation, i.e. at launch time with configuration and deployment scripts), the association of non-functional properties with application components composed of several internal components (we limited ourselves to primitive components), or the management of heterogeneity (our prototype is language-specific, but it would be usefull to be able to implement extensions in any language).

References

1. Bruneton E, Riveill M. JavaPod: une plate-forme à composants adaptable et extensible. Tech. Rep. RR-3850, INRIA, 2000.
2. Bruneton E, Riveill M. JavaPod: an adaptable and extensible component platform. In *Workshop on Reflective Middleware (RM'2000)*. New-York, USA, 2000.
3. Bruneton E, Riveill M. Reflective implementation of non-functional properties with the JavaPod component platform. In *Workshop on Reflection and Metalevel Architectures (RMA'2000)*. Cannes, France, 2000.

4. ODP reference model: Foundations. ITU-T Recommendation X.902 | ISO/IEC International Standard 10746-2, 1995.
5. ODP reference model: Architecture. ITU-T Recommendation X.903 | ISO/IEC International Standard 10746-3, 1995.
6. CORBA 3.0 CCM FTF draft ptc/99-10-04, 1999.
7. Enterprise Java Beans.
   URL http://java.sun.com/products/ejb/
8. Balacheff N. Teaching, an emergent property of eLearning environments. In *The Information Society for All (IST)*. Nice, France, 2000.
9. Bracha G, Cook W. Mixin-based inheritance. In *Object Oriented Programming Systems Languages and Applications (OOPSLA)*. Ottawa, Canada, 1990.
10. Ungar D, Smith RB. Self: The power of simplicity. In *Object Oriented Programming Systems Languages and Applications (OOPSLA)*. Orlando, USA, 1987.
11. Bergmans LM. The composition filters object model. Departement of Computer Science, University of Twente, 1994.
12. Gamma E, Helm R, Johnson R, Vlissides J. *Design Patterns, Elements of Reusable Object-Oriented Software*. Addison-Wesley, 1995 pp. 175–184.
13. Martin R, Riehle D, Buschmann F, eds. *Pattern Languages of Program Design 3*. Addison-Wesley, 1998 pp. 79–88.
14. Harrison N, Foote B, Rohnert H, eds. *Pattern Languages of Program Design 4*. Addison-Wesley, 2000 pp. 15–32.
15. Truyen E, Vanhaute B, Joosen W, Verbaeten P, Joergensen BN. Dynamic and selective combination of extensions in component-based applications. In *23rd International Conference on Software Engineering (ICSE'2001)*. Toronto, Canada, 2001.
16. McAffer J. Meta-level architecture support for distributed objects. In *International Workshop on Object-Orientation in Operating Systems*. Lund, Sweden, 1995.
17. Singhai A, Sane A, Campbell R. Reflective ORBs: Supporting robust, time-critical distribution. In *ECOOP'97 Workshop on Reflective Real-Time Object-Oriented Systems*. Jyväskylä, Finland, 1997.
18. Hayton R, Herbert A, Donaldson D. FlexiNet: a flexible, component oriented middleware system. In *European Workshop Support for Composing Distributed Applications*. Sintra, Portugal, 1998.
19. Hayton R, Bursell MH, Donaldson D, Herbert A. Mobile Java objects. In *International Conference on Distributed Systems Platforms and Open Distributed Processing (MIDDLEWARE)*. The Lake District, UK, 1998.
20. Blair GS, Coulson G, Robin P, Papathomas M. An architecture for next generation middleware. In *International Conference on Distributed Systems Platforms and Open Distributed Processing (MIDDLEWARE)*. The Lake District, UK, 1998.
21. Costa FM, Blair GS, Coulson G. Experiments with reflective middleware. In *ECOOP'98 Workshop on Reflective Object-Oriented Programming and Systems*. Brussels, Belgium, 1998.
22. Blair GS, Coulson G, Costa F, Duran HA. On the design of reflective middleware platforms. In *Workshop on Reflective Middleware (RM'2000)*. New-York, USA, 2000.

DJ: Dynamic Adaptive Programming in Java

Doug Orleans and Karl Lieberherr

Northeastern University, Boston, MA 02115, USA
{dougo,lieber}@ccs.neu.edu

Abstract. DJ is a new pure-Java library for adaptive programming that allows traversal strategies to be constructed and interpreted dynamically at run-time, as opposed to existing adaptive programming tools that are strictly static. Traversal strategies can be used with adaptive visitors (similar to the Visitor pattern) or in a generic programming style by adapting them to the Java Collections framework. The DJ library makes heavy use of Java reflection and we give some details of this implementation.

1 Introduction

Traversing complex object structures is a common operation in object-oriented programs, yet traversal code can be tedious to write and is often brittle with respect to an evolving object model. **Adaptive programming** [8] is a development method in which each traversal is specified succinctly as a **traversal strategy** [10]. A traversal strategy describes a traversal at a high level, only referring to the minimal number of classes in the program's object model: the root of the traversal, the target classes, and waypoints and constraints in between to restrict the traversal to follow only the desired set of paths. The methods needed to implement a traversal can be generated from a traversal strategy and a description of the object model, either by hand or automatically with a tool such as DemeterJ [9]. If the object model changes, often the traversal strategy doesn't need to be changed; the traversal methods can simply be re-generated in accordance with the new model, and the behavior can adapt to the new structure.

With the addition of reflection to Java [5], it became possible to interpret a traversal strategy at run-time. DJ is a pure-Java library developed by the Demeter team that provides this capability. This makes it easier to add traversal strategies to a Java program, because there is no need to modify the compilation process to run the DemeterJ code generator or to convert the source code to its input language syntax. Instead traversal strategies can simply be expressed as literal strings in ordinary Java code, or even constructed dynamically from an external source not known at compile time.

This paper begins by presenting an example program that uses the DJ library, leading into an overview of the interface of DJ. The relation of DJ to DemeterJ is discussed, followed by some details of the implementation, a survey of related work, and a brief indication of future research directions.

A. Yonezawa and S. Matsuoka (Eds.): REFLECTION 2001, LNCS 2192, pp. 73–80, 2001.
© Springer-Verlag Berlin Heidelberg 2001

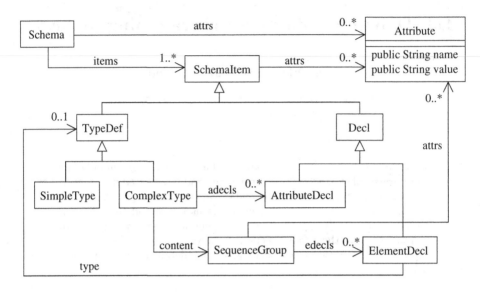

Fig. 1. UML diagram for XML schemas.

2   Example

The example domain for this paper will be that of processing XML Schema
definitions [3]. An XML schema defines the structure of a class of XML doc-
uments, by enumerating the element types allowed and what attributes and
subelements they may contain. The relation between an XML schema and a
conforming XML document is analogous to an object model and a graph of instance objects. An XML document consists of a list of elements, each with a
list of attributes (name/value pairs) and a list of subelements (which may themselves contain attributes and subelements). An XML schema (which is itself an
XML document) consists of a list of type definitions and element and attribute
declarations. A simple type definition defines a type of attribute or element with
no subelements, while a complex type definition defines a type of element with
subelements; each type definition has a name, stored as the value of an attribute
with name **name**. An element or attribute declaration has a name and a type,
stored as values of attributes with names **name** and **type**; an element declaration
may contain a local type definition instead of a reference to a previously defined
type. Figure 1 shows a UML [2] class diagram that represents a small subset of
the XML Schema definition language.

A simple task that one might want to implement is checking a schema for
undefined types. This task involves two traversals of the object structure representing the schema definition: one to collect all the types defined in the schema,
and one to check each type referenced by a declaration to see if it's in the set of
defined types. Figure 2 shows some definitions on the **Schema** class that implement these two traversals.

```
static final ClassGraph cg = new ClassGraph();
public Set getDefinedTypeNames()
{ final Set def = new HashSet();
  cg.traverse(this, ''from Schema via ->TypeDef,attrs,* to Attribute",
              new Visitor() { void before(Attribute host)
                                  { if (host.name.equals("name"))
                                       def.add(host.value); }});
  return def; }
public Set getUndefinedTypeNames()
{ final Set def = getDefinedTypeNames(), undef = new HashSet();
  cg.traverse(this, ''from Schema via ->Decl,attrs,* to Attribute",
              new Visitor() { void before(Attribute host)
                                  { if (host.name.equals("type")
                                       && !def.contains(host.value))
                                       undef.add(host.value); }});
  return undef; }
```

Fig. 2. Using traverse from the DJ library.

The getDefinedTypeNames method collects the set of all type definition names in a schema: it traverses the object structure rooted at the Schema object to every Attribute object reachable through the attrs field of a TypeDef object, and adds the attribute value if the attribute name is "name". The getUndefined-TypeNames method collects the set of all type references which are not in the set of defined names: it traverses to every Attribute object reachable through the attrs field of a Decl object, and adds the attribute value if the attribute name is "type" and the value is not the name of a defined type.

The static cg variable in Fig. 2 is initialized to the default class graph, which consists of all the classes in the default package. A ClassGraph object is a simplified representation of a UML class diagram; its nodes are types (classes and primitive types) and its edges are associations (has-a relations) and generalizations (is-a relations). A traversal is performed by calling the traverse method on a ClassGraph object. It takes three arguments: the root of the object structure to be traversed; a string specifying the traversal strategy to be used; and an **adaptive visitor** object describing what to do at points in the traversal.

A traversal strategy specifies the end points of the traversal, using the from keyword for the source and the to keyword for the target(s). In between, any number of constraints can be specified with via or bypassing. The two traversals in figure 2 both traverse from Schema to Attribute, but differ in their constraints: the first traversal only looks at attributes of type definitions (TypeDef objects), while the second traversal only looks at attributes of declarations (Decl objects). The ->TypeDef,attrs,* syntax is a pattern specifying the set of association edges in the object graph whose source is a TypeDef object and whose label (field name) is attrs; the asterisk means that an edge in the set can have any target type.

Traversal strategy interpretation is done as described in [10], with a few modifications whose details will be presented in a future paper. The general idea is that the object structure is traversed recursively, but associations (including inherited associations) which cannot possibly lead to a target object (subject to any constraints specified in the traversal strategy) are skipped. For example, in our XML Schema example, a `Schema` object contains a collection of `SchemaItem` objects; this collection may contain `TypeDef` objects, since `TypeDef` is a subclass of `SchemaItem`, so the elements of the collection are traversed as part of the `getDefinedTypes` traversal. However, some of the elements may be `AttributeDecl` objects, and there is no possible path to a `TypeDef` object; if one of these elements is encountered in the collection, no further traversal of that object is performed. The `adecls` association of `ComplexType` is never traversed at all, since it can only contain a collection of `AttributeDecl` objects.

An adaptive visitor class is a subtype of the `Visitor` class in the DJ library; it implements the Adaptive Visitor pattern described in [8, pp. 426-427]. The Adaptive Visitor pattern differs from the Visitor pattern as presented in [4] in two ways: only a minimal set of methods needs to be defined, namely those describing the functional behavior to be performed at points along the traversal, rather than one method each for every class in the traversal; and no `accept` methods need to be defined on the classes being traversed, nor does traversal behavior need to be defined in the visitor methods. These two differences result in a unit of behavior that can adapt both to changes in the object model and to changes in the traversal.

In place of the `visitFoo` methods in the Visitor pattern, an adaptive visitor can define one or more `before` or `after` methods, each with a single argument of the type being visited. These are executed at the beginning and ending, respectively, of traversals of objects of that type. The `Visitor` subclasses defined inline in figure 2 define one `before` method each, which is executed at `Attribute` objects, the end point of the traversal.

DJ also can be used with Java's Collections framework [6]: the `asList` method on `ClassGraph` makes a `List` from an object structure and a traversal strategy. The object structure is viewed as a list of objects whose type is the target of the traversal strategy; the list iterator performs the traversal incrementally (lazily) with each call to `next` (or even backwards, with `previous`). Changes to the `List` object "write through" to the object structure. This allows a traversal to be performed anywhere a `List` is generically traversed, such as the algorithms provided by the Collections framework like `sort`, `reverse`, or `shuffle`.

3   DJ and DemeterJ

The DJ library is based on DemeterJ, a development tool for adaptive programming. DemeterJ takes as input a **class dictionary file**, which is a textual definition of a class diagram, along with one or more **behavior files**, which contain method definitions. The methods defined in the behavior files can be plain Java methods or **adaptive methods**; an adaptive method definition consists of a method signature, a traversal strategy, and a set of visitor methods to be executed during the traversal. From these input files, DemeterJ generates a set of plain Java files, which can then be compiled by an ordinary Java compiler.

DJ is not meant to replace DemeterJ, but to complement it. For those programmers who can't or don't want to develop in a language other than plain Java, the DJ library provides an easy way to integrate adaptive programming into their code. DJ also allows more flexible dynamic traversals than DemeterJ can support, due to being able to build class graphs and interpret traversal strategies at run-time; for example, classes can be loaded at run-time, perhaps downloaded from the network or constructed dynamically, and traversed using DJ. Traversal strategies might be defined at run-time as well, perhaps based on user input such as a database query. Also, this reification of adaptive programming concepts enables the creation of more generic traversal components with DJ: a method that performs a traversal can take as parameters the class graph, the traversal strategy, the list of classes to be visited, or visitor method callbacks.

However, these dynamic traversals suffer from the performance penalty of using Java's reflection facilities. Preliminary timing tests have indicated that a DJ traversal runs approximately 25 to 30 times slower than the corresponding DemeterJ traversal; however, we conjecture that this can be improved to be only 10 times slower. There is also the space overhead of keeping the reified objects in memory. The other main advantage of using DemeterJ is that it provides more development support by being able to automatically generate class definitions from the class dictionary file, as well as generate utility methods for parsing, printing, copying, and comparing object structures. Of course DemeterJ and DJ can be used together, since DJ is just a Java package, adding the dynamic flexibility benefits of DJ to a regular DemeterJ program.

Three features of DJ are new additions to adaptive programming—they are not in DemeterJ currently but could be added. One is the ability to traverse classes for which the programmer does not have source code, or is not able or willing to modify the source code; DemeterJ only generates traversal code on the classes defined in the class dictionary file, but it could allow traversal strategies to "cut across" library packages by generating traversal code that uses the public interface of the packages. For example, an adaptive method could traverse a compound GUI object made up of classes from the Swing library. The second is the `asList` method that makes a `List` view of a traversal; there is no easy way to pause an adaptive method, or go backwards, but the list iterator does exactly this. Third is the ability to create a new class graph that is a subgraph of another class graph, determined by a traversal strategy; in essence, this allows strategies to be composed by intersection, which is not supported in DemeterJ. For example, if you have a complicated strategy `from A via B via C...to Z` but you want to bypass all edges named `cache`, in DemeterJ you would have to add the bypassing constraint between each pair of classes in the traversal strategy; in DJ, you could create a new `ClassGraph` object from the main class graph and the traversal strategy `from * bypassing ->*,cache,* to *` and then traverse that class graph using the other traversal strategy.

4 Implementation Details

When the `ClassGraph` constructor is called, it creates a graph object containing reflective information about all the classes in a package. For each class in the package, it calls `Class.forName` with the class name, which causes the JVM to load the class if it hasn't already been loaded. Once a `Class` object is obtained, its fields are retrieved using `getDeclaredFields`; then, for each `Field` object, its name and type class are retrieved using `getName` and `getType`, respectively. A corresponding association edge from the defining class to the type class is then added to the graph, labeled with the field name. (Optionally, a class's accessor methods can be used instead of or in addition to the fields. This allows for extra computation to be performed when traversing an edge, as well as allowing "virtual" edges in the class graph.) Generalization edges are also added for each superclass and interface, retrieved from a `Class` object using `getSuperclasses` and `getInterfaces`, respectively.

Given an object o of class C to be traversed and a visitor object v of class V, the `traverse` method performs the following steps: first, for each class C' starting at `Object` and going down the inheritance hierarchy to C, and for each class V' starting at V and going up the inheritance hierarchy to `Visitor`, the `Class` object for V' is queried using `getDeclaredMethod` to see if there is a method named `before` with one argument of type C'. (The query result is cached, to avoid repeated introspection, because it is very expensive in Java—an exception is thrown if there is no such method, and even though the exception is immediately caught, the JVM must fill in the complete stack trace on the exception object. There is no `hasDeclaredMethod` to determine whether a method exists without throwing an exception.) If a `before` method exists, it is run using `invoke`(v,o) on the `Method` object.

Then, for each class S starting at C and going back up the inheritance hierarchy to `Object`, and for each edge to be traversed from S, the corresponding field or accessor method is retrieved from the `Class` object for S using `getDeclaredField` or `getDeclaredMethod` (these are also kept in a cache to avoid repeated introspection). The target object o' of the edge is then retrieved by either calling `get`(o) on the `Field` object or `invoke`$(o,$`null`$)$ on the `Method` object; o' is then recursively traversed with v.

Finally, for each class C'' starting at C and going up the inheritance hierarchy to `Object`, and for each class V'' starting at V and going up the inheritance hierarchy to `Visitor`, the `Class` object for V'' is queried to see if there is a method named `after` with one argument of type C''. If such a method exists, it is run using `invoke`(v,o) on the `Method` object.

The implementation of `asList` is somewhat trickier than regular traversal: the list iterator must return in the middle of the traversal whenever a target object is reached, and then resume where it left off (perhaps going backwards) when `next` is called again. An earlier version created an ad-hoc continuation-like object that was saved and restored at each iteration, but this was error-prone and not very efficient; the current version uses a separate Java thread as a coroutine, suspending and resuming at each iteration. An additional provided method `gather` can be used to copy all the target objects into an `ArrayList`, which is faster still, but the list returned by `asList` has two advantages: calls to `set` on the iterator can replace target objects in the original object structure, and modifications made to the object structure while a traversal is paused can be seen when the traversal resumes.

5   Related Work

An Adaptive Object-Model [11] is an object model that is interpreted at run-time. If an object model is changed, the system changes its behavior. Java's object model can't be changed at run-time (other than dynamic class loading) but DJ interprets the object model when doing traversals.

DJ's `Visitor` class is similar to the reflective visitor described by Blosser [1] and the `Walkabout` class of Jay and Palsberg [7], though all three approaches were developed independently. Blosser describes a programming technique for implementing the Visitor pattern that uses reflection to choose which visitor method to call at each visit in the traversal. Jay and Palsberg improve on this by making a single generic `Walkabout` class that handles the reflective lookup and can be subclassed to provide the visitor methods. In addition, the `Walkabout` class performs the traversal of the object structure, also using reflection. However, it can only traverse the entire object structure; there is no mechanism analogous to traversal strategies for customizing the traversal to a particular subgraph.

6   Summary and Future Work

We have presented DJ, a pure-Java library supporting dynamic adaptive programming. It is more flexible and dynamic than the preprocessing approach taken by DemeterJ, by interpreting traversal strategies at run-time and using reflection to traverse object structures with adaptive visitors, at the expense of performance.

The Demeter team is currently working on a number of enhancements to DJ. One is the ability to write visitor methods that get executed whenever certain edges in the class graph are traversed (currently, visitor method execution depends only on the class of the object being traversed). Another is the ability to write **around** methods on visitors that are executed in place of a traversal step and get passed a thunk that can be executed to continue the traversal. Both of these enhancements would allow visitors to have more control over the behavior that gets executed during a traversal.

There are many optimizations that could be made to traversal interpretation. Some of the reflective overhead of calling `Field.get` and `Method.invoke` could be avoided by generating a new class (at run-time) that invokes the appropriate fields and methods directly; although generating a class would be a one-time performance hit, overall performance would be much better if the same visitor and traversal strategy were used together multiple times. Other applications of partial evaluation to speed up the traversal may be possible as well.

Visit the Demeter home page for more information about DJ, DemeterJ, and adaptive programming: `http://www.ccs.neu.edu/research/demeter/`.

Acknowledgements

Josh Marshall designed and implemented the early versions of DJ. Johan Ovlinger designed and implemented the predecessor to DJ, TAO (Traversals As Objects), and suggested the run-time generation of a class to avoid reflective overhead. Pengcheng Wu is implementing several enhancements to DJ, including **around** visitor methods and visitor methods on edges. Thanks to Lars Hansen for suggesting the use of threads as coroutines for the `asList` iterator. The XML Schema example is a simplified version of an XML-Schema-to-Java tool being developed by Adak Prasenjit. Thanks to Erik Ostrom, Robert Stroud, Greg Sullivan, and the anonymous reviewers, who provided many insightful comments and suggestions. Research supported by Defense Advanced Research Projects Agency under agreement F33615-00-C-1694 (PCES Program).

References

1. Jeremy Blosser. Java Tip 98: Reflect on the visitor design pattern. *JavaWorld*, July 2000.
2. Grady Booch, James Rumbaugh, and Ivar Jacobson. *The Unified Modeling Language User Guide*. Object Technology Series. Addison Wesley, 1999. ISBN 0-201-57168-4.
3. David C. Fallside. *XML Schema Part 0: Primer*. W3C, October 2000.
4. Erich Gamma, Richard Helm, Ralph Johnson, and John Vlissides. *Design Patterns: Elements of Reusable Object-Oriented Software*. Addison-Wesley, 1995.
5. JavaSoft. *Java Core Reflection*, 1998.
6. JavaSoft. *Collections Framework Overview*, 1999.
7. Barry Jay and Jens Palsberg. The essence of the visitor pattern. In *COMPSAC'98, 22nd Annual International Computer Software and Applications Conference*, pages 9–15, Vienna, 1998.
8. Karl J. Lieberherr. *Adaptive Object-Oriented Software: The Demeter Method with Propagation Patterns*. PWS Publishing Company, Boston, 1996. 616 pages, ISBN 0-534-94602-X.
9. Karl J. Lieberherr and Doug Orleans. Preventive program maintenance in Demeter/Java (research demonstration). In *International Conference on Software Engineering*, pages 604–605, Boston, MA, 1997. ACM Press.
10. Karl J. Lieberherr and Boaz Patt-Shamir. Traversals of Object Structures: Specification and Efficient Implementation. Technical Report NU-CCS-97-15, College of Computer Science, Northeastern University, Boston, MA, Sep. 1997.
11. Joseph W. Yoder and Reza Razavi. Metadata and adaptive object-models. In *ECOOP 2000 Workshop Reader*, volume 1964 of *Lecture Notes in Computer Science*. Springer Verlag, 2000.

The K-Component Architecture Meta-Model
for Self-Adaptive Software

Jim Dowling and Vinny Cahill

Distributed Systems Group
Department of Computer Science
Trinity College Dublin
Jim.Dowling@cs.tcd.ie, Vinny.Cahill@cs.tcd.ie

Abstract. Software architectures have recently emerged as a level of design concerned with specifying the overall structure of a system. Traditionally, software architectures only provide static descriptions of the participants and interaction structures in a system. Dynamic software architectures, however, can be reconfigured at runtime and therefore provide support for building dynamically adaptable applications. Software architectures can be specified using architectural reflection. In this paper we introduce an architecture meta-model that realises a dynamic software architecture. The architecture meta-model reifies the configuration graph of the architecture and is automatically generated from our component definitions and implementation language source-code. We show how graph transformations that re-write the architecture's configuration graph can be implemented as reflective programs, called adaptation contracts. Adaptation contracts are written in a separate programming language, thus cleanly separating the adaptation code from the computational code. Adaptation contracts can even be replaced at run-time. They are deployed in a run-time meta-level architecture that addresses issues of system safety, integrity and overhead during graph transformation. The paper also describes a prototype implementation of our model called K-Components.

1 Introduction

Architectural structures have always been present in object-oriented software, but their importance has increased with the advent of complex, distributed object systems. Modelling complex systems can be done informally with system diagrams or more formally using an Architecture Description Language (ADL) [SG96]. Traditionally ADLs were developed for representing and reasoning about the static structures and interactions in a software architecture [AdlSei]. However, since there are many classes of systems that are dynamic, including evolving systems that require on-line software upgrades, adaptive systems whose provided behaviour adapts to resource availability in their current operating environment, and learning or knowledge-based systems, there has recently emerged a field of study concerned with dynamic software architectures.

Dynamic software architectures can be used to build dynamic systems by supporting the self-management and reconfiguration of the dynamic system's architecture at run-time [Allen98]. Current approaches to specifying dynamic software architectures use ADLs with Architecture Modification Languages [Darwin95, OGT99, Rapide95, Werm00] or Co-ordination Languages [Cuesta01]. Another approach to specifying dynamic software architectures is to use *architectural reflection* [Caz00]. A system that supports architectural reflection reifies its architectural features as an *architecture meta-model* [Blair01] that can be inspected and modified at run-time. Modifications of the architecture meta-model result in modifications of the software architecture itself, and the architecture is therefore reflective. The architecture meta-model is not only concerned with the architectural features it reifies but also with an associated set of *architectural constraints* [Blair01], describing how and when to safely reconfigure the software architecture.

The architecture meta-model introduced in this paper realises a dynamic software architecture. Our architecture meta-model reifies the software architecture as a typed, directed configuration graph, where interfaces are the vertices, components the type labels and connectors are directed edges. We present a novel approach to generating the architecture meta-model. Rather than force programmers to explicitly specify the software architecture's configuration graph with an ADL, we automatically generate the meta-level configuration graph by building a dependency graph from both the component definitions, in Interface Definition Language-3 (IDL-3) [CCM99], and the connections between them, defined in the system implementation language.

A. Yonezawa and S. Matsuoka (Eds.): REFLECTION 2001, LNCS 2192, pp. 81–88, 2001.
© Springer-Verlag Berlin Heidelberg 2001

The architectural constraints over the architecture meta-model enforce the dynamic properties of or assertions about the software architecture and are encapsulated in reflective programs called *adaptation contracts*. We use the more general term *adaptation code* to mean the architectural constraints of a system. To obtain a clean separation of concerns between the adaptation code and computational code at design time, we provide a separate *adaptation contract description language* for specifying the adaptation code as adaptation contracts.

Adaptation contracts can reason about the system's architecture, state and external dependencies using adaptation events and reconfigure the system's architecture and external dependencies using reconfiguration operations. Since adaptation contracts invoke reconfiguration operations on the architecture meta-model that result in modifications of the software architecture itself, adaptation contracts are reflective programs. Adaptation contracts are separate meta-level objects and they can be loaded and unloaded at run-time. A container, called a configuration manager, provides a deployment and execution environment for the adaptation contracts and also allows for the injection of new adaptation contracts at runtime.

In summary, we model dynamic reconfiguration as the transformation of a system's architecture meta-model and use adaptation contracts to separate adaptation code from computational code.

2   Background and Related Work

Dynamic systems are systems that can adapt their behaviour while executing, relative to some context information. Dynamic systems come in two flavours: *closed dynamic systems* and *open dynamic systems* [OGT99]. For closed dynamic systems both the complete system behaviour and the behaviour that describes adaptations are specified at build time. Open dynamic systems, on the other hand, allow system behaviour to evolve after build time and are necessary if unanticipated adaptations are to be performed at run-time. Techniques for implementing open dynamic systems include dynamic linking mechanisms, dynamic object technology (including class loaders) and dynamic programming languages [OGT99].

It is also important to make the distinction between adaptable and self-adaptive systems. *Adaptable* systems can be adapted to a particular deployment environment [Czarn00], whereas *self-adaptive* systems adapt themselves to their operating environment [OGT99]. Adaptable systems support their *explicit adaptation* by an external actor [Werm00] using either a procedural or declarative interface [Blair01]. Adaptable systems with procedural interfaces are open dynamic systems and can support arbitrary or evolutionary adaptations [MG99].

Self-adaptive systems, however, are subject to *implicit adaptation*, triggered by changes in either their internal state or their environment. Self-adaptive systems possess adaptation logic. *Adaptation logic* is the code that monitors a representation of the system's internal state and environment and then adapts that representation resulting in a reconfiguration of the actual system. Adaptation logic is by nature reflective. Self-adaptive systems are normally closed dynamic systems. A closed self-adaptive system is said to support programmed adaptation [MG99]. If a self-adaptive system is to be open dynamic, it has to support the dynamic loading of adaptation logic. Self-adaptive systems require no support from external actors, and so can be adapted transparently to users of the system. Implicit adaptation is required to achieve *adaptation transparency*. Application-transparent adaptation is desirable when the conditions for adaptation can be known a-priori. Fig.1 shows an architecture that supports both its explicit and implicit adaptation.

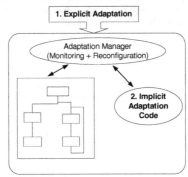

Fig. 1. Explicit and Implicit Adaptation with an Adaptation Manager

2.1   Adaptation Logic

Adaptation logic for a system is usually made up of two main parts – *monitoring* and *reconfiguration* code, as can be seen in [Silva00, QuO00]. Monitoring code is responsible for identifying operating region-transitions [QuO00] in a system. Operating regions define the different operating modes of a system and each one generally requires a different configuration of the system. Operating region transitions can be triggered either by some internal state change in the system or by a change in a system that it is dependent on [Kon01]. Operating region transitions identify adaptation events, events that signal the need for a reconfiguration of the system. For example, when resource managers can no longer provide their managed resource to clients at some quality of service level they will generate adaptation events that are both handled internally and sent to resource-aware client systems. Systems can generate and receive adaptation events, handle them internally and forward them to interested clients.

While adaptable systems possess only monitoring code and an interface for invoking reconfiguration commands, self-adaptive systems contain both monitoring and reconfiguration code. Thus, the intelligence for when and how to reconfigure the system is either supplied externally by a user and is, therefore, modifiable at run-time (i.e. adaptable systems), or else it is supplied internally and known at design time (i.e. self-adaptive systems). Systems can be both adaptable and self-adaptive.

The run-time infrastructure that manages the monitoring and reconfiguration aspects of the system can be either centralised (as in an adaptation manager, see Fig.1) or distributed (as in self-organising architectures) [MG99]. Variations of the adaptation manager for self-adaptive systems can be found in the configuration manager [KM90, Werm00] and in the configurer [Allen98, Kon01].

2.2   Separating Adaptation Code from Computational Code

To obtain a clean separation of concerns between the adaptation code and the computational code at design time, a separate language can be used to specify the adaptation logic. Examples of this include the configuration programming philosophy [KM98] that advocates using two languages for configuration programming: a configuration language for the structural description and change logic and a separate programming language for basic component programming. Similarly, BBN's Quality Objects uses separate Quality Description Aspect Languages [QuO99] to write a distributed object's quality of service contracts. Techniques such as aspect-oriented programming [Czarn00] and reflection can enable the use of separate languages to represent separate concerns in a program.

2.3   Dynamic Software Architectures

Dynamic software architectures represent a principled method for the construction of adaptable and self-adaptive systems. Software architectures represent static metadata about the components, the connectors and the architectural configuration of a system and they are often specified explicitly using an Architecture Definition Language (ADL) [SG96]. To support dynamic software architectures, there is a need to support adaptation logic and provide mechanisms for managing the system's integrity and dependencies during reconfiguration. There is, however, little consensus in the research community on what architectural features a dynamic software architecture should contain. Different approaches to the specification and construction of dynamic software architectures include Event Systems [Rapide95, OGT99], process algebras in Wright [Allen98], graph grammars [LeMet98], rewriting logic [Werm00] and architecture meta-models [Caz00, Blair01, Cuesta01].

Adaptation logic in software architectures is captured in both architectural constraints and reconfiguration operations. Architectural constraints are properties of or assertions about configurations, component or connectors, the violation of which will render the software architecture unacceptable (or less desirable) to one or more stakeholders [MT00]. Examples of reconfiguration operations include the addition and removal of components and their linking and unlinking via connectors [Werm00].

In the case of mobile systems, a good deal of the adaptation logic is known in advance, indicating that they would benefit from application-transparent adaptation. But in order to adapt to unforeseen and exceptional system states, there is also a requirement for dynamic updating of their adaptation logic. Currently no dynamic software architecture provides support for the dynamic loading and unloading of programs with adaptation logic (i.e. as architectural constraints) and we propose the use of adaptation contracts for this purpose.

2.4   Architectural Reflection

We define architectural reflection as being concerned with the observation and manipulation of the configuration graph of a software architecture and its constituent vertices and edges. Just as there is no consensus on what architectural features should be in an ADL, there is no consensus on what constitutes the vertices and edges in a software architecture's configuration graph. For example, the configuration graph's vertices and edges are components and connectors in [MOT00], interfaces and connectors in [Rapide95] and interfaces (labelled with an implementation component) and connectors in [Werm00], representing a typed configuration graph. Behavioural reflection is concerned with the reification of a system's computation. In software architectures, each configuration graph represents a particular computational instance of the system. We define behavioural reflection for software architectures as the ability to rewrite the system's configuration graph of components and connectors at runtime. Structural reflection for software architectures is concerned with introspecting the architecture's configuration graph and constituent components, connectors and interfaces.

3   Architecture Meta-Model

An architecture meta-model reifies the architectural features of a system. The main issues in designing an architecture meta-model for a dynamic software architecture include what architectural features to represent in the meta-level (e.g. the architecture's configuration graph, components and connectors), how to represent the adaptation code, what mechanisms to provide for integrating the adaptation code into the system, and how to manage system integrity and consistency during dynamic reconfiguration. The following sections introduce the features in our architecture meta-model.

3.1   Architecture Meta-Model's Configuration Graph

We reify a software architecture configuration as a typed, connected graph, where the vertices are interfaces, labelled with component instances, and the edges are connectors, labelled with connector properties. A vertex is modelled as an interface and implementation (component) pair, (i,c). An edge is modelled as a triple $i ->_l j$, which contains the source and target vertices ids i and j, and the edge label l. The edge label represents reconfigurable properties of the connector such as the ability to change its communication protocol or set of installed interceptors. The root vertex of a configuration graph is a special type of vertex, the entry point in the program. It is normally the main() of a C++/Java implementation. Cycles are allowed in the graph and are modelled with cyclic connectors. A meta-level component, called the configuration manager, is responsible for the storage and management of the software architecture's configuration graph.

3.2   Dynamic Reconfiguration as Configuration Graph Transformation

We represent dynamic reconfiguration as conditional graph transformations, specified in reflective programs called adaptation contracts. A graph transformation is a rule-based manipulation of the configuration graph [Werm00]. The interfaces and connectors that represent the vertices and edges in our graph describe the static structural part of the system that is preserved during a graph transformation. The component instances and connector properties that represent the labels of the vertices and edges in our graph respectively describe the dynamic structural part of the graph that is rewritten during a graph transformation.

Since graph transformations ensure that the result of a rule is again a graph, we can guarantee the integrity and consistency of the system if the graph rules are *transactional operations* over the graph. In practice, however, graph transformations may affect only part of the configuration graph and a *reconfiguration protocol* [KM90] can be used to ensure that only those vertices that are affected by the transformation must be in a *safe state* [Werm00]. We follow this approach and use a reconfiguration protocol as it helps reduce the length of the reconfiguration phase and allows concurrent client invocation during the reconfiguration phase on components that are not "frozen". Computation and adaptation code are related through the reconfiguration protocol as it *freezes* computation in components involved in a reconfiguration. Component state can only be changed by computation, not by reconfiguration operations. One of the other advantages of our reconfiguration protocol is the maintenance of system state integrity by transferring component state from the old component to the new one. The successful transfer of component state requires that component developers implement a copy constructor interface for their component. The meta-level configuration manager is responsible for implementation of the reconfiguration operations and the correct operation of the reconfiguration protocol.

3.3   Managing Dynamic Reconfiguration

The configuration manager [KM90, Werm00] is a meta-level adaptation manager that stores the reified configuration graph and implements the reconfiguration (graph rewrite) operations and reconfiguration protocol. The configuration manager is a run-time container for the deployment, scheduling and execution of adaptation contracts, see Fig. 2. The configuration manager provides a procedural interface for the loading/unloading of adaptation contracts at runtime. In order to guarantee the safety of the code being introduced into the system, the new adaptation contracts must be developed and tested in the original, trusted development environment. The procedural interface verifies that the new adaptation contract is trusted from its XML descriptor.

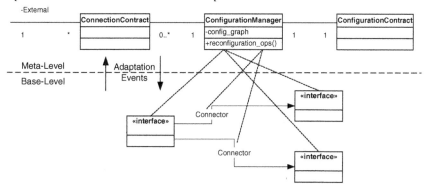

Fig. 2. Configuration Manager as a Meta-Level Adaptation Manager

4   Adaptation Contracts

Adaptation contracts are used to specify meaningful transformations of an architecture meta-model's configuration graph. They can be used to provide the adaptation logic for self-adaptive systems. Adaptation contracts are reflective as they invoke reconfiguration operations on the architecture meta-model that results in modifications of the software architecture itself. They are represented at runtime by meta-level objects and are deployed in and managed by a configuration manager, see Fig. 2.

An adaptation contract contains a series of conditional rules for the transformation of the meta-level configuration graph. Adaptation contracts are used to specify a system's architectural constraints. Since architectural constraints represent properties of or assertions about configurations, components or connectors, our adaptation contracts require a mechanism for accessing these properties and assertions. We provide *adaptation events* as a mechanism for allowing contracts to poll architectural constraint information from meta-level configurations and base-level components and connectors. Architectural constraints can be specified using adaptation events with conditional statements.

Adaptation events also have the advantage of decoupling the meta-level adaptation contract from the base-level components and connectors, see Fig. 2. In effect, they provide a run-time separation of concerns between the adaptation code and the computation code. This allows adaptation contracts to be dynamically loaded and unloaded, since they have no clients directly dependent on them.

During the reconfiguration of a software architecture, the management of the *incoming* and *outgoing dependencies* of a system (the systems/users that depend on it and the systems that it depends on, respectively) is crucial to the safety and integrity of both the system and its dependent systems [Kon01, Dow00]. Because of the two different types of dependencies, adaptation contracts come in two forms: *configuration contracts* that manage internal resources and incoming dependencies from clients, and *connection contracts* that manage outgoing dependencies to components the system is dependent on.

Table 1. Adaptation Contract Description Language Syntax

```
/* Automatically generated from XML configuration descriptor */
configuration   configuration*          ::= configuration -descriptor.xml
interface       interface*              ::= component-descriptor.xml

/* Automatically generated from component XML descriptors */
component       component-name*         ::= component-descriptor.xml
consumes        user_defined_handler*   ::= component-descriptor.xml
emits           adaptation_event*       ::= component-descriptor.xml
handler         handler*                ::= reconfiguration_op | user_defined_handler
reconfiguration_op                      ::= change_component | change_configuration |
                                            install_interceptor | remove_interceptor | rollback |
                                            callback_client
/* User-defined below here*/
contract configuration configuration
{
       /*      Conditional statements and reconfiguration operations        */
}

contract connection connection-contract*       ::=
       [component client_name] [interface port_name] [component provider_name]
{
       /*      Conditional statements and reconfiguration operations        */
}
```

Configuration contracts are specified in the Adaptation Contract Description Language, see Table 1. They consist of a series of conditional statements, testing for the occurrence of adaptation events, and associated reconfiguration operations. There is support for managing incoming dependencies in the form of a contract renegotiation. A contract renegotiation informs dependent clients of a reconfiguration in the system. In our model, configuration contracts can only be defined for a single-address space. *Connection contracts* represent architectural constraints for individual connections between the system and components it is dependent on (potentially outside the address space of the system). Similar to configuration contracts, they consist of a series of conditional statements and reconfiguration operations. A *configuration tool* takes adaptation contracts, the components and connectors in the software architecture and produces an implementation in a concrete language, i.e. in our prototype C++. It performs refinement transformations by allowing the specialisation and concretisation of the abstract meta-level components in the K-Component framework.

5   The K-Component Framework

K-Components are components with an architecture meta-model and adaptation contracts to support their dynamic reconfiguration. Our prototype implementation is in C++. The following section describes the component and connector models, how the software architecture is automatically generated from the implementation programming language and how to attach the adaptation contracts to architectures.

5.1   The Component Model

We leverage existing component syntax to define components. IDL-3 [CCM99] is used to define components with explicit dependency management, through `provides` and `uses` interfaces. IDL-3 `emits` and `consumes` events [CCM99] are used to specify base-level adaptation events. Component skeletons are generated by the IDL-3 compiler by specialising and templating abstract components in the K-Component framework. Components can be either *primitive* or *composite* components [Darwin95]. Only composite K-Components have their own architecture meta-model, configuration contract and configuration manager.

Our C++ framework supports the *dynamic evolution* [MT00] of components using component subtyping, factory objects [COM+99] and dynamic linked libraries (DLLs). Components also have interfaces that are used by the reconfiguration protocol: a traversal interface for traversing the configuration graph and a copy constructor for migrating connectors and state during component replacement. Reference counting is used to guarantee a safe-state during the reconfiguration phase and for the safe removal of components. To overcome the cyclic reference counting problem [COM+99], programmers explicitly specify connectors as being either normal or cyclic connectors.

We do not need full introspective meta-level information about components at runtime in order to rewrite the configuration graph, therefore we do not represent components as full meta-level objects. They are represented in the meta-level by a typed reference in the configuration manager, used for reconfiguration operations and adaptation event processing. Component meta-information, for use in the adaptation contract description language, is stored in an XML component descriptor [CCM99] that is generated from the component's IDL-3 definition. The programmer fills in additional details such as component packaging and deployment information.

5.2   Connectors as First-Class Entities

In K-Components, connectors are implemented as typed objects relating `provides` and `uses` interfaces on components. Connectors are generated from IDL-3 component definitions by specialising and templating abstract connectors in the K-Component framework. There are two types of connectors: *client-side* and *provider-side connectors*. Client-side connectors can connect directly to a component, unless it is external to the system in which case it connects to a provider-side connector on the target component. For correct functioning of the reconfiguration operations, programmers have to ensure that they explicitly represent cycles in their configuration graphs as cyclic connectors. Connectors provide a reconfiguration interface, with operations such as `link_component` and `unlink_component`, and the configuration manager uses this interface to implement its graph rewrite operations.

5.3   Writing and Configuring K-Components

C++ is used instead of an ADL to specify the software architecture. Several abstractions and programming idioms are used in our C++ prototype implementation for representing concepts commonly found in an ADL, such as interfaces, connectors and binding operations. In addition to this programming guidelines are specified, e.g. for services offered by an interface can only be accessed via connectors.

Rather than force programmers to explicitly specify the software architecture's configuration graph with an ADL, we automatically generate the static part of the meta-level configuration graph by building a dependency graph from the C++ source-code. Similar to how a C++ compiler generates a dependency graph from C++ header files, the configuration tool parses the C++ source code from its entry point for connectors (edges) and their target interfaces (vertices). Each interface's header file is then parsed in turn for more connectors and interfaces until leaf interfaces are reached and a full parse-tree of the system is built. The configuration tool then produces a typed, directed configuration graph of the system with interfaces as vertices and connectors as edges as an XML configuration descriptor.

The programmer can bind the interfaces to actual components by editing the interface labels in the configuration descriptor. Once component implementations have been specified for all the interfaces in the configuration graph and adaptation contracts have been attached, the software architecture can be instantiated by the configuration tool.

6   Conclusions

Without a mechanism for achieving a separation of concerns, dynamic systems' adaptation-specific code becomes tangled with its functional code. We provide an adaptation contract description language that separates the adaptive behaviour of systems from their functional behaviour. We are able to provide a separate language for the adaptation code since dynamic reconfiguration is implemented using reflective programs called adaptation contracts. Architectural reflection enables this separation of concerns.

Our architecture meta-model reifies the software architecture of a system as a typed, directed configuration graph with interfaces as vertices, labelled with component instances, and edges as connectors. We model dynamic reconfiguration as a transformation of a system's configuration graph, and use a reconfiguration protocol to guarantee the consistency and integrity of both the reconfiguration operation and the system. Meta-level graph rewriting programs, called adaptation contracts, perform conditional graph transformations. Adaptation contracts allow programmers to write adaptation transparent applications.

Our model of dynamic reconfiguration is constrained to replacing the components in a system's configuration graph. The alternative of allowing new services to be introduced to a system at runtime leaves open the problem of how existing components in the system and existing clients of the system become aware of and access these new service interfaces at runtime. For self-adaptive software, we do not see our model of dynamic reconfiguration as being overly restrictive. In fact, it can help programmers by constraining the system's possible dynamic reconfigurations to meaningful ones.

References

[AdlSei] Carnegie Mellon Software Institute, *Architecture Description Languages*, URL = http://www.sei.cmu.edu/str/descriptions/adl_body.html.

[Allen98] Robert J. Allen, Remi Douence, and David Garlan, "Specifying and Analyzing Dynamic Software Architectures", *Conference on Fundamental Approaches to Software Engineering, March 1998*.

[Blair01] Gordon Blair et Al., "The Design and Implementation of Open ORB v2", DS Online Vol. 2, No. 6 2001.

[Caz00] Walter Cazzola, Andrea Savigni, Andrea Sosio, and Francesco Tisato, "Explicit Architecture and Architectural Reflection". In *Proceedings of the 2nd International Workshop on Engineering Distributed Objects* (EDO 2000), LNCS. Springer-Verlag.

[CCM99] OMG, *The CORBA Component Model*, orbos/99-07-01.

[COM+99] Guy and Henry Eddon, *Inside COM+ Base Services*, Mircosoft Press, 1999.

[Corra96] A. Corradini, U. Montanari, F. Rossi, H. Ehrig, R. Heckel, M. Loewe, "Algebraic Approaches to Graph Transformation, Part I: Basic Concepts and Double Pushout Approach", Technical Report: TR-96-17, University of Pisa, 1996.

[Cuesta01] Carlos E. Cuesta, Pablo de la Fuenta and Manuel Barrio Solrazano, "Dynamic Coordination Architecture through the use of Reflection", *Coordination Models, Languages and Applications Special Track of ACM SAC*, 2001.

[Czarn00] Krzysztof Czarnecki and Ulrich W. Eisenecker, *Generative Programming*, Ad. Wesley 2000.

[Darwin95] J. Magee, N. Dulay, S. Eisenbach and J. Kramer, "Specifying Distributed Software Architectures", In *Proceedings of 5th European Software Engineering Conference*, Sept. 1995.

[DSC00] Jim Dowling, Tilman Schaefer, Vinny Cahill, "Using Reflection to Support Dynamic Adaptation of System Software: A Case Study Driven Evaluation", In *Proceedings of Software Engineering and Reflection 2000*, LNCS 1826.

[Dow00] Jim Dowling and Vinny Cahill, "Building a Dynamically Reconfigurable minimumCORBA Platform with Components, Connectors and Language-Level Support", In *IFIP/ACM Middleware'2000 Workshop on Reflective Middleware*, New York, USA, April 2000.

[KLL97] Gregor Kiczales et Al., "Open Implementation Guidelines", *19th International Conference on Software Engineering (ICSE)*, ACM Press, May 1997.

[KM98] Jeff Kramer and Jeff Magee, "Analysing Dynamic Change in Distributed Software Architectures", *IEEE Proceedings – Software*, 145(5):146-154, October 1998.

[Kon01] Fabio Kon, Tomonori Yamane, Christopher K. Hess, Roy H. Campbell and M. Dennis Mickunas, "Dynamic Resource Management and Automatic Configuration of Distributed Component Systems", *USENIX COOTS'2001*.

[LeMet98] D. Le Metayer, "Describing software architecture styles using graph grammars", *IEEE Transactions on Software Engineering*, 24(7):521–553, July 1998.

[MG99] Kaveh Moazami-Goudarzi, *Consistency Preserving Dynamic Reconfiguration of Distributed Systems*. PhD Thesis, Imperial College London, March 1999.

[MOT00] Nenad Medvidovic, Peyman Oreizy, Richard Taylor, Rohit Khare, and Michael Guntersdorfer, "An Architecture-Centered Approach to Software Environment Integration", Tech Report UCI-ICS-00-11, Dept. of Info. and Computer Science, University of California, Irvine, March 2000.

[MT00] Nenad Medvidovic and Richard N. Taylor, "A Classification and Comparison Framework for Software Architecture Description Languages", *IEEE Transactions on Software Engineering*, January 2000.

[OGT99] Peyman Oreizy et Al., "An Architecture-Based Approach to Self-Adaptive Software", *IEEE Intelligent Systems*, May/June 1999.

[QuO00] Pal PP, Loyall JP, Schantz RE, Zinky JA, Shapiro R, Megquier J., "Using QDL to Specify QoS Aware Distributed Application Configuration", In *Proceedings of ISORC 2000*, March 2000.

[Rapide95] David C. Luckham and James Vera, "An Event-Based Architecture Definition Language", *IEEE Transactions on Software Engineering*, Vol 21, No 9, pp.717-734. Sep. 1995.

[SG96] M. Shaw and D. Garlan, *Software Architecture: Perspecitves on an Emerging Discipline*. Prentice Hall, Englewood Cliffs, NJ, 1996.

[Silva00] Francisco Jose da Silva, M. Endler, F. Kon, Roy Campbell and Dennis Mickunas, "Modeling Dynamic Adaptation of Distributed Systems", UIUCDCS-R-2000-2196, December 2000.

[Werm00] Michel Wermelinger, *Specification of Software Architecture Reconfiguration*, PhD Thesis Universidade Nove de Lisboa, 2000.

Separation of Concerns
in Mobile Agent Applications

Naoyasu Ubayashi[1] and Tetsuo Tamai[2]

[1] Systems Integration Technology Center, Toshiba Corporation, Tokyo, Japan,
naoyasu.ubayashi@toshiba.co.jp
[2] Graduate School of Arts and Sciences, University of Tokyo, Tokyo, Japan,
tamai@graco.c.u-tokyo.ac.jp

Abstract. Using mobile agent systems, cooperative distributed applications that run over the Internet can be constructed flexibly. However, there are some problems: it is difficult to understand collaborations among agents and travels of individual agents as a whole because mobility/collaboration functions tend to be intertwined in the code; it is difficult to define behaviors of agents explicitly because they are influenced by their external context dynamically. Many aspects of mobility/collaboration strategies including traveling, coordination constraints, synchronization constraints and security-checking strategies should be considered when mobile agent applications are constructed.
In this paper, the concept of RoleEP(Role Based Evolutionary Programming) is proposed in order to alleviate these problems. In RoleEP, a field where a group of agents roam around hosts and collaborate with each other is regarded as an *environment* and mobility/collaboration functions that an agent should assume in an environment are defined as roles. An object becomes an agent by binding itself to a role that is defined in an environment, and acquires mobility/collaboration functions dynamically. RoleEP provides a mechanism for separating concerns about mobility/collaboration into environments and a systematic evolutionary programming style. Distributed applications based on mobile agent systems, which may change their functions dynamically in order to adapt themselves to their external context, can be constructed by synthesizing environments dynamically.

1   Introduction

Recently, cooperative distributed applications based on mobile agent systems are increasing. Most of these applications are implemented in Java so that they can run on any platform[18]. Using mobile agents, cooperative distributed applications can be developed that run over the Internet more easily and more flexibly than before. However, there are problems as follows: it is difficult to understand collaborations among agents and travels of individual agents as a whole because mobility/collaboration functions tend to be intertwined in the code; it is difficult to define behaviors of agents explicitly because they are influenced by the external context. Many aspects of mobility/collaboration strategies including

A. Yonezawa and S. Matsuoka (Eds.): REFLECTION 2001, LNCS 2192, pp. 89–109, 2001.

traveling, task executions, coordination constraints, synchronization constraints, security-checking strategies and error-checking strategies should be considered when mobile agent applications are constructed.

This paper proposes the concept of RoleEP(Role Based Evolutionary Programming) in order to alleviate the above problems. In RoleEP, a field where a group of agents roam around hosts and collaborate with each other is regarded as an *environment* and mobility/collaboration functions that an agent should assume in an environment are defined as roles[28]. Mobile agent applications that may change their functions dynamically in order to adapt themselves to their external context can be constructed by synthesizing multiple environments dynamically. There are two contributions in this paper: 1) RoleEP provides a mechanism for separating concerns about mobility/collaboration in mobile agent applications; 2) RoleEP gives a systematic and dynamic evolutionary programming style. In this paper, problems that may occur when distributed applications are designed by using traditional construction approaches are pointed out in section 2. In section 3, the concept of RoleEP is introduced to address these problems. The framework *Epsilon/J*[1] that realizes RoleEP on Java is explained in section 4, and examples described in Epsilon/J are shown. Section 5 shows how to implement Epsilon/J using a reflection mechanism. Section 6 is a discussion on RoleEP. In section 7, reference is made to a number of works related to RoleEP. Lastly, in section 8, we conclude this paper.

2   Problems of Constructing Cooperative Mobile Agent Applications

In this section, a distributed information retrieval system—a typical example of cooperative distributed applications based on mobile agent systems—is described by using traditional approaches, and problems that may occur in those approaches are pointed out. An example is illustrated in Figure 1.

Example. A user requests an agent to search information on specified topics. The agent divides the request into several subtasks according to the kinds of topics and assigns them to searcher agents that are dispersed over the Internet by roaming around hosts and executing the contract-net protocol[25] at each host. The contract-net protocol is a protocol for assigning tasks to objects through negotiations. In the contract-net protocol, managers and contractors exist. First, a manager announces a task to all contractors. Then, each contractor compares its own condition with a condition shown by the manager, and if the former condition satisfies the latter condition, the contractor sends its bid to the manager. The manager selects a contractor that shows the most satisfactory bid-condition and awards the contract to it. There are two aspects to be considered in this example. One is a mobility aspect and the other is a collaboration aspect (contract-net protocol). We want to describe these two aspects as separately as possible.

---

[1] This name originates from the head letter of *environment*.

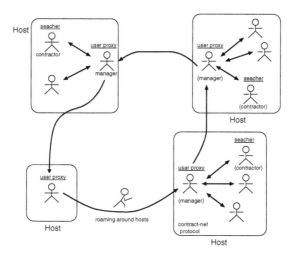

Fig. 1. Distributed information retrieval system

2.1   Case1: Orthodox Approach

In the orthodox approach, a program description maps domain structures to program structures. The following program is written in quasi-code similar to Java.

```
/**
 *  User Proxy
 */
public class UserProxy{
 public UserProxy(){
   roam();
 }
 public void roam(){
   // Move to the next host
   //    and execute the method ''contractNet_start".
 }
 public void contractNet_start(){
   // Multicast a task-announcement message ''contractNet_taskAnnounce"
   //    to all information searchers that exist in the current host.
 }
 public void contractNet_bid(InfoSearcher i){
   // Receive responses from information searchers.
   // Select the ''best_contractor"
   //    if all bids are finished.
   best_contractor.contractNet_award(this);
 }
 public void contractNet_end(Result r){
   // Save the information from the ''best_contractor".
   // Move to the next host
   //    and execute the method ''contractNet_start" again.
   roam();
 }
}
```

```
/**
 *  Information Searcher
 */
public class InfoSearcher{
 public InfoSearcher(){}
 public void contractNet_taskAnnounce(UserProxy u){
   // Compare my condition with a condition shown by the user proxy.
   // Send a message ''contractNet_bid" to the user proxy
   //   if the searcher's condition satisfies the user proxy's condition.
   u.contractNet_bid(this);
 }
 public void contractNet_award(UserProxy u){
   // Execute task
   //   and return the result to the user proxy.
   u.contractNet_end(executeTask());
 }
 public Result executeTask(){
   // Search information.
 }
}
public class Result{}
```

This program is described based on weak mobility[10] in which only program code and instance data are moved. This program starts from the constructor *UserProxy()* that calls *roam* method. In the *roam* method, the agent moves to the next host and executes the *contractNet_start* method. In the *contractNet_start* method, the agent (as a manager) broadcasts a task announcement to all agents (as contractors) that exist in the host. The manager agent receives responses from other contractor agents by the *contractNet_bid* method and selects the best contractor agent. Then, the manager agent awards the contract to the contractor agent. The manager agent saves results of the task execution in the *contractNet_end* method and moves to the next host.

It is difficult to understand behaviors of this program as a whole since mobility/collaboration functions that compose a program are not described separately. Code for roaming around hosts is mixed with code for executing the contract-net protocol. Moreover, it is difficult to extend program code. If another function is added to this program, the *contractNet_start* method and the *contractNet_bid* method may have to be changed to adapt itself to the new function. These methods will include code that is not related to the contract-net protocol. The problem with this approach is that the program code becomes more complex as new functions are added to the code.

2.2   Case2: Design-Pattern Approach

Next, we take the design-pattern[11] approach that may alleviate the problems that are pointed out in Case1. Recently, design patterns focused on mobile agents are proposed. For example, Aridor and Lange propose design patterns for Aglets[15][22], a typical mobile agent system based on Java, as follows[3]:

1. Traveling Patterns: Itinerary, Forwarding, Ticket, etc.
2. Task Patterns: Master-Slave, Plan, etc.
3. Collaboration Patterns: Meeting, Locker, Messenger, Facilitator, Organized Group, etc.

The following Aglets program is described using the *Itinerary* pattern, a design pattern for roaming around hosts and executing a task at each host. In Aglets, a mobile agent is defined as an instance created from a subclass of the *Aglets* class. In this pattern, information for roaming is encapsulated in an instance of the *Itinerary* class. It is only necessary to change the content of the instance when host addresses for roaming are changed.

```
/**
 * User Proxy Aglet
 */
public class UserProxy extends Aglets{

 public void onCreation(Object init){
    // Initialize the aglet.
    // Only called the very first time this aglet is created.

    roam();
 }

 public void roam(){
    // Set sequential planning itinerary.
    SeqPlanItinerary itinerary = new SeqPlanItinerary(this);
    itinerary.addPlan(HostAddress1, ''contractNet_start");
    itinerary.addPlan(HostAddress2, ''contractNet_start");
      :
    itinerary.addPlan(HostAddressN, ''contractNet_start");

    // Start the trip.
    itinerary.startTrip();
 }
 public void contractNet_start(){}
 public void contractNet_bid(InfoSearcher i){}
 public void contractNet_end(Result r){}
}
/**
 * Information Searcher Aglet
 */
public class InfoSearcher{
 public void onCreation(Object init){}
 public void taskAnnounce(UserProxy u){}
 public void award(UserProxy u){}
 public Result executeTask(){}
}
```

In Aglets, a constructor is specified by the *onCreation* method. The *onCreation* is only called the very first time an aglet is created. In this program, *onCreation* calls *roam* method in which an instance is created from the *SeqPlanItinerary* class that is a subclass of the *Itinerary* class and host addresses for roaming and methods that are executed at each host are specified in the *addPlan* method. Here, N host addresses and the *contractNet_start* method are specified. An agent starts to roam around hosts when an instance of the *SeqPlanItinerary* class receives a *startTrip* message.

Although a mobility function (code for roaming around hosts) is separated from a collaboration function (code for executing the contract-net protocol), both of these two functions must be described as methods of an agent. So, separations of mobility/collaboration descriptions are limited only within an agent. If the user proxy agent must have other collaboration functions in addition to the contract-net protocol, the code of this agent will be more complex. The mix-in approach is often used in order to address this kind of problems. In this case, functions requested for a manager can be described in a superclass. If an agent has many roles, the agent must inherit corresponding superclasses statically. So, program code must be modified whenever roles requested for an agent are added or deleted. Moreover, multiple inheritances are not allowed in Java.

2.3   Case3: Role Model & AOP Approach

AOP(Aspect Oriented Programming)[17][13][8] is a programming paradigm such that a concern that cross-cuts a group of objects is modularized as an aspect. A compiler, called *weaver*, weaves aspects and objects together into a system. Concerns including error-checking strategies, synchronization policies, resource sharing, distribution concerns and performance optimizations are examples of aspects.

AspectJ[4], AOP language, is an aspect-oriented extension to Java. A program in AspectJ is composed of aspect definitions and ordinary Java class definitions. An aspect is defined by *aspect* that is an AspectJ specific language extension to Java. Aspects and classes are woven together by AspectJ weaver. Main language notions in AspectJ are *introduces* and *advises*. *Introduces* adds a new method in which cross-cutting code is described to a class that already exists. *Advises* modifies a method that already exists. *Advises* can append cross-cutting code to a specified method. *Before* is used in order to append code before a given method, and *after* is used in order to append code after a given method.

Kendall proposed role model designs and implementations with AspectJ in [16]. In the role model, an object has core intrinsic attributes/methods and a role that adds extrinsic attributes/methods provides perspectives that can be used by other objects. Kendall recommended an approach: 1) introduce the interface for the role specific behavior to the core class; 2) advise the implementation of the role specific behavior to instances of the core class; 3) add role relationships and role contexts in the aspect instance. The contract-net protocol can be described as follows[2].

---

[2] The syntax of this program is based on AspectJ 0.8beta3.

UserProxy.

```
/**
 *  User Proxy Aglet
 */
public class UserProxy extends Aglets{
 public void onCreation(Object init){
   roam();
 }
 public void roam(){
   SeqPlanItinerary itinerary = new SeqPlanItinerary(this);
     :
 }
}
/**
 *  Manager Aspect
 */
aspect Manager extends Role{
 // Role relationships in aspect
 protected Contractor[] contractor;
 // Introduce empty behavior to the class UserProxy.
 public void UserProxy.start(){}
 public void UserProxy.bid(InfoSearcher i){}
 public void UserProxy.end(Result r){}
 // Advise an instance of the class UserProxy.
 before(UserProxy u): instanceof(u) && receptions(public void start){
   // Multicast a task-announcement message ``taskAnnounce"
   //   to all information searchers that exist in the current host.
 }
 before(UserProxy u): instanceof(u) && receptions(public void bid){
   // Receive responses from information searchers.
   // Select the best one ``best_contractor"
   //   if all bids are finished.
   best_contractor.award(this);
 }
 before(UserProxy u): instanceof(u) && receptions(public void end){
   // Save the information from the ``best_contractor".
 }
}
```

InfoSearcher.

```
/**
 *  Information Searcher Aglet
 */
public class InfoSearcher extends Aglets{
 public void onCreation(Object init){}
 public Result executeTask(){}
}
/**
 *  Contractor Aspect
 */
aspect Contractor extends Role{
 // Role relationships in aspect
 protected Manager manager;
```

```
// Introduce empty behavior to the class InfoSearcher.
public void InfoSearcher.taskAnnounce(UserProxy u){}
public void InfoSearcher.award(UserProxy u){}
```

```
// Advise an instance of the class InfoSearcher.
before(InfoSearcher i): instanceof(i) && receptions(public
void taskAnnounce){
    // Compare my condition with a condition shown by the user proxy.
    // Send a message ''bid" to the user proxy
    //   if the searcher's condition satisfies the user proxy's condition.
    u.bid(this);
}
before(InfoSearcher i): instanceof(i) && receptions(public void award){
    // Execute task
    //   and return the result to the user proxy.
    u.end(executeTask());
}
}
```

Although a mobility function is completely separated from a collaboration function in this approach, the following problems still remain.

1. Description of aspects depends on specific core classes. The name *UserProxy* appears in the definition of the aspect *Manager*. So, the description of *Manager* cannot be applied to other core classes.
2. Description of role behavior depends on method names of core classes. That is, when a role uses a method of a core class, the role must call the method directly. In the aspect *Contractor*, *InfoSearcher.award()* must call *executeTask()* that is a method of the core class *InfoSearcher*. In general, there are many kinds of contractors that implement their own task execution methods whose names may be different. For example, a contractor that has an information searching function may have a task execution method named *searchInfo*. On the other hand, a contractor that has an information delivering function may have a task execution method named *deliverInfo*.
3. An aspect must be defined per role. A description that cross-cuts roles may be dispersed in several aspects.

3   RoleEP

3.1   Basic Concepts

In this section, RoleEP, an approach that addresses the problems pointed out in section 2, is proposed. RoleEP provides the following for constructing mobile agent applications: 1) a mechanism for separating concerns about mobility/collaboration including traveling, task executions, coordination constraints, synchronization constraints, security-checking strategies and error-checking strategies; 2) a systematic and dynamically evolvable programming style.

RoleEP is composed of model constructs including agents, roles, objects and environments as shown in Figure 2. Agents can roam around hosts, collaborate

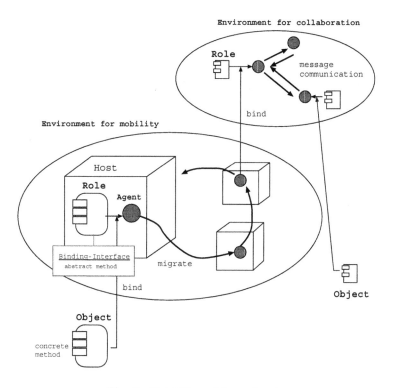

Fig. 2. RoleEP model constructs

with other agents that exist in the same environment by sending messages to each other and execute their original functions. These functions requested to agents can be separated to mobility/collaboration functions and original functions. Original functions are common to all kinds of environments and do not contain mobility/collaboration functions that are given by specific environments. Corresponding to the example shown in section 2, functions for roaming around hosts can be regarded as mobility functions and functions for the contract-net protocol can be regarded as collaboration functions. A function that is executed by the *executeTask* (in Case 3) can be regarded as an original function that is commonly used by not only the contract-net protocol but also other kinds of collaborations. Original functions are functions that are not related to travels or collaborations directly. In the contract-net protocol, functions of the *executeTask* vary according to target applications. It is desirable to separate original functions from mobility/collaboration functions. If concrete functions of the *executeTask* can be described separately, applications that use the contract-net protocol can be implemented by changing the description of *executeTask*. In RoleEP, these two kinds of functions are described separately. Environments and roles are model constructs that describe mobility/collaboration functions, and objects are model constructs that describe original functions[28]. An agent is composed dynamically by binding an object to a role that belongs to an environment. Syntactic definitions of environments, roles, agents and objects are as follows[3]:

```
environment ::= [environment attributes, environment methods, roles]
role ::= [role attributes, role methods, binding-interfaces]
agent ::= [roles, object]
object ::= [attributes, methods]
```

3.2   Environment and Role

An environment is composed of environment attributes, environment methods and roles. A role, which can move between hosts that exist in an environment, is composed of role attributes, role methods and binding-interfaces. Mobility/collaboration functions including tours around hosts and message communications among agents are described by role attributes and role methods. Role attributes and role methods are only available in an environment to which the role belongs. A binding-interface, which is similar to an abstract method interface, is used when an object binds itself to a role. The mechanisms of binding-interfaces and binding-operations are explained later. Common data and functions that are used in roles are described by environment attributes and methods. Directory services such as role-lookup-services are presented as built-in environment methods. A travel or collaboration is encapsulated by an environment and roles. The notion of roles in RoleEP extends the role model in 2.3 so that roles can have not only collaboration functions but also mobility functions.

3.3   Object and Agent

An object, which cannot move between hosts, is composed of attributes and methods. Although an object cannot move between hosts, it can move by binding itself to a role that has mobility functions. An object becomes an agent by binding itself to a role that belongs to an environment, and can collaborate with other agents within the environment. An object can participate in a number of environments simultaneously. The agent identifier is the same as the object identifier. Role identifiers can be regarded as aliases of the object identifier. An agent can be referenced by its role identifier from other agents that exist in the same environment.

3.4   Binding-Operation

Figure 3 shows the notion of the *binding-operation* that binds binding-interfaces of roles to concrete methods of objects. The binding-interface defines the interface in order to receive messages from other roles existing in the same environment. Using the binding-interface, collaborations among a set of roles can be described separately from each object. The binding-operation is permitted only

---

[3] Environment, role, agent and object are instances. The symbol ::= means that the left-hand side is defined by the right-hand side.

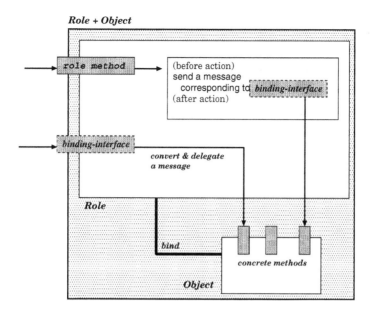

Fig. 3. Binding-operation

when an object has methods corresponding to the binding-interface. Binding-operations are implemented by creating delegational relations between roles and objects dynamically. That is, if a role receives a message corresponding to its binding-interface from other roles or itself, the role delegates the message to an object bound to the role. For example, if the binding-interface *executeTask* defined in a role is bound to the *searchInfo* method defined in an object, the message "executeTask" received by the role is renamed "searchInfo" and delegated to the object. Many kinds of collaborations can be described by changing combinations of roles and objects. Binding-operations correspond to *weaver* in AOP, and binding-interfaces correspond to *join points* that are weaving points in AOP.

3.5   Example

Figure 4 illustrates the example in section 2 using the notion of RoleEP. In step 1, the user proxy object binds itself to the *visitor* role in the *Roaming* environment at host 1 and becomes the agent. This agent can roam around hosts using mobility functions given by the *visitor* role. In step 2, the user proxy agent binds itself to the *manager* role in the *ContractNet* environment at host 2 and can execute the contract-net protocol using collaboration functions given by the *manager* role. Step 3 shows that the user proxy agent acquires other kinds of role functions after step 2. Figure 4 shows dynamic compositions of environments. Environments of the user proxy agent are composed by *Roaming*, *ContractNet* and so on.

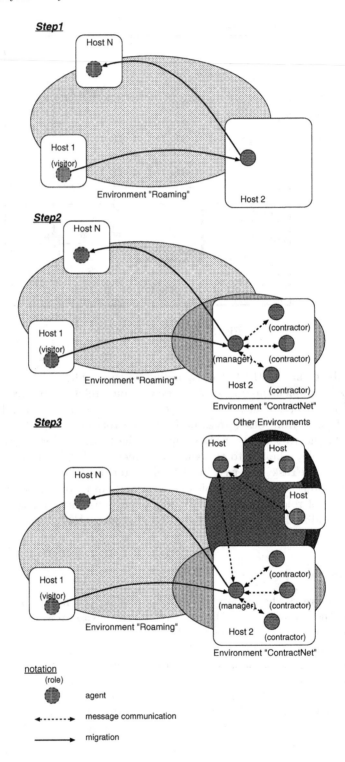

Fig. 4. Dynamic evolution of environment

In general AOP, aspects that construct a system are statically defined when the system is designed, and do not change from the beginning of computation to the end. On the other hand, environments proposed in RoleEP can be defined separately and compositions of environments can be re-arranged dynamically. A distributed application based on mobile agents is composed of environments that can be added or deleted dynamically. Number, kinds and topologies of collaborations among agents may change dynamically. Compositions of environments can be re-arranged dynamically as a distributed application evolves its functions dynamically in order to adapt itself to its external context. Participating in environments, an agent can engage in multiple roles and collaborate with other agents of each environment.

4   Java RoleEP Framework Epsilon/J

Epsilon/J is a framework that supports RoleEP concepts including environment and roles. This framework is implemented on Aglets. In this section, features of Epsilon/J are explained by describing the example presented in section 2.

4.1   Environment Descriptions

In Epsilon/J, an environment class is defined as a subclass of the *Environment* class, and a role class is defined as a subclass of the *Role* class. The *Role* class is implemented as a subclass of the *Aglets* class that has mobility functions. The following is a program that defines the environment class *Roaming* and *ContractNet*. In the *Roaming* environment class, the *Visitor* role class is defined. An object becomes an agent that can roam around hosts by binding itself to a role instantiated from the *Visitor* class. On the other hand, in the *ContractNet* environment class, the *Manager* role class and the *Contractor* role class are defined. An agent, which arrives from another host, acquires new functions that are necessary for behaving as a manager by binding itself to a role instantiated from the *Manager* role.

The *Roaming* environment class

```
public class Roaming extends Environment{
  public void onEnvironmentCreation(String environmentName){}
  public class Visitor extends Role{
    public void onRoleCreation(String roleName){
      // Add this role whose name is specified by ''roleName"
      //    to the ''Roaming" environment.
      Roaming.this.addRole(roleName, this);
      addBindingInterface("executeTask");
    }
    public void roam(){
      SeqPlanItinerary itinerary = new SeqPlanItinerary(this);
        :
    }
  }
}
```

The *onEnvironmentCreation* is a constructor that is called when an environment is instantiated. The *onRoleCreation* is a constructor that is called when a role is instantiated. These names are based on the name of the Aglet's constructor *onCreation*. The role's name, the parameter of the *onRoleCreation*, is an identifier of a role instance. This name identifies roles instantiated from the same *Visitor* role class. Roles that belong to the same role class can exist in the same environment. Epsilon/J presents directory services based on role names. The environment name in the *onEnvironmentCreation* is treated in the same manner.

In the *Visitor* role class, the binding-interface *executeTask*, which is an interface of a method that is invoked when an agent arrives at a host, is added dynamically. An agent, which is composed of an object and an instance created from the *Visitor* role class, roams around hosts and executes the *executeTask* at each host.

The *ContractNet* environment class

```
public class ContractNet extends Environment{
  public void onEnvironmentCreation(String environmentName){}
  public class Manager extends Role{
    public void onRoleCreation(String roleName){
      ContractNet.this.addRole(roleName, this);
    }
    public void start(){}
    public void bid(Contractor c){}
    public void end(Info info){}
  }
  public class Contractor extends Role{
    public void onRoleCreation(String roleName){
      ContractNet.this.addRole(roleName, this);
      addBindingInterface("executeTask");
    }
    public void taskAnnounce(Manager m){}
    public void award(Manager m){
      m.end(executeTask());
    }
  }
}
```

4.2   Object Descriptions

The following is a program that defines the class *UserProxy* and the class *SearchInfo*. An object instantiated from the *UserProxy* class is bound to a visitor role instantiated from the *Visitor* class and a manager role instantiated from the *Manager* class. A class of an Epsilon/J's object is defined as a subclass of the *EpsilonObj* class that presents functions for binding-operations. The *onEpsilonObjCreation* is a constructor that is called when an EpsilonObj is instantiated.

The *UserProxy* **class**

```
public class UserProxy extends EpsilonObj{
  public void onEpsilonObjCreation() {
    // Search a visitor role ''visitorRole"
    //   and bind this user proxy to the visitor role.
    // This user proxy becomes an agent that can roam around hosts.
    visitorRole.bind(this, ''executeTask", ''executeContractNet");
    visitorRole.roam();
  }
  public void executeContractNet() {
    // Search a manager role ''managerRole"
    //   and binds this user proxy to the manager role.
    // This user proxy becomes an agent that can act as a manager.
    managerRole.bind(this);  // there are not binding-interfaces.
    managerRole.start();
  }
}
```

The *InfoSearcher* **class**

```
public class InfoSearcher extends EpsilonObj{
  public void onEpsilonObjCreation() {
    // Search contractor roles existing
    //   in the environment ''contractnetEnv"
    //   that is instantiated from ''ContractNet".
    Contractor [] allContractorRoles
      = contractnetEnv.searchRole("Contractor");
    // Select a role ''contractorRole" from ''allContractorRoles"
    //   and bind this information searcher to the role.
    // This information searcher becomes an agent
    //   that can act as a contractor in the ''contractnetEnv".
    contractorRole.bind(this, ''executeTask", ''searchInfo");
  }
  public void searchInfo(){...}
  public void search2Info(){...}
}
```

5   Reflection and Epsilon/J Implementation

5.1   Epsilon/J Implementation

Epsilon/J presents built-in classes including *Environment, Role* and *EpsilonObject*. Mechanisms such as binding-interfaces and binding-operations are contained in these built-in classes that are implemented by using Java core reflection APIs (Application Programming Interfaces). Using a reflection mechanism, method signatures defined in objects/roles/environments can be introspected and invoked dynamically. If a message received by a role corresponds to a binding-interface, the message is transformed to a signature that is specified as an argument in a binding-operation[4] and delegated to an object bound to the role. This

---

[4] In the current implementation, a transformation of a signature is limited to renaming a message name.

approach is similar to the Composition Filters(CF)[1][8] approach. In CF, an object consists of an interface layer that contains input/output message filters and a kernel object. A role in RoleEP corresponds to a message filter in CF. As shown in Figure 3, binding-interfaces can be wrapped with before/after actions that describe synchronization constraints, error checking strategies, security checking strategies, coordination constraints and so forth.

Since mechanisms of binding-interfaces and binding-operations are implemented very simply in Epsilon/J, decline in performance caused by adding RoleEP features of this kind to the original Aglets mobile agent system is slight. In Aglets, moreover, a dynamic method dispatching mechanism is already used in order to realize a message as an object. Other features such as implementation of environment methods/attributes may prompt discussion. In Epsilon/J, information on an environment such as role references, role host addresses and environment methods/attributes is stored intensively in a host where the environment is instantiated. If a role does not reside in a host where the corresponding environment exists, the role has to execute remote-accessing in order to use the above kinds of information. In Epsilon/J, the notion of *messenger role* is introduced to realize role-to-role remote communication and role-to-environment remote communication. A messenger role is a special role that brings a message object from one host to another host. In Epsilon/J, an API function for message communication is prepared to encapsulate existence of messenger roles. This API function decides automatically whether communication is remote or local. If communication is remote, the API function uses a messenger role. Otherwise, the function sends a message normally. The mechanism of a messenger role may cause some kind of decline in performance.

5.2   Reflection Facilities in Epsilon/J

Epsilon/J gives reflection facilities that can introspect environments and roles —for example, a list of environment instances/names, a list of method names in an environment, a list of role instances/names in an environment, a list of method/binding-interface names in a role. Using these facilities, dynamic aspects of programs can be described easily: 1) An object can search an environment that the object wants to adapt to; 2) An object can check if the object is able to bind to a role. The object must have methods corresponding to binding-interfaces of the roles. Environments in RoleEP can be considered as execution environments for objects. Binding-operations and facilities for introspecting environments/roles can be regarded as some kinds of MOPs (Metaobject protocols) that are provided as Epsilon/J class libraries. For example, a binding-operation is implemented in *Role* class and a customized binding-operation such as a binding-operation with security checking can be described by defining a subclass of *Role* class.

6   Discussion

6.1   Merits of RoleEP

RoleEP addresses problems pointed out in section 2 as follows:

- Mobility/collaboration functions can be separated from original functions completely and can be encapsulated within environment descriptions. This solves problems that appeared in Case 1 and 2.
- The problem that descriptions of role behavior depend on interface names of core classes in Case 3 can be solved by the binding-interface mechanism.

  Moreover, there are attractive properties as follows:

- Construction mechanism for mobility/collaboration components: RoleEP is beneficial for constructing mobility/collaboration components. For example, the environment class *ContractNet* can be reused in many distributed applications based on mobile agent systems. Environment classes can be regarded as mobility/collaboration components.
- Evolution mechanism for agents: In RoleEP, an object becomes an agent by binding itself to a role that belongs to an environment. An object can dynamically evolve to an agent that can play multiple roles. Using RoleEP, programs that adapt to external context can be described easily.
- Agentification mechanism: Genesereth and Ketchpel show three approaches for converting objects into agents[12]: 1) an approach that implements a transducer that mediates between an object and other agents, 2) an approach that implements a wrapper, and 3) an approach that rewrites an original object. In RoleEP, a role corresponds to a transducer that accepts messages from other agents and translates them into messages that an object can understand. Although general agentifications are implemented statically, a connection between an object and a transducer is created dynamically through a binding-operation in RoleEP. RoleEP can be regarded as one of the dynamic agentification mechanisms. In RoleEP, mobility/collaboration functions needed for mobile agents are described in terms of roles and other functions are described in terms of objects. In order to separate these two kinds of functions completely, roles have facilities as transducers that translate message interactions among roles to message interactions among objects.

6.2   Comparisons with AOP

Table 1, which extends an AOP comparison method proposed in [6], compares RoleEP with AOP. RoleEP emphasizes dynamic aspect syntheses and dynamic evolution. Although AOP and RoleEP have common viewpoints, there is a big difference between them. In AOP, an executable program can be constructed only by objects even if there are no aspects that add cross-cutting properties to

Table 1. AOP vs RoleEP

viewpoint	AOP	RoleEP
aspects	aspects	environments and roles
components	components	objects
join points	join points	binding-interfaces
(between aspects and components)		
weaving method	weaver	binding-operation
aspect reuse	emphasized	emphasized
dynamic evolution	not emphasized	emphasized

objects. On the other hand, objects cannot organize a program without environments in RoleEP.

In RoleEP, the use of binding-operation eliminates the necessity of AOP style weaving. *Introduces* weaving in AspectJ can be replaced by adding role methods through binding-operation. However, *advises* weaving does not correspond to any model constructs in RoleEP. This is a weak point of RoleEP, and reduces the ability to prevent code duplication. From the viewpoint of static evolution, *advises* weaving is very useful because it prevents code duplication. From the viewpoint of dynamic evolution, however, *advises* weaving is slightly risky because it is difficult to understand real behaviors. In Kendall's approach, *introduces* weaving only adds a method interface, and the body of the method is added through *advises* weaving. This kind of *advises* weaving can be realized by the binding-operation.

6.3   Comparisons with the Pluggable Composite Adapter

Mezini, Seiter and Lieberherr propose a new language construct, called a *pluggable composite adapter*, for expressing component gluing[23]. In the pluggable composite adapter, a component is a set of collaborating classes that defines some functionality. A pluggable composite adapter defines how to dynamically extend a component with a new collaboration. The component is adapted dynamically to play roles in the collaboration without changing the component's classes. In addition, a pluggable composite adapter defines how to glue together two independently developed components C1 and C2, where C2 is an abstract collaboration. The following is the structure of the pluggable composite adapter.

```
adapter A {
  Field_Method_Defs
  Helper_Class_Defs
  { adapter R adapts C1.B [extends C2.S] adaptation_body }*
}
```

C1.B is a class of a component C1. Through *adapts* relation, an instance of *C1.B* acquires a function given in adaptation_body. An instance of *adapter R* is created only when an instance of *C1.B* comes into R's scope. *Adapter A* and *adapter R* correspond to an environment and a role in RoleEP respectively. Adaptations are similar to binding-operations in RoleEP. Using the pluggable composite adapter, the contract-net protocol can be described as follows.

```
adapter ContractNet {
  adapter Manager adapts UserProxy {
    public void start(){...}
    public void bid()   {...}
    public void end()   {...}
  }
  adapter Contractor adapts InfoSearcher {
    public void taskAnnounce(){...}
    public void award(){ InfoSearcher.this.searchInfo(); }
  }
}
```

Notions of the pluggable composite adapter are quite similar to RoleEP. However, there are some differences between them as follows: 1) A relation between an adapter and an adaptee is described statically in the the pluggable composite adapter; 2) Descriptions of adapter's behavior depend on interface names of adaptee's class in the the pluggable composite adapter.

7   Related Works

Bardou shows comparisons between AOP and related approaches, namely Role Modeling[2], Activities and roles[21], Subject-Oriented Programming[14], Split objects[5] and Us "a subjective version of SELF"[26] in [6]. Besides Role modeling, a lot of other research has been done concerning role concepts[19][20][9][27]. Van Hilst and Notkin propose the idea of role components, which are described by C++ templates, to implement collaboration-based design[29]. This approach is similar to the mix-in approach. In *Coordinated Roles* proposed in [24], descriptions of collaborations are separated from descriptions of objects by using role concepts. Although this approach is similar to the binding-interface concepts, there is no concept of dynamic binding between an object and a role in *Coordinated Roles*. In these approaches, dynamic evolution or dynamic synthesis of collaboration structures is not emphasized. Split objects and Us are based on a delegation mechanism that enables dynamic evolution.

On the other hand, adaptations to external context are studied from the viewpoint of how a single object evolves dynamically—for example, how a person acquires methods and attributes when he/she does a job, marries and so on. In the Subject Oriented Programming, an object acquires new functions by participating in subjects. The concept of subjects is similar to the concept of environments in RoleEP. *Mobile Ambients* is a model that gives a layered agent structure[7]. In this model, agents run on fields constructed by synthesizing contexts (environments) dynamically.

8   Conclusions

Distributed applications that reside in the Internet environment, whose structures change dynamically, are spreading rapidly. Most applications are implemented in traditional programming languages, and have many embedded logics according to individual environments. These applications must switch to new logics as environments change. As a result, these applications need to be restructured drastically when they have to adapt to new environments. New computation paradigms and programming languages are necessary in order to alleviate this requirement. RoleEP that we have proposed in this paper is one approach to address this issue. In this paper, the effectiveness of RoleEP was discussed from the viewpoint of mobile agent applications. However, the notion of RoleEP is quite general and can be applied to other kinds of applications that need mechanisms for *separation of concerns*.

References

1. Akist, M. and Tripathi, A.: Data Abstraction Mechanisms in Sina/ST, *Proceedings of the Conference on Object-Oriented Programming Systems, Language, and Applications (OOPSLA'88)*, pp.265-275, 1988.
2. Andersen, E.P. and Reenskaug, T.: System Design by Composing Structures of Interacting Objects, *Proceedings of the European Conference on Object-Oriented Programming (ECOOP'92)*, Lecture Notes in Computer Science, Springer, vol.615, pp.133-152, 1992.
3. Aridor, Y. and Lange, D.B.: Agent design patterns: Elements of agent application design, *Proceedings of Agents'98*, 1998.
4. AspectJ. http://aspectj.org/.
5. Bardou, D. and Dony, C.: Split Objects: a Disciplined Use of Delegation within Objects, *Proceedings of the Conference on Object-Oriented Programming Systems, Language, and Applications (OOPSLA'96)*, pp.122-137, 1996.
6. Bardou, D.: Roles, Subjects and Aspects: How do they relate?, *Proceedings of the Aspect-Oriented Programming Workshop at ECOOP'98*, 1998.
7. Cardelli, L. and Gordon, A.D.: Mobile Ambients (Extended Abstract), *the proceedings of the workshop on Higher Order Operational Techniques in Semantics*, 1997.
8. Czarnecki, K. and Eisenecker, U.W.: *Generative Programming*, Addison-Wesley, 2000.
9. Fowler, M.: Dealing with Roles, *Proceedings of the 4th Annual Conference on Pattern Languages of Programs*, 1997.
10. Fuggetta, A., Picco, G.P.d, and Vigna, G.: Understanding Code Mobility, *IEEE Transactions on Software Engineering*, vol.24, No.5, pp.342-361, 1998.
11. Gamma, E., Helm, R., Johnson, R., and Vlissides, J.: *Design Patterns*, Addison-Wesley Publishing Company, Inc., 1995.
12. Genesereth, M.R. and Ketchpel, S.P.: *Software Agents*, *Communications of the ACM*, vol.37, No.7, pp.48-53, 1994.
13. Guerraoui, R. et al.: Strategic Directions in Object-Oriented Programming. *ACM Computing Surveys*, Vol.28, No.4, pages 691-700, 1996.
14. Harrison, W. and Ossher, H.: Subject-oriented Programming, *Proceedings of the 8th Conference on Object-Oriented Programming Systems, Language, and Applications (OOPSLA'93)*, pp.411-428, 1993.
15. IBM: *Aglets   Software   Development   Kit   Home   Page*, http://www.trl.ibm.co.jp/aglets/index.html, 1999.

16. Kendall, E.A.: Role Model Designs and Implementations with Aspect-oriented Programming, *Proceedings of the Conference on Object-Oriented Programming Systems, Language, and Applications (OOPSLA'99)*, pp.353-369, 1999.

17. Kiczales, G., Lamping, J., Mendhekar A., Maeda, C., Lopes, C., Loingtier, J., and Irwin, J.: Aspect-Oriented Programming, *Proceedings of the European Conference on Object-Oriented Programming (ECOOP'97)*, Lecture Notes in Computer Science, Springer, vol.1241, pp.220-242, 1997.

18. Kiniry, J. and Zimmerman, D.: A Hands-On Look at Java Mobile Agents, *IEEE Internet Computing*, vol.1, No.4, 1997.

19. Kristensen, B.B.: Object-oriented Modeling with Roles, *Proceedings of the 2nd International Conference on Object-oriented Information Systems (OOIS'95)*, 1996.

20. Kristensen, B.B. and Osterbye, K.: Roles: Conceptual Abstraction Theory and Practical Language Issues, *Special Issue of Theory and Practice of Object Systems (TAPOS) on Subjectivity in Object-oriented Systems*, 1996.

21. Kristensen, B.B. and May, D.C.M.: Activities: Abstractions for Collective Behavior, *Proceedings of the European Conference on Object-Oriented Programming (ECOOP'96)*, Lecture Notes in Computer Science, Springer, vol.1098, pp.472-501, 1996.

22. Lange, D. and Oshima M.: *Programming and Deploying Java Mobile Agents with Aglets*, Addison-Wesley, 1998.

23. Mezini, M., Seiter, L. and Lieberherr, K.: Component Integration with Pluggable Composite Adapters, *Software Architectures and Component Technology: The State of the Art in Research and Practice, Mehmet Aksit, editor*, Kluwer Academic Publishers, 2000.

24. Murillo, J.M., Hernandez, J., Sanchez, F., and Alvarez, L.A.: Coordinated Roles: Promoting Re-usability of Coordinated Active Objects Using Event Notification Protocols, *COORDINATION'99 Proceedings*, pp.53-68, 1999.

25. Smith, R.G.: The Contract Net Protocol: High-Level Communication and Control in a Distributed Problem Solver, *IEEE Trans. on Computers*, vol.29, No.12, pp.1104-1113, 1980.

26. Smith, R.B. and Ungar, D.: Programming as an Experience: The Inspiration for Self, *Proceedings of the European Conference on Object-Oriented Programming (ECOOP'95)*, Lecture Notes in Computer Science, Springer, vol.952, pp.303-330, 1995.

27. Tamai, T.: Objects and roles: modeling based on the dualistic view, *Information and Software Technology*, Vol. 41, No. 14, pp. 1005–1010, 1999.

28. Ubayashi, N. and Tamai, T.: An Evolutional Cooperative Computation Based on Adaptation to Environment, *Proceedings of Sixth Asia Pacific Software Engineering Conference (APSEC'99)*, IEEE Computer Society, pp.334-341, 1999.

29. VanHilst, M. and Notkin, D.: Using Role Components to Implement Collaboration-Based Designs, *Proceedings of the Conference on Object-Oriented Programming Systems, Language, and Applications (OOPSLA'96)*, pp.359-369, 1996.

Dynamic Adaptability: The MolèNE Experiment

Jacques Malenfant[1], Maria-Teresa Segarra[2], and Françoise André[2]

[1] IRISA, Triskell Action, and Université de Bretagne sud
[2] IRISA, Solidor Project
Campus universitaire de Beaulieu, F-35042 Rennes Cedex, France
{Jacques.Malenfant,Maria-Teresa.Segarra,Francoise.Andre}@irisa.fr,
http://www.irisa.fr/solidor/work/molene.html

Abstract. Dynamic adaptability of applications to their execution evironment is growingly important in mobile, WAN-based and distributed embedded systems. In this paper, we present MolèNE , an object-oriented middleware framework enabling the construction of dynamically adaptable mobile applications, coping with temporary memory restrictions, variations in network bandwith, etc. We then come back on MolèNE to compare it with other similar systems, in order to draw lessons towards reflective middleware and system designers.

1 Introduction

The dynamic adaptability of applications to variations in their run-time environment is acknowledged as a major challenge in mobile, WAN-based, and distributed embedded systems. Mobile systems exhibit rapid and drastic changes in otherwise limited resources availability: power, network connectivity, ... Moreover, mobility itself triggers drastic modifications of available services: printers, database servers, etc. In WAN computing, applications experience significant variations in network bandwith. More and more embedded systems are distributed and face similar variations in workload and resources availability.

To face these challenges, new systems and middleware are developed with dynamic adaptability as their primary goal. MolèNE is an object-oriented middleware framework enabling the construction of dynamically adaptable applications running on mobile computing devices [SA00a]. Similar systems, such as QuO [PLS00,LAS01], Sumo-CORE and Sumo-ORB [BS98] in the field of quality of service as well as 2K [KYH01] for dynamic (re)configuration, have been developed to address similar issues. But few reflective approaches have been proposed that address the specific means for context-based adaptation triggered by dynamic changes on the execution environment. For example, dynamicTAO [KRL00,WKS00] and Lancaster next generation middleware [BCC99] consider adaptations triggered by events external to the computation itself, while the only reflective language that explicitly addresses issues of context-based adaptations is LEAD++ [AW99].

The goal of this paper is to gather experience and lessons learned from MolèNE and other similar systems designed for dynamic adaptability, towards designers of reflective languages, middlewares and operating systems.

A. Yonezawa and S. Matsuoka (Eds.): REFLECTION 2001, LNCS 2192, pp. 110–117, 2001.

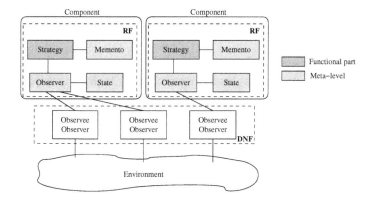

Fig. 1. Structure of the Dynamic Adaptation Framework

2   A General Overview of MolèNE

MolèNE's design aims at coping with variations in resources availability to offer a sustained level of quality of service while keeping aplications core well isolated from variations management code. In order to achieve this, it considers applications as sets of components which behavior can be changed at run-time according to resource availability and provides a dynamic adaptation framework which is divided into two subframeworks: the *Detection/Notification Framework* (DNF), which monitors resources and notify components of changes, and the *Reactive Framework* (RF) which is encapsulated on each adaptive component and is responsible for changing the component behavior in order to make it better-suited to the new execution conditions.

Adopting the perspective of design patterns [GHJV95], the architecture of the dynamic adaptation framework can be understood as illustrated in Figure 1. A two-leveled *observer* pattern is used which events trigger state changes for a *state* pattern, which in turn uses a *strategy* pattern to adapt the algorithm used in the functional part of the component. When interchanging strategies, a *memento* and an *adapter* pattern are used to transfer contextual run-time information from the old algorithm to the new one.

MolèNE has been fully implemented and totals around 200 Java classes and 320 KB of code. Three mobile applications have contributed to the development and validation of MolèNE. Two of them, a file system called MFS [AS99] and an e-commerce application called METIS [AP98] have allowed us to identify a large number of functionalities to manage mobile environments. As they were developed in parallel with the MolèNE prototype, they do not fully benefit from MolèNE mechanisms. The third experiment, the reengineering of a medical prescriptions application towards mobility, called Charcot [AP00], has allowed us to validate the MolèNE's dynamic adaptation framework in real settings and has raised a number of open issues such us reactions coordination, instabilities, and error management.

3   Resource Monitoring and Notification

The Detection/Notification Framework (DNF) provides the necessary means to make MolèNE components environment-aware. It implements asynchronous notification of changes by letting reaction mechanisms register monitoring conditions, and polling as information about the environment can be directly accessed.

The DNF is organized into two well-defined layers. The low-level one, implemented by base monitors (BMs), maintains basic information about physical and software resources and monitors the environment in order to detect variations. The amount of available network bandwidth or memory of each station is managed at this level. Base monitors are instances of the `BaseMonitor` class which provides methods to let reaction mechanisms (i) access measures of the environment and (ii) register monitoring requests. High-level monitors (HLMs) are entities of the high-level layer and are defined by the designer of the adaptation strategy by subclassing the `HLMonitor` abstract class. They collect and synthesize informations from BMs and other HLMs in order to obtain an abstraction of the environment state. Network connection quality is an example of a high-level information expressed in terms of the available bandwidth, the error rate, or a combination of both. The synthesized information is made available either by polling or by asynchronous notification.

4   Reactive Component

Dynamic adaptability means reacting to changes in the environment that happen asynchronously to the execution of the application. In order to make components adaptive, MolèNE clearly separates their functional part from the reaction mechanisms. The former is provided by two objects classes (see Figure 2) which relation is defined by the *strategy* pattern [GHJV95]: an `Interaction` object that manages communication with other components and an `Implementation` object which effectively realizes the component task. Reaction mechanisms are embedded in a *reactive entity* that extends the structure of a component. They are responsible for (i) deciding about changes to be performed on the `Implementation` object, and (ii) controlling the execution of such changes. They register monitoring requests on the DNF and receives notifications when they are satisfied by the execution conditions.

The reactive entity architecture is made up of two types of objects. The `Controller` object effectively executes changes on the functional part of the component. These changes are performed according to the adaptation strategy designed for the component and reified by the `Adaptation Strategy` object as an automaton which states represent execution conditions and provide the implementation to be used on them and transitions determine the reaction to be performed when changing from one state to another. Reactions may concern the change of the value of some parameters of the `Implementation` object or the replacement of the `Implementation` object itself.

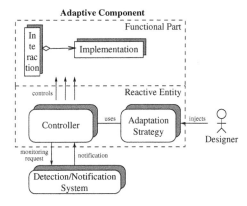

Fig. 2. Structure of an Adaptive Component

5   Dynamic Behavior Replacement

Dynamic adaptability requires multiple implementations, which in turn mean different data structures, and translation of state when changing from the old to the new implementation. The `Controller` object is responsible for executing reactions described in the `Adaptation Strategy` object. It registers monitoring requests on the concerned DNS monitors and decides about reactions to be performed on the functional part of the component according to the information provided by the `Adaptation Strategy` object. The *observer* design pattern [GHJV95] defines relations between the `Controller` object and monitors.

While executing a reaction, the `Controller` object should prevent functional requests from being lost. In order to achieve this, it asks the `Interaction` object to block requests from other components and to memorize them. When operations on the behavior are finished, the `Controller` object relinquishes the `Interaction` object and the stored requests will be processed.

When a behavior replacement reaction is executed a major issue concerns the transfer of information between `Implementation` objects. MolèNE manages this issue by letting the `Controller` object execute a three-phased protocol that involves the *Interaction*, the *Implementation*, and a *State Adapter* objects. During the first phase, the current `Implementation` object finishes its ongoing tasks and builds its *internal state*. Designers of *Implementation* sub-classes are responsible for deciding which infor mation should be included in the state. The *memento* design pattern [GHJV95] is used to achieve this. Once this state is available, the `Controller` object launches the second phase during which the built state is passed to the `State Adapter` object associated to the reaction being executed. This object adapts the state of the replaced `Implementation` object so that the new one is able to correctly interpret its contents. This adaptation may concern complex tasks that involve contents of the state. At t he end of this phase, the `Controller` object allows the `Interaction` one to transfer requests to the new `Implementation` object.

6   Related Work

QuO [PLS00,LAS01] is a middleware that enables applications to dynamically adapt to variations in the quality of service offered by their execution environment. Similar to monitors of MolèNE, QuO's *system condition objects* provide both a query interface and an event-based notification service. QuO implements reactions in specific stub objects called *delegate objects*, which adapts their treatment of sent and received messages. Contracts define negotiated and measured regions of QoS values as well as reactions, using a set of specification languages collectively called QDL (QoS Description Languages). These contracts are compiled into delegate objects. Transitions between measured regions are triggered by changes in the environment noticed either by querying or by receiving an event from system condition objects.

2K [KYH01] is a network-centric operating system built for managing dynamism through an adaptable software architecture. In 2K, a resource management service monitors the state of resources, negotiates and allocates resources to components, and notifies the reaction entities upon changes. 2K implements reactions in *component configurator objects*, which reify configuration strategies by expressing dependencies towards resources, services and loaded components. According to these dependencies, the component configurator negotiates with the resource managers to perform the QoS- and resource-aware configuration. This configuration includes the choice of an "optimal" implementation given the resource awarded during the negotiation phase. When a change of implementation is needed for a dynamic reconfiguration, 2K uses the *memento* pattern [GHJV95] to deliver the internal state of the replaced implementation to the newly loaded one.

Sumo [BS98] proposes a framework for the dynamic adaptability in distributed multimedia. Crucial to the approach are signal interfaces and stream bindings as first-class objects. A stream binding represents a multimedia flow between two endpoints. Adaptation in this model is ensured by reactive objects that coordinate sets of streams and application objects by receiving events emitted by streams and application objects at specific points in the computation. Reactive objects encode QoS monitoring in their reactions to these events and trigger adaptation when something goes wrong according to the expected QoS. Reactive objects are programmed using a synchronous language, Esterel, which runs under the hypothesis of instantaneous processing of incoming events (avoiding a possible metaregression to control the QoS of reactive objects).

DART [RL98] is another distributed middleware that introduces adaptive methods to provide several different implementations of the same method selected at runtime according to predefine adaptation policies triggered by events. A restriction is however imposed on adaptive methods since all of their implementations share the same object state representation. Coordination of distributed adaptations in DART is being investigated. Odyssey [NS99] deals with dynamic adaptation for mobile system and puts forward, through real experiments, the need for coordination of individual adaptive entities.

LEAD++ [AW99] is a reflective language based on Java that implements authors' DAS model for dynamic adaptability. In LEAD++, resources are reified by *environmental objects*, which are monitored using *event objects* invoking specific callback methods in applications when changes occur. A LEAD++ method is defined as an adaptable procedure, which is a set of methods qualified by selection conditions depending on the state of the execution environment. Selection itself is performed by a two-level dispatch. Invocation of a method triggers the execution of a *dispatch object* at the meta-level. The dispatch object instantiates a *strategy object*, itself an adaptable procedure defining the base-level selection strategy, and selects the strategy according to the current state of execution, which is then applied to select the method in the base-level adaptable procedure that will process the message. This two-level dispatch elegantly applies the basic adaptability mechanism to also adapt the meta-level.

Few papers discuss adaptation policies in the light of control theory in the context of reflection. De Meer [dM00] considers reflection for continuous QoS control systems, and he shows how concepts of automatic control can be applied to define correct and optimal adaptation policies. Efstratiou and Cheverst [EC00] identify rather than solve the issues raised by coordination of adaptation policies. Global coordination in distributed systems is also considered by these authors. Li and Nahrstedt [LN99] do not consider reflection, but they propose an ambitious attempt in the area of control theoretic models for QoS enforcement to formulate a series of recommendations for applications to make them amenable to a formal analysis using control theory concepts and tools.

More generally, Braux and Noyé [BN99] consider objects that change their behavior depending on the state of other objects and propose a composition of *strategy* and *observer* patterns as a general architecture for that purpose. Ferreira and Rubira [FR98] go further and propose a *reflective state* pattern where the automaton representing states and transitions is implemented at the meta-level.

7   Discussion, Conclusion and Perspectives

We have presented MolèNE, a middleware framework for adaptable mobile systems, and we have compared and contrasted it with similar systems. From this comparison, a canonical software architecture for dynamic adaptability emerges that includes monitoring, reaction and adaptable components. The experience that has been gathered helps to identify the set of concepts and technology dedicated to dynamic adaptability:

Monitoring: An extensible monitoring subsystem allows programmers to query the state of resources (for rapidly changing values) and to subscribe to event-based notifications (for values that change infrequently [LAS01]). Low-level monitors are responsible for the measurements of raw resources parameters. High-level monitors express conditions meaningful to the applications, and should be expressed in a declarative way to allow for reasoning and verification of adaptable applications.

Reaction: Reactive meta-objects, in the line of Sumo's, control adaptations at run-time by reacting to events external to the current computation. Reactive meta-objects should implement contracts in the line of QuO's, expressing the adaptation strategies. The current challenge is to generate reactive meta-objects from higher level expressions of applications needs in resources, QoS, and meaningful external events. More declarative contract languages are still needed, to provide programmers with a high-level view of adaptation.

Adaptable entities: Abstractions for adaptable objects include many different implementations targeted to specific run-time conditions. Such adaptable objects must provide as a basic service a semantic-based protocol for transfering state information between their different implementations. More than simply applying a *memento* pattern on a per object basis, the MolèNE experiment has stressed the idea that interchangeable implementations of interface compliant services are an inherent and integral part of adaptation. The granularity of adaptable entities must be a trade off between individual methods, as in LEAD++, and whole components as in 2K.

Adaptation policies: Our experiments show that even simple adaptable systems are hard to implement correctly. When conditions triggering adaptation vary rapidly, even as a consequence of the adaptation itself, incorrect adaptation policies lead to oscillation or to a form of trashing, i.e. doing nothing else than adapt repeatedly. Global coordination of adaptations is needed, but more generally theories of adaptation must be sought to ensure system-wide correctness properties. Control theory, where controllability and stability have been studied for years, can help, but the complexity of distributed adaptable systems challenges the current theory. Neural networks provide another path to explore, as done in the control of complex systems.

Our experiments in dynamic adaptability put forward the relatively new idea of using events in reflection. This naturally leads to a novel *asynchronous reflective model* where reflective computations are no longer triggered by events internal to the execution (i.e. synchronous), but rather by external events (i.e. asynchronous). Such a model will have deep impacts on reflection. Going back to debates in the early '90s, event-based reflective models can solve issues about concurrency and causal connection between base-level and meta-objects. The base-level and meta-objects can run concurrently and use events to notify changes in a causally connected fashion. More specifically, event-based reflection can help us to stop thinking about the meta link as an implementation relationship, and see it as a more or less tightly coupled representation link, as Smith was argueing in his seminal paper at the OOPSLA'90 Workshop [Smi90].

References

AP98. F. André and E. Saint Pol. A Middleware for Transactional Internet Applications on Mobile Networks. In *Proc. of the Conf. PDPTA*, 1998.

AP00. F. André and E. Saint Pol. A middleware for transactional hospital applications on local wireless networks. In *Proc. of the Conf. PDPTA*, 2000.

AS99.   F. André and M.T. Segarra. On Building a File System for Mobile Environ-
           ments Using Generic Services. In *Proc. of the 12th Conf. PDCS*, 1999.
AW99.   N. Amano and T. Watanabe. An Approach for Constructing Dynamically
           Adaptable Component-Based Software Systems using LEAD++. In *Elec-
           tronic Proc. of the OOPSLA'99 Workshop OORaSE '99*, pages 1–16. 1999.
BCC99.   G. Blair, F. Costa, G. Coulson, H. Duran, N. Parlavantzas, F. Delpiano,
           B. Dumant, F. Horn, and J.-B. Stéfani. The Design of a Resource-Aware
           Middleware Architecture. In *Proc. of Reflection'99*, number 1616 in Springer-
           Verlag LNCS, pages 115–134. 1999.
BN99.   M. Braux and J. Noyé. Changement dynamique de comportement par com-
           position de schémas de conception. In *Proceedings of "Langages et Modèles
           à Objets, LMO'99"*, Hermès, 1999. in french.
BS98.   G. Blair and J.-B. Stéfani. *Open Distributed Processing and Multimedia*.
           Addison-Wesley, 1998.
dM00.   J. de Meer. On the Construction of Reflective System Architectures. In
           Electronic Proc. of the Reflective Middleware Workshop, 2000.
EC00.   C. Efstratiou and K. Cheverst. Reflection: A Solution for Highly Adaptive
           Mobile Systems. In *Elec. Proc. of the Reflective Middleware Workshop*, 2000.
FR98.   L.L Ferreira and C.M.F. Rubira. Reflective Design Patterns to Implement
           Fault Tolerance. In *Proc. of the OOPSLA'98 Workshop on Reflective Pro-
           gramming in C++ and Java*, pages 81–85. 1998.
GHJV95.   E. Gamma, R. Helm, R. Johnson, and J. Vlissides. *Design Patterns: Ele-
           ments of Reusable Object-Oriented Software*. Addison-Wesley, 1995.
KRL00.   F. Kon, M. Ròman, P. Liu, J. Mao, T. Yamane, L.C. Magalhæs, and R.H.
           Campbell. Monitoring, Security, and Dynamic Configuration with the dy-
           namicTAO Reflective ORB. In *Proc. of Middleware 2000*, number 1795 in
           Springer-Verlag LNCS, 2000.
KYH01.   F. Kon, T. Yamane, C.K. Hess, R.H. Campbell, and D. Mickunas. Dy-
           namic Resource Management and Automatic Configuration of Distributed
           Component Systems. In *Proc. of USENIX COOTS*, 2001.
LAS01.   J.P. Loyall, A.K. Atlas, R.E. Schantz, C.D. Gill, D.L. Levine, C. O'Ryan,
           and D.C. Schmidt. Flexible and Adaptive Control of Real-Time Distributed
           Object Computing Middleware. submitted for publication, 2001.
LN99.   B. Li and K. Nahrstedt. A Control-Based Middleware Framework for Qual-
           ity of Service Adaptations. *Journal on Selected Areas in Communications*,
           17(9):1632–1650, 1999.
NS99.   B.D. Noble and M. Satyanarayanan. Experience with adaptive mobile ap-
           plications in Odyssey. *Mobile Networks and Applications*, 4:245–254, 1999.
PLS00.   P. Pal, J. Loyall, R. Schantz, J. Zinky, R. Shapiro, and J. Megquier. Using
           QDL to Specify QOS Aware Distributed (QuO) Application Configuration.
           In *Proc. of ISORC'00*, IEEE, 2000.
RL98.   P.-G. Raverdy and R. Lea. DART: a Distributed Adaptive Run-Time. In
           Proceedings of Middleware'98, IFIP, Springer-Verlag, 1998.
SA00a.   M.T. Segarra and F. André. A Framework for Dynamic Adaptation in
           Wireless Environment. In *Proc. of TOOLS Europe 2000*, 2000.
Smi90.   B.C. Smith. What do you mean, *meta*? In *Informal Proc. of the First
           Workshop on Reflection in OOP, OOPSLA/ECOOP'90*, 1990.
WKS00.   N. Wang, M. Kircher, and D.C. Schmidt. Towards a Reflective Middleware
           Framework for QoS-Enabled CORBA Component Model Applications. In
           Electronic Proc. of the Reflective Middleware Workshop, 2000.

A simple security-aware MOP for Java

Denis Caromel, Fabrice Huet and Julien Vayssière

INRIA - CNRS - I3S
Université de Nice Sophia-Antipolis
First.Last@sophia.inria.fr

Abstract. This article investigates the security problems raised by the use of proxy-based runtime meta-object protocols (MOPs) for Java and provides an approach for making meta-level code transparent to base-level code, security-wise. We prove that, but giving all permissions only to the kernel of the MOP and by using Java's built-in mechanism for propagating security contexts, the permissions required by base-level and meta-level code do not interfere. We illustrate this result in the context of a simple proxy-based runtime MOP that we wrote.

1 Introduction

Different authors have suggested using Meta-Object Protocols (MOPs) as an elegant solution for implementing security mechanisms. However, studying the security issues *raised by* MOPs has never been adressed as a problem on its own.

A previous work [2] provided a set of rules for combining together the permissions associated with the different protection domains of a typical reflective component-based application. One of the main results was that a proxy-based runtime MOP implied fewer constraints than other types of MOPs.

This article presents an approach that makes it possible to have, security-wise, a completely transparent meta-level in the context of a simple proxy-based runtime MOP that we designed and implemented for Java.

The paper is organised as follows. Section 2 introduces related work. Our simple proxy-based runtime MOP is described in section 3, while section 4 proposed a technique for making this MOP transparent with respect to security, and section 5 concludes.

2 Related Work

In this section we first present an overview of the different kinds of MOPs that exist for Java, then review some related work on meta-programming and security.

2.1 Different kinds of MOPs

MOPs come in multiple flavours. Depending on the criterion used, many different classification of MOPs are possible. Ferber [4], for example, first proposed

A. Yonezawa and S. Matsuoka (Eds.): REFLECTION 2001, LNCS 2192, pp. 118–125, 2001.

to separate between *structural* and *computational* reflection. The former is concerned with the structure of a program, that is its classes, inheritance relations and so forth, while the later deals with elements that only exist at runtime, such as method invocation or object creation. Alternatively, it is possible to make a distinction between *implicit* and *explicit* reflection, which indicates whether the shifts to the meta-level are visible from the base level or not.

However, we have chosen to follow here a third classification of MOPs that uses as a criterion the period in the life of a program when meta-objects are actually in use. The three periods of time we consider are *compile-time, load-time* and *runtime*. A specific MOP may use meta-objects at more than one period in the life of a program. This is why we end up with six different cases (see Fig. 1), which range from the most static compile-time MOPs to the most dynamic run-time MOPs.

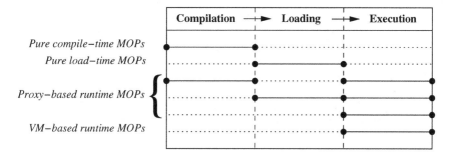

Fig. 1. A classification of MOPs based on when meta-objects are actually in use

Pure compile-time MOPs perform source-to-source transformations. The difference with usual pre-processors is that the translation itself is expressed as a Java program which handles meta-objects that represent classes, methods, loops, statements, etc. OpenJava [3] is an example of such a MOP.

Pure load-time MOPs perform bytecode-to-bytecode transformations. Like for pure compile-time MOPs, the translation uses meta-objects for providing an object view of the bytecode representation of a class. Most of the time, load-time MOPs are implemented through a specialised classloader object.

Proxy-based MOPs introduce hooks into the program in order to reify runtime events such as method invocation or access to fields. The hooks are introduced either at compile-time, for example by using a compile-time MOP, or at load-time by modifying the bytecode for a class (see Kava [10]) or even at runtime [7] by using objects that implement the *proxy* pattern (also called *wrapper* objects). These MOPs do not require any modification to the JVM, which explains why some low-level events cannot be reified.

VM-based Runtime MOPs rely on a modified JVM in order to intercept things that only exist at runtime, such as method invocations. On occurrence of such events, control is transferred to meta-level objects that are standard Java objects. MetaXa [6], Guaraná [7], and Iguana/J [9] are such MOPs.

2.2 Security and MOPs

The idea of using MOPs for implementing security mechanisms has been explored in a number of different works [1, 11]. However, the problem of studying the security problems raised by MOPs received little attention so far.

On several occasions, MOP implementors addressed the issue of security in their work, but mostly as a side note. Oliva and Buzato in [8] present some ideas on how to discipline the interaction between base-level and meta-level objects in their VM-based runtime MOP Guaraná, especially with respect to dynamic reconfiguration of the binding between the two levels. Welch and Stroud in [10] also present some security issues raised by their proxy-based run-time MOP Kava. They introduce the idea of making a clear separation between classes of the kernel of the MOP that are trusted and untrusted meta-object classes developed by third parties.

3 A simple proxy-based MOP

The purpose of our MOP is to reify two elements of the execution environment of a Java program: method invocations on objects[1] and calls to constructors.

3.1 Mapping base-level objects to meta-objects

Deciding which objects are reified and which are not is done on a per-object basis: for a given class, non-reified instances are created, as usual, using the `new` operator of the Java language, while reified instances are created using a call to the static method `MOP.newInstance` of our library.

One of the originalities of our MOP lies in the way the programmer declares which meta-level class is to be used when a reified instance of a given base-level class is created. Unlike other MOPs, which use a separate file for declaring such mappings, we have chosen to use the interface construct of the Java language instead. More specifically, we have an open-ended set of marker interfaces[2] which all inherit, either directly or indirectly, from `Reflect` (see Fig. 2). Each interface has a static `String` field that contains the name of a meta-level class and that can be overridden by sub-interfaces.

A base-level class implements one of these interfaces in order to declare which meta-object should be associated with a reified instance of this class. When it is not possible to modify the base-level class, the programmer can subclass the

---

[1] as opposed to the invocation of `static` methods.

[2] Marker interfaces are interfaces that do not declare any methods but 'flag' a class with a specific property. The use of marker interfaces has become an idiom of the Java language, as exemplified by the `Serializable` or `Cloneable` interfaces.

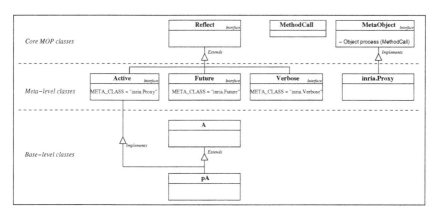

Fig. 2. Class diagram of the core MOP classes, meta-level classes and base-level classes.

base-level class in order to implement the marker interface in the subclass. This is the case shown in figure 2 where the base-level class pA inherits from class A and also implements the marker interface Active. If this, in turn, is not possible, the programmer can still specify which meta-level class to use by passing its name as a parameter of the call to newInstance.

3.2 Meta-level classes

Meta-level behaviours are expressed in meta-level classes that all implement the interface MetaObject. Each time a call to a reified object is intercepted by the MOP, it is reified into an instance of class MethodCall and passed to the meta-object associated with the reified object as a parameter to the call to the method process declared in interface MetaObject.

Our MOP does not impose any constraint on the organisation of the meta-level. It is up to the meta-level objects to handle the creation and organisation of the computations that take place at the meta-level.

3.3 Implementation

We implemented our MOP with two main design goals in mind: to provide a non-intrusive reification mechanism and to induce as few modifications of the source code as possible when retro-fitting existing code with meta-level behaviour.

Transparent interception of method calls is achieved through the use of *stub objects*. Stub objects are created and returned by the MOP as the result of the creation of a reified object and represent the reified object for its clients. Stub objects are instantiated from stub classes that are type-compatible with the class of the reified object. Then, it becomes possible to use the stub object wherever the original non-reified object is expected. What a stub class actually does is simply to redefine all the methods it inherits from its superclass[3] in order to, within the body of each such method, build an object that represents the call and pass this object to the meta-object associated with the stub. If needed, stub classes can be generated on-the-fly by our MOP: the source code is generated and written to the local file system, compiled and loaded just like any other locally-available Java class.

4   Security and MOP in a single address space

In this section we first present a quick overview of the security architecture of Java 2 and then show how, within a single virtual machine and under certain conditions, we obtain an interesting result: using our MOP for adapting base-level components is perfectly transparent with respect to security.

4.1   The Security Architecture of Java

The security architecture of Java 2 [5] is mostly concerned with *access control*, i.e. protecting access to critical local resources such as files, sockets, or the windowing system. An application is composed of a number of *protection domain*, which correspond to a URL where classes can be downloaded from or to a set of certificates that can be used for signing classes. Each protection domain has an associated set of *permissions*, each permission consists of a resource (say, a file) that we want to protect access to, and an access mode (such as read, write, ...).

At runtime, each of the classes loaded inside the virtual machine is associated with a specific protection domain. Whenever a thread performs a call that requires a specific permission, the security manager computes the *intersection* of the permission sets of all the protection domains on the execution stack of the thread. If the resulting set of permissions contains the permission needed for accessing the resource, the access is granted, otherwise an exception is thrown.

The security architecture of Java also provides the `doPrivileged` construct that limits the computation of the intersection of the permissions of the protection domains where `doPrivileged` is invoked, and those invoked from it.

4.2   A security-aware MOP

In the context of an component-based application that runs within a single virtual machine, we want the following property to hold:

In a reified call that crosses the boundary between two protection domains, the set of permissions under which the reified call is actually executed in the second protection domain after meta-level processing should be exactly the same as if the call had not been reified at all.

---

[3] Of course, `final` classes and `final` methods of non-final classes cannot be reified, which is a limitation of our MOP.

We will now prove that this property holds with our MOP, given that reasonable permissions are given to the different components.

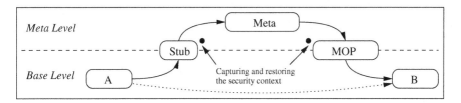

Fig. 3. Chain of calls in a reified call and handling of the security context

Let us consider that we have a component A that calls a method on a component B. This method performs an operation that requires an access check, therefore the set P_{std} of the permissions that are needed for the call to succeed in the standard case is the intersection of the permissions of A and the permissions of B. If the call from A to B is reified with a proxy-based runtime MOP like ours, we obtain the chain of calls described in figure 3, which lead to the permission set P_{ref}. If we call P the function that maps protection domains to their set of permissions, we have

$$P_{std} = P(A) \cap P(B) \text{ and } P_{ref} = P(A) \cap P(Stub) \cap P(Meta) \cap P(MOP) \cap P(B)$$

We will now explain step by step how, by making sensible choices with respect to which permissions are granted to each of the protection domain in the above equation, we can build a MOP for which $P_{std} = P_{ref}$.

Capturing and restoring a security context. With the security architecture of Java 2, it is possible to take a snapshot of the set of permissions associated with the current thread with a call to `AccessController.getContext()`. This call returns a `AccessControlContext` object that represents the permissions available to the current thread at the moment of the call. This object can be used later in a call to `doPrivileged` in order to perform a call under the security context captured within the `AccessControlContext` object.

We use this feature for capturing the security context when the call is reified (in the stub object), and restoring it later when the reified call is actually performed on the reified object, that is when the `execute` method is called on the `MethodCall` object that belongs to the *MOP* protection domain (see Fig. 3).

The security context $P_{captured}$ at the moment of the reification of the call is re-injected inside the component *MOP*, which leads to

$$P_{captured} = P(A) \cap P(Stub) \text{ and } P_{ref} = P_{captured} \cap P(MOP) \cap P(B)$$

$$\text{and hence } P_{ref} = P(A) \cap P(Stub) \cap P(MOP) \cap P(B)$$

Which is already an improvement over the previous value of P_{ref} because we have managed to remove the term $P(Meta)$ that corresponds to the permission set of the meta-object. Capturing and restoring a security context does not require any modification to the base-level classes or to the meta-object component $Meta$, but only to the classes of the MOP.

In the MOP we trust By nature, the classes of the MOP perform security-sensitive operations. This includes such different things as, for example, reading standard user properties, writing the source file of stub classes to the local file system and calling the compiler, or using the Reflection API for invoking non-public methods, which also requires a specific permission.

For all those reasons, we advocate that the protection domain that contains the base classes for the MOP should be granted all permissions. This means that, when using a MOP in a component-based application, the MOP must be fully trusted, which, by the very nature of a MOP, is very much needed anyway. This does not mean at all that the meta-level classes that implement the meta-level behaviour ($Meta$ in our example) will all be granted all permissions because those classes actually belong to a different protection domain. As the $MethodCall$ class belongs to the protection domain of the MOP, we have

$$P(MOP) = \infty$$

Granting permissions to stub classes With our MOP, stub classes can be generated either statically or dynamically. If stub classes are generated statically, it can be assumed that those classes will be bundled with the components that use them. In our case, this means that stub classes will belong to the same protection domain as A, and hence

$$P(A) \cap P(Stub) = P(A) \text{ if stubs are generated statically}$$

If, on the other hand, stubs are generated dynamically, they all go into the same directory on the local file system, which then becomes a protection domain of its own. As the stub classes are generated by the MOP itself, we believe they should be granted all permissions. It is the MOP that controls what goes into the code of stub classes, and granting all permissions to stub classes should arise from granting all permissions to the MOP classes. As a matter of fact, stub classes never perform any action that may require a permission, all they do is build meta-objects for reifying calls and forwarding them to the meta-level. As a consequence, granting all permissions to the protection domain of the stubs is not a dangerous thing to do, and in terms of permission sets we have:

$$P(Stub) = \infty \text{ and hence } P(A) \cap P(Stub) = P(A)$$

which means that in both cases, either static or dynamic, we end up with the same relation. The term P_{ref} then rewrites to:

$$P_{ref} = P(A) \cap P(B) \text{ which is enough for stating that } P_{std} = P_{ref}$$

and we have proved that using our MOP with the strategy and permissions we have implemented does not add or remove permissions to base classes.

5   Conclusion

Within the context of a proxy-based runtime MOP for Java, we proved that it is possible to prevent the security constraints of the base-level and these of the meta-level from interfering, given that the classes for the MOP (but not the classes that implement meta-level behaviors) are given all permissions. In the near future, we plan to widen the scope of the results presented in this paper and work on designing a general security model for reflective applications.

References

1. M. Ancona, W. Cazzola, and E. B. Fernandez. Reflective authorization systems: Possibilities, benefits, and drawbacks. *LNCS*, 1603:35–50, 1999.
2. Denis Caromel and Julien Vayssière. Reflections on MOPs, Components, and Java Security. In J. Lindskov Knudsen, editor, *Proceedings of ECOOP 2001*, volume 2072 of *LNCS*, pages 256–274, Budapest, Hungary, June 2001. Springer-Verlag.
3. Shigeru Chiba and Michiaki Tatsubori. Yet another java.lang.class. In *ECOOP'98 Workshop on Reflective Object-Oriented Programming and Systems*, Brussels, Belgium, July 1998.
4. J. Ferber. Computational reflection in class based object-oriented languages. *ACM SIGPLAN Notices*, 24(10):317–326, October 1989.
5. Li Gong. *Inside Java 2 platform security: architecture, API design, and implementation*. Addison-Wesley, Reading, MA, USA, june 1999.
6. J. Kleinoeder and M. Golm. Metajava: An efficient run-time meta architecture for java. Techn. Report TR-I4-96-03, Univ. of Erlangen-Nuernberg, IMMD IV, 1996.
7. A. Oliva and L. E. Buzato. The design and implementation of Guaraná. In *Proceedings of the Fifth USENIX Conference on Object-Oriented Technologies and Systems*, pages 203–216. The USENIX Association, 1999.
8. Alexandre Oliva and Luiz Eduardo Buzato. Designing a secure and reconfigurable meta-object protocol. Technical Report IC-99-08, icunicamp, February 1999.
9. B. Redmond and V. Cahill. Iguana/J: Towards a dynamic and efficient reflective architecture for Java. In *ECOOP 2000 Workshop on Reflection and Metalevel Architectures*, June 2000.
10. I. Welch and R. Stroud. From Dalang to Kava — the evolution of a reflective Java extension. In Pierre Cointe, editor, *Proceedings of the second international conference Reflection'99*, number 1616 in LNCS, pages 2 – 21. Springer, July 1999.
11. I. Welch and R. J. Stroud. Using reflection as a mechanism for enforcing security policies in mobile code. In *Proceedings of ESORICS'2000*, number 1895 in Lecture Notes in Computer Science, pages 309–323, October 2000.

Reflective Middleware Solutions for Context-Aware Applications

Licia Capra, Wolfgang Emmerich and Cecilia Mascolo

Dept. of Computer Science
University College London
Gower Street, London, WC1E 6BT, UK
{L.Capra|W.Emmerich|C.Mascolo}@cs.ucl.ac.uk

Abstract. In this paper, we argue that middleware for wired distributed systems cannot be used in a mobile setting, as the principle of transparency that has driven their design runs counter to the new degrees of awareness imposed by mobility. We propose the marriage of reflection and metadata as a means for middleware to give applications dynamic access to information about their execution context. Finally, we describe a conceptual model that provides the basis of our reflective middleware.

1 Introduction

Recent advances in wireless networking technologies and the growing success of mobile computing devices, such as laptop computers, third generation mobile phones, personal digital assistants, watches and the like, are enabling new classes of applications that present challenging problems to designers. Devices face temporary and unannounced loss of network connectivity when they move; they discover other hosts in an ad-hoc manner; they are likely to have scarce resources, such as low battery power, slow CPU speed and little memory; they are required to react to frequent changes in the environment, such as new location, high variability of network bandwidth, etc.

When developing distributed applications, designers should not have to deal explicitly with problems related to distribution, such as heterogeneity, scalability, resource sharing, and the like. *Middleware* developed upon network operating systems provides application designers with a higher level of abstraction, hiding the complexity introduced by distribution. Existing middleware technologies, such as transaction-oriented, message-oriented or object-oriented middleware [4] have been built adhering to the metaphor of the *black box*, i.e., distribution is hidden from both users and software engineers, so that the system appears as a single integrated computing facility. In other words, distribution becomes *transparent*. These technologies have been designed and are successfully used for stationary distributed systems built with fixed networks, but they do not appear to be suitable for the mobile setting. Firstly, the interaction primitives, such as distributed transactions, object requests or remote procedure calls, assume a high-bandwidth connection of the components, as well as their constant

A. Yonezawa and S. Matsuoka (Eds.): REFLECTION 2001, LNCS 2192, pp. 126–133, 2001.

availability. In mobile systems, in contrast, unreachability and low bandwidth are the norm rather than an exception. Moreover, object-oriented middleware systems, such as CORBA, mainly support synchronous point-to-point communication, while in a mobile environment it is often the case that client and server hosts are not connected at the same time. Secondly, and most notably, completely hiding the implementation details from the application becomes both more difficult and makes little sense. Mobile systems need to detect and adapt to drastic changes happening in the environment, such as changes in connectivity, bandwidth, battery power and the like. By providing transparency, the middleware must take decisions on behalf of the application. The application, however, can normally make more efficient and better quality decisions based on application-specific information. This is particularly important in mobile computing settings, where the 'context' (e.g., the location) of a device should be taken into account [2].

In this paper, we propose the joint use of reflection and metadata in order to develop middleware targeted to mobile settings. Through metadata we obtain separation of concerns, that is, we distinguish what the middleware does from how the middleware does it. Reflection is the means that we provide to applications in order to inspect and adapt middleware metadata, that is, influence the way middleware behaves, according to the current context of execution.

2   Principles of Reflective Middleware

In this section, we introduce the basic principles that have driven the design of our reflective middleware.

Applications running on a mobile device need to be aware of their execution context. By context, we mean everything that can influence the behaviour of an application. Under this general term, we can identify two more specific levels of awareness, already encountered in our case study: *device awareness* and *environment awareness*. Device awareness refers to everything that resides on the physical device the application is running on; for example, memory, battery power, screen size, processing power and so on. We call these entities *internal resources*. Environment awareness refers to everything that is outside the physical device, that is bandwidth, network connection, location, other hosts (or services) in reach, and so on. We call these entities *external resources.*

On one hand, being aware of the execution context requires the designer to know, for instance, the location of the device, the hosts in reach, and, in general, any piece of information that is collected from the network operating system. On the other hand, we do not want the application designers to build their applications directly on the network OS, as this would be extremely tedious, error-prone and lead to non-portable applications. Instead a middleware should be used to solve these issues. The middleware must interact with the underlying network operating system and keep updated information about the execution context in its internal data structures. This information has to be made available to the applications, so that they can listen to changes in the context (i.e., *inspection*

of the middleware), and influence the behaviour of the middleware accordingly
(i.e., *adaptation* of the middleware).

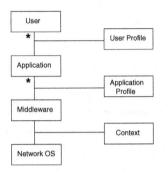

Fig. 1. User and application profiles.

*Reflection and metadata are the means we rely on to build middleware sys-
tems that support context-aware applications.* As Fig. 1 shows, there may be
several applications running on the same middleware, and many different users
using the same application. Each user may customize the application in many
different ways; users can, for example, customize the task bar of the application
interface using some icons instead of others; but they can also do more sophisticated things like asking the application to be silent when the user is in particular
places (e.g., in a movie theatre, on a train, etc.), automatically disconnect from
the network when the battery power is too low, etc. To do so, the user sets up
a *user-profile* that instructs the application on how to behave in different circumstances. From an application point of view, we call 'data' the subject of its
own computation or, we could say, of its functional requirements (e.g. a product
catalogue for an e-shopping application). The user-profile is instead what we
define as application metadata. The application filters out the settings it can
manage alone in a context-independent way (e.g., layout of the task bar), and
translates the other ones into an *application profile* that is then passed down
to the middleware. From a middleware point of view, the context is its own
data (e.g., value of the bandwidth, status of the network connection, status of
the battery power, etc.), while the application profile is its own metadata (see
Fig. 2). From now on, it is the middleware that is in charge of maintaining a
valid representation of the context, directly interacting with the network operating system; whenever a change in the execution context is detected, it consults
its metadata to find out how the application has asked it to behave in such a
configuration. Now the question is whether it is reasonable to assume that the
application fixes its own profile once and for all at the time of installation and
never changes it after. The answer is no. Both the needs of the user and the
context change quite frequently, and we cannot expect the application designers
to foresee all the possible configurations. We therefore need to provide the mid-

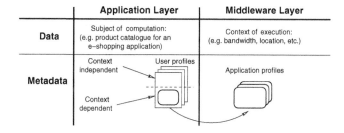

	Application Layer	**Middleware Layer**
Data	Subject of computation: (e.g. product catalogue for an e–shopping application)	Context of execution: (e.g. bandwidth, location, etc.)
Metadata	Context independent ⟶ User profiles / Context dependent ⟶	Application profiles

Fig. 2. Application and Middleware data/metadata.

dleware with an initial profile, and then grant the application dynamic access to it. Here is where reflection comes into play. By definition [3], reflection allows a program to access, reason about and alter its own interpretation. The principle of reflection has been mainly adopted in programming languages, in order to allow a program to access its own implementation (see the reflection package of Java or the interface repository in CORBA). The use of reflection in middleware is more coarse-grained and, instead of dealing with methods and attributes, it deals with middleware data and metadata. Metadata store information about *how* the middleware has to behave *when* executing in a particular context. Applications use the reflective mechanisms provided by middleware to access their own profile, so that changes in this information immediately reflect into changes in the middleware behaviour.

3   Reflective Conceptual Model

The last section has left us with an open question: *what* information do we need to encode in the application profile, that is, in the middleware metadata, and *how*? We now provide an answer.

The application profile is written by the application designer and then managed by the underlying middleware, that is, there must be an agreement between the two parts about the representation of the profile. We believe that the eXtended Markup Language (XML)[1], and related technologies (in particular XML Schema) can be successfully used to model this information. In our scenario, middleware defines the *grammar*, that is the rules that must be followed to write profiles, in an XML Schema; the application designer then encodes the profile in an XML document that is a valid *instance* of the grammar. Every change done later to the profile must respect the grammar, and this check can be easily performed using available XML parsers.

To understand what information to encode, we distinguish two different ways in which the application influences the behaviour of the middleware.

1. *Changes in the execution context.* The application can ask the middleware to listen to changes in the execution context and react accordingly, independently of the task the application is performing at the moment. For example, the application may ask the middleware to disconnect when the bandwidth is

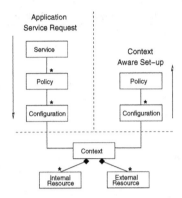

Fig. 3. Application profile.

fluctuating, or when the battery power is too low. We establish an association between particular context configurations that depend on the value of one or more resources the middleware monitors, and policies that have to be applied, as shown on the right-hand side of Fig. 3. Fig. 4 illustrates a simple example of an XML document for this kind of information.

```
<RESOURCE name="battery">
    <STATUS operator="lessEqual" value=x/>          % context configuration
    <BEHAVIOUR policy="disconnect"/>                % policy
</RESOURCE>
```

Fig. 4. XML encoding of a context aware set-up.

Middleware interacts with the underlying network operating system in order to keep an updated configuration of the context. Whenever a change in the context happens, it looks up in the application profiles of running applications whether one or more of them have registered an interest in the changed resources, and triggers the corresponding actions.

2. *Service request.* The application can ask the middleware to execute a service; for example, to access some remote data it has not cached locally. There are many different ways a service can be provided; for example, the service 'access data' can be delivered using at least two different policies, 'copy' (i.e., a physical copy of the bunch of data is created locally) and 'link' (i.e., a network reference to the master copy is created). The circumstances under which an application may want to use them are different: a physical copy of data may be preferred when there is a lot of free space on the device, while a link may become necessary when the amount of available memory prevents us from creating a copy, and the network connection is good enough to allow reliable read and write operations across it. Therefore, for every service the application may ask the middleware, the application profile specifies the policies that have to be applied and the re-

quirements that must be satisfied in order to choose which of them to apply. These requirements are expressed in terms of the execution context (left-hand side of Fig. 3). Fig. 5 gives an example of how to express this information in the application profile in XML.

```
<SERVICE name="accessData">
    <BEHAVIOUR policy="copy">
        <RESOURCE name="memory">
            <STATUS operator="greaterEqual" value=x/>
        </RESOURCE>
    </BEHAVIOUR>
    <BEHAVIOUR policy="link">
        <RESOURCE name="bandwidth">
            <STATUS operator="greaterEqual" value=y/>
        </RESOURCE>
        <RESOURCE name="memory">
            <STATUS operator="less" value=x/>
        </RESOURCE>
    </BEHAVIOUR>
</SERVICE>
```

Fig. 5. XML encoding of an application service request.

Particular services that middleware systems must provide to all the supported applications include trading and binding services. A *trading service* is put in place to find out which host provides a specific service requested by an application. In a mobile setting, hosts may come and leave quite rapidly; the services available when a host disconnects from the network can be completely different from the ones the host finds in the context when it reconnects. Therefore, on every host there must be a trader that keeps track of all the services provided by the hosts that are in reach at the moment. In general, there may be more than a provider of the same service; for example, if the service we are looking for is "access data x", there can be more than one host holding a replica of x in our neighborhood. In such a situation, the trader needs to choose which one to contact, and this decision can be taken using many different strategies (e.g., contact the closest host, contact the host on the cheapest link, etc.). Every application specifies (in its own profile) how the trading service must be delivered to it, that is, which policy the trader must apply when selecting service providers for the requests coming from this application.

Once the service provider to be contacted has been chosen, the middleware needs to decide which policy to apply to serve the request it is dealing with. If the application has not specified a particular policy, a *binding service* is invoked; the binder is in charge of checking the requirements related to each policy and deciding which one to adopt. Again, there may be circumstances where more than one policy can be followed; the selection is driven by the strategy (i.e., policy) specified by the application in its own profile under the voice "binding service" (e.g., use the policy that requires the least amount of resources, the one that provides the best quality of service, and so on).

For the reflective principle, middleware must grant applications dynamic access to their profiles: whenever a profile is modified, the middleware runs a validating parser that parses the document and checks whether it is a valid XML instance of the grammar provided by the middleware to the application. Also the grammar, that is, the XML schema, can be updated and the middleware is in charge of verifying the consistency of the updates: for example, if a new policy P is introduced, the code for it must be provided[1]. In this way, we can both reconfigure the middleware to adapt to unpredictable situations, and extend the set of behaviours it provides with great flexibility.

4   Discussion and Related Work

We have described a middleware for context-aware mobile applications based on the principle of reflection and metadata. Through metadata, we achieve separation of concerns, that is, we distinguish what the middleware does from how the middleware does it. Reflection is then used to provide applications dynamic access to middleware metadata.

The principle of reflection has already been investigated by the middleware community during the past years, mainly to achieve flexibility and dynamic configurability of the ORB. Examples include OpenCorba, dynamicTAO, the work done by Blair et al., etc. Even though we adhere to the idea of using reflection to add flexibility and dynamic configurability to middleware systems, the platforms developed to experiment with reflection were based on standard middleware implementations (i.e., CORBA), and therefore not suited for the mobile environment.

Other middleware systems have been built to support mobility, without using the reflective principle. However, we observe that only partial solutions have been developed to date, mainly focused on providing support for location awareness (e.g., Nexus and Teleporting), and for disconnected operations and reconciliation of data (e.g., Bayou and Odyssey).

Tuple space coordination primitives, initially suggested for Linda, have been employed in a number of mobile middleware systems such as Jini/JavaSpaces, Lime, and T Spaces, to facilitate component interaction for mobile systems. Although addressing in a natural manner the asynchronous mode of communication characteristic of ad-hoc and nomadic computing, all these systems are bound to very poor data structures (i.e., flat unstructured tuples), which do not allow complex data organization and therefore can hardly be extended to support metadata and reflection capabilities. We believe that XML, and in particular its associated hierarchical tree structure, allows semantically richer data and metadata formatting, overcoming this limitation.

---

[1] If everything is implemented in Java, the existence of a class P (to be dynamically loaded by the Java Class Loader) can be required.

5   Future Work and Concluding Remarks

The growing success of mobile computing devices and networking technologies, such as WaveLan and Bluetooth, call for the investigation of new middleware that deal with mobile computing requirements, in particular with context-awareness. Our goal in this paper has been to outline a global model for the design of mobile middleware systems, based on the principle of reflection and metadata. The choice to use XML to represent metadata comes from our previous experience with XMIDDLE [5], an XML-based middleware for mobile systems that focuses on data reconciliation and synchronization problems and solves them exploiting application-specific reconciliation strategies. Our plan is to extend the previously built prototype to fully support the reflective model presented here.

Other issues to be investigated are the followings. Conflicting policies: what happens if two applications ask the middleware to behave differently when executing in the same context? What if the same application requires conflicting behaviors when changes related to different resources happen at the same time (e.g., "disconnect when battery is low" vs. "connect when bandwidth is high")? All these questions are currently under investigation

Another major problem is security. Portable devices are particularly exposed to security attacks as it is so easy to connect to a wireless link. Reflection seems somehow to worsen the situation. Reflection is a technique for accessing protected internal data structures and it could cause security problems if malicious programs break the protection mechanism and use the reflective capability to disclose, modify or delete data. Security is a major issue for any mobile computing application, and therefore proper measures need to be included in the design of any mobile middleware system. We plan to investigate this issue further.

References

1. T. Bray, J. Paoli, and C. M. Sperberg-McQueen. Extensible Markup Language. Recommendation http://www.w3.org/TR/1998/REC-xml-19980210, World Wide Web Consortium, March 1998.
2. L. Capra, W. Emmerich, and C. Mascolo. Middleware for Mobile Computing: Awareness vs. Transparency (Position Summary). In *Proceedings of the 8th Workshop on Hot Topics in Operating Systems (HotOS-VIII)*, Schloss Elmau, Germany, May 2001.
3. F. Eliassen, A. Andersen, G. S. Blair, F. Costa, G. Coulson, V. Goebel, O. Hansen, T. Kristensen, T. Plagemann, H. O. Rafaelsen, K. B. Saikoski, and W. Yu. Next Generation Middleware: Requirements, Architecture and Prototypes. In *Proceedings of the 7th IEEE Workshop on Future Trends in Distributed Computing Systems*, pages 60–65. IEEE Computer Society Press, December 1999.
4. W. Emmerich. Software Engineering and Middleware: A Roadmap. In *The Future of Software Engineering - 22nd Int. Conf. on Software Engineering (ICSE2000)*, pages 117–129. ACM Press, May 2000.
5. Cecilia Mascolo, Licia Capra, and Wolfgang Emmerich. An XML-based Middleware for Peer-to-Peer Computing. In *Proc. of the International Conference on Peer-to-Peer Computing (P2P2001)*, Linkopings, Sweden, August 2001. To appear.

Testing MetaObject Protocols Generated by Open Compilers for Safety-Critical Systems

Juan Carlos Ruiz, Jean-Charles Fabre and Pascale Thévenod-Fosse

LAAS-CNRS
7, Avenue du Colonel Roche
31400 – Toulouse Cedex 4 (France)
{ruiz, fabre, thevenod}@laas.fr

Abstract. Although broadly used in many application domains, the use of reflection in safety-critical systems remains questionable due to the little work reporting on validation aspects. This paper defines an approach for testing MetaObject Protocols (MOPs) generated using open compiler facilities. These protocols are defined in terms of a set of analysis and generation rules, which are used to specialize the MOP implementation according to the features supplied by object definitions. The proposed test strategy classifies these analyses and generation rules. Testing objectives and conformance checks are defined for each type of rule. Along the paper, the approach will be illustrated through a real MOP implemented using OpenC++ and extracted from the $\mathcal{FRIENDS}$ architecture, an architecture devoted to the implementation of fault-tolerant systems. The test experiments performed show the interest of the strategy since they have revealed some errors in the considered protocol implementation.

1 Introduction

As has been shown in [1][2][3], reflection [4] is a design concept of great interest for the development of fault-tolerant architectures. In these architectures, a so-called MetaObject Protocol [5] (MOP) defines the system reflective mechanisms enabling fault-tolerance strategies (considered as non-functional mechanisms) to be applied on functional components. The efficiency of these fault-tolerance strategies is thus strongly dependent on the adequate implementation of the system MOP. From a safety viewpoint, that implementation is an error-prone task that requires specific programming skills.

Open compilers [6][7] provide an interesting solution to automate the implementation of runtime MOPs [8]. These compilers apply the notion of reflection at compile-time in order to provide facilities for customizing the compilation process of a program. Open compiler facilities can thus be exploited in order to define a set of rules for analyzing and transforming programs in order to customize MOP implementations for a given collection of object features. This solution has two main

This work was supported in part by France-Telecom (contract ST.CNET/DTL/ASR/97049/DT) and the European Community (project IS-1999-11585: DSOS - Dependable Systems of Systems).

A. Yonezawa and S. Matsuoka (Eds.): REFLECTION 2001, LNCS 2192, pp. 134–152, 2001.

benefits. On one hand, it minimizes the effort required for providing customized MOP implementations; the rules defining the MOP are defined only once and they can be later used on any program. On the other hand, the approach also provides transparency of the MOP implementation to the application programmer; this avoids the participation of unskilled programmers in the development of such critical and error-prone mechanisms.

Despite the interest of the above approach, its use in safety-critical systems remains questionable. To the best of our knowledge, there is a lack of work reporting on the verification of such type of MOPs. Most research work focused on the verification of MOP-based reflective architectures reports on the definition of high-level architectural models using formal languages [9][10]. These models can be analyzed in terms of consistency, completeness, deadlocks and refinement checks. However, the level of abstraction used is too generic to be helpful in finding problems associated with the implementation of the considered MOP.

Testing, which is a dynamic verification technique that consists in exercising the implementation by supplying it with test case input values, is thus an essential complementary verification technique. Testing MOPs gathers the well-known problems related to both protocol testing [11] and object-oriented testing [12][13]. In a recent paper [14], we have defined a general strategy for testing MOPs in fault-tolerant reflective architectures. This strategy abstracts from a particular MOP implementation and it defines a systematic and incremental order for testing (in general) the reflective capabilities of the system. Obviously, the instantiation of the test strategy must comply with the implementation of the considered MOP. That is the aspect of the problem handled in this paper. We focus here on the refinements that the general approach requires for testing MOPs whose implementations are automatically generated using open compiler facilities. These refinements are specified in terms of guidelines for checking the rules governing the generation and the instantiation of the considered MOPs. Our approach provides solutions to three major testing problems:

- In what order should the rules defining the MOP be activated?
- Which class features should be used for the activation of these rules?
- Which conformance checks should be performed for deciding whether or not the rules defining the MOP are correct?

The proposed approach will be exemplified along the paper on a real MOP [8] implemented using OpenC++ v2 [6] and extracted from the $\mathcal{FRIENDS}$ architecture [1].

The next section defines the notion of MOP used all through the other sections. Section 3 addresses the problems concerning the test of the MOPs defined in Section 2. Section 4 presents our solutions to these problems and exemplifies the proposed approach. Section 5 gives some results obtained from the test experiments performed. Section 6 discusses the lessons learnt. Finally, Section 7 presents conclusions.

2   MOP-Based Safety-Critical Systems

Safety-critical systems use reflection as a design concept for defining a clear separation between the application components of the system (running at the system *base-level*), and the system components devoted to the implementation of non-functional requirements, which are executed at the *meta-level*. A major input to the meta-level is the image of the structural and behavioral features of its base-level. This image (also called *meta-model*) must be *causally connected* to the base-level, which means that any change in one of them leads to the corresponding effect upon the other. This meta-model enables the meta-level to reason about and act on its base-level.

From a design viewpoint (see Fig. 1), one can distinguish four different processes in a reflective system. The *reification* process corresponds to the process of exhibiting to the meta-level the occurrence of events at the base-level. The *introspection* process provides means to the meta-level for retrieving base-level structural information. Finally, the *intercession* process enables the meta-level to act on the base-level behavior (*behavioral intercession*) or structure (*structural intercession*). The term *behavioral reflection* will refer from here to both reification and behavioral intercession. Symmetrically, *structural reflection* will be used to designate both introspection and structural intercession mechanisms. The *reflective mechanisms* of the system are thus those mechanisms providing either behavioral or structural reflection.

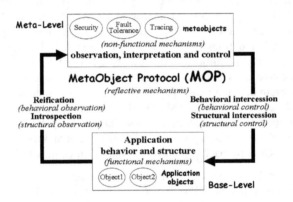

Fig. 1. High-level view of a reflective architecture

In most systems mixing the object-oriented approach and the notion of reflection, a so-called Metaobject Protocol (MOP) handles the interactions between the base- and the meta-level entities, respectively called *objects* and *metaobjects*. In general, MOPs are defined according to the level of observability and controllability required at the meta-level for interpreting and acting on the behavior and the structure of the application objects. In the context of safety-critical systems, various MOPs have been defined and used for the implementation of fault-tolerance mechanisms at the meta-level. The MAUD [2] and GARF [3] architectures propose simple reflective mechanisms for intercepting events at the meta-level (redirecting messages by renaming destinations in the first case, and making a tricky use of the Smalltalk exception handling mechanisms in the second case). The *FRIENDS* [1] architecture relies on a more sophisticated MOP enabling both behavioral and structural reflection. The reflective capabilities of this protocol are, however, limited and they are expressed in terms of object method invocations and data containers defined for objects' states.

A major issue in the development of the above architectures is the implementation of the MOP's reflective mechanisms, which must be specialized on a case-per-case basis according to the features (behavior and state) of each application object. The work presented in [8] showed the interest of using open compiler facilities to automate that specialization process.

2.1 Open Compilers and Runtime MOPs

Open compilers, like [6][7], are macro systems providing means to perform source-to-source transformations. Fig. 2 provides a high-level view of the compilation process proposed by this type of compilers. The supplied facilities provide means to reason about and act on object-oriented programs, which are handled as a compound of classes with methods and attributes. However, these facilities do not apply by themselves any transformation to the input source code. This is the role of the *meta-program*, which uses the open compiler facilities for defining rules that (1) analyze the structure of the input source code, and (2) transform this structure according to the needs. Along this paper, these rules will be referred as *analysis and transformation rules*. It is worth noting that meta-programs may also generate error messages. When no error message is generated by the meta-program, the customized code finally produced can be compiled using a regular compiler.

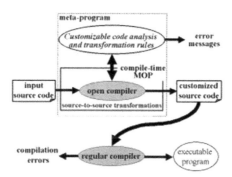

Fig. 2. Open compilation process

In our context, the above analysis and transformation rules are specialized for the generation of reflective code from non-reflective one. The source code supplied to the open compiler is customized in order to provide an output code that (1) encapsulates the original source code, and (2) adds a specialization of the MOP reflective mechanisms for each class definition contained in the input program. The generation of an error message signals the violation of one of the programming conventions imposed by the meta-program. These programming conventions are filters applied to the input programs for checking whether or not these programs can be correctly managed by the generation rules.

2.2   A Runtime MOP for Fault-Tolerance

For safety reasons, the systems that we consider map objects and metaobjects on different (and independent) fault-containment regions (processes in the implementation). These processes interact using a communication channel that is established between each object and its metaobject when the object is instantiated. The reflective mechanisms of the MOP make intensive use of this communication channel, which is exercised in every object-metaobject interaction (see Fig. 3).

Service requests are systematically intercepted by metaobjects through the MOP reification mechanisms (step 1). These interceptions enable metaobjects to add pre- and post-computation to the execution of the invoked method. In $\mathcal{FRIENDS}$ [1], for instance, those pre- and post-computations are specialized in order to implement fault-tolerance and security strategies. Fault-tolerance strategies are replication-based strategies (like the primary-backup and the leader-follower strategies) that require both behavioral and structural reflection for implementing checkpointing and cloning. Security strategies exploit behavioral reflection to check the specific access rights of client objects and authorize or deny consequently the execution of the invoked method. Through the behavioral intercession mechanisms of the MOP (step 2), metaobjects are able to act on their objects to trigger the execution of the reified method invocations. The MOP has to distinguish public methods (the ones belonging to the *Service* interface) from non-public methods (the others). The activity of these non-public methods (step 3) must not be reified to the object's metaobject. Steps 4 and 5 show the path followed by the generated output values.

From a structural point of view, metaobjects consider objects as data containers. The introspection mechanisms of the MOP fill such data containers with the current set of object attribute values. These containers are required, for instance, for cloning server objects. In that case, the data containers retrieved by introspection are used for updating (by intercession) the states of the server's replicas.

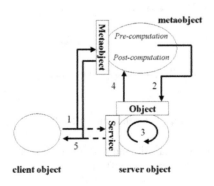

Fig. 3. Runtime MOP interactions

The above interactions are performed through two interfaces called the *reflective interfaces*. The first one, the *Metaobject* interface, is used in order to reify to metaobjects the events governing the behavior of their objects. The second interface, the *Object* interface, is reserved to metaobjects for acting on their objects. Through that interface, metaobjects inspect the state of their object, modify that state and trigger the execution of their object's methods. These mechanisms are activated by metaobjects according to the needs associated with the non-functional requirements of the system. For the time being, the presented runtime MOP does not consider multi-threaded objects and other sources of non-determinism: base-level objects are hence assumed deterministic and mono-threaded system components.

3 Test Strategy Overview

The use of reflective solutions in safety-critical systems is strongly dependent on the degree of confidence on that type of solutions. The definition of verification strategies is thus an essential issue to enlarge the application of the reflective approach to critical domains.

3.1 Related work

Main research work focused on the verification of reflective architectures reports on the definition of high-level models for such architectures, using formal languages. In [10], the authors propose a model based on an architectural description language, called WRIGHT. This language describes a system as a set of architectural components linked by connectors (MOPs). The notion of MOP used in that work is, however, different from the one considered in this paper since it encapsulates both the reflective capabilities of the system and the system meta-level. A different model based on -calculus is proposed in [9]. It describes a reflective system as a system composed of agents (objects and metaobjects), which communicate by exchanging messages. The MOP is implicitly defined in this model as the protocol handling interactions between objects and metaobjets.

Both models can be analyzed using tools specifically developed for the associated formal languages. The results obtained are useful to ensure a certain number of high-level properties, for instance the absence of deadlocks in the MOP. However, the level of description used in these models is too generic to be helpful in finding problems associated with a particular MOP implementation.

We have already proposed in [14] a general strategy for testing MOPs in fault-tolerant reflective architectures. The approach is aimed at reducing the testing effort by promoting a gradual increment of the observability and controllability of the MOP under test. In accordance with this goal, the test order proposed (see Table 1) takes into account the dependencies existing between the MOP reflective mechanisms to define a consistent order among testing levels. This order enables the reuse of those mechanisms that have been already tested for verifying the remaining ones. It differentiates testing issues regarding particular MOP implementations (grouped in the testing level 0) from ones concerning the verification of the MOP reflective mechanisms (handled in testing levels 1 to 4).

The above strategy was defined with the goal of being generic and thus applicable to any MOP of the family described in Section 2.2. Hence, the approach omits implementation details and focuses on the description of testing levels 1 to 4. For each one of these testing levels, the requirements to be checked and the test environments needed for these checks are clearly identified. Testing concerns related to particular MOP implementations were not discussed since they must be faced up in a case- per-case basis.

Testing level 0.	Testing preceding the activation of the MOP (implementation dependent testing concerns);
Testing level 1.	Reification mechanisms;
Testing level 2.	Behavioral intercession mechanisms;
Testing level 3.	Introspection;
Testing level 4.	Structural intercession mechanisms.

Table 1. Incremental test order for a MOP

This paper focus on verifications that can be performed during the testing level 0 of the general strategy when the considered MOP is implemented using open compiler facilities. The major goal of this testing work must be the verification of the communication channel used by objects and metaobjects to interact. This very first step is critical for a later reliable testing of the reflective mechanisms using that communication channel. Next section addresses that issue and reports on additional verification that can be also performed. Concretely, the use of an open compiler provides the possibility of checking separately and incrementally: (1) the generation of the MOP's reflective code, (2) its compilation and (3) finally, the communication channel generated from the instantiation of this code. These phases define what we consider as the *MOP implementation process*.

3.2 On Testing MOPs Generated by Open Compilers

From a high-level viewpoint, testing the rules defining the MOP can be viewed as checking the mapping between the (informal) MOP specification and the rules defined for applying that specification on a particular program. By fixing errors in these rules, the gap between the specification and the rules is reduced and thus the risk of introducing errors, through those rules, in the MOP implementation.

To facilitate the incremental verification of the MOP implementation process, we decompose that process in three successive phases (see Fig. 4): (1) the generation phase, (2) the compilation phase, and finally (3) the instantiation phase.

Generation phase – In this first phase, the MOP specification is specialized for a given set of class features according to the directives provided by the defined set of analysis and transformation rules. Since we focus on the verification of these rules, we consider open compilers as being error-free, i.e., they do not introduce by themselves errors in the generation process. For testing purposes, we propose to distinguish three types of analysis and transformation rules in the MOPs defined in Section 2:

- *Code-filtering rules*: These rules are introduced in the MOP for enforcing programming conventions, which are mandatory for an adequate implementation of fault-tolerance strategies at the system meta-level. When these programming conventions are not respected, the reflective mechanisms of the MOP cannot be correctly generated. Hence, the MOP filtering rules stop the compilation process and produce a *code-filtering message* that identifies the detected problem.
- *Runtime support generation rules*: These rules specialize the software infrastructure required for executing the MOP. For instance, MOPs providing structural reflection requires data containers for saving and restoring object states. These containers must be specialized according to the structural features of each base-level object. The generated runtime support is finally stored in the runtime support repository[1] of the system.
- *Reflective mechanisms generation rules*: The third type of rules generates the code associated with the reflective mechanisms of the MOP. Among these code generation rules, one can distinguish rules regarding behavioral reflection and rules concerning structural reflection. The formers are rules producing reification and behavioral mechanisms. The others generate introspection and structural intercession mechanisms.

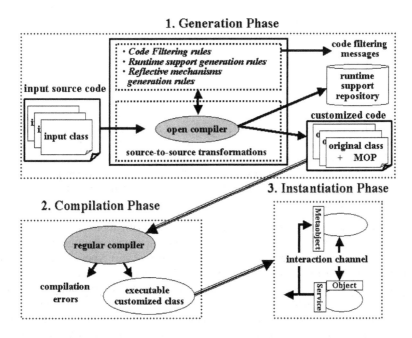

Fig. 4. High-Level view of the proposed approach

---

[1] The notion of repository is used here with a large sense and must be specialized for each considered MOP. This repository could be, for instance, a directory or a library.

Compilation Phase – This phase regards the compilation of each customized class generated by the above rules. Regular compilers are also considered as being error-free, that is, we consider that they always generate executables that conform to the supplied source code. From a testing viewpoint, this regular compiler performs additional checks by verifying the syntactical correctness of the transformations applied on the original source code.

Instantiation Phase – The instantiation of each class leads to the creation of a communication channel that is used by objects and metaobjects to interact. If this channel is not correctly created, then the MOP cannot adequately handle the interactions between object and metaobjects. This justifies the importance of checking that communication channel before testing the reflective mechanisms of the MOP.

4 Case Study

This section defines the test objectives and the conformance checks to be performed in each one of the three phases previously identified. Along the section, a real MOP extracted from the $\mathcal{FRIENDS}$ architecture [1] is used to illustrate the proposed approach. This protocol, generated using OpenC++ v2 [6], provides both behavioral and structural reflection mechanisms and it complies with the MOP model defined in Section 2.

4.1 Generation Phase

The three types of analysis and transformation rules defined in Section 3.2 must be verified in this phase. Each type of rules must meet a different set of requirements and thus a different set of test objectives and conformance checks. We propose to conduct the verification of the considered rules in three successive steps: (1) the filtering rules, (2) the runtime support generation rules, and finally (3) the rules generating the reflective mechanisms of the MOP. The relevance of this order will appear evident through the next paragraphs.

Code-filtering rules – The test objective of this verification step is to determine the ability of the filtering rules to reveal violations of the programming conventions defined by the MOP. This verification requires the use of two types of classes: classes providing forbidden features and classes supplying features that respect the defined programming conventions. It must be underlined that the programming conventions imposed by the rules under test may vary according to the object model and the flexibility supplied by the considered programming language. As an example, Table 2 provides some of the programming conventions imposed by the $\mathcal{FRIENDS}$ MOP to C++ classes in order to ensure a strong object attribute encapsulation.

> Friend classes and functions;
> Pointer arithmetic;
> Use of global or class variables;
> Multiple-level pointers.

Table 2. C++ forbidden programming features in *FRIENDS*

As stated in Section 2.1, every violation of the considered programming conventions must lead to the generation of a filtering message. An exhaustive list of these messages is thus also required in order to decide whether or not the filtering rules pass the test.

According to this, a test succeeds, i.e. an error is detected in the filtering rules of the of the MOP, when (1) in spite of the use of class features respecting the programming conventions a filtering message is generated, or (2) despite the use of forbidden class features, no filtering message is generated or the generated message is not the specified one.

Runtime support generation rules – In order to facilitate the verification of these rules, one can distinguish the rules defining runtime support for behavioral reflection from rules providing support for structural reflection. MOPs providing behavioral reflection require the definition of the data containers for marshalling and un-marshalling the parameters supplied to method invocations. We call these data containers *Invocation containers*. Symmetrically, structural reflection requires data containers for saving and restoring the state of base-level objects. These containers are named *State containers.*

Rules generating Invocation containers must be exercised using classes providing methods with different signatures. On the other side, rules producing State containers must be activated using classes with different sets of attributes. In any case, the activation of each one of the considered rules must lead to the verification of both the existence of the expected data containers and the correctness of their structure.

The existence of each container requires the exploration of the repository storing the runtime support of the system. For each input class, the rules under test must include in the repository one State container for the class and one Invocation container for each class method. According to that point, an error is detected when the number of State and Invocation containers generated does not conform to the one defined by the MOP specification. Those errors may have two possible sources: (1) a wrong implementation of the activated rule, or (2) a requirement of the MOP that has not been implemented (rule omission).

The correct structure of each generated container must be verified according to the information supplied by the MOP specification. In the *FRIENDS* MOP (see Fig. 5):

- Invocation containers, like *Point3DistanceMethod*, are structures providing one field for each method parameter. As the example shows, an additional field (called *returnValue*) is included in the structure when a method returns a value.
- State containers, like *Point2DState*, are also structures that must supply one field for each class attribute (*x* and *y* in the example). Inherited attributes are handled by recursion. In our example, *Point3DState* has a field of type *Point2DState*, which is a container for storing the state of its super-class.

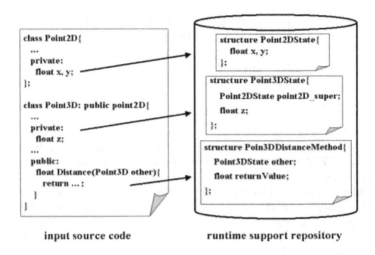

input source code   runtime support repository

Fig. 5. Runtime support generation in ℱℛℐℰℕ𝒟𝒮

It is worth noting that the above verifications cannot be made by hand when testing real-size MOPs. Code analysis facilities are thus necessary to assist testers during these verifications. Concretely, the introspection capabilities of an open compiler can be exploited with this aim.

Reflective mechanisms generation rules - One can differentiate two major types of rules devoted to the generation of reflective mechanisms: rules regarding behavioral reflection and rules providing structural reflection. A clear identification of these rules in the MOP specification reduces the testing effort to be applied since it provides means to separate the activation (and thus the test) of each type of rules.

- *Testing rules providing behavioral reflection:* As explained in Section 2.2, objects provide, from the viewpoint of the MOP, two types of methods: public methods (whose activation should be handled at the meta-level) and non-public methods (whose existence should be hidden to the meta-level). Rules implementing behavioral reflection should only act on public methods. During the test experiments, the rules under test must thus be exercised using: (1) classes providing public methods, (2) classes supplying non-public methods and (3) classes providing both public and non-public methods. The first type of classes should be modified by the activated rules. The second type of classes should not be customized at all. Finally, the third type of classes must be used in order to check the ability of the rules for handling both types of methods at the same time.

    Consequently, every input class providing public methods require the verification of the transformations applied to its code. The goal is to verify the conformity of the generated mechanisms to the MOP specification. In the ℱℛℐℰℕ𝒟𝒮 MOP, for instance, behavioral reflection is implemented using a technique called *method wrapping* [15]. As shown in Fig. 6, this technique generates, for each method of the original class (method *distance* of class *Poin3D*), three different methods in the customized class:

1. The *WrappedDistance* method, which contains the code of the original *Distance* method;
2. The *Distance* method, which rewrites the code of the original method in order to reify method invocations to the metaobject;
3. The *ActivateDistance* method, which is used by metaobjects for activating (by intercession) the original code of the method.

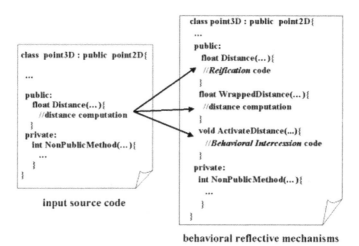

behavioral reflective mechanisms

Fig. 6. Behavioral reflection in *FRIENDS*

Testers can check the adequate application of the above transformations using code analysis tools. First, the code of each input class must be analyzed in order to determine, according to the MOP specification, which methods are public and which ones are non-public. This information is stored in a table that associates the signature of each original method to the signatures of the methods that the transformed class should contain. Through this table, the tester is able to verify, on the customized class, that every (public and non-public) method has been adequately managed by the rules under test.

– *Rules providing structural reflection:* Rules providing structural reflection must generate serialization facilities for marshalling (un-marshalling) objects' states to (from) State containers.

These rules must be exercised using classes providing different collections of attributes. For the activation of these rules, two important concerns are inheritance and encapsulation. It is important to check the ability of these rules to handle inherited attributes and attributes defined using different levels of visibility. However, these concerns are not tackled in the same way in every MOP. For instance, the *FRIENDS* MOP handles inherited attributes by recursion. Fig. 7 provides an example of the type of serialization mechanisms generated for the *FRIENDS* MOP. The Point2D *SaveState* method saves the value of each attribute in the associated field of the *Point2DState* container. On the other hand, the *RestoreState* method restores the value of each attribute value using the values supplied by the *Point2DState* container. *Point3D* serialization methods make a similar job although in that case, the state of the Point3D super-class is saved and restored by recursion, i.e., using the serialization methods of *Point2D* in the example.

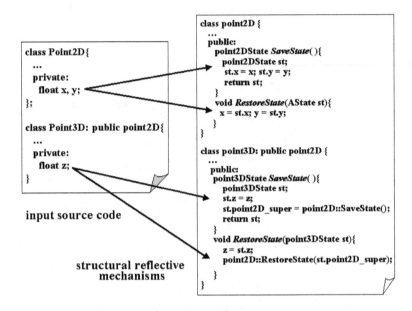

Fig. 7. Structural reflection in $\mathcal{FRIENDS}$

The verifications required for these rules are similar to the ones described for rules providing behavioral reflection. The input source code of each class must be analyzed in order to define a table containing the name and the type of the class attributes. The table also contains information in order to distinguish the inherited attributes from the non-inherited ones. Using that table, the tester analyzes the generated output code in order to determine if the applied transformation complies with the MOP specification. As already said, these code analyses can be assisted by open compiler facilities.

4.2 Compilation Phase

Once the MOP implementation has been specialized for the features supplied by the input class, the resulting code must be compiled in order to detect any syntactical error introduced by the exercised rules. The goal is to check the ability of the exercised rules for producing syntactically correct code. The regular compiler acts in that phase as an oracle checking the correct syntax of the code under compilation.

Compilation errors can be directly associated with errors generated by the MOP rules, since the compiler and the original class are both assumed to be error-free.

4.3 Instantiation Phase

As introduced in Section 3, the implementation of the reflective mechanisms defining the MOP can only be exercised (and thus tested) once a high confidence can be placed on the channel interconnecting objects to metaobjects. The MOP model presented in Section 2 specifies that each server object must be handled by only one metaobject (*unity requirement*). Another requirement regards the capacity of an object to interact with its metaobject and vice versa (*interaction requirement*). From an abstract viewpoint, objects and metaobjects are able to interact if they have correctly exchanged their *references*. A reference can be defined as a compound of information unambiguously identifying a system entity. For instance, a reference in *FRIENDS* corresponds to a set of four elements: an object identifier, the PID of the system process running the object, the IP address of the host executing that object and finally the port number on which the object listens for incoming messages.

  In *FRIENDS*, an object is interconnected with its metaobject (and vice versa) during its instantiation. Objects are instantiated through runtime services called *Object factories*. Symmetrically, *Metaobject factories* are used to create metaobjects. Fig. 8 shows the test environement we defined for checking the process followed for interconnecting objects to metaobjects. This environment is defined in terms of the entities participating in the test experiments (i.e., object, metaobject, object and metaobject factories, test driver and oracle objects), the interactions among these entitites, and the conformance checks to be performed in order to decide whether the interconnection channel has been correctly generated. The role of the *oracle object* is to verify that the test executions meet the specified requirements: it analyzes the test results according to an *oracle procedure* that implements conformance checks. The *test driver object* manages the test experiments: (i) it asks to the object factory for the instantiation of an object and, (ii) it notifies the oracle object of the end of the instantiation process.

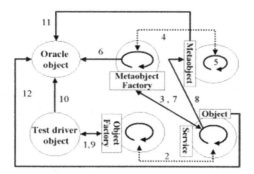

Fig. 8. Testing the interconnection channel in *FRIENDS*

When the test driver asks to the *Object factory* for the creation of an object (step 1), the object constructor is activated (step 2). That activation leads to the creation of the object's metaobject (step 3). The object includes in that request of creation its own reference, which is delivered by the *Metaobject Factory* to the new instantiated metaobject (step 4). Once created, the metaobject stores that reference in order to get connection with its object (step 5). The *Metaobject Factory* sends to the oracle object the reference of the metaobject and the reference of its associated object (step 6). The reference of the metaobject is also returned to the object (step 7), which stores it. This exchange of references leads both the object and its metaobject to get interconnection. The activation of the class constructor can then be reified to the meta-level (step 8). Once the object has been instantiated, its reference is returned to the test driver object (step 9), which notifies the oracle object of the end of the instantiation process (step 10).

The oracle procedure checks the identity of the references supplied by the *Metaobject factory* (step 6) and the references finally stored by the object and its metaobject. It is worth noting that the procedure followed to obtain the second set of references varies from one MOP to another. In general, MOPs designed for being easily testable should provide facilities for consulting that type of information. In *FRIENDS*, these references can be obtained through the reflective interfaces of the MOP (steps 11 and 12). The oracle procedure considers that an object and its metaobject are able to interact if they have correctly exchanged (and stored) their respective references.

Finally, the unity requirement is respected when the notification performed in step 6 of the test environment is performed only once during the instantiation of the object. More than one notification implies the instantiation of more than one metaobject for the object, which violates the unity requirement.

5 Results of Test Experiments

The proposed approach has shown its interest during the test experiments performed on the *FRIENDS* MOP since some errors have been detected in the analysis and transformation rules defining the protocol. We illustrate in the following paragraphs four examples of the errors detected (and fixed) during the experiments. These errors are presented according to the type of rule generating them. The first three errors of the list were detected during the generation phase; the latter was discovered during the instantiation phase.

A code-filtering rule error – The test experiments performed on code-filtering rules showed that these rules handle correctly all the specified programming conventions. Only one error concerning the use of array-type attributes was discovered. The cause of this error was a rule that confuses array-type and pointer class attributes. In C++, array-type variables can be also viewed as pointers pointing to the first element of the array. The *FRIENDS* MOP was supposed to handle arrays but, at the same time, it was also supposed to forbid the use of pointers (other than char and class pointers). However, rules checking class attribute types did not make that distinction. Thus, array-type attributes were rejected as being pointers. The problem was easily fixed by extending the concerned code-filtering rules in order to determine when pointers are arrays. A filtering message is now generated only for C++ pointers that are not arrays.

An omission error in the runtime generation support rules - The runtime generation support rules presented a problem concerning the generation of Invocation containers for methods with an empty list of parameters. The same problem was revealed for rules generating State containers when the analyzed class was stateless, i.e., it did not contain any attribute. In both cases, the rules under test did not generate any container at all. However, the MOP specification states that empty containers should be generated in both cases. That rule omission error was fixed by adding the required generation rules in the meta-program defining the MOP implementation.

An error in the rules providing structural reflection – These rules do not correctly handle the distinction between subobjects and references [16]. That problem is the one of differentiating class attributes whose values at runtime will be an instance of the class (notion of *subobject*) from the class attributes whose values will be a reference to such instance (notion of *reference attribute*). Hence, the serialization facilities of the MOP must handle subobjects by deep-copy (deep-restore), i.e., by a recursive duplication (restoration) of the entire state of the subobject. Conversely, reference attributes must be handled by shallow-copy (shallow-restore), i.e., only the reference is copied (restored) but not the content it refers. That content will be handled by the metaobject associated to the referenced class instance.

The problem was related to both the introspection and the structural intercession mechanisms of the *FRIENDS* MOP. The problem was detected by code analysis, which revealed that both types of attributes were handled using deep-copy (deep-restore) facilities. That bug was fixed by introducing rules for providing shallow-copy (shallow-restore) facilities to handle reference attributes.

An error regarding the rules supplying behavioral reflection – This error was identified during the test experiments performed at the instantiation phase. It consists in a violation of the unity requirement when using inheritance for the definition of a base-level object. Using the test environment described in Section 4.3, the oracle object has observed that the instantiation of such base-level objects leads to the instantiation of more than one metaobject per object. Concretely, a different metaobject was created for each class of the inheritance hierarchy of the object. For instance, the instantiation of an inheritance hierarchy made of two classes leads to the creation of two metaobjects linked to the same object. This violates the unity requirement imposed by the MOP specification. The problem was fixed by systematically providing the type of the object under instantiation as a parameter of each class constructor. Code is also inserted in class constructors in order to compare that type to the one associated to the class. Thus, only the class representing the type of the object under instantiation asks the metaobject factory for the creation of the necessary metaobject. A rule implementing that solution was included in the MOP meta-program.

6 Lessons Learnt

The approach defined in this paper provides guidelines for conducting the verification of compile-time analysis and transformation rules defined for generating runtime reflective components. This problem is slightly different from the one of testing the implementation of the MOP reflective mechanisms since our test targets are not the mechanisms themselves but the rules driving the generation of their implementation. Hence, our approach enables to check the mapping between the MOP specification and the rules defined for automating the generation of the MOP implementation.

The considered MOP implementation process has been decomposed in three phases: the generation phase, the compilation phase and finally the instantiation phase. In fact, these phases can be identified in the development process of any meta-program defined using open-compiler facilities. That's why we propose a verification approach built around these three phases.

Four major lessons can be extracted and generalized from the work presented in this paper for testing meta-programs:

1. We have identified three major types of rules in a meta-program: (1) rules filtering input source code, (2) rules providing runtime support to the generated code and finally, (3) code analysis and generation rules providing output customized implementations for input code. Obviously, this classification can be refined (or maybe also extended) according to each meta-program specification. In general, that classification work is difficult to automate.

2. A clear set of conformance checks must be defined for each type of rules in order to determine whether the transformations applied by the meta-program on the supplied source code conform (or not) the ones originally specified. However, due to the nature of the rules under verification, the conformance checks applied on the generated mechanisms involve a lot of code analysis. In order to assist the testers in this analysis, the introspection facilities supplied by open-compilers (and currently by some programming languages) are very useful. When these facilities are used, these conformance checks can be made semi-automatically.

3. Conventional compilers are also useful tools to check the syntactic correctness of the code generated by a meta-program. In conventional programs, compilation errors are a direct consequence of programmer implementation errors. In a meta-program, compilation errors are due to the defined analysis and transformation rules. Hence, compilation errors are valuable outputs to fix problems in the meta-program rules.

4. Verifications at the instantiation phase are very important specially when the transformations defined by the meta-program rules act on objects' constructors, i.e., on the code starting up objects. These transformations may lead to the introduction of critical errors in the applications since these errors may lead to an incorrect instantiation of the object. From a verification viewpoint, an object incorrectly instantiated cannot be adequately tested later. As stated in Section 4.3, testing environments can be defined for automating

the verifications to be performed. Nevertheless, this automation requires a certain level of observability and controllability on the system under test.

7 Conclusions

Reflection is a powerful design concept for promoting a clear separation of concerns in complex safety-critical systems. However, the use of this technology in that kind of systems is very dependent on the degree of confidence that one can place on the supplied mechanisms. The definition of verification strategies is thus essential to increase this confidence and enlarge the application of the reflective approach to critical domains. The testing approach defined in this paper constitutes a step forward in that direction for MOPs generated using open-compiler facilities. The interest of the proposed solution relies in the identification of general guidelines for conducting the verification of aspects that are, in most cases, highly dependent on the considered set of analysis and transformation rules. A general classification of these rules has been defined. Then, the identified types of rules have been ordered for testing purposes. Fixing potential faults in successive testing stages minimizes the risk of side effects of the applied corrections on other fixes that could be required during the next phases.

The efficiency of such a progressive and debugging strategy was noticeable all along the experiments conducted on the *FRIENDS* MOP. Indeed, these experiments were carried out in parallel with the definition of the analysis and transformation rules used to generate the MOP implementation. Some of the features included in the MOP were specifically defined for supporting testing. As said in Section 4.4, for instance, the reflective interfaces of the *FRIENDS* MOP provide to the oracle object the required means for retrieving the references stored by objects and metaobjects during the instantiation phase. These facilities are defined in order to facilitate the verification of the MOP instantiation process. In other words, the *FRIENDS* MOP includes facilities for increasing its testability. That is what we call "design for validation", which is a key issue in safety-critical systems.

References

[1] Fabre J.-C. and Pérennou T., "A Metaobject Architecture for Fault-Tolerant Distributed Systems: the FRIENDS Approach", in *IEEE Transactions on Computers*. Special issue on Dependability of Computing Systems, vol. 47, pp. 78-95, 1998.

[2] Agha G., Frolund S., Panwar G. and Sturman D., "A Linguistic Framework for Dynamic Composition of Dependability Protocols", in *Dependable Computing for Critical Applications 3 (DCCA-3)*, Vol. 8, in the Series on Dependable Computing and Fault-Tolerant Systems, Springer-Verlag, 1993, pp. 345-363.

[3] Garbinato B., Guerraoui R. and Mazouni K., "Implementation of the GARF Replicated Objects Platform", in *Distributed Systems Engineering Journal*, vol. 2, pp. 14-27, 1995.

[4] Pattie Maes, "Concepts and experiments in computational reflection", in *Object-Oriented Programming Systems, Languages and Applications (OOPSLA'87)*, Orlando, 1987, pp. 147-155.

[5]   Kiczales G., Rivières J. and Bobrow D.G. *The Art of the Metaobject Protocol*. MIT Press, ISBN 0-262-61074-4,1991.

[6]   Chiba S., "Macro Processing in Object-Oriented Languages", in *Technology of Object-Oriented Languages and Systems (TOOLS Pacific '98)*, Australia, IEEE Press, 1998, pp. 113-126.

[7]   Tatsubori M., Chiba S., Killijian M.-O and Itano K., "OpenJava : A Class-based Macro System for Java", in *Reflection and Software Engineering*, W.Cazzola, R.J. Stroud, and F.Tisato, Eds., Lecture Notes in Computer Science 1826, Springer-Verlag, July, 2000, pp.119-135.

[8]   Killijian M.-O. and Fabre J.C., "Implementing a Reflective Fault-Tolerant CORBA System", in *IEEE Symposium on Reliable Distributed Systems (SRDS'2000)*, Germany, 2000, pp. 154-163.

[9]   Marsden E., Ruiz J.C. and Fabre J.-C., "Towards Validating Reflective Architectures: Formalization of a MetaObject Protocol", in *IFIP/ACM International Conference on Distributed Systems Platforms and Open Distributed Processing, Workshop on Reflective Middleware (RM 2000)*, New York, 2000, pp. 33-35.

[10] Welch I. and Stroud R., "Adaptation of Connectors in Software Architectures", in *Object-Oriented Programming Systems, Languages and Applications (OOPSLA'98), Workshop on Component -Oriented Programming (WCOP'98)*, Brussels, 1998, pp. 145-146.

[11] Bochmann G.V. and Petrenko A., "Protocol testing: review of methods and relevance for software testing", in *International Symposium on Software Testing and Analysis (ISSTA '94)*, Seattle, 1994, pp. 109-124.

[12] Kung D., Hsia P. and Gao J. (eds). *Testing Object-Oriented Software*. IEEE Computer Society, 1998.

[13] Binder R.V. *Testing Object-Oriented Systems*. Addison-Wesley, 1999.

[14] Ruiz J.C., Thévenod-Fosse P. and Fabre J.C., "A Strategy for Testing MetaObject Protocols in Reflective Architectures", in *2nd IEEE Conference on Dependable Systems and Networks (DSN 2001)*, Göteborg (Sweden), July 2001.

[15] Brant J., Foote B., Johnson R.E. and Roberts D., "Wrappers to the Rescue", in *ECOOP'98*, Brussels, 1998, pp. 396-417.

[16] Meyer B., *Object-Oriented Software Construction,* 2nd Edition, Prentice Hall Professional Technical Reference, 1997.

Supporting Formal Verification
of Crosscutting Concerns

Torsten Nelson, Donald Cowan, and Paulo Alencar

Computer Systems Group, University of Waterloo
{torsten,dcowan,alencar}@csg.uwaterloo.ca

Abstract. This paper presents an approach to formal verification of the properties of systems composed of multiple crosscutting concerns. The approach models
concerns as sets of concurrent processes, and provides a method of composition
that mimics the composition operators of existing multiple-concern implementation languages. A case study demonstrates the composition process and shows
how formal verification of different composition strategies can detect potential
problems. We also discuss the need for a general model of concerns that can be
handled by different formal languages.

1 Introduction

Recent research in separation of concerns has recognized the need for a dimension of
decomposition where features of systems *crosscut* the objects and functions of a system.
Techniques that expand upon the object-oriented paradigm, such as subject-oriented
programming [4], aspect-oriented programming [7], and composition filters [1] explore
the possibilities of this additional dimension of decomposition.

Most existing crosscutting concern approaches address implementation level issues
and provide implementation languages. Our work addresses the use of crosscutting
concerns in formal specifications. The use of formal models and verification tools is
particularly important when dealing with crosscutting concerns, as the composition
mechanisms provided by languages like AspectJ [7] and HyperJ [14] are quite powerful,
but often result in a composed system that alters the properties of the isolated concerns.
Different compositions that may seem equivalent can also turn out to have different
properties, and these are often difficult to detect using visual inspection or testing.

Therefore, it is important to have mechanisms through which we can specify the
concerns in a formal language, verify their desired properties, compose these concerns
into a unified description, and again verify whether the properties hold in the composed
system. We should use composition operators that are semantically equivalent to the operators found in implementation languages for crosscutting concerns, so that the formal
models of the concerns and the composed system have corresponding implementations.

In Section 2 we discuss the issues involved in the composition of crosscutting concerns. In Section 3 we discuss modeling concerns using formal methods. Section 4
contains a case study - the formal definition and analysis of a bounded buffer with three
crosscutting concerns. The case study will demonstrate how formal verification can be
used to detect the effects of different compositions of the same concerns.

A. Yonezawa and S. Matsuoka (Eds.): REFLECTION 2001, LNCS 2192, pp. 153–169, 2001.

2   Crosscutting Concerns

The kind of crosscutting concerns we deal with in this work can be viewed as an added dimension of decomposition, orthogonal to the function and object dimensions. This notion dates back to Brian Smith's work on reflection [12] and was recently refined as a multidimensional conceptual space by Tarr *et al* [14]. Intuitively, we see function decomposition as a breakdown of the problem space according to its relevant verbs. Object decomposition, on the other hand, is a breakdown according to concrete nouns. In object-oriented systems, object decomposition is said to be the *dominant* decomposition, as the problem space is first divided into the relevant data elements, or objects, and then each object is divided into functions.

Crosscutting concerns are an attempt to deal with drawbacks of the object-oriented model such as scattering, tangling, and class explosion [14] [7]. The idea is to add a new dimension of decomposition where the problem space is divided according to abstract nouns or adjectives. Each of these divisions, or "concerns", is then divided according to the relevant objects and functions. Figure 1 depicts our interpretation of the three dimensions of decomposition, with a sample problem space (a bounded buffer) decomposed into concerns, objects, and functions.

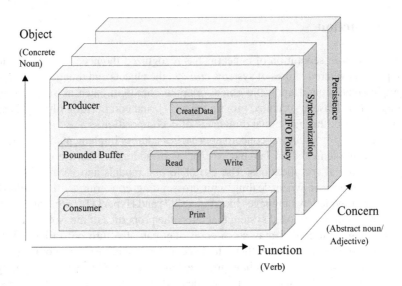

Fig. 1. Decomposing a problem into crosscutting concerns

There are other approaches that deal with the drawbacks of object-orientation without leaving the boundaries of the object-oriented paradign, such as design patterns [3]. However, these approaches present their own set of drawbacks [14] and crosscutting concerns are emerging as new paradigm.

While decomposition of systems into concerns is conceptually simple, the challenge is putting the concerns back together to form a coherent whole. We will look at how functions and objects are composed, and then examine the issues involved in composing concerns.

2.1   Function- and Object-Level Composition

When a system is divided into functions, the functions are made to interoperate through the mechanism of *function call*, where a function transfers control to other functions during its execution. The functions perform operations over shared data. A common mechanism is for the functions to pass data to one another through the function call. Thus, a function call serves two purposes: transfer of control, and ferrying of data.

When we divide a system into objects, we still use the mechanism of function call to make them work together. Methods from an object call methods from other objects, sending data back and forth. When using objects we also have additional composition operators at our disposal. Rather than working at the functional level, like function call, these operators work at the object level. Two examples of object-level composition operators are specialization (inheritance) and aggregation.

Object-level composition operators are mainly structural. They affect the accessibility and organization of data and functions in the system. Behavioral composition is accomplished through function call. However, the effect of function calls can vary depending on the structure of the system, due to polymorphism. Thus, the object-level composition operators affect behavior as well.

2.2   Concern-Level Composition

After defining crosscutting concerns of a system, we need to compose them. Object-orientation is marked by the use object-level composition operators. We also need operators with which we can structurally join concerns, and the same time describe the behavior of their interactions.

In order to define any kind of concern-level composition operator, there are three issues that must be addressed: *correspondence, behavioral semantics*, and *binding*.

Correspondence refers to matching elements across concerns. A concern is a slice through the problem domain that addresses a single issue. This implies that, if the problem is decomposed into a set of concerns, there will be elements of the problem (data and functions) that will appear in more than one concern. To compose the independent concerns, we must identify these elements.

Data correspondence means that data defined in more than one concern represent the same entities. Function correspondence means that different parts of a function are distributed across various concerns, and executing the function should involve all of its parts.

There doesn't have to be a one-to-one matching of elements across concerns. When we define a crosscutting concern, we find that many elements of a concern match a single element of another concern. An example of this is a function logging concern. If all function calls in a system are to be logged, the actual code that does the logging is the same, no matter which function is called. The function logging concern, then, needs to have only a single function that corresponds to the logging portion of all the functions in the system.

Behavioral semantics refers to the consequences of establishing the correspondence. This is generally associated with function correspondence. Most approaches to crosscutting concern composition allow at least two possibilities: function merge and function override. Function merge means all corresponding functions will be executed when the system receives a request to execute any of them. Override means that when a request is received for any one of a set of corresponding functions, only one of the set (previously defined) will be executed, not necessarily the one requested. Merge-type operators often involve some form of temporal ordering of the functions. For example, in the case of the function logging concern, we may decide that the semantics of the correspondence is for the logging function to execute immediately after any one of the functions in its corresponding set is executed.

Binding refers to the time when correspondence is established, or when the behavioral semantics of the correspondence takes effect. This can be either *static* or *dynamic*. With static binding, correspondence is made explicit in the system's description and lasts through the system's lifetime. With dynamic binding, correspondence can be determined at runtime, and elements can be connected or disconnected under program control. For instance, if our logging example uses dynamic binding, we may display a menu at runtime so that the user can determine which functions should be logged.

2.3   Composition in Implementation Languages

Existing implementation languages that offer support for crosscutting concerns differ in terms of how much emphasis is placed on each of the three issues described above.

One of AspectJ's greatest strengths, for instance, lies in its mechanisms for establishing correspondence. The language allows the user to define *pointcuts*, which are sets of program execution points. A variety of operators allow the definition of pointcuts that are resolved either statically or dynamically. For instance, a pointcut could be defined as the static set of calls to methods with a given signature. Wildcard characters can be used to broaden the set of methods that match the signature, and set operations such as union and intersection can be used to combine pointcuts. Dynamically resolved pointcuts are possible with the use of operators such as *cflow*, which denotes the program's flow of control starting at a given method.

HyperJ, on the other hand, has a more limited set of correspondence operators. However, correspondence is not limited to methods, as in AspectJ, but extends to data elements as well. HyperJ also separates concerns from correspondence and composition expressions, where in AspectJ these are all mixed in the code. HyperJ also has concern-level operators, where correspondence of multiple elements of two concerns is established according to some criteria such as lexical equivalence.

Some approaches use a layered model to lay out the concerns in relation to each other. One of these, *Composition Filters* [1], allows one-to-many correspondence between functions placed in different concerns, as well as dynamic binding. *GenVoca* [2] has a simplified model that uses one-to-one lexical correspondence, but still exhibits most of the features related to support for crosscutting concerns.

Though approaches to correspondence and binding vary in these languages, the semantics of composition operators are similar. All allow some form of ordered operation merge, where corresponding elements in different concerns are all executed in some order. Some also allow operation override, where corresponding elements are executed selectively.

3 Modeling Concerns in Formal Languages

Formal methods are often used in the specification of safety-critical systems. However, their use is not limited to this field. Formal analysis of concurrent systems is quite useful, as testing these systems is difficult. Systems with complex data models can also benefit from formalization, as desired properties of the system can be verified early in the lifecycle, saving possibly costly code restructuring.

When we introduce concern-level composition operators into a programming language, as described in section 2.2, the need for formal verification becomes even greater. These operators often have far-reaching and subtle effects in the code. The possibility of concerns overriding the functionality of one another can lead to violations of local properties.

Our approach is based on a five step procedure to specification and verification:

1. Specify each concern using a formal language
2. Verify desired local properties of each concern
3. Compose the various concerns into a single integrated specification, using composition operators that have semantics equivalent to the operators found in implementation level languages
4. Verify whether the local properties of the concerns still hold after the composition
5. Verify desired global properties

The key idea is determining a representative set of concern-level composition operators, and devising means of using these operators in one or more formal languages.

The choice of a formal language for verification depends mostly on the problem and on the type of properties to be verified. At this point work concentrates on composition using two different formal languages. The first is Alloy [6], a subset of the Z language [13] suitable for systems with complex relationships between data elements. The second is based on Labeled Transition Systems (LTS) [8] and is geared toward concurrent systems.

Alloy uses first-order logic based on the set-relational model. It is an adequate language for representing data-centric systems, where the major source of complexity lies in the structure of the data. Object-oriented systems map particularly well to Alloy. The language is somewhat limited in representing program states – operations can only refer to the current state and the next state, making it difficult to verify properties that require the execution of several operations in sequence.

Concerns specified in Alloy can be composed in different ways, since there is substantial flexibility in the possible kinds of data correspondence. Subclassing and aggregation are possible. Temporal composition of functions using *merge-* and *override-* type operators is also feasible.

Labeled transition systems are suitable for modeling systems as state machines. While the LTS have practically no data modeling, they are suitable for the analysis of the behavior of sequences of function calls, and for concurrent systems.

Concerns specified in LTS are composed through *merge-* and *override-* type operators, with or without temporal orderings. Section 4 will show the use of LTS in concern composition through a case study.

4   Formal Verification of a Bounded Buffer with Three Crosscutting Concerns

We will use a bounded buffer problem to illustrate the decomposition of a Java program into multiple concerns and the subsequent composition of these concerns using a simple composition operator. The composed system is slightly different than the original. In order to test whether the composed system is deadlock-free, we will then model each concern using a formal language, compose the concerns using a process that is equivalent to the one used to compose the Java program, and test the composed system using a model checking tool.

4.1   Problem Description

The system consists of a FIFO bounded buffer accessed by multiple reader and writer threads. Access to the buffer is mutually exclusive. If a reader thread attempts to read from the buffer when it is empty, the thread blocks. The same happens when a writer thread attempts to write to a full buffer.

4.2   Java Implementation

Single Concern Implementation The object-oriented implementation of the buffer in Java is straightforward, and is shown in figure 2. By analyzing the implementation, we find three crosscutting concerns, which are highlighted in the figure. The first is the concern that actually inserts and removes elements from the buffer, implementing the FIFO policy. The second concern deals with the buffer's behavior when it is empty. The final concern deals with the behavior of a full buffer.

Each concern is scattered through both of the buffer's methods, *read* and *write*, and each method consists of a tangling of all three concerns. Note that the first line of the *write* method belongs to both the full buffer and FIFO policy concerns.

Multiple Concern Implementation Separating the buffer into concerns isolates each concern in a single package, making changes to a concern easier. It also allows us to substitute concerns. For instance, if we need a LIFO stack instead of a FIFO buffer, everything we need to change is in the FIFO policy concern. Likewise, if instead of blocking writers when the buffer is full, we decide to drop the write request and not block the thread, we need only change the full buffer concern; the others are not affected.

Each concern consists of the class declaration, the data items the concern requires, and *read* and *write* methods. Figure 3 shows the FIFO policy and full buffer policy concerns.

```
class BlockingBuffer {
  final int size = 1000;
  int first, last;
  int[] buf = new int[size];

  public synchronized int read( ) {

    while (first == last) {
      try {
        wait( );
      } catch (InterruptedException e) { }
    }

    int element = buf[first];
    first = (first + 1) % size;

    notify();

    return element;

  }
```

```
public synchronized void write(int element) {

  int nextposition = (last+1) % size;

  while ( nextposition == first) {
    try {
      wait();
    } catch (InterruptedException e) { }
    nextposition = (last+1) % size;
  }

  last = nextposition;
  buf[last] = element;

  notify();

}
}
```

- Empty buffer policy
- Full buffer policy
- FIFO policy

Fig. 2. Java implementation of the bounded buffer

```
concern FIFOPolicy {
  class BlockingBuffer {
    final int size = 1000;
    int first, last;
    int[] buf = new int[size];

    public synchronized int read( ) {
      int element = buf[first];
      first = (first + 1) % size;
      return element;
    }
    public synchronized void write(int element) {
      int nextposition = (last+1) % size;
      last = nextposition;
      buf[last] = element;
} } }
```

```
concern FullPolicy {
  class BlockingBuffer {
    int size, first, last;

    public synchronized int read( ) {
      notify();
    }
    public synchronized void write(int element) {
      int nextposition = (last+1) % size;
      while ( nextposition == first) {
        try {
          wait();
        } catch (InterruptedException e) { }
        nextposition = (last+1) % size;
} } } }
```

Fig. 3. Implementations of the *FIFOPolicy* and *FullPolicy* concerns

4.3   Composing the Multiple Concerns

As discussed in section 2.2, any approach to composing concerns must address three
issues: correspondence, behavioral semantics, and binding. For our example, we will
use the following strategies to address the three issues:

- **correspondence**
  Lexical - elements in different concerns correspond to each other if they have the
  same name.
- **behavioral semantics**
  In order to determine the order in which the concerns should be executed, we will
  use a single composition operator, "*followed-by*", (described in our previous work
  [9]).

– binding
Static - all composition is performed at compile time

The followed-by operator. The *followed-by* operator is one of the simplest possible concern-level operators. It represents the first of a set of operators that together should mirror, at the specification level, the sets of operators found in implementation approaches.

The operator determines the semantics that should be attached to elements that correspond across concerns. Corresponding data represents shared memory; variables with the same name are representations of the same variable. Corresponding methods are executed in the order given by the *"followed-by"* operator. For instance, given two concerns A and B, both with a method M, composed as A *followed-by* B, the execution of the composed method M will result in the execution of A.M followed by the execution of B.M. The operator *followed-by* has semantics equivalent to that of operators of implementation-level languages, such as AspectJ's *before* and HyperJ's *order before*.

Possibilities for composition. In practical terms, we compose the concerns by creating a single BoundedBuffer class with *read* and *write* methods. The data members of the class are the union of the data members of all three concerns. The body of each method is formed by copying the bodies of the corresponding method of each concern, in the order given by the composition expression.

There are six possible ways to compose the three concerns. Since the composition operator *"followed-by"* defines a temporal ordering of the concerns, we are only interested in the compositions where the FIFO policy is executed last, because it would be meaningless to read from the buffer before checking whether it is empty, or writing to it before checking whether it is full. Thus, we have two possible compositions: {*FullPolicy followed-by EmptyPolicy followed-by FIFOPolicy*}, and {*EmptyPolicy followed-by FullPolicy followed-by FIFOPolicy*}. Which composition to choose is uncertain – it seems likely that both will have the same behavior.

When performing either of the previous compositions, one of the composed methods will not have exactly the same sequence of statements as in the original implementation. For instance, if we use the composition {*EmptyPolicy followed-by FullPolicy followed-by FIFOPolicy*}, the *read* method is similar to the original, but the composed *write* method is slightly different. Since the empty buffer policy comes first, the line *"notify();"* will be the first line of the method, rather than the last. Choosing the other composition would not affect the *write* method, but we'd find the same issue in the *read* method.

Figure 4 shows a Java class consisting of the composition of the three concerns using the expression {*EmptyPolicy followed-by FullPolicy followed-by FIFOPolicy*}.

Is this a problem? The answer is not clear from examining the code. Since access to the buffer is mutually exclusive, perhaps it does not matter if the blocked threads are notified before or after the element is actually written to the buffer. However, the fact that the writing thread may block after notifying may prove to be a problem. Testing can be done to try to detect faults, but testing concurrent systems is challenging. An alternative is to use formal modeling tools that can perform automated analysis of the composed system and detect potential problems.

```
class BlockingBuffer {
  final int size = 1000;
  int first, last;
  int[] buf = new int[size];

  public synchronized int read( ) {

    while (first == last) {
      try {
        wait( );
      } catch (InterruptedException e) { }
    }

    notify();

    int element = buf[first];
    first = (first + 1) % size;
    return element;
  }
}
```

```
public synchronized void write(int element) {

  notify();

  int nextposition = (last+1) % size;
  while ( nextposition == first) {
    try {
      wait();
    } catch (InterruptedException e) { }
    nextposition = (last+1) % size;
  }

  last = nextposition;
  buf[last] = element;

  }
}
```

- Empty buffer policy
- Full buffer policy
- FIFO policy

Fig. 4. Java implementation of the result of composing the three bounded buffer concerns with composition expression {*EmptyPolicy followed-by FullPolicy followed-by FIFOPolicy*}

4.4   Labeled Transition System (LTS) Model

The choice of a formal method was guided by the system's concurrent nature. Any problems that arise after composition are likely to be related to the multiple accesses to the buffer by reader and writer threads. Therefore, we chose to use Labeled Transition Systems (LTS), as these are suitable for modeling the interactions between concurrent processes. Another reason was tool availability - we used Magee and Kramer's LTS Analyser tool (LTSA)[8], which is capable of performing checks for liveness, safety and fairness violations.

We will use the tool to check whether the system is deadlock free, which is a liveness property. Other properties we could check are whether writes to a full buffer never happen (a safety property) or whether elements can always be written to the buffer when there is space (a liveness property).

Multiple Concern Model   The specifications of the three concerns of a two-element buffer using LTSA are shown in figure 5. Each concern defines three processes: BUFFER, READER, and WRITER. A process has a set of states. Each state defines the transitions (actions) it accepts. For example, the line *read → read.suspend → EMPTY* under state EMPTY in figure 5(a) defines that from this state the process can perform a *read* transition, leading to an intermediate state where the only acceptable transition is *read.suspend*, which leads the process back to state EMPTY. LTSA makes no distinction between labeled states such as EMPTY and NOT-EMPTY, and intermediate states such as the one between the *read* and *read.suspend* transitions. However, our approach makes that distinction. We call the labeled states *principal* states. These are states that will be considered when determining the set of states in the composed system. A *transition sequence* connects two principal states.

```
BUFFER = EMPTY,
  EMPTY =
    ( read → read.suspend → EMPTY
    | write → read.notify → NOT-EMPTY ),
  NOT-EMPTY =
    ( read → NOT-EMPTY
    | read → EMPTY
    | write → read.notify → NOT-EMPTY
    | read.resume → NOT-EMPTY
    | read.resume → EMPTY ).

READER = ( read → READAUX | read.resume → READER ),
  READAUX = ( read.suspend → read.notify → READRESUME
        | read.notify → READAUX
        | doread → READER ),
  READRESUME = (read.resume → READAUX | read.notify → READRESUME).

WRITER = ( write → WRITER ).
```

(a) Empty buffer policy

```
BUFFER = NOT-FULL,
  NOT-FULL =
    ( read → write.notify → NOT-FULL
    | write → NOT-FULL
    | write → FULL
    | write.resume → NOT-FULL
    | write.resume → FULL ),
  FULL =
    ( read → write.notify → NOT-FULL
    | write→ write.suspend → FULL ).

WRITER = ( write → WRITEAUX | write.notify → WRITER ),
  WRITEAUX = ( write.suspend → write.notify → WRITERESUME
        | write.notify → WRITEAUX ),
  WRITERESUME = (write.resume → WRITEAUX | write.notify → WRITERESUME).

READER = ( read → READER ).
```

(b) Full buffer policy

```
BUFFER = EMPTY,
  EMPTY = ( read→ ERROR
        | write→ dowrite → ONE ),
  ONE = ( read→ doread → EMPTY
        | write→ dowrite → FULL ),
  FULL = ( read → doread → ONE
        | write→ ERROR ).

READER = ( read → doread → READER ).

WRITER = ( write → dowrite → WRITER ).
```

(c) FIFO policy

Fig. 5. LTS specifications of bounded buffer concerns: (a) Empty buffer policy; (b) Full buffer policy; (c) FIFO policy

Transitions with the same label in different processes are *shared actions*. If a shared action executes, all processes that share the action must perform the transition simultaneously. Thus, a process will block upon reaching a shared action until all processes that share it also reach the equivalent action.

Each concern models only what is needed in order to address its particular needs. For instance, the concern that handles the empty buffer policy (figure 5a) has only two states of interest: buffer empty and buffer not empty. How many actual elements are in the buffer is irrelevant. The processes use non-determinism to deal with their incomplete specifications. For instance, in the empty buffer policy concern (figure 5a), a *read* transition when the buffer is not empty can lead either to state EMPTY or to state NOT-EMPTY, since the buffer may have had a single element, or more than one. During verification, the model checker gives equal weight to each possibility. In other words, if a non-deterministic choice occurs infinitely often, then each possibility will occur infinitely often.

The state ERROR in figure 5(c) is a built-in error state that terminates a process. Ideally, after composition all transitions to error states should disappear.

Having specified each concern, we have completed step 1 of the five-step procedure outlined in section 3. The next step is to verify local properties of each concern. Since the property we are interested in verifying here is the presence of deadlock, we used the LTSA tool to show that each of the concern specifications is deadlock-free. This completes step 2.

4.5   Composing the Formal Models

We now need to compose the three LTSA concerns in a way that preserves the semantics of the composition operator defined in section 4.2. While creating the composed Java program using the operator was straightforward, composing the LTSA specifications is a more elaborate process. The composition expression used in this example is {*EmptyPolicy followed-by FullPolicy followed-by FIFOPolicy*}.

The composed system consists of three processes: BUFFER, READER, and WRITER. Each process in the composed system is formed by combining the corresponding processes of each concern.

Before composing the concerns, we must establish the correspondence and behavioral semantics for the composition process. In an LTS description, there are two kinds of elements that may correspond across concerns: states and transitions. We will use lexical correspondence for both, meaning that elements with the same names in different concerns are considered equivalent.

The *followed-by* operator is a merge-type composition operator. In the case of LTS descriptions, this implies that all transitions that appear in the concerns must appear in the composed system. The semantics of *followed-by* are such that transitions belonging to concerns that come first in the composition expression must come first in the composed system.

Conceptually, the composition of the three concerns is similar to the execution of all of their processes in parallel. To understand this better, imagine that all three BUFFER processes are running. All three share the *read* and *write* actions. If we execute a *write* transition from the initial state, all three must participate in the action, according to

LTSA rules. Following this action we have several choices. The empty buffer concern can perform the *read.notify* action, or the FIFO concern can perform the *dowrite* action. Since we are simulating concurrent processes, both actions can occur at the same time. However, this is not what we want – we are trying to create a single, sequential bounded buffer process. The two actions above must both be executed, but in a well-defined order. The composition, therefore, will be equivalent to *one* of the possible sequential orderings of events in the parallel execution of all processes in the concerns.

The result of the composition will be a static specification that we can verify using the LTSA tool. Note that while the composition process simulates parallel execution, it is not sufficient to simply test the execution of all concerns in parallel, since this effectively allows invalid sequential orderings. Thus, building a composed specification is essential.

The actual composition procedure has two steps: finding equivalent states, and merging transition sequences.

States of the composed system. Each state in a composed system is formed of a set of states, with one state from each of the concerns. Concern states that correspond must belong to the same set, otherwise the set will not represent a state in the composed system. For example, we cannot have a state in the composed system that is formed by combining state EMPTY from the EmptyPolicy concern (EB), state NOT-FULL from the FullPolicy concern (FB), and state ONE from the FIFO concern (FIFO), since state EMPTY also appears in the FIFO concern and therefore must be present in the set if EMPTY from EmptyPolicy is present. One of the states in the composed system will be the initial state. This state must correspond to the initial states of all processes, otherwise the composition is impossible.

Given these rules, it is possible to establish correspondence automatically, and determine the set of states in the composed system. However, at the time of writing there is no tool support for this. We manually determined that there are only three sets of compatible states in the composed bounded buffer. The new states are labeled B0, B1, and B2. State B0 contains the initial states of all three processes, so it is the initial state of the composed system.

```
B0:  (EB.EMPTY,     FB.NOT-FULL,  FIFO.EMPTY)
B1:  (EB.NOT-EMPTY, FB.NOT-FULL,  FIFO.ONE)
B2:  (EB.NOT-EMPTY, FB.FULL,      FIFO.FULL)
```

Transitions of the composed system. Having the set of states of the composed buffer, we need to determine the set of transition sequences from each state. In order to determine this set, we simulate the concurrent execution of the concerns following LTSA rules.

For example, to find the transitions from B0, we simulate the parallel execution of EmptyPolicy starting at EMPTY, FullPolicy starting at NOT-FULL, and FIFOPolicy starting at EMPTY.

We now determine all possible sequences of transitions from these states. If, at some instant during execution, there is a choice between two or more transitions, we must choose the one from the concern that comes earlier in the composition expression {*EmptyPolicy followed-by FullPolicy followed-by FIFOPolicy*}. If the transition sequence leads the processes to states that are not compatible (that is, that together do not form one of the states in the composed system), the entire transition sequence is discarded.

As an example, to find the transition sequences from state B0, we'll simulate the parallel execution of the concerns starting from its three corresponding states. One of the possible actions from these states is *write*. All three processes execute the action synchronously at first, and the action is added to the composed transition sequence. Note that in the FullPolicy concern we have two possibilities for the transition, as there is a non-deterministic choice. We must create one transition sequence for each of the choices. Next, we have a choice of action *read.notify* from the EmptyPolicy concern, or action *dowrite* from the FIFO concern (the FullPolicy concern has finished its sequence, no matter what choice we made). Since the EmptyPolicy concern comes before the FIFO concern in the composition sequence, the rule dictates that we must choose the *read.notify* action. Now, only the *dowrite* action is left, and we are left with two possible transition sequences:

write → read.notify → dowrite → (EB.NOT-EMPTY, FB.FULL, FIFO.ONE)
write → read.notify → dowrite → (EB.NOT-EMPTY, FB.NOT-FULL, FIFO.ONE)

Since the first combination of states (EB.NOT-EMPTY, FB.FULL, FIFO.ONE) does not correspond to a state in the composed process, it must be discarded, leaving us with the second transition sequence from state B0 to state B1.

Transition-level operators. The *followed-by* operator has so far been used at the concern level. That is, it affects all the transitions of the operand concerns. However, there are cases in which concern-level operators are too coarse to handle all the expected behaviors of a system. In cases like this, we need to override the semantics of the concern-level operators with transition-level operators that handle the exceptions.

In the case of the bounded buffer specification, there are two types of transitions that must be handled differently so that composition succeeds. These are *suspend* and *resume* transitions. The reason for this special treatment is that the "suspend-notify" synchronization protocol used in the bounded buffer introduces function entry and exit points. That is, a process may enter the *read* and *write* functions not only through a function call, but also by receiving a notification from another thread after being suspended, in which case execution starts at the function location that immediately follows the suspend command.

We need to take multiple entry points into consideration because of the time-ordered nature of the composition. If a *suspend* transition is found in a concern, the execution should stop at that concern. Likewise, after a *resume* transition, the execution should proceed starting from the concern where the equivalent *suspend* occurred.

The behavior of *resume* transitions can be handled at the correspondence level. So far, we have used lexical correspondence. That is, states and transitions in different concerns correspond if they have the same names. However, we wish to add an additional correspondence: resume transitions correspond to their equivalent function-entry transitions. The *corresponds-to* operator can be used to establish correspondence between individual transitions. For instance,

```
EmptyPolicy(read.resume) corresponds-to FullPolicy(read)
```

The above states that *read.resume* transitions in concern *EmptyPolicy* should be treated as equivalent to *read* transitions in concern *FullPolicy* for the purpose of composition. The above example is necessary in the composition *EmptyPolicy followed-by FullPolicy followed-by FIFOPolicy*.

The *suspend* transitions affect the behavior of the composition. We must specify that transitions that would ordinarily follow a *suspend* should not be executed. We can use the *followed-by* operator applied at the transition level to state this:

```
EmptyPolicy(read.suspend) followed-by null
FullPolicy(write.suspend) followed-by null
```

Ordinarily, when a *read.suspend* transition happens in the *EmptyPolicy* concern, it should be followed by a transition in the next concern in the composition expression. However, here we are overriding that behavior by stating that these transitions should not be followed by any other concerns. Instead, the system should end the transition sequence and move to a principal state.

Figure 6 shows a full expression for the composition of the three concerns.

```
Correspondence:
  Lexical except {
    EmptyPolicy(read.resume) corresponds-to FullPolicy(read)
  }

Behavior:
  (EmptyPolicy followed-by FullPolicy followed-by FIFOPolicy) except {
    EmptyPolicy(read.suspend) followed-by null
    FullPolicy(write.suspend) followed-by null
  }
```

Fig. 6. Composition expression for the bounded buffer concerns

The composed model. Figure 7 shows the result of composing the three concerns of the bounded buffer following the composition expression {*EmptyPolicy followed-by FullPolicy followed-by FIFOPolicy*} and the composition procedure outlined above. It is interesting to note how the transitions to ERROR from the FIFOPolicy concern don't appear in the composed specification. This is because the special semantics we have assigned to the *suspend* transitions have made reaching the error states impossible.

4.6   Verifying the Composed Model

Having the composed model, we used the LTSA tool to try to detect possible deadlocks. We also generated different composed specifications from the concern specifications and compared their effects.

```
BUFFER = B0,
  B0 =
    ( read → read.suspend → B0
    | write → read.notify → dowrite → B1
    | write.resume → dowrite → B1 ),
  B1 =
    ( read → write.notify → doread → B1
    | write → read.notify → dowrite → B2
    | read.resume → write.notify → doread → B0
    | write.resume → dowrite → B2 ),
  B2 =
    ( read→ write.notify → doread → B1
    | write→ read.notify → write.suspend → B2
    | read.resume → write.notify → doread → B1 ).

READER = ( read → READAUX | read.notify → READER),
  READAUX = ( read.suspend → read.notify → READRESUME
        | doread → READER
        | read.notify → READAUX ),
  READRESUME = (read.resume → READAUX | read.notify → READRESUME).

WRITER = (write → WRITEAUX | write.notify → WRITER ),
  WRITEAUX = ( write.suspend → write.notify → WRITERESUME
        | write.notify → WRITEAUX
        | dowrite → WRITER ),
  WRITERESUME = (write.resume → WRITEAUX | write.notify → WRITERESUME).
```

Fig. 7. Result of composing the three bounded buffer concerns

In addition to the specification shown in figure 7, we tested the specification {*Full-Policy followed-by EmptyPolicy followed-by FIFOPolicy*}. The specifications shown so far assume an infinite number of read and write functions. In order to test more realistic boundary cases, we created two modified specifications that read and write exactly three elements, one more than the buffer size. Table 1 shows the results of testing the four specifications for deadlock using the LTSA tool.

Table 1. Result of checking composed buffer for deadlocks using the LTSA tool

Composition	Infinite accesses	Finite accesses
{*FullPolicy followed-by EmptyPolicy followed-by FIFOPolicy*}	No deadlock	No deadlock
{*EmptyPolicy followed-by FullPolicy followed-by FIFOPolicy*}	No deadlock	DEADLOCK

The results are interesting as only one of the compositions resulted in deadlock, and only when the reader and writer threads halt after a finite number of transactions. Deadlock happens in the following situation: the writer thread writes two elements to the buffer; in the third write attempt, the buffer is full; it notifies the reader and suspends; the reader thread reads two elements, notifying the writer; in the third read attempt, it suspends; the writer thread writes the last element and quits, leaving the reader suspended with an element available for reading in the buffer.

The deadlock doesn't happen with the other composition because the buffer begins in the empty state. If the initial state of the buffer had been full, we would find the opposite situation: the first composition would deadlock, and the second would not.

5   Related Work

The idea of specifying the composition of parallel processes in terms of transition orderings can be found in other formal approaches such as C-YES [10], where concurrent system protocols are specified by stating event ordering constraints.

Ku [11] is a formal object-oriented language for composing crosscutting concerns currently under development at Imperial College. While similar in goals, our work differs substantially from *Ku*. Our approach consists of finding a representative set of concern-level composition operators, and showing how to use these operators to compose concerns written in existing formal modeling languages. *Ku*, on the other hand, is an attempt at building a new formal modeling language capable of adequately expressing crosscutting concerns.

Another issue of interest is whether or not the use of crosscutting concerns is beneficial in decomposing formal specifications. This topic has been addressed by Daniel Jackson [5] and others, and while there seem to be indications that specifications written in this fashion are easier to write and understand, more research is necessary before conclusions can be drawn.

6   Summary

We have presented our current work on providing support for formal modeling and verification of crosscutting concerns. Any composition method that supports crosscutting concerns must address three main issues: correspondence between concerns, semantics of the composition, and binding time. Existing implementation-level methods differ in how they address each of these issues. However, the number of different concern composition operators is relatively small.

To provide support for concern-level composition in a formal language, we must show how the same operators that appear at the implementation level can be incorporated into the language, and how multiple formal specifications of crosscutting concerns can be composed into an integrated specification.

Our work currently involves mechanisms to allow the composition of crosscutting concerns written in two formal languages: Alloy and LTSA. We have shown through a case study how concerns written using LTSA can be integrated using composition operators. The case study illustrates how formal methods can be used to test properties (such as the presence of deadlock) of different compositions a set of concerns, and how compositions that are similar in nature can turn out to have subtly different behaviors.

The case study used lexical correspondence and a single composition operator called *followed-by*. This operator uses simple merge semantics, and represents the first of a more complete set. In particular, operators are needed that offer support for more sophisticated forms of correspondence, such as one-to-many matches, and other composition semantics, such as function override.

References

1. M. Aksit, K. Wakita, J. Bosch, L. Bergmans, and A. Yonezawa. Abstracting object-interactions using composition-filters. In R. Guerraoui, O. Nierstrasz, and M. Riveill, editors, *Object-Based Distributed Processing*, pages 152–184. Springer-Verlag, 1993.

2. Don Batory. Subjectivity and GenVoca generators. In *Proceedings of the Fourth International Conference on Software Reuse*, Orlando, Florida, April 1996.

3. Erich Gamma, Richard Helm, Ralph Johnson, and John Vlissides. *Design Patterns: Elements of Reusable Object-Oriented Software*. Addison-Wesley, 1995.

4. William Harrison and Harold Ossher. Subject-oriented programming (a critique of pure objects). In *Proceedings of OOPSLA '93*, pages 411–428. ACM, 1993.

5. Daniel Jackson. Structuring Z specifications with views. *ACM Transactions on Software Engineering and Methodology*, 4(4):365–389, October 1995.

6. Daniel Jackson. Alcoa: the alloy constraint analyzer. In *Proceedings of ICSE 2000*, Limerick, Ireland, 2000. http://sdg.lcs.mit.edu/alloy/.

7. Gregor Kiczales, J. Lamping, A. Mendhekar, C. Lopes, J. Loingtier, and J. Irwin. Aspect-oriented programming. In *Proceedings of ECOOP '97*, 1997.

8. J. Magee and J. Kramer. *Concurrency: State Models and Java Programs*. John Wiley & Sons, 1999.

9. Torsten Nelson, Donald Cowan, and Paulo Alencar. A model for describing object-oriented systems from multiple perspectives. In *Fundamental Approaches to Software Engineering, FASE 2000*, volume 1783 of *Lecture Notes in Computer Science*, Berlin, Germany, 2000. Springer.

10. R. Pande and J. Browne. A compositional approach to concurrent object-oriented programming. In *Proceedings of the International Conference on Compilers and Languages*, Paris, France, May 1994.

11. Mark Skipper. A model of composition oriented programming. In *Proceedings of the ICSE 2000 Workshop on Multi-Dimensional Separation of Concerns in Software Engineering*, 2000.

12. B. Smith. Reflection and semantics in lisp. In *Proceedings of PoPL'84: The Eleventh Annual ACM Symposium on Principles of Programming Languages*, January 1984.

13. Spivey. *The Z Notation: A Reference Manual*. Prentice Hall, 1987.

14. Peri Tarr, Harold Ossher, William Harrison, and S. Sutton. N degrees of separation: Multi-dimensional separation of concerns. In *Proceedings of the 21st International Conference on Software Engineering*, pages 107–119, 1999.

A formal definition of crosscuts[*]

Rémi Douence, Olivier Motelet, Mario Südholt

École des Mines de Nantes
4 rue Alfred Kastler, 44307 Nantes cedex 3, France
www.emn.fr/{douence,motelet,sudholt}

Abstract Crosscutting, i.e. relating different program points is one of
the key notions of Aspect-Oriented Programming. In this article, we consider a general and operational model for crosscutting based on execution
monitors.
A domain-specific language for the definition of crosscuts constitutes the
core of the article. The semantics of this language is formally defined by
means of parser operators matching event patterns in execution traces.
We define an operational semantics of the matching process by means
of rules relating the operators. The use of the language is exemplified
by several sophisticated crosscut definitions. We sketch a prototype implementation in JAVA which has been systematically derived from the
language definition.

1 Introduction

Aspect-Oriented Programming (AOP) [9] is an emerging programming paradigm
providing explicit support for separation of concerns. Once different concerns
have been identified, two main questions arise. Where non-functional concerns
must be inserted in the base program (aka. the functional aspect)? How the
non-functional aspects interact with the functional one and with one another?
In this article, we focus on the first question. More specifically, we are interested in an operational definition of crosscuts, i.e., relating different points in
the execution of a sequential program. We argue for a formal definition of crosscuts for two reasons. First, well-defined crosscutting is a mandatory requirement
for the understanding of AOP tools. Second, a formal definition enables aspect
composition and compilation to be treated systematically.

In this article, we argue for execution monitors as a general and operational
model for AOP and, in particular, crosscutting. Indeed, the "points of interest"
of the execution can be abstracted as events and a specialized language enables
quite general relations between events to be defined. Moreover, this language
provides an operational semantics for crosscut detection.

The article is structured as followed: Section 2 introduces execution monitoring as a model for AOP. Section 3 presents a rigorous treatment of the framework, formally defines our crosscutting language and presents several examples

---

[*] This work has been partially funded by the EU project "EasyComp"
(www.easycomp.org), no. IST-1999014191.

A. Yonezawa and S. Matsuoka (Eds.): REFLECTION 2001, LNCS 2192, pp. 170–186, 2001.

of crosscut definitions. Related work is discussed in Section 4. Section 5 concludes and lists future work.

2 AOP from a monitoring perspective

Crosscutting is one of the key notion of AOP. In the context of this paper, we define crosscuts as relating different program points or execution points, such that functionality can be parameterized with information from some of these points and inserted at others. The relations between program points can be quite diverse. For instance, an aspect for method logging requires only individual calls to be identified in order to construct and write the corresponding log message. On the other hand, multi-step security protocols require more complex relationships. During execution of a securized application, such protocols relate points where certificates are generated, points where authentication based on certificates is done and points where resource accesses require that specific rights have been granted after authentication.

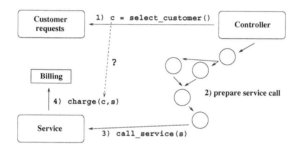

Figure 1. Billing in a loosely-coupled client-server system

In this article, we use *billing* in (what we call) "loosely-coupled client-server systems" as a running example. In such client-server systems, communication is initiated and mediated by a controller. Figure 1 shows a controller that is intended to manage a communication between customers and services which should not or cannot communicate directly. A typical scenario of such a system architecture is the following: first select a customer request, second prepare the service call by performing a potentially complex computation (e.g. establishing communication statistics or performing configuration tasks) and third call a service. In such an application, the last selected customer is not available when a service is called. However, this information is mandatory in order to upgrade the application such that the service (not the controller!) can bill the customer.

A conventional solution to this problem is to propagate the customer identity by threading this piece of information through the complex computation code (e.g. add an extra argument to all functions implementing this code). Obviously, such a modification can be quite tedious depending on the size of the code.

An AOP-like solution is to define a billing crosscut that relates a customer request selection to the corresponding service called. Such systems thus provide an interesting and complex example for crosscutting with realistic applications.

2.1   Overview of the framework

The examples we just discussed motivate several essential characteristics any framework for AOP should have: first, a mechanism which allows programs (i.e. program code) or program executions to be abstracted to "points of interests," i.e., points where information is needed from or points where new behavior is to be inserted. Second, a part of the framework that must be able to relate such points of interests. Third, this part must also be able to gather the information provided at the points of interest and insert the new behavior, i.e., to perform actions.

Monitor-based AOP. We advocate the use of execution monitors as a framework for AOP. A monitor has a global view on the program execution. In this context, the framework characteristics are materialized as follows:

1. The points of interest of a program execution are defined in terms of *events* emitted during program execution.
2. Points of interest that relate to one another are denoted by *patterns of events* to be *matched.*
3. Once a pattern has been matched, the program execution is suspended and an *action* may be executed.

We claim that execution monitors are highly appropriate as a framework for AOP. They provide a natural abstraction in terms of events, enable the explicit definition of complex crosscuts by means of event patterns and accommodate very general actions. In this article, we are mainly interested in substantiating this claim by giving a formal definition of crosscutting as event patterns and the process of pattern matching.

Crosscut definitions. In order to get a first intuitive understanding of the kind of crosscuts we are interested in let us consider the billing example introduced above. The essence of this example is to relate customer selections to service calls despite the loose coupling between clients and servers. Let us therefore assume that two corresponding events *select_customer*() and *call_service*(s) are generated during program execution. Once these events are generated, we may want to match the following event patterns:

- A pair consisting of a customer selection and the next service call.
- A (possibly infinite) sequence of such pairs — e.g., to cope with iteration in the controller.

- Sequences of overlapping pairs of selection and call — e.g., to cope with buffering in the controller: a number of customer selections is followed by the corresponding service calls. By means of overlapping pairs, we can disambiguate the sequence of events

$$c_1 = select\_customer() \ldots c_2 = select\_customer()$$
$$\ldots call\_service(s_1) \ldots call\_service(s_2)$$

as relating c_1 to s_1 as well as c_2 to s_2 (but not, e.g., c_1 to s_2).
- Nested pairs of customer selections and service calls — e.g., to cope with recursion in the controller: a customer selection may require that another customer service pair is executed first.

Aspect definitions. An aspect can then be defined as a rule   *pattern* $\Rightarrow$ *action* and several aspects can be defined simply as concurrent rules. A billing aspect, for instance, could be expressed by the rule

$$c = select\_customer(); call\_service(s) \Rightarrow charge(c, s)$$

which can be interpreted as follows: monitor the application execution in order to detect the next call to the *select_customer*() function, pause the execution, store the value of the variable c, resume execution, monitor the execution in order to detect the next call to the *call_service*() function, pause the execution, store the value of the variable s, call the function *charge*() and resume execution. Hence, the pattern on the left-hand side of the rule relates every customer selection to the next service called during program execution.

3 A formal definition of crosscuts

In this section we propose a formal definition of crosscuts: Section 3.1 shows how the main notions of our framework can be formalized. Section 3.2 presents our domain-specific language for crosscutting and the properties of its operators. Finally, Section 3.3 applies this language to the billing example and sketches how formal properties of the pattern operators can be used.

In the following, we present a formalization using the functional language HASKELL [6]. We introduce its syntactic elements on the fly as needed. The full implementation defining our framework can be found in Appendix A.

3.1 A formal framework for AOP

In our framework an event represents a point in the program execution. The following type synonym models events by a pair consisting of a name tag and a time stamp.[1]

---

[1] A more realistic event definition — extending the one given in this section — is discussed along with the presentation of our JAVA prototype in Section 3.4.

```
type Event = (String, Int)
```

The complete trace of the execution is defined as a list of events.

```
type Trace = [Event]
```

A program is a sequential computation that produces a trace, one event at a time.

```
data Program = Over | Cont (Tick -> (Event, Program))
```

This is modeled by the following algebraic data type: either the program terminates (represented by the constructor Over) or it is a continuation (Cont) that at each step (represented by Tick) returns the next event and the remainder of the program.

A crosscut is defined as a list of events representing different points in the program execution which are to be related.

```
type Crosscut = [Event]
```

A monitor is a program that performs event pattern matching, one event at a time. It can be defined as a function mapping an event to a pair consisting of a list of crosscuts detected at this event and the monitor continuation.[2]

```
data Monitor = M (Event -> ([Crosscut], Monitor))
```

The program and the monitor implement a producer-consumer pair. In order to compose them, we define a function run[3] that returns the list of all crosscuts detected during program execution:

```
run :: Program -> Monitor -> [Crosscut]
run Over          _              = []
run (Cont program) (M monitor) =
        let (event,program')     = program Tick
            (crosscuts,monitor') = monitor event
        in crosscuts ++ (run program' monitor')
```

When the program execution is over, an empty list of crosscuts is returned. Otherwise, the program generates an event which is passed to the monitor and the list of detected crosscuts at this point is concatenated (++) with the crosscuts to come (recursive call to run).

Note that we focus on the definition and detection of crosscuts in this article. So, we do not model actions which are to be interleaved with the program execution each time a crosscut is detected. However, in order to define the framework completely, aspect actions could be modeled as functions mapping a crosscut and the current program state to another program state:

```
type Action = Crosscut -> Program -> Program
```

---

[2] In HASKELL, type synonyms cannot be recursive and the constructor M is thus needed for technical reasons.

[3] In HASKELL, a function definition is preceded by its type (introduced by ::).

3.2   A domain-specific language for crosscut definition

Rephrasing the definition of the type `Monitor` above, we can say that the monitor is a function of past events. This function can be as complex as needed in order to detect sophisticated crosscuts. However, in order to support a concise definition of crosscuts, we argue for a domain-specific language (DSL) to define event patterns.

```
data Pattern =
       -- sequential patterns
       Return Crosscut
     | Bind (Crosscut -> Pattern)
     | Pattern 'Seq' Pattern
       -- filtering patterns
     | Filter (Event -> Bool) Pattern
       -- abortable patterns
     | Abort
       -- parallel patterns
     | Pattern 'Par' Pattern
     | First Pattern
```

Figure 2. DSL for crosscut definition

In Figure 2, we present such a DSL for crosscut definitions that is based on the notion of event patterns. Pattern constructors are classified in four categories: sequential patterns, filtering patterns, abortable patterns and parallel patterns.

Informally, our constructions can be interpreted as follows: `Return c` returns c as a result; `Bind f` applies the function f to the previous result (and thus binds it to a variable); p1 `'Seq' p2`[4] matches first p1 and then p2; `Filter pred p1` filters out the next event that satisfies `pred` while matching p1; `Abort` aborts the current sequential pattern; p1 `'Par'` p2 matches p1 and p2 simultaneously; `First p` returns the result of the first sequential pattern of (a `Par`-expression) p that matches.

In order to familiarize the reader with this language, we present a few basic pattern/crosscut definitions. (More sophisticated patterns are presented in the following section.)

– A pattern defining a crosscut consisting only of the next event.

```
nextEvent :: Pattern
nextEvent = Bind (\[e] -> Return [e])
```

This pattern binds the next event to the variable e[5] and returns it as a crosscut.

---

[4] In HASKELL, 'C' denotes infix application of C.

[5] In HASKELL, the lambda abstraction \arg->exp denotes the function $\lambda arg.exp$.

- A pattern that matches the next event satisfying a predicate `pred`.

```
nextP :: (Event -> Bool) -> Pattern
nextP pred = Bind (\[e]-> if (pred e) then Return [e]
                                      else nextP pred)
```

The pattern `nextP` binds the next event and returns it as a crosscut if the predicate is satisfied, otherwise the pattern is called recursively.

- A pattern that matches the next two events and returns the corresponding crosscut.

```
nextThenNext :: Pattern
nextThenNext = nextEvent 'Seq' Bind (\[e1] ->
               nextEvent 'Seq' Bind (\[e2] ->
               Return [e1,e2]))
```

- A pattern that matches the second event satisfying a predicate by filtering out the first one.

```
second :: (Event -> Bool) -> Pattern
second pred = Filter pred (nextP pred)
```

- A pattern that matches the next event and returns it provided the event does not satisfy a predicate, but does not return a crosscut otherwise.

```
no :: (Event -> Bool) -> Pattern
no pred = nextEvent 'Seq' Bind (\[e] ->
          if (pred e) then Abort
                      else return [e])
```

Note that this pattern is different from `nextP (not . pred)`[6] that returns the next event that does not satisfies `pred`. Indeed, if the next event satisfies `pred`, `no pred` aborts, while `nextP (no . pred)` skips the event.

- A pattern that matches the next event satisfying `pred1` *and* matches the next event satisfying `pred2`. Note that in this case, two different crosscuts are returned.

```
and :: (Event -> Bool) -> (Event -> Bool) -> Pattern
and pred1 pred2 = nextP pred1 'Par' nextP pred2
```

- A pattern that matches *either* the next event satisfying `pred1` *or* the next event satisfying `pred2` whichever matches first. In this case only one crosscut is returned.

```
or :: (Event -> Bool) -> (Event -> Bool) -> Pattern
or pred1 pred2 = First (and pred1 pred2)
```

---

[6] In HASKELL, ' .' denotes function composition.

Formal semantics. Figure 3 lists the equivalence rules which the pattern operators obey. The sequential composition of pattern is associative (R1). A sequence
of Return and Bind is equivalent to applying the function to the returned result
(R2). Abort terminates a sequence (R3) but does not interfere with the parallel
composition (R8). The parallel composition of patterns is associative (R4) and
commutative (R5) and is distributive with respect to sequential composition (R6,
7). Rules R9-16 deal with First and Filter. Rules R9, 13 state how results are
propagated under one of these two constructions. The remaining rules define the
semantics of First (that returns the result of the first sequential pattern that
matches within a Par-expression) and Filter (that filters out the next event
that satisfies a predicate).

```
R1      p1 'Seq' (p2 'Seq' p3) = (p1 'Seq' p2) 'Seq' p3
R2      Return es 'Seq' Bind f = f es
R3      Abort 'Seq' p2 = Abort
R4      p1 'Par' (p2 'Par' p3) = (p1 'Par' p2) 'Par' p3
R5      p1 'Par' p2 = p2 'Par' p1
R6      p1 'Seq' (p2 'Par' p3) = (p1 'Seq' p2) 'Par' (p1 'Seq' p3)
R7      (p1 'Par' p2) 'Seq' p3 = (p1 'Seq' p3) 'Par' (p2 'Seq' p3)
R8      Abort 'Par' p2 = p2
R9      p1 'Seq' First p2 = First (p1 'Seq' p2)
R10     First (Abort) = Abort
R11     First (Return e) = Return e
R12     First (Return e 'Par' p2) = Return e
R13     Return e 'Seq' Filter pred p2
            = p2                                -- if (pred e)
            = Filter pred (Return e 'Seq' p2)   -- otherwise
R14     Filter pred (Abort) = Abort
R15     Filter pred (Return e) = Return e
R16     Filter pred (Return e 'Par' p2) = Return e 'Par' Filter pred p2
```

Figure 3. Equivalence rules for the event pattern operators

The equivalence rules shown in Figure 3 can be used as the essential building
block of an interpreter for pattern terms. In the HASKELL implementation shown
in Appendix A, the function monitor :: Pattern -> Monitor interprets terms
of type Pattern by reducing a term of the form Return [e] 'Seq' pattern
where e is the current event. The function monitor implements a term-rewriting
system obtained from the equivalence rules (see the definition of the function
step in Appendix A).

3.3 Crosscut definitions

In this section, we formally define the *billing* crosscuts introduced in Section 2
and exemplify how formal properties of the pattern operators can be used in

this application context. We assume in the remainder of this section that customer selections and service calls are modeled by events tagged "c" and "s", respectively. The trace "ccss" thus models the program execution

$$c_1 = select\_customer() \ldots c_2 = select\_customer()$$
$$\ldots call\_service(s_1) \ldots call\_service(s_2)$$

A first simple crosscut for billing consists in matching a customer selection followed by the next service selection.

```
billing :: Pattern
billing =
    next "c" 'Seq' Bind (\[e1] ->
    next "s" 'Seq' Bind (\[e2] ->
    Return [e1,e2]))
```

where next n matches (by calling nextP) the next event named n. Matching the pattern billing in the trace "cscs" yields the single crosscut [("c",1),("s",2)].

Of course, there can be multiple occurrences of this pattern in the execution trace. In order to detect all the crosscuts, it is necessary to introduce recursion:

```
billingS :: Pattern
billingS =
        next "c" 'Seq' Bind (\[e1] ->
        next "s" 'Seq' Bind (\[e2] ->
        Return [e1,e2] 'Par' billingS))
```

With this new definition, every time a crosscut is found, a new one is looked for. Note that we used Par, which returns several results, rather than Seq. However, the crosscut instances must be sequential. Indeed, overlapping customer selections and service calls are not recognized as they should. For example, matching billingS on the trace "ccss" yields the single crosscut [("c",1),("s",3)] because after the first "c" has been matched, the pattern looks for the next "s" and skips the second "c".

In order to detect the different instances of the billing crosscut in the presence of overlapping, the pattern definition must be modified to:

```
billing0 :: Pattern
billing0 =
    next "c" 'Seq' Bind (\[e1] ->
    billing0' e1)

billing0' :: Event -> Pattern
billing0' e1 =
    First (next "c" 'Par' next "s") 'Seq' Bind (\[e2] ->
    if (isName "s" e2)
      then Return [e1,e2]
      else billing0' e1 'Par'
            Filter (isName "s") (billing0' e2))
```

In this case, we get the expected behavior: matching `billing0` on the trace `"ccss"` yields two crosscuts: `[("c",1),("s",3)]` and `[("c",2),("s",4)]`. The first definition `Billing0` matches the next c and passes it as a parameter to the auxiliary definition `billing0'`. This second crosscut definition matches either the next `"s"` or the next `"c"` whichever comes first. If `"s"` is matched, a crosscut has been found and it is returned. If `"c"` is matched, the beginning of a new instance has been detected and a new pattern must be matched in parallel. Note that, in this latter case, the next event `"s"` must not be taken into account by the newly created pattern (i.e. the second argument of `Par`). This is achieved with the help of the `Filter` construction. Hence, overlapping customer-service pairs are matched. (A crosscut definition `billingNS` matching nested pairs can be found at the end of Appendix A.)

Another crosscut definition is inspired by ASPECTJ [10]. In ASPECTJ, it is possible to define a *restricted* version of the billing crosscut as follows:

```
billingCflow = cflow(customer.select()) &&
               execution(service.call())
```

This definition denotes crosscuts that relate each call to `service.call()` with the previous call to `customer.select()` that has not yet returned (i.e., the top-most call to `customer.select()` in the execution stack). Such a crosscut can be repeated and nested. For example, let `"c"` represents a call to `customer.select()`, `"r"` the corresponding return-statements and `"s"` a call to `service.call()`. Then, `cflow()` should yield three crosscuts for the trace `"ccssrsrs"`: `[("c",2), ("s",3)]`, `[("c",2), ("s",4)]` and `[("c",1), ("s",6)]`.

There is currently no formal definition of ASPECTJ's crosscut language. In fact, one of the initial motivations of our work was to be able to understand crosscutting in ASPECTJ without inspecting the code produced by the weaver. Using our framework, `cflow()` could be formally defined as follows (rather than having recourse to a new primitive pattern constructor):

```
billingCflow :: Pattern
billingCflow =
  next "c"                 'Seq' Bind (\[e1] ->
  billingCflow' e1 billingCflow)

billingCflow' :: Event -> Pattern -> Pattern
billingCflow' e1 k =
  First (next "c" 'Par' next "r" 'Par' next "s")
  'Seq' Bind (\[e2] ->
    if (isName "s" e2)
       then Return [e1,e2] 'Par' (billingCflow' e1 k)
       else if (isName "r" e2)
              then k
              else billingCflow' e2 (billingCflow' e1 k))
```

In the definition of `billingCflow'`, a continuation k is used in order to deal with nested crosscuts. Event `e1` represents the last customer selection that has not yet returned. Three cases have to be considered. First, if "s" is matched a crosscut starting at e1 has been found, is returned and further crosscuts — still relating to the customer selection e1 — are searched for. If "r" is matched the continuation is used to restore the previous value of e1. Finally, if "c" is matched new crosscuts starting with the current selection e2 have to be looked for and the value of e1 is stored in the continuation. Note that this definition makes explicit the complex relationship (inherent to the cflow()-construction) between the points involved.

One advantage of such a formalization is that non-trivial properties can be *proven*, for instance, for optimization purposes. In our framework, a program execution (trace) can be modeled as a sequence of Return-statements. For example, the expression

```
prog :: Int -> Pattern
prog ts = prog (ts+3) 'Seq' Return [("r", ts+2)]
                      'Seq' Return [("s", ts+1)]
                      'Seq' Return [("c", ts)]
```

models a program repeatedly performing a customer selection and a service call before returning from the customer selection[7]. Our formal definition allows the following property to be proven by means of the rules shown in Figure 3 (The proof can be found in [2].):

(prog ts) 'Seq' billingCflow = (prog ts) 'Seq' billingS

This property enables a more complex pattern (billingCflow whose continuation could, e.g., be implemented using a stack) to be replaced by a simpler one (billingS which does not need a stack) in the context prog.

3.4   A JAVA Prototype

We have developed a prototype of our framework in JAVA. This prototype is single-threaded: the original JAVA program execution and the monitor execution are interleaved. In order to treat the billing-example, our prototype deals only with two kind of events: method-call events and method-return events. These events are represented by objects that contain the following fields: receiver, method name, arguments, result, and time stamp. Before and after each method call in the monitored JAVA program, the corresponding event object is created and the pattern-matching method of the monitor is called.

The monitor implementation in JAVA has been derived from the HASKELL source code in Appendix A. The Pattern data type has been translated to a set of Java classes such that a pattern is represented by a tree of objects (an abstract syntax tree). Each node of the tree provides a method step() in order to perform term rewriting as shown in Figure 4 for expressions involving the operator Par.

---

[7] Note that in HASKELL infinite data structures are constructed lazily. Hence, the above function models a stream of events.

HASKELL code (excerpt from function `step`, see Appendix A):

```
step (Abort 'Par' p2) = p2
step (p1 'Par' Abort) = p1
step (p1 'Par' p2) = step p1 'Par' step p2
```

Derived JAVA code:

```
class Par extends Pattern {
  Pattern p1, p2;
  Pattern step() {
    if (p1 instanceof Abort) return p2;
    if (p2 instanceof Abort) return p1;
    return new Par(p1.step(), p2.step());
  }
  ...
}
```

Figure 4. Rewriting Par-expressions

Every time an event is emitted (i.e. the monitor is called), the current term is rewritten and the resulting crosscuts are extracted. Actions (i.e. Java code) can then be called with the event objects as parameters. In the context of the billing example, such an action could charge a customer for a service. Finally, the pattern-matching method of the monitor returns and the original program resumes its execution.

This prototype has allowed us to implement the different examples presented in this paper in JAVA. Because the prototype has been derived from the HASKELL definition, the prototype implementation was quite easy and its correctness should be simpler to investigate. A more detailed description of the JAVA prototype (event model, code instrumentation, etc.) can be found in the companion technical report [2].

4   Related Work

In this section, we briefly discuss the relationship of our work to other work on AOP, execution monitoring, monadic programming and reflection.

Formal approaches to AOP. Few work has been done on formal approaches to AOP. Notable exceptions are the frameworks presented by Lämmel [12], Fradet and Südholt [5] and De Meuter [14]. The first two articles discuss the introduction of aspects into program texts by means of source transformations. They are less general than our approach because they do not allow to relate arbitrary execution points. This limitation enables efficient woven code to be produced, in particular by taking into account static analysis techniques. The third article presents monadic programming as a framework for AOP which allows the introduction of new behavior in a structured manner but does not include any support for crosscut definitions.

AOP tools. ASPECT-J [10] provides a development environment for AOP in JAVA. In particular, it includes a language for crosscut definitions which enables points in the execution of JAVA programs (called "pointcuts") to be denoted. Pointcuts can be atomic such as "method call" or "field assignment" pointcuts but can also denote *sets* of execution points (as, e.g., the cflow() pointcuts). The language also includes a limited number of operators (most notably, set union and intersection) for the composition of pointcuts.

In contrast to our proposal, ASPECTJ's crosscut definition language is intimately tied to (the execution model of) JAVA and is limited in scope. In fact, the pointcut cflow(customer.select()) denotes only points occurring between the call to select() and the corresponding return statement, which does not allow to define the billing crosscut as presented here. Furthermore, the understanding of ASPECTJ's crosscut language is hampered by lack of a precise definition.

HYPER/J [17] is another aspect weaver for JAVA providing substantial support for multiple domains with class- and method-granularity. However, it does not have a clear semantics and cannot relate execution events (e.g., there is no equivalent to cflow()).

Execution monitoring for security purposes. Event monitoring has been mainly used recently for security-relevant tasks, especially *intrusion detection* [11,13]. The language RUSSEL [15], for instance, is a turing-complete DSL describing algorithms on sequential streams of security-relevant events. It provides a rule-based language to define intrusion-detection based on conditions and associated actions. In contrast to our approach, such languages do not provide descriptive means to relate arbitrary events: RUSSEL definitions are formulated in a purely imperative style and it essentially relies on an ad-hoc mechanism for the definition of chained rule applications which is specifically-designed with intrusion detection in mind. Efficiency concerns are also a major issue with respect to using execution monitoring for security purposes. Hence, compilation techniques for merging monitors into monitored programs are an important research issue (see e.g. Colcombet and Fradet [1]).

Monadic parsing and postmortem trace analysis. Our DSL was strongly influenced by monadic parser libraries [7]. Indeed our pattern constructors are closely related to the monadic operators: our Return (resp. Abort, Par) corresponds to the monadic result (resp. zero, plus) and our pattern p1 'Seq' Bind p2 corresponds to the monadic expression p1 'bind' p2.

The main difference comes from our interaction model: each time an event is emitted, the monitor must decide if a pattern has been detected. This lazy producer-consumer behavior is mandatory in order to be able to suspend the program execution to perform an action. So, multiple patterns composed with Par must be detected by proceeding in a lock-step manner. This is why we introduced an extra constructor Bind representing a closure (a partially matched pattern). The producer-consumer behavior also prohibits backtracking behavior. Hence, work on postmortem trace analysis as used for debugging in PROLOG [4] cannot be reused directly.

Reflection. Reflective systems, in particular those based on Meta-Object Protocols (MOP) [8], can be seen as programmable monitoring systems: the so-called hooks define points of interest and the metaobjects monitor the execution and perform actions. However, a MOP defines a fixed set of hooks and does not allow to denote arbitrary execution points (METAJ [3] weakens this restriction by providing a technique to construct specially-tailored MOPs). Furthermore, since a metaobject is only concerned with "events" relating to the objects it is associated to, metaobjects do not have a completely global view of the execution. Finally, since formal treatment of MOP-based systems is rather difficult, they do not seem suitable as a model. They provide, however, a potentially valuable implementation platform.

5 Conclusion

In this article, we introduced a general and operational model for crosscut definitions based on execution monitors. Principally, we presented a formally-defined domain-specific language for crosscut definitions and we defined sophisticated crosscuts useful in realistic applications. This work also allowed us to propose a formal definition for ASPECTJ's crosscut constructor `cflow()`. Finally, we briefly presented a JAVA prototype which has been derived from the formal DSL definition.

Future work. The work presented in this article provides numerous opportunities for future work.

First, we should experiment with our DSL by developing libraries of useful crosscuts. Alternative pattern languages (e.g. based on regular expressions) could be investigated. A JAVA-like syntax for pattern definitions should be developed. More declarative definitions, e.g. based on temporal logic [16] should also be explored. Second, in order to guide the user, static analysis techniques dealing with cost measures (e.g. based on measures for pattern complexity) and interactions between aspects (e.g. patterns that overlap) should be designed. Third, for efficiency concerns, the monitor should be compiled into the monitored program and the elimination of superfluous events should be studied.

Finally, we focused on crosscut definitions in this article. As far as actions are concerned, a taxonomy of actions based on realistic applications should be built and a DSL for action composition should be provided to users (e.g. subsuming ASPECTJ's `before, after, around, dominate, ...`).

References

1. T. Colcombet and P. Fradet. Enforcing trace properties by program transformation. In *Proceedings of the 27th ACM SIGPLAN-SIGACT Symposium on Prin-*

ciples of Programming Languages (POLP-00), pages 54–66, N.Y., January 19–21 2000. ACM Press.

2. R. Douence, O. Motelet, and M. Südholt. A formal definition of crosscuts. Technical Report 01/3/INFO, École des Mines de Nantes, 2001.

3. R. Douence and M. Südholt. A generic reification technique for object-oriented reflective languages. *The Journal of Higher-Order and Symbolic Computation*, 14(1), 2001.

4. M. Ducasse. Opium: An extendable trace analyser for Prolog. *The Journal of Logic programming*, 1999.

5. P. Fradet and M. Südholt. AOP: towards a generic framework using program transformation and analysis.

6. P. Hudak, S. Peyton Jones, P. Wadler, et al. Report on the programming language HASKELL. *ACM SIGPLAN Notices*, 27(5), March 1992. HASKELL home page: www.haskell.org.

7. G. Hutton and E. Meijer. Monadic parsing in HASKELL. *Journal of Functional Programming*, 8(4):437–444, July 1998.

8. G. Kiczales, J. des Rivieres, and D. G. Bobrow. *The Art of the Meta-Object Protocol*. MIT Press, Cambridge (MA), USA, 1991.

9. G. Kiczales et al. Aspect-oriented programming. In Mehmet Aksit and Satoshi Matsuoka, editors, *11th Europeen Conference on Object-Oriented Programming*, volume 1241 of *LNCS*, pages 220–242. Springer Verlag, 1997.

10. G. Kiczales et al. An overview of ASPECTJ. In *Proceedings of the European Conference on Object-Oriented Programming (ECOOP)*, 2001. To appear, preprint version: see ASPECTJ home page, www.aspectj.org.

11. C. Ko, G. Fink, and K. Levitt. Automated detection of vulnerabilities in privileged programs by execution monitoring. In *Proceedings of the Computer Security Application Conference*, 1994.

12. R. Lämmel. Declarative aspect-oriented programming. In *Partial Evaluation and Program Manipulation*, 1999.

13. U. Lindqvist and P. Porras. Detecting computer and network misuse through the production-based expert system toolset (P-BEST). In *Proceedings of the IEEE Symposium on Security and Privacy (SSP '99)*, pages 146–165. IEEE, May 1999.

14. W. De Meuter. Monads as a theoretical foundation for AOP.

15. A. Mounji. *Languages and Tools for Rule-Based Distributed Intrusion Detection*. PhD thesis, Université de Namur, 1997.

16. Amir Pnueli. The temporal logic of programs. In *Proceedings of the 18th IEEE Symposium on the Foundations of Computer Science (FOCS-77)*, pages 46–57. IEEE, 31– 2 1977.

17. P. Tarr and H. L. Ossher. HYPER/J user and installation manual. Technical report, IBM Corp., 2000.

A   Haskell implementation of a DSL for crosscutting

```haskell
type Event = (String, Int)
type Crosscut = [Event]

data Pattern =
          Return Crosscut
        | Bind (Crosscut -> Pattern)
        | Seq Pattern Pattern
        | Filter (Event -> Bool) Pattern
        | Abort
        | Par Pattern Pattern
        | First Pattern

step :: Pattern -> Pattern
step (Return e 'Seq' (Bind f))        = f e                              -- R2
step (Abort 'Seq' p2)                 = Abort                            -- R3
step (p1 'Seq' First p2)              = First (p1 'Seq' p2)              -- R9
step (First Abort)                    = Abort                            -- R10
step (First (Return e))               = Return e                         -- R11
step (First (Return e 'Par' p2))      = Return e                         -- R12
step (First p)                        = First (step p)        -- propagate
step (Return [e] 'Seq' Filter pred p2) =
            if (pred e) then p2                                          -- R13
                      else Filter pred (Return [e] 'Seq' p2)            -- R13
step (Filter pred Abort)              = Abort                            -- R14
step (Filter pred (Return e))         = Return e                         -- R15
step (Filter pred (Return e 'Par' p2)) = Return e 'Par' Filter pred p2   -- R16
step (Filter pred p)                  = Filter pred (step p) -- propagate
step (p1 'Seq' (p2 'Par' p3))         = (p1 'Seq' p2) 'Par' (p1 'Seq' p3) -- R6
step ((p1 'Par' p2) 'Seq' p3)         = (p1 'Seq' p3) 'Par' (p2 'Seq' p3) -- R7
step (p1 'Seq' (p2 'Seq' p3))         = step ((p1 'Seq' p2) 'Seq' p3)    -- R1
step ((p1 'Par' p2) 'Par' p3)         = p1 'Par' (p2 'Par' p3)           -- R4
step (Return e 'Par' p2)              = Return e 'Par' p2                -- R5
step (p1 'Par' Return e)              = Return e 'Par' p1                -- R5
step (p1 'Par' (Return e 'Par' p2))   = Return e 'Par' (p1 'Par' p2)     -- R5
step (Abort 'Par' p2) = p2                                               -- R8
step (p1 'Par' Abort) = p1                                               -- R8
step (p1 'Seq' p2)                    = step p1 'Seq' step p2
step (p1 'Par' p2)                    = step p1 'Par' step p2
step (Return e)                       = Return e
step (Bind f)                         = Bind f
step (Abort)                          = Abort

run :: Program -> Monitor -> [Crosscut]
run Over           _          = []
run (Cont program) (M monitor) = let (event,program') = program ()
                                     (crosscuts,monitor') = monitor event
                                 in crosscuts ++ (run program' monitor')
```

```
run' :: Pattern -> String -> [Crosscut]
run' p s = run (program s) (monitor p)


data Program = Over | Cont (() -> (Event,Program))

program :: String -> Program
program s = program' s 1

program' :: String -> Int -> Program
program' ""     _ = Over
program' (c:cs) n = Cont (\() -> (([c],n), program' cs (n+1)))


data Monitor = M (Event -> ([Crosscut],Monitor))

monitor :: Pattern -> Monitor
monitor p = M (\event -> let p' = reduce (Return [event] `Seq` p)
                         in (getReturns p', monitor (removeReturns p')))

reduce :: Pattern -> Pattern
reduce p = fixPoint step p
        where fixPoint f x = if (f x == x) then x else fixPoint f (f x)


removeReturns :: Pattern -> Pattern
removeReturns (Return _)       = loop where loop = Bind (\e -> loop)
removeReturns (p1 `Par` p2)    = removeReturns p1 `Par` removeReturns p2
removeReturns (p)              = p

getReturns :: Pattern -> [Crosscut]
getReturns (Return e)          = [e]
getReturns (p1 `Par` p2)       = getReturns p1 ++ getReturns p2
getReturns _                   = []

next :: String -> Pattern
next s = Bind (\[e]-> if (isName s e) then Return [e] else next s)

isName :: String -> Event -> Bool
isName n (n',_) = n==n'

billingNSTest = run' billingNS "ccscsscs"
-- [[("c",2),("s",3)],[("c",4),("s",5)],[("c",1),("s",6)],[("c",7),("s",8)]]

billingNS = next "c"                  `Seq` Bind (\[e1] ->
        billingNS' e1 billingNS)

billingNS' e1 k =
        First (next "c" `Par` next "s") `Seq` Bind (\[e2] ->
        if (isName "s" e2)
                then Return [e1,e2] `Par` k
                else  billingNS' e2 (billingNS' e1 k))
```

Process-Algebraic Foundations of Aspect-Oriented Programming

James H. Andrews

Dept. of Computer Science, Univ. of Western Ontario
London, Ontario, CANADA N6A 5B7
andrews@csd.uwo.ca

Abstract. Process algebras are proposed as a foundation for aspect-oriented programming. A particular process algebra is described, and programs illustrating its use in programming are given. It is argued that the framework clarifies the notion of equivalence between programs and correctness of aspect-weaving algorithms. The question of which notion of equivalence is most appropriate is discussed from theoretical and practical points of view. An aspect-weaving algorithm is presented and proven correct. A simple imperative aspect-oriented language is presented and translated into the given process algebra.

"The Analytical Engine weaves Algebraical patterns just as the Jacquard loom weaves flowers and leaves." – Ada Augusta, Countess of Lovelace

1 Introduction

Aspect-oriented programming (AOP) offers the promise of "additive, rather than invasive, software development" [CG99]: development in which various aspects of the program can be considered and added one by one without wholesale modification of existing code. Approaches to AOP have been variously formulated and have borne various other names, such as "hyperslices" and "advanced separation of concerns". However, the general technique is the same: aspects are programmed separately and then combined into a single program, for instance by an intelligent compiler which "weaves together" the aspects into a single body of code. Recent examples of AOP languages include AspectJ [KLM+97] and Hyper/J [TOHJ99], in which statement-level and code-fragment-level weaving can be done.

1.1 Motivation of Formal Foundations

In current implementations, the role of the compiler as weaver of aspects is central to AOP. But how can we tell (or even define) whether the aspect-weaving that a compiler does is correct? One approach is to simply define the weaving algorithm used by a particular compiler as correct. This is ultimately unsatisfying, as it leaves open issues such as how to modify the algorithm to consistently

A. Yonezawa and S. Matsuoka (Eds.): REFLECTION 2001, LNCS 2192, pp. 187–209, 2001.

incorporate new features, how to change features newly revealed to be undesirable, how to build one weaving algorithm based on another, what the merits of different weaving algorithms are, and what the intended behaviour of the final program is "supposed" to be. Analogous questions would arise with approaches to implementing AOP not using an aspect-weaving compiler (for instance, using an aspect-enabled bytecode interpreter).

Another approach, then, is to define precisely the intended behaviour of aspect-oriented programs, the intended behaviour of final "woven" programs, and a notion of equivalence of behaviours; and then to argue (or even prove formally) that a particular compiler transforms a program in a manner consistent with this notion of equivalence.

Previous researchers [NCA99, Ski00] have approached the problem of defining the foundations of AOP. These approaches define the notion of aspect or concern, and associate with it sequences of actions in execution paths for the program. They then show how re-combination of the aspects works to build a single program.

1.2   Aspects and Process Algebras

In this paper, we show how process algebras [Mil80, Hoa85] tailored to the purpose can provide a formal foundation for such an action-sequence view of AOP. A process algebra consists of a definition of the syntax of a process term, together with rules for how a particular process term can evolve into another, performing an action. A computation by a process is a sequence of these evolution steps and the actions that are performed. The various syntactic operators for building up a process term represent various ways of extending and combining the behaviours of simpler process terms.

We take the view here that processes of a process algebra can be used to stand for aspects, and that combinations of processes can be used to stand for the re-combination of aspects[1]. There are two main advantages to this view. First, aspects, programs, and expected behaviour can be represented using a relatively small number of operators and simple rules. Second, when we link aspects to process algebras, we can tap into a rich literature of well-studied notions in process algebra in order to study issues like equivalence of programs and correctness of weaving algorithms.

The central metaphor of this view of AOP is tabulated in Fig. 1. A process represents an aspect, and a set of process definitions (associations of process names with processes) represents a program. The main function of an aspect-oriented program is represented by some "root" process made up of processes combined with a synchronization operator. Actions in the processes can represent variously sections of code, join points at which aspects synchronize, or communication between aspects via free variables in the action terms.

---

[1]   Note that this view should not be confused with representing aspects by operating-system-level processes or threads. Indeed, what we ultimately want in most cases is to get a single, monolithic program out of the separated and recombined aspects.

Aspect-oriented notion	Process algebra notion
Aspect/concern/hyperslice	Process
Program	Definitions of processes
Main function (recombination of aspects)	Processes combined with synchronization into a root process
Section of code	Unsynchronized action
Synchronization at join points	Processes taking the same synchronized action
Communication between aspects	Processes taking the same synchronized action with unbound variables
Aspect weaving	Transformation of a program and a root process to eliminate synchronization

Fig. 1. The central metaphor mapping aspect-oriented notions to process-algebra notions

Finally, in this metaphor, the activity of weaving aspects into a finished program corresponds to an algorithm which systematically *removes* all synchronization operators from the program, resulting in an equivalent program without synchronization. To do this, the algorithm must interleave actions of the process-algebraic terms in a manner reminiscent of Ada Lovelace's famous description of the Analytical Engine as "weaving algebraical patterns".

This paper expands on and solidifies this metaphor. Our purpose is to show that process algebra can supply a foundation which resolves such issues as correctness of weaving algorithms. We would eventually like to see this work applied to existing aspect-oriented languages and to the design of new languages; however, we leave this to future work.

The remainder of this paper is organized as follows. Section 2 presents the syntax and operational semantics of the process algebra which we propose as a possible foundation for AOP. Section 3 discusses the central notion of equivalence, and presents some useful equivalences between processes. Section 4 describes a weaving algorithm, based on the equivalences, which eliminates synchronization operators from programs. Section 5 completes the bridge to aspect-oriented programming by defining a simple imperative aspect-oriented language, and showing how programs in that language could be translated into the process algebra used in this paper. Section 6 discusses related work, and Section 7 presents conclusions and suggestions for future directions.

2   Process Language

The language we study here is based on the subset of the CSP process algebra [Hoa85] with prefixing, synchronization on a set, and external choice. We tailor this language to our purpose by using terms as actions, and adding an existential quantifier for introducing variables and an *if* construct for conditional choice; these additions will be important in allowing us to perform the weaving operation. (*Terms* in the language are just first order terms, built up from variables and constants in the usual manner using function symbols of given arities.) We have chosen these features in an attempt to find the smallest set that will allow us to do everything we want to do.

In this section, we first describe the syntax and behaviour of the process algebra we will consider, give more detail about the form of sets of terms used in the language, and then give some examples of aspect-oriented programs written using it.

2.1   Syntax and Behaviour

The syntax and informal meanings of processes is as follows.

- *nil* is the process which can do nothing[2].
- $p[t_1, \ldots, t_n]$, where p is a process identifier and the t_is are terms, is a reference to a defined process (see below; analogous to a function call with its actual parameters). (We sometimes write, e.g., $\vec{t}$ for $t_1, \ldots, t_n$ when the number of elements in the list is not important.)
- $t{-}{>}P$, where t is a term (standing for an action) and P is a process, is the process which can perform a t action and then act like the process P.
- $P \Box Q$, where P and Q are processes, is the process which can (nondeterministically) behave either like P or like Q. Two or more nondeterministic processes combined with the synchronization operator can effectively become deterministic.
- $\exists x.P$, where P is a process, is the equivalent of the infinite sum $P[x := t_1] \Box P[x := t_2] \Box P[x := t_3] \cdots$, where $t_1, t_2, t_3, \ldots$ is the enumeration of all the ground terms.
- *if* (*c*) *then* P *else* Q is the process that can act like P if the condition c is true, and otherwise act like Q. c here is a *constraint* of the form $s = t$, $s \in S$, or $\neg c'$, where s and t are terms, S is a set of terms, and c' is a constraint. Equality constraints are interpreted consistent with Clark's Equality Theory, CET [Cla78]; that is, two terms are equal iff they are syntactically identical.
- $P \,|S|\, Q$, where P and Q are processes and S is a set of terms, is the process which can do the actions of P and Q interleaved, except that any action in the set S must be taken jointly at the same time by the two processes. Here S is referred to as the *synchronization set* or *sync set*. For instance, $(a{-}{>}nil \Box b{-}{>}nil)|\{a, b, c\}|(b{-}{>}nil \Box c{-}{>}nil)$ is the process which can do only the action b, since that is the only action in the sync set which both of the subprocesses can take. We assume that $|S|$ associates to the right; that is, that $P \,|S|\, Q \,|T|\, R$ is parsed as $P \,|S|\, (Q \,|T|\, R)$.

---

[2] We use the CCS-style *nil* rather than the CSP-style *STOP* here to avoid confusion concerning what the effective "end" of the program is; see Sect. 4.2.

Action:
$$\frac{}{t{-}{>}P \xrightarrow{t} P}$$

$\exists$:
$$\frac{P[x := s] \xrightarrow{t} P'}{\exists x.P \xrightarrow{t} P'}$$

where s is a ground term

If/1:
$$\frac{\vdash c \quad P \xrightarrow{t} P'}{if \ c \ then \ P \ else \ Q \xrightarrow{t} P'}$$

If/2:
$$\frac{\vdash \neg c \quad Q \xrightarrow{t} Q'}{if \ c \ then \ P \ else \ Q \xrightarrow{t} Q'}$$

$\square$/1:
$$\frac{P \xrightarrow{t} P'}{P \square Q \xrightarrow{t} P'}$$

$\square$/2:
$$\frac{Q \xrightarrow{t} Q'}{P \square Q \xrightarrow{t} Q'}$$

Defined:
$$\frac{P[\vec{x} := \vec{s}] \xrightarrow{t} P'}{p[\vec{s}] \xrightarrow{t} P'}$$

Sync/1:
$$\frac{P \xrightarrow{t} P' \quad Q \xrightarrow{t} Q' \quad \vdash t \in S}{(P \ |S| \ Q) \xrightarrow{t} (P' \ |S| \ Q')}$$

where $(p[\vec{x}] = P)$ is in $\mathcal{P}$

Sync/2:
$$\frac{P \xrightarrow{t} P' \quad \vdash t \notin S}{(P \ |S| \ Q) \xrightarrow{t} (P' \ |S| \ Q)}$$

Sync/3:
$$\frac{Q \xrightarrow{t} Q' \quad \vdash t \notin S}{(P \ |S| \ Q) \xrightarrow{t} (P \ |S| \ Q')}$$

Fig. 2. Operational semantics of processes. See Fig. 3 for the rules for constraints, of the form $\vdash c$

A *process definition (defining p)* is an expression of the form $p[x_1, \ldots, x_n] = P$, where p is a process identifier, the x_is are distinct variables (formal parameters), and P is a process having no free variables not in $x_1, \ldots, x_n$. A *(process) program* is a collection of process definitions defining distinct process names. Generally we will omit mention of the program when its existence can be assumed.

The formal operational semantics of processes is given by rules for the $\rightarrow$ relation in Fig. 2, which is a relation between two processes and a term. Intuitively, $P \xrightarrow{t} P'$ if process P can do an action t and evolve into process P'. Figure 3 shows the rules for deciding when a constraint is true.

2.2 Sets

We have expressed the operational semantics so that sets in the set membership constraints $(s \in S)$ and the synchronization processes $(P \ |S| \ Q)$ can be any set of ground terms. However, for the implementation of our formalism, we have found it convenient to restrict the form of sets used; this restricted form will be used throughout the rest of the paper. Here we explain the restricted form in more detail.

A *set* is a finite collection of *patterns*. The collection of patterns is the smallest collection such that:

$=:$ $$\overline{\vdash (t = t)}$$ $\neq:$ $$\overline{\vdash \neg(s = t)}$$

where s and t are non-identical terms

$\in:$ $$\overline{\vdash (t \in S)}$$ $\notin:$ $$\overline{\vdash \neg(t \in S)}$$

where t is in the set S where t is not in the set S

$\neg\neg:$ $$\frac{\vdash c}{\vdash \neg\neg c}$$

Fig. 3. Proof rules for constraints. All terms are assumed to be ground

- *any*, or equivalently "*_*", is a pattern.
- If f is a function symbol and $p_1, \ldots, p_n$ are patterns, for $n \geq 0$, then $f(p_1, \ldots, p_n)$ is a pattern.

Note that the second form of pattern encompasses constant patterns, which are nullary function symbols applied to 0 patterns.

We say that a term *matches* a pattern in the following situations.

- Any term matches *any*.
- The term $f(t_1, \ldots, t_n)$ matches the pattern $f(p_1, \ldots, p_n)$ if t_i matches p_i for all i, $1 \leq i \leq n$.
- Otherwise, the term does not match the pattern; i.e., $f(t_1, \ldots, t_n)$ does not match $g(p_1, \ldots, p_m)$ if either f is not g, n is not m, or some s_i does not match p_i.

A term is considered to be in a set if it matches one of the patterns in the set. Thus, examples of sets, with the notation we use for them, are: $\{c\}$, the set containing only the constant c; $\{f(\_), g(f(\_), \_)\}$, the set containing all terms of the form $f(s)$ or $g(f(s), t)$, for any terms s, t; and $\{\}$, the empty set.

Other implementations of CSP and related formalisms have used other approaches to defining sets. In the Concurrency Workbench of North Carolina [CPS93], a set is any finite list of identifiers, or any intersection, union or difference of sets. In Machine Readable CSP [Sca98], users can define a much richer range of sets, including sets of terms satisfying a given boolean expression. Our sets are intermediate in expressiveness between these approaches, and have been sufficient for our purposes so far.

2.3 Examples

As a first example, consider the program in Fig. 4, part of a hypothetical program for controlling a microwave oven. The process *button*[ ] defines the behaviour of the on/off button, which either locks the door and turns the oven on, or turns the oven off and unlocks the door. This definition encapsulates the aspect

Definitions:

$$button[\,] = \quad lock(door) \text{--} > turn(on) \text{--} > button[\,]$$
$$\square\ turn(\mathit{off}) \text{--} > unlock(door) \text{--} > button[\,]$$
$$seq[\,] \quad = \quad turn(on) \text{--} > turn(\mathit{off}) \text{--} > seq[\,]$$

Root:

$$button[\,]$$
$$|\{turn(\_)\}|$$
$$seq[\,]$$

Fig. 4. The microwave oven program, MWAVE

saying that the button can do one of two things, while abstracting away the aspect concerning the sequence in which those things can be done. The process $seq[\,]$ similarly encapsulates the aspect saying that the sequence of turning the oven on and off must follow the pattern $on, \mathit{off}, on, \mathit{off}, \ldots$. The root process (the "main program", as far as we are concerned) combines the two processes, insisting on synchronization on all actions of the form $turn(\_)$. Because of the synchronization between the two processes, the only infinite sequence of actions that the entire program can engage in is the one consisting of repetitions of the sequence $lock(door), turn(on), turn(\mathit{off}), unlock(door)$.

Figure 5 shows HW and HWR, two versions of a more complex program, corresponding to the option-processing task cited by Carver as a model task for separation of concerns [Car00]. The two programs have identical process definitions but different root processes. The program HW takes no options; it prints the message "hello world". The program HWR takes one option, "rev" (for "reverse"); it prints the message "hello world" if the option is not set, and "world hello" if it is. Both versions print a usage message and terminate if an invalid option is specified by the user. The actions and their corresponding intended meanings are described in Fig. 6.

Note that the only difference between the programs is that the *revopt* process has been added to HWR and a larger sync set is used to synchronize the *choice* process with the rest of the processes. However, the *revopt* process has effected both additive and substitutive changes to the program. Consider the following traces (sequences of actions):

1. *endopt, mode(reg), write(hello), write(world), end*
2. *opt(verbose), invalid(verbose), usage, end*
3. *opt(verbose), invalid(verbose), usage, write(revValidOpt), end*
4. *opt(rev), invalid(rev), usage, end*
5. *opt(rev), valid(rev), endopt, mode(alt), write(world), write(hello), end*

Trace 1 is a trace of both the HW and the HWR program, indicating that both can operate in regular mode without options. Traces 2 and 3, of the HW and HWR programs respectively, show that the (undefined) *verbose* option is rejected by both processes, but that HWR adds to its usage message the information that

Definitions:

$$choice[\,] \quad = \quad \exists x.opt(x)\text{–>}invalid(x)\text{–>}usage\text{–>}end\text{–>}nil$$
$$\Box\ \exists x.opt(x)\text{–>}valid(x)\text{–>}choice[\,]$$
$$\Box\ endopt\text{–>}mode(reg)\text{–>}write(hello)\text{–>}write(world)\text{–>}end$$
$$\text{–>}nil$$
$$\Box\ endopt\text{–>}mode(alt)\text{–>}end\text{–>}nil$$
$$invalidOpt[\,] \quad = \quad \exists x.invalid(x)\text{–>}invalidOpt[\,]$$
$$regularMode[\,] = \quad mode(reg)\text{–>}regularMode[\,]$$
$$revopt[val] \quad = \quad valid(rev)\text{–>}revopt[yes]$$
$$\Box\ usage\text{–>}write(revValidOpt)\text{–>}end\text{–>}nil$$
$$\Box\ if\ (val = yes)\ then$$
$$(mode(alt)\text{–>}write(world)\text{–>}write(hello)\text{–>}end\text{–>}nil)$$
$$else\ (mode(reg)\text{–>}end\text{–>}nil)$$

HW Root:

$$choice[\,]$$
$$|\{valid(\_), invalid(\_), mode(\_)\}|$$
$$invalidOpt[\,]$$
$$|\{\}|$$
$$regularMode[\,]\ )$$

HWR Root:

$$choice[\,]$$
$$|\{valid(\_), invalid(\_), mode(\_), usage, end\}|$$
$$revopt[no]$$
$$|\{invalid(rev), mode(reg)\}|$$
$$invalidOpt[\,]$$
$$|\{\}|$$
$$regularMode[\,]$$

Fig. 5. HW and HWR, two versions of the hello-world program

Action	Intended meaning
$opt(x)$	Read option x from the command line
$endopt$	Reach the end of the option list
end	Reach the end of program execution
$valid(x)$	Decide internally that x is a valid option
$invalid(x)$	Decide internally that x is an invalid option
$mode(x)$	Decide internally on the program mode (reg or alt)
$usage$	Print a usage message
$write(x)$	Write a constant

Fig. 6. The intended meanings of the actions in the HW and HWR programs

rev is a valid option. Trace 4 is a trace only of the HW program, which rejects *rev* as also being invalid. Trace 5 is a trace only of the HWR program, showing that the *revopt* process has the effect of changing the behaviour of the program to deciding that *rev* is valid and printing a different message to the user ("world hello").

3   Equivalence

The precise notion of equivalence that we use is important to showing the correctness of our aspect-weaving algorithm. In this section, we argue that *trace equivalence* is the most appropriate notion of equivalence between programs for our purposes. We then show various classes of equivalences between processes which are useful to aspect weaving.

3.1   Trace Equivalence and Bisimilarity

We extend the standard notion of trace equivalence to account for free variables in processes. A sequence $t_1, t_2, \ldots, t_n$ of terms is a *trace* of a process P (with respect to a program $\mathcal{P}$) if there are processes $P_0 (= P), P_1, P_2, \ldots, P_n$ such that $P_{i-1} \xrightarrow{t_i} P_i$ wrt $\mathcal{P}$ for every i, $1 \leq i \leq n$. Two processes P, Q are *trace equivalent* (with respect to a program $\mathcal{P}$), in symbols $P \cong Q$, if for every grounding substitution θ, every trace of $P\theta$ wrt $\mathcal{P}$ is a trace of $Q\theta$ wrt $\mathcal{P}$ and vice versa.

Trace equivalence is a simple and intuitive notion of equivalence, but has been criticized as too weak. Consider the two processes $a{-}{>}(b{-}{>}nil \square c{-}{>}nil)$ and $(a{-}{>}b{-}{>}nil)\square(a{-}{>}c{-}{>}nil)$. The first retains the capability of taking action b after taking action a, but the second (depending on the choice made for the $\square$ operator) might not retain that capability. The notion of *bisimilarity* [Par81, Mil90] does not consider these processes equivalent, insisting that two bisimilar processes each be able to simulate the actions of the other step by step.

However, we believe that trace equivalence is more appropriate for our purposes than bisimilarity. In the context of writing a program, users would almost certainly like the aspect weaver eventually to *transform* a section of code of the form $(a{-}{>}b{-}{>}nil)\square(a{-}{>}c{-}{>}nil)$ into the more capable code $a{-}{>}(b{-}{>}nil \square c{-}{>}nil)$; thus they would prefer that the transformation algorithm *not* preserve bisimilarity. We therefore employ equivalences in our aspect weaver such as that of $(P_1 \square P_2 \; |S| \; Q)$ with $(P_1 \; |S| \; Q) \; \square \; (P_2 \; |S| \; Q)$, which are valid under trace equivalence but not under bisimulation. If we require the final program to be maximally capable, then we could apply further transformations as described above to get a program which is trace-equivalent to, but more capable than, the result of the weaving algorithm.

In order to use trace equivalence as a useful notion for transforming programs, we must show that subprocesses can be substituted by equivalent processes; that is, that trace equivalence is a congruence. Space does not permit us to show the proof here, but it follows the lines of the usual proofs in the literature.

3.2   Useful Equivalences

Specific equivalences of processes are used in our aspect-weaving algorithm in order to transform the program and root process into a trace-equivalent program and process without syncs. Here we highlight two of the most important classes of equivalences.

Sync Reduction Equivalences. The *sync reduction* equivalences, when applied as rewrite rules to subprocesses of a process, have the effect of pushing a synchronization operator lower in a process. These will be used for systematically reducing syncs to the simplest form possible.

1. $(nil \; |S| \; nil) \cong nil$
2. $(nil \; |S| \; t{-}{>}Q) \cong if \; (t \in S) \; then \; nil \; else \; t{-}{>}(nil \; |S| \; Q)$
3. $(t{-}{>}P \; |S| \; nil) \cong if \; (t \in S) \; then \; nil \; else \; t{-}{>}(P \; |S| \; nil)$
4. $((if \; c \; then \; P_1 \; else \; P_2) \; |S| \; Q) \cong if \; c \; then \; (P_1 \; |S| \; Q) \; else \; (P_2 \; |S| \; Q)$
5. $(\exists x.P \; |S| \; Q) \cong \exists x'.(P[x := x'] \; |S| \; Q)$
   where x' does not appear free in P, Q
6. $(P_1 \Box P_2 \; |S| \; Q) \cong (P_1 \; |S| \; Q) \Box (P_2 \; |S| \; Q)$
7. $(P \; |S| \; Q) \cong (Q \; |S| \; P)$ where Q is of the form $if \; c \; then \; Q_1 \; else \; Q_2, \; \exists x.Q_1,$
   or $Q_1 \Box Q_2$
8. $(s{-}{>}P \; |S| \; t{-}{>}Q) \cong if \; (s \in S) \; then$
   $$if \; (t \in S) \; then$$
   $$if \; (s = t) \; then$$
   $$t{-}{>}(P \; |S| \; Q)$$
   $$else \; nil$$
   $$else \; t{-}{>}(s{-}{>}P \; |S| \; Q)$$
   $$else \; if \; (t \in S) \; then$$
   $$s{-}{>}(P \; |S| \; t{-}{>}Q)$$
   $$else \; (s{-}{>}(P \; |S| \; t{-}{>}Q)) \Box (t{-}{>}(s{-}{>}P \; |S| \; Q))$$

Note here the role of the *if* operator, whose introduction has allowed us to push the sync operator lower in three cases.

We define an *irreducible* process $P \; |S| \; Q$ as one where either P or Q is a defined process call, and the other of P and Q is either *nil*, a defined process call, or a process of the form $t{-}{>}P'$. We define a *sync-reduced* process as one which has no sync operators, except in irreducible subprocesses. When the above equivalences are applied as rewrite rules in a left-to-right manner, they result in a trace-equivalent sync-reduced process.

Constraint Simplification Equivalences. The *constraint simplification* equivalences have the effect of cutting away branches of *if* processes that can never be reached due to enclosing *if*s. For instance, consider the process $if \; (x = a) \; then \; (if \; (x = b) \; then \; P \; else \; Q) \; else \; R$; because the variable x cannot be equal to both the constant a and the constant b, this process must be trace-equivalent to $if\ (x = a)\ then\ Q\ else R$. In this subsection, we define a function which generalizes this simplification operation in a constraint-based manner.

A substitution θ grounding a constraint c *satisfies* c if $\vdash c\theta$ is provable. A substitution θ grounding each constraint in a set C of constraints satisfies C if it satisfies each constraint in C. We say that $C \supset c$, in words "C implies c", if every substitution satisfying C also satisfies c. We say that two processes P, Q are *trace-equivalent with respect to* a constraint set C if for every grounding substitution θ satisfying C, $P\theta \cong Q\theta$.

The function $cs(C, P)$, returning a process, where C is a set of constraints and P is a process, is the least function satisfying the following.

1. $cs(C, nil) = nil$
2. $cs(C, t{\to}P) = t{\to}cs(C, P)$
3. $cs(C, if\ c\ then\ P\ else\ Q) = cs(C, P)$ if $C \supset c$
4. $cs(C, if\ c\ then\ P\ else\ Q) = cs(C, Q)$ if $C \supset \neg c$
5. $cs(C, if\ c\ then\ P\ else\ Q) = if\ c\ then\ cs(C \cup \{c\}, P)\ else\ cs(C \cup \{\neg c\}, Q)$ if neither $C \supset c$ nor $C \supset \neg c$
6. $cs(C, \exists x.P) = \exists x'.cs(C, P[x := x'])$ where x' does not appear free in C or P
7. $cs(C, P \Box Q) = cs(C, P) \Box cs(C, Q)$
8. $cs(C, P\ |S|\ Q) = cs(C, P)\ |S|\ cs(C, Q)$
9. $cs(C, p(\vec{t})) = p(\vec{t})$

Theorem 1. $cs(C, P)$ *is trace-equivalent to* P *with respect to* C.

Proof. By induction on the size of P. Cases are on the outermost operator and are straightforward. □

Corollary 1. $cs(\{\}, P) \cong P$.

We can thus replace any subprocess P in a process definition body by the equivalent process $cs(\{\}, P)$, in order to cut down on unreachable subprocesses. This turns out to be valuable to the weaving algorithm because many of the branches of the ifs generated by sync reduction are unreachable.

4   Aspect Weaving

Given our central metaphor, aspect-weaving corresponds to elimination of synchronization operators from a program. In this section, we give an algorithm for doing this, and prove its correctness. We show that it terminates in the absence of function symbols, and exhibit a program with function symbols for which it does not terminate. We have implemented our algorithm (in Prolog) and applied it to example programs with good preliminary results; in this section we also offer some discussion on this topic.

– While R contains a subprocess of the form $(P \,|S|\, Q)$, where P and Q contain no syncs:

1. Let p be a new process name. Let $\vec{x}$ be all the free variables of $(P \,|S|\, Q)$. Add a definition of $p[\vec{x}]$ with body $(P \,|S|\, Q)$ to $\mathcal{P}$, add a process equivalence $\langle p[\vec{x}], (P \,|S|\, Q) \rangle$ to E, and replace $(P \,|S|\, Q)$ in R by $p[\vec{x}]$.

2. While some process definition body in $\mathcal{P}$ contains a sync operator:
   (a) Replace each defined process call inside syncs in $\mathcal{P}$ by the corresponding bodies.
   (b) Apply the sync reduction equivalences.
   (c) Apply the constraint simplification equivalences.
   (d) For each remaining sync process within a process definition body, of the form $(P \,|S|\, Q)$:
       • If there is an equivalence $\langle p[\vec{x}], P' \rangle \in E$ such that $(P \,|S|\, Q)$ is $P'[\vec{x} := \vec{t}]$ for some $\vec{t}$, then replace the sync in the process body by $p[\vec{t}]$.
       • Otherwise, let p be a new process name. Let $\vec{x}$ be all the free variables of $(P \,|S|\, Q)$. Add a definition of $p[\vec{x}]$ with body $(P \,|S|\, Q)$ to $\mathcal{P}$, add a process equivalence $\langle p[\vec{x}], (P \,|S|\, Q) \rangle$ to E, and replace $(P \,|S|\, Q)$ in the process body by $p[\vec{x}]$.

Fig. 7. The aspect-weaving algorithm, given a program $\mathcal{P}$, a root process R, and a set E of defined process equivalences

4.1 Weaving Algorithm

The weaving algorithm is given a root process R and a program $\mathcal{P}$ not containing syncs, and must transform it into a root process R' not containing syncs and a program $\mathcal{P}'$ not containing syncs in process definition bodies. The algorithm can be extended straightforwardly to account for syncs in the original program.

The algorithm is assisted by a set of known equivalences. A *defined process equivalence* for a given program $\mathcal{P}$ is a pair $\langle P, Q \rangle$ of processes, in which P is of the form $p[\vec{x}]$, Q is a process containing no free variables not in $\vec{x}$, and for which $P \cong Q$ with respect to $\mathcal{P}$. A process equivalence is used to permanently record equivalences between defined processes and irreducible sync processes.

Given a program $\mathcal{P}$, root process R, and set E of defined process equivalences, the basic aspect-weaving algorithm is given in Fig. 7. (We omit mention of some other equivalence-based transformations included to reduce the size of the resulting program.) The algorithm repeatedly reduces syncs in process definition bodies, and defines new processes for each of the irreducible syncs in the bodies. When an old irreducible sync comes up again in a process body, it is replaced by an already-defined equivalent process (as remembered by the defined process equivalences). Figure 8 shows the result of this algorithm on the MWAVE program from Fig. 4; the final program is indeed trace-equivalent to the original but contains no syncs.

The algorithm does not always terminate, but we can prove it correct if it does.

Definitions:

$$Root001[\ ] = lock(door)\text{->}turn(on)\text{->}Sync002[\ ]$$
$$Sync002[\ ] = lock(door)\text{->}nil$$
$$\square\ turn(off)\text{->}Sync003[\ ]$$
$$Sync003[\ ] = unlock(door)\text{->}Root001[\ ]$$

Root: $Root001[\ ]$

Fig. 8. The result of the weaving algorithm applied to MWAVE

Theorem 2. *If the aspect-weaving algorithm terminates, then it transforms a root process R and program $\mathcal{P}$ into a process R' and $\mathcal{P}'$ such that the set of traces of R' wrt $\mathcal{P}'$ is the same as the set of traces of R wrt $\mathcal{P}$.*

Proof. At each transformation, the algorithm either adds harmless new definitions to the program, or replaces subprocesses in the root process or program by other trace-equivalent processes. ☐

When the language of terms t contains no function symbols other than a finite number of constants, then each process is equivalent to a nondeterministic finite automaton, and the process of weaving aspects is equivalent to finding the product of given automata. Therefore it is reassuring that our algorithm terminates in this case:

Theorem 3. *If the language of terms consists only of variables and a finite number of constants, then the aspect-weaving algorithm terminates.*

Proof (sketch). Let π be the set of process names in the program at the start of step 2 of the algorithm. The sync reduction step (2b) eliminates all syncs except those of the form $nil\ |S|\ q[\vec{t}]$ or of the form $(t_1\text{->}t_2\text{->}\ldots\text{->}t_n\text{->}p[\vec{s}])\ |S|\ q[\vec{t}]$, where $p, q \in \pi$. There is a bound on n, and this bound holds through each execution of step 2. However, there are a finite number of sync processes of the form $(t_1\text{->}t_2\text{->}\ldots\text{->}t_m\text{->}p[\vec{s}])\ |S|\ q[\vec{t}]$, where $m \le n$ and $p, q \in \pi$, and the loop in step 2 will terminate (at the latest) when all such processes get equivalent defined processes. Therefore the loop in step 2 always terminates, and therefore the whole algorithm terminates. ☐

However, our algorithm does not terminate for all programs. Consider the program consisting of the process definitions $p[x] = a\text{->}s(x)\text{->}p[s(x)]$ and $q[\ ] = a\text{->}q[\ ]$, and the root process $(p[0]\ |\{a\}|\ q[\ ])$. Then the algorithm successively creates new process definitions for processes equivalent to $(p[0]\ |\{a\}|\ q[\ ])$, $(p[s(0)]\ |\{a\}|\ q[\ ])$, $(p[s(s(0))]\ |\{a\}|\ q[\ ])$, etc. We discuss this problem below.

4.2 Dead Trace Elimination

Given a program, we may find in transforming it that certain undesirable traces are reproduced in the final, transformed program. For instance, the original

MWAVE program can follow the trace *lock(door)*, *turn(on)*, *lock(door)*, ending in the blocked process

$$(turn(on).button[\ ]|\{turn(\_)\}|turn(off).seq[\ ])$$

The problematic trace is faithfully reproduced by the result of the weaving algorithm shown in Fig. 8.

We therefore define a *dead trace* as a trace which does not end in the distinguished action *end*. (We thus reserve *end* for the situation in which a program may make a deliberate decision to terminate). We can eliminate dead traces from our program by repeatedly replacing a process of the form $t{-}{>}nil$, where t is not *end*, by *nil*.

The resulting program is *not* trace-equivalent to the original program, since we have lost possible traces. Nevertheless, we have found that the program with dead traces eliminated is often closer to the intended behaviour of our program than the original transformed program.

4.3   Discussion

We have implemented the given algorithm and obtained good preliminary results. The algorithm finds programs with no syncs equivalent to the MWAVE, HW, and HWR programs, and several other small programs.

Whether the algorithm scales or not is an open question; clearly it is possible to get an exponential blowup in the size of the program, due to the well known state space explosion problem. Another open question is whether we can find a weaving algorithm which terminates on all inputs. This may be impossible due to reduction to some undecidable problem such as the word problem[3].

However, we should recall that we are trying to model and provide a basis for the task of separating and recombining aspects in the creation of a program, a task that is already being performed by compilers. It may well be that the aspects used in typical aspect-oriented programming do not tend to lead to exponential blowup or non-termination. We may also find that it is reasonable for the aspect-weaving algorithm to report failure of the weaving process when some time or space bound has been reached. As is often the case, theory and practice must interact in order to come to a fuller understanding of what the important issues are.

5   Translation of Imperative Aspect-Oriented Programs

In this section, we directly relate the process language which we have analyzed to a simple imperative aspect-oriented language, by giving a translation from imperative programs to process programs. We argue that giving such a translation clarifies certain issues in the implementation of the aspect-oriented language.

---

[3] Thanks to Sheng Yu for pointing out this possibility.

$\langle program \rangle$ ::= $\{\langle procDefn \rangle\} * [\langle aDefn \rangle]*$
$\langle procDefn \rangle$ ::= $p(\langle var \rangle, \ldots, \langle var \rangle)$ "{" $\langle stmtList \rangle$ "}"
$\langle stmtList \rangle$ ::= ϵ empty list
             | $\langle stmt \rangle$; $\langle stmtList \rangle$ statements
$\langle stmt \rangle$ ::= $\langle var \rangle := \langle term \rangle$ assignment
             | $p(\langle var \rangle, \ldots, \langle var \rangle)$ procedure call
             | if ($\langle constr \rangle$) then $\langle stmtList \rangle$ else $\langle stmtList \rangle$ if-then-else
             | match ($\langle term \rangle := \langle term \rangle$) then $\langle stmtList \rangle$ match
               else $\langle stmtList \rangle$
             | while ($\langle constr \rangle$) do $\langle stmtList \rangle$ while loop
$\langle adefn \rangle$ ::= before call($p(\langle var \rangle, \ldots, \langle var \rangle)$) $\langle stmtList \rangle$ before advice
             | after   call($p(\langle var \rangle, \ldots, \langle var \rangle)$) $\langle stmtList \rangle$ after advice
             | around call($p(\langle var \rangle, \ldots, \langle var \rangle)$) $\langle stmtList \rangle$ around advice

Fig. 9. Syntax of IAO, the imperative aspect-oriented language to be translated

Work on translating imperative programs to processes dates back to Milner's original book [Mil80]; a recent example (using the π-calculus to model a concurrent language) is [RS99]. These approaches generally represent variables by standalone processes, because the process languages on which they are based have no explicit variables. Because our language does have variables (introduced via the $\exists$ operator), the variables of the imperative language can be translated directly into (sequences of) variables in the process language. Our translation is thus similar in some respects to translations of imperative languages into logic programming languages, dating back to Clark and van Emden [CvE81].

We first present the syntax of a simple imperative aspect-oriented language, and then explore the translation of each of the syntactic constructs of the language into processes and process definitions in the process language. We end with a discussion of the significance of the translation.

5.1   Syntax of IAO Programs

Here we give a syntax for the programs, procedure definitions and aspect definitions for the imperative aspect-oriented language we will translate. This language will be referred to as IAO (Imperative Aspect-Oriented) in order to distinguish it from the process programs used in the main body of this paper.

Figure 9 gives the syntax of IAO programs. A program is a non-empty list of procedure definitions $\langle procDefn \rangle$, possibly followed by a list of aspect definitions $\langle aDefn \rangle$. Procedure definitions and statements are in standard format, except for the match statement (see below). An aspect definition associates "advice" with a given procedure call, in the style of AspectJ [KLM+97]; advice can be "before" advice (code to be executed before the procedure call), "after" advice (code to be executed after the procedure call), or "around" advice (code which may replace the procedure call).

Because we are working with a simple language of first order terms, we must have a facility for extracting subterms from bound variables. The match statement allows us to do this. match ($t_1 := t_2$) then Z_1 else Z_2 binds all free variables in t_1; if t_1 can be matched with t_2, the statement does so and executes the statement sequence Z_1, and otherwise it executes Z_2. By "matching", we mean assigning all free variables in t_1 whatever values will cause t_1 to be equal to t_2. For instance, if x is bound to the term $g(a, b)$, then the statement match $(g(y, z) := x)$ then Z_1 else Z_2 will bind y to a and z to b, and then execute Z_1.

For simplicity, we make some assumptions about the language which do not significantly decrease its expressivity. All parameters in procedure calls are distinct variables; parameters are passed by reference. A procedure can call only a procedure declared earlier in the program. Thus, no recursion is possible, though while loops are possible, making the language Turing-complete. The last procedure defined is the main procedure. Without loss of generality we assume that this last procedure's name is main, and has no arguments. Finally, we allow only one piece of advice in an aspect, although different aspects may apply to the same procedure.

5.2   Translation

Here we give details of the translation of each of the elements of IAO into processes and process programs.

The process representing a given program consists of a process corresponding to the original primary code, with processes corresponding to each aspect layered above it, and a final "caller" process at the top of the stack (see Fig. 10). Each aspect layer i communicates with the layer below it via synchronization on terms of the form $call(i-1, t)$ and $return(i-1, t)$, and with the layer above via synchronization on $call(i, t)$ and $return(i, t)$. The subterm t in these terms represents a procedure call. Essentially, each aspect translates lower-level calls and returns into higher-level calls and returns, adding its own code around the aspect code. The top-level caller then makes the "base calls" that actually run the procedures in the primary code.

We first describe the top-level translation of an imperative program, and then describe the translations of a procedure definition into a process definition, a list of statements into a process, and an aspect definition to a process. Finally, we describe the top-level caller.

Top-Level Translation. The top-level translation of an imperative program I with procedure definitions $D_1, \ldots, D_n$ (defining procedures $p_1, \ldots, p_n$) and aspects $A_1, \ldots, A_m$ is as follows. (All $[\![\ldots]\!]$ constructs will be defined below.)

- The program associated with I is the process program $pdpd[\![D_1]\!]$, $\ldots, pdpd[\![D_n]\!]$, with, in addition, any other process definitions made during the course of the translation, as described below.
- The root process associated with I is the process

$$(\ldots ((primary|S_0|adp[\![A_1, 1]\!])|S_1|adp[\![A_2, 2]\!]) \ldots$$
$$\ldots |S_{m-1}|adp[\![A_m, m]\!])|T|caller[\ ]$$

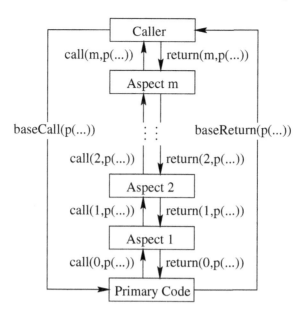

Fig. 10. Schematic diagram of the translation of an aspect-oriented program

where:
- *primary* is the process $(p_1[\ ]|\{\}|p_2[\ ]|\{\}|\dots|\{\}|p_n[\ ])$, which runs in parallel all of the processes associated with the procedure definitions;
- S_i is the set $\{call(i, \_), return(i, \_)\}$, for $0 \le i \le m-1$;
- $adp[\![A_i, i]\!]$, defined below, is the process representing aspect i of the original program; and
- T is the set $\{call(m, \_), return(m, \_), baseCall(\_), baseReturn(\_)\}$, representing the messages on which the *caller*[ ] process (defined below) synchronizes with the top-level aspect and the primary code.

The process associated with the primary code thus consists of one process associated with each of the procedures. When these processes want to "call" the procedures associated with other processes, they take the action $call(0, p(\vec{x}))$ to initiate the call, followed by $return(0, p(\vec{y}))$ in order to retrieve the return values. The calls rise up the stack of aspects, ultimately causing base calls back to some other process in the primary code; the returns repeat this action in reverse.

***pdpd*: Procedure Definition to Process Definition.** We will translate each definition of a procedure p into a definition of a process $p[\ ]$, which starts with an action of the form $baseCall(p(\vec{x}))$ and ends with an action of the form $baseReturn(p(\vec{y}))$ before looping to handle the next call.

The translation $pdpd[\![D]\!]$ of a procedure definition D of the form $p(\vec{x}) \{Z\}$ is the process definition

$$p[\ ] = \exists\vec{x}(baseCall(p(\vec{x}))\text{->}[\![Z, 0, (baseReturn(p(\vec{x}))\text{->}p[\ ])]\!])$$

where $[\![Z, i, P]\!]$ (as defined below) is the process which executes the code in Z at level i of the aspect stack, and then becomes process P. Thus, the definition is a process which endlessly loops, fielding base calls to the procedure and sending base returns back. Note that p here is overloaded (without loss of generality) as a procedure name, a process name and a function symbol.

Note also that this process will call other procedures by $call(0, \ldots)$ actions. Procedures are restricted to not being recursive because while the process is in the middle of fielding a base call, it cannot field another base call to itself until it has finished processing the original one.

Statement List to Process. $[\![Z, i, P]\!]$, the translation of a statement list Z into a process at level i of the stack with final process P, is as follows.

- $[\![\epsilon, i, P]\!]$ is the process P.
- $[\![(x := t; Z), i, P]\!]$ is the process $\exists x'(if\ (x' = t)\ then\ [\![Z', i, P']\!]\ else\ nil)$ where x' is a fresh variable name, Z' is Z with x replaced by x', and P' is P with x replaced by x'.
- $[\![(p(\vec{x}); Z), i, P]\!]$ is the process
  $$call(i, p(\vec{x})) {-}{>} \exists \vec{y}(return(i, p(\vec{y})) {-}{>} [\![Z', i, P']\!])$$
  where $\vec{y}$ are fresh, Z' is Z with $\vec{x}$ replaced by $\vec{y}$, and P' is P with $\vec{x}$ replaced by $\vec{y}$.
- $[\![((if(c)\ then\ Z_1\ else\ Z_2); Z_3), i, P]\!]$ is the process $if(c)\ then\ [\![(Z_1; Z_3), i, P]\!]$ $else\ [\![(Z_2; Z_3), i, P]\!]$.
- $[\![((while(c)\ do\ Z_1); Z_2), i, P]\!]$ is the defined process call $q[\vec{x}]$, where: $\vec{x}$ are all the free variables of c, Z_1, Z_2 and P; q is a fresh process name; and $q[\vec{x}]$ is defined as the process $if(c)\ then\ [\![Z_1, i, (q[\vec{x}])]\!]\ else\ [\![Z_2, i, P]\!]$.

As an example of this translation, consider a procedure `mult` for multiplying two Peano numerals (terms of the form 0 or $s(N)$, where N is a Peano numeral). This procedure can be implemented as follows; we assume that the procedure call `addto(z, y)` adds the value of y to z, and the procedure call `decr(x)` decreases the value of x.

```
mult(x, y, z) = {
  z := 0;
  while (!(x = 0)) {
    addto(z, y);
    decr(x);
  }
}
```

The translation of this IAO program into a process program would be:

$$mult[\ ] = \exists x, y, z(baseCall(mult(x, y, z)) {-}{>}$$
$$\exists z_1\ if(z_1 = 0)then\ (q[x, y, z_1])else\ nil)$$

where

$$q[x, y, z_1] = if(\neg(x = 0))\ then\ P\ else\ baseReturn(mult(x, y, z_1))$$

and P is the process
$$call(0, addto(z_1, y)) \rightarrow$$
$$\exists z_2, y_1 (return(0, addto(z_2, y_1)) \rightarrow$$
$$call(0, decr(x)) \rightarrow$$
$$\exists x_1 (return(0, decr(x_1)) \rightarrow$$
$$q[x_1, y_1, z_2]))$$

***adp*: Aspect Definition to Process.** $adp[\![A, i]\!]$, the translation of aspect A into a process at level i of the stack, is the process $a_i[\,]$, where $a_i[\,]$ is defined as follows.

- If A is of the form (**before** $call(p(\vec{x}))$ Z), then

$$a_i[\,] = \exists t (call(i-1, t) \rightarrow$$
$$\exists \vec{x} (if (t = p(\vec{x})) then [\![Z, i, (call(i, t) \rightarrow a_i[\,])]\!]$$
$$else(call(i, t) \rightarrow a_i[\,])))$$
$$\square \ \exists t (return(i, t) \rightarrow return(i-1, t) \rightarrow a_i[\,])$$

In other words, a_i is the process which passes on all calls to the layer above and all returns to the layer below, except calls to its focus procedure, which it handles by first executing the aspect code and then passing on the call.

- If A is of the form (**after** $call(p(\vec{x}))$ Z), then

$$a_i[\,] = \exists t (call(i-1, t) \rightarrow call(i, t) \rightarrow a_i[\,])$$
$$\square \ \exists t (return(i, t) \rightarrow$$
$$\exists \vec{x} (if (t = p(\vec{x})) then [\![Z, i, (return(i-1, t) \rightarrow a_i[\,])]\!]$$
$$else(return(i-1, t) \rightarrow a_i[\,])))$$

In other words, a_i is the process which passes on all calls to the layer above and all returns to the layer below, except returns from its focus procedure, which it handles by first executing the aspect code and then passing on the return.

- If A is of the form (**around** $call(p(\vec{x}))$ Z), then

$$a_i[\,] = \exists t (call(i-1, t) \rightarrow$$
$$\exists \vec{x} (if (t = p(\vec{x})) then [\![Z, i, (a_i[\,])]\!]$$
$$else(call(i, t) \rightarrow a_i[\,])))$$
$$\square \ \exists t (return(i, t) \rightarrow return(i-1, t) \rightarrow a_i[\,])$$

This process is identical to the **before** advice process, except that the process does not automatically pass on the focus procedure call to the layer above. If the aspect code wants to call the focus procedure, it can do so with a normal procedure call. This will be handled like any other procedure call in the aspect code (see discussion below).

Caller Process. The top-level caller process is $caller[\,]$, where the relevant definitions are:

$$caller[\,] \quad = baseCall(main)\!\!-\!\!>\!caller Aux[\,]$$
$$caller Aux[\,] = \exists t(call(m,t)\!\!-\!\!>\!baseCall(t)\!\!-\!\!>\!caller Aux[\,])$$
$$\quad\quad\quad\quad \square\; \exists t(baseReturn(t)\!\!-\!\!>$$
$$\quad\quad\quad\quad\quad\quad if(t = main())\; then\; (end.nil)$$
$$\quad\quad\quad\quad\quad\quad else\; (return(m,t)\!\!-\!\!>\!caller Aux[\,]))$$

where m is the number of aspects in the program.

Thus, the caller process does the initial base call to the main procedure of the program, and then goes into a loop of fielding calls from the last (topmost) aspect and passing them on as base calls, and fielding base returns and passing them on as returns to the last aspect. Finally, when it receives the base return from the main procedure, it terminates (does an "end" action and becomes nil).

5.3   Discussion

Here we discuss the significance of the translation given in this section, both as a proof of concept for the foundations of aspect-oriented languages and as a way of clarifying the semantics of the particular language given.

We have presented one possible semantics for an aspect-oriented imperative language. This semantics shows that an aspect-oriented program can be translated as a process-algebraic process representing the primary code, with processes representing aspects added to it non-invasively. Clearly the language is only one possible point in the space of AOP languages, but it does have the characteristics of such languages: a definition of join points (in IAO's case, points in the program text), a means of designating join points (by procedure name), and a means of affecting them (with the three types of advices). Whether the given semantics is the best one is a matter for opinion and discussion; many other approaches to the semantics of AOP are possible, even within the general framework of process algebra.

However, describing any semantics precisely has the effect of clarifying certain issues, and defining exactly what approach is taken to them. One issue clarified in the present semantics is what happens to procedure calls in advice code itself. If a call to some procedure p appears in an advice, it is not clear whether advice code for p in another aspect should be applied to it. This could result in recursive aspect code, if advice for p calls q and advice for q calls p. The given semantics handles this issue by essentially saying that the only advices applied to advice code in aspect k are advices in aspects $k + 1$ and later.

Another issue is what to do about multiple advices applied to the same procedure. What order do they go in, and how does **around** advice (which may never call the procedure in question) affect the application of **before** and **after** advice? The given semantics takes the view that later aspects are "closer" to the base call and return of the procedure. Thus, multiple **before** advices on the same procedure are executed in order, and multiple **after** advices are executed in reverse order. Since an **around** advice is free to execute a call to the focus procedure if the programmer so chooses, this call is treated as any other call – later advices can apply to it, but not previous advices. However, previous advices do surround the `around` advice code itself. Different policies could be implemented by modifying the semantics accordingly.

6   Related Work

We are not aware of any work related to the metaphor of aspects as process-algebraic processes. The work most closely related to ours is the following.

Architecture description languages (ADLs) such as Wright [AG94], also based on CSP, allow us to describe the high-level structure of a software system. Pict [PT97] is a programming language based on the pi-calculus (a successor process algebra to CCS). Neither ADLs nor Pict have, to our knowledge, been studied in the context of systematic transformation to eliminate synchronization.

Nelson, Cowan and Alencar [NCA99] and Skipper [Ski00] have both defined foundations for AOP based on sequences or trees of traces, with composition operators to define the precise ways in which aspects can be recombined. The present work can be seen as extending their work with notions such as □ nondeterminism, and relating it to the literature on process algebras in order to clarify notions of equivalence. It would be interesting to explore precise connections between our work and the previous work.

Finally, the original motivation for this work was the observation that a program in the language LFAL [AZ00], used for checking the results of tests on software, can be used to actually simulate the software it is intended to check. An LFAL program is essentially a process of a process algebra expressed as a collection of state machines. We chose a process algebra setting for the present work in order to make clearer the notion of equivalence of programs.

7   Conclusions and Future Work

We have shown that giving a process-algebraic foundation for aspect-oriented programming has several advantages, the chief one being the clarification of the notions of equivalence of processes and correctness of aspect-weaving algorithms. We have described a small language which allows us to express, in processes, a program with aspects and to recombine the aspects, and we have given a correct aspect-weaving algorithm which transforms such a program into a conventional one. Finally, we have given a translation from a simple imperative aspect-oriented language to the process language, in order to complete the bridge between our formalism and aspect-oriented languages.

Space has not permitted us to explore certain issues, such as the role of the external choice (□) operator in final, woven programs, or the precise constraint satisfaction algorithms used. We wish to explore these issues more fully in future work. Future work also includes more in-depth study of the properties of, and alternatives to, the weaving algorithm; exploration of the analysis of process programs with CSP analysis tools such as FDR; construction of an AOP language more practical than the simple syntax given here; and studying the precise relationships of process algebras to existing aspect-oriented languages.

Acknowledgements

Thanks to Homy Dayani-Fard, Lila Kari and Sheng Yu for interesting discussions on this work. Thanks also to Gregor Kiczales, Carolyn Talcott, and the anonymous referees for valuable corrections and suggestions. This research is supported by Natural Sciences and Engineering Research Council of Canada (NSERC) individual grant 203247-98.

References

AG94.   Robert Allen and David Garlan. Formalizing architectural connection. In *Proceedings of the Sixteenth International Conference on Software Engineering*, pages 71–80, Sorrento, Italy, May 1994.

AZ00.   James H. Andrews and Yingjun Zhang. Broad-spectrum studies of log file analysis. In *Proceedings of the 22nd International Conference on Software Engineering (ICSE 2000)*, Limerick, Ireland, June 2000.

Car00.   Lee Carver. A practical hyperspace application: Lessons from the option-processing task. In *Workshop on Multi-Dimensional Separation of Concerns in Software Development, ICSE 2000*, Limerick, Ireland, June 2000.

CG99.   Lee Carver and William G. Griswold. Sorting out concerns. In *First Workshop on Multi-Dimensional Separation of Concerns in Object-Oriented Systems (OOPSLA '99)*, Denver, Col., November 1999.

Cla78.   K. L. Clark. Negation as failure. In *Logic and Data Bases*, pages 293–322, New York, 1978. Plenum Press.

CPS93.   Rance Cleaveland, Joachim Parrow, and Bernhard Steffen. The concurrency workbench: A semantics-based tool for the verification of concurrent systems. *ACM Transactions on Programming Languages and Systems*, 15(1):36–72, January 1993.

CvE81.   Keith Clark and Maarten van Emden. Consequence verification of flowcharts. *IEEE Transactions on Software Engineering*, SE-7(1):52–60, January 1981.

Hoa85.   C. A. R. Hoare. *Communicating Sequential Processes*. Prentice-Hall, Englewood Cliffs, NJ, 1985.

KLM+97.   Gregor Kiczales, John Lamping, Anurag Mendhekar, Chris Maeda, Cristina Lopes, Jean-Marc Loingtier, and John Irwin. Aspect-oriented programming. In Mehmet Akşit and Satoshi Matsuoka, editors, *ECOOP '97 — Object-Oriented Programming 11th European Conference*, volume 1241, pages 220–242, Jyväskylä, Finland, 1997. Springer-Verlag.

Mil80.   Robin Milner. *A Calculus of Communicating Systems*, volume 92 of *Lecture Notes in Computer Science*. Springer-Verlag, Berlin, 1980.

Mil90.   Robin Milner. Operational and algebraic semantics of concurrent processes. In J. van Leeuwen, editor, *Handbook of Theoretical Computer Science: Volume B: Formal Models and Semantics*, pages 1201–1242. Elsevier, Amsterdam, 1990.

NCA99.   Torsten Nelson, Donald Cowan, and Paulo Alencar. Towards a formal model of object-oriented hyperslices. In *First Workshop on Multi-Dimensional Separation of Concerns in Object-Oriented Systems (OOPSLA '99)*, Denver, Col., November 1999.

Par81.   David Park. Concurrency and automata on infinite sequences. In *5th GI Conference*, volume 104 of *LNCS*, Berlin, 1981. Springer.

PT97.   Benjamin C. Pierce and David N. Turner. Pict: A programming language based on the pi-calculus. Technical Report CSCI Technical Report 476, Indiana University, March 1997.

RS99.   Christine Röckl and Davide Sangiorgi. A pi-calculus procsss semantics of concurrent idealised ALGOL. In *Proceedings of FOSSACS 1999*, number 1578 in LNCS, pages 306–321. Springer, 1999.

Sca98.   J. Bryan Scattergood. *The Semantics and Implementation of Machine-Readable CSP*. PhD thesis, Oxford University, 1998.

Ski00.   Mark Skipper. A model of composition oriented programming. In *Workshop on Multi-Dimensional Separation of Concerns in Software Development, ICSE 2000*, Limerick, Ireland, June 2000.

TOHJ99.   Peri Tarr, Harold Ossher, William Harrison, and Stanley M. Sutton Jr. *n* degrees of separation: Multi-dimensional separation of concerns. In *21st International Conference on Software Engineering*, Los Angeles, May 1999.

UML Reflections

François Pennaneac'h, Jean-Marc Jézéquel,
Jacques Malenfant, and Gerson Sunyé

IRISA, Campus de Beaulieu, F-35042 Rennes Cedex, France
{pennanea,jezequel,malenfant,sunye}@irisa.fr

Abstract. The UML shares with reflective architectures the idea that self-definition of languages and systems is a key principle for building and maintaining complex systems. The UML is now defined by a four-layer metalevel structure, enabling a flexible and extensible definition of models by metamodels, and even a self-description of the meta-metamodel (the MOF). This metalevel dimension of UML is currently restricted to structural reflection. But recently a new extension to the UML, called the *Action Semantics* (AS), has been proposed for standardization to the OMG. This paper explores how this proposed extension brings a behavioural reflection dimension to the UML. Indeed, we show that it is not only possible but quite effective to use the AS for manipulating UML models (including the AS metamodel). Besides elegant conceptual achievements, such as a metacircular definition of the AS, reflective modeling with the AS leverages on the UML metalevel architecture to provide the benefits of a reflective approach, in terms of separation of concerns, within a mainstream industrial context. A complete model can now be built as an ideal model representing the core concepts in the application, to which non-functional requirements are integrated as fully traceable transformations over this ideal model. For example, this approach paves the way for powerful UML-defined semantics-based model transformations such as refactoring, aspect weaving, application of design patterns or round-trip engineering.

1 Introduction

The UML (Unified Modeling Language) shares with reflective architectures the idea that self-definition of languages and systems is a key principle for building and maintaining complex systems. In its recent versions, the UML adopted a four-layer metalevel structure, which has enabled a flexible and extensible definition of models through metamodels, and even a self-description of the meta-metamodel. We concur with Bézivin and Lemesle [1] that this metalevel architecture is both a sign that models are now becoming first-class entities, but also that modeling now challenges the role of programming as the central activity in software development. But this metalevel dimension of the UML is currently restricted to structural reflection, a restriction that, in our view, holds up this mutation. Fortunately, new additions to the standard are now introducing behavioural reflection capabilities that will, again in our opinion, play a major role in this software development shift.

A. Yonezawa and S. Matsuoka (Eds.): REFLECTION 2001, LNCS 2192, pp. 210–230, 2001.

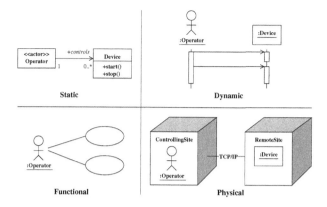

Fig. 1. Uml Dimensions

Until recently, the UML lacked precise and formal foundations for several constructs such as transition guard expressions or method bodies, for which it resorted to semantic loopholes in the form of "uninterpreted" strings. Some tools use general purpose programming languages or specific proprietary languages, but yet this is a rather ad hoc and non-standard answer to the problem. Because this was hampering the acceptance of the UML in some industrial circles (e.g., the aerospace or telecom industry), where the strong emphasis on the criticality of software is coped with using precise behaviour description languages and formal verification tools, the Action Semantics (AS) [10] has been proposed for standardization to the Object Management Group (OMG). The AS aims at filling this gap by providing means to annotate UML models with action statements as well as a model of execution for these statements. The AS is introduced as a metamodel integrated into the UML metamodel. Building over what already exists in the CCITT Specification and Description Language (SDL) community [6,11], the integration of the Action Semantics into the UML standard should promote interoperability among tools, and allow for executable modeling and simulation, as well as full code or test cases generation.

This paper explores how this proposed extension brings a behavioural reflection dimension to the UML. While the purpose of the AS is to annotate models with executable specifications for applications source code, we show in this paper that it is not only possible but quite effective to use the AS for manipulating UML models, including even the AS metamodel. Besides providing grounds for neat conceptual achievements, such as a metacircular minimal definition of the AS itself, reflective programming with the AS leverages on the UML metalevel architecture (the UML metamodel is itself an UML model) to provide the benefits of a reflective approach within a mainstream industrial context. Indeed, a model can now be built as an ideal model representing the core concepts in the application, to which non-functional requirements are integrated as transformations over this ideal model.

This novel approach to metamodeling builds on the strong commitment towards separation of concerns that UML also shares with approaches such as AOP (Aspect Oriented Programming) and SOP (Subject Oriented Programming). With its nine views which are like projections of a whole multi-dimensional system onto separate plans, some of them being orthogonal, the UML indeed provides the designer with an interesting separation of concerns, covering four main dimensions of software modeling (see Fig. 1): functional (use cases diagrams express the requirements), static (class diagrams), dynamic (statecharts, sequence diagrams for the specification of behavioural aspects) and physical (implementation diagrams). By applying the AS reflectively to models and metamodels, we have been able to show how designers can carry on, within the UML notational context, activities such as behaviour-preserving transformations [23] (see § 4.2), design pattern application [12] (§ 4.3) and design aspects weaving [15] (§ 4.4).

The rest of the paper is structured as follows. Section 2 recalls the principles of the UML metalevel architecture ; besides explaining the architecture itself, this section also discusses the parallel with well-known object-oriented programming languages metalevel architectures. Section 3 reviews the Action Semantics as it is currently submitted for standardization at the OMG and it explains how it can be used for reflective modeling. Section 4 shows the interest of using the Action Semantics at the metamodel level for specifying and programming model transformations in several contexts. Related work are discussed in Section 5, and a conclusion summarizes our contributions.

2   The UML with the Action Semantics

2.1   From Modeling to Metamodeling

The UML is all about defining models for executable software artifacts, and more precisely objects. Commonly, the UML is used to define models for objects that will eventually execute on some computer to carry on a computation. A model usually abstracts implementation details of executable objects into entities, which are depicted using a graphical notation and, more and more importantly, a standard XMI serialization format. On the other hand, a model can provide more information that a crude program, mainly by representing and by giving details about relationships between objects, which are implemented by only a few expressible relationships in programming languages (client, inheritance, sometimes agregation and a few others).

If models can describe executable objects and their relationships, it has been soon recognized that they could as well describe other artifacts, and more precisely models. After all, models are built of entities and relationships. Hence, models of models, or metamodels, can describe what kinds of entities and relationships are found in models. Without surprise, metamodels being themselves models, the idea of describing them using metametamodels comes immediately to minds. To avoid a potential infinite metaregression, a fixed-point must be sought to define precisely and completely a modeling architecture.

2.2   A Standard Four-Layer Metalevel Architecture

The UML follows a four-layer modeling architecture, each layer being a model of the layer under, the last one being a model of itself. The first layer, called M_0, holds the executable ("living") entities when the code generated from the model is executed, i.e. running objects, with their attribute values and links to other objects. The second layer M_1 is the modeling layer. It represents the model as the designer conceives it. In UML, this is the place where well-known classes, associations, state machines,... are defined (via the nine views, quoted above). The running objects are "instances" of the classes defined at this level. The third level M_2 is the metamodel level, i.e. a description of what a syntactically correct model is. Finally the fourth level M_3 is the meta-metamodel level, i.e. the definition of the metamodel syntax, such as the syntax of the UML metamodel. UML creators chose a four-layer architecture because it provides a basis for aligning the UML with other standards based on a similar infrastructure, such as the widely used Meta-Object Facility (MOF).

This four-level architecture brings a form of structural reflection to the UML. Each level defines the syntax and semantic constraints of models one level below. Defining UML as a metamodel allows for easy extension of UML to serve specific modeling needs, while the MOF serves as a unique root to define several modeling languages, perhaps adapted to specific application areas. Bézivin and Lemesle have explored the underpinnings and consequences of this metalevel architecture and predict a mainstream role to modeling in future software development processes [1].

In terms of structural reflection, however, the UML architecture is somewhat restricted. As the major restriction, notice that the relationship between levels is neither explicitly defined nor explicitly used in the definition of UML [1]. This relationship is not precisely instantiation, since it is a many-to-many relationship, many elements of one level usually concur to the definition of one or more elements one level below. Moreover, a more traditional instantiation relationship can be depicted between elements of adjacent levels, such as between classes defined at level M_1 and the objects at level M_0. Bézivin and Lemesle suggest the term "based-on" to name this relationship between levels, a convention we adopt here. Again, we concur with these authors that the two relationships, "based-on" and "instance-of", will have to be reified into UML and the MOF for this metalevel architecture to fully bear fruits.

2.3   Comparisons with Other Reflective Architectures

Unsurprisingly, the metalevel architecture of UML is reminescent of several well-known architectures in reflective languages and systems. Loops [3] has a metaclass/class/instance architecture where the metaclass `Metaclass` is the root of the instantiation hierarchy, playing a role similar to the one of the MOF. The metaclass `Class` defines the structure and behaviour of a Loops class and therefore plays a role similar to the one of the UML metamodel, which defines the syntax of a UML model.

The question of whether the UML four-level architecture can collapse into three levels, in a similar way as Briot and Cointe did for Loops with the ObjVLisp architecture [4,5,9] comes immediately to the mind; we will return to this next. Maintaining a four-level architecture though has the strong advantage of allowing many different metamodels that still share the same basis for their definition (see [1]).

The fact that many different model elements concur to define one particular object is also reminiscent of metalevel architectures for concurrent object-oriented languages such as CodA [21], among others. The organization of these model elements in nine views is similar to the multi-model reflection framework of AL-1/D [22], which has been adopted by many object-oriented reflective middleware, such as OpenORB [2], and operating systems, such as μChoices [27].

2.4   Metamodeling in Practice

As models are becoming growingly complex, the use of sophisticated tools to build and manipulate them is now mandatory in industrial contexts. Thanks to the metalevel architecture of UML, more and more of these tools are built around this reflective representation of models and metamodels. For practical reasons though, full-fledged four-level tools are still rare. One of the potential simplification when the tools choose to specialize themselves into UML modeling is to collapse the level M_3 onto the level M_2, as we have pointed out before.

Although there is no strict one-to-one mapping between all of the MOF meta-metamodel elements (M_3) and the UML metamodel elements, the two models are interoperable. In fact, the UML core package metamodel and the MOF are structurally quite similar. A reason explaining this similarity is that self-described UML metamodels have been proposed before the standardization of the MOF. Adding the obvious influence of UML on the design of the MOF explains a relatively tight compatibility between a subset of the UML metamodel and a subset of the MOF. This design implies that the UML metamodel (a set of class diagrams) is itself a UML model (pretty much in the same way that the metaclass `Class` in ObjVlisp is self-describing and therefore an instance of itself). The Fig. 2 shows this inclusion. The chief interest of this property, as tools are concerned, is the fact that tools built to manipulate UML models can very well, and indeed do apply equally well to metamodels, a specificity we heavily rely on for our study, as we will see shortly.

3   The Action Semantics and Its Reflective Properties

3.1   Motivations for an Action Semantics in UML

Traditional modeling methods which do not have support for any action language to specify the behaviour of model elements have focused on separating analysis and design, i.e. the *what the system has to do* and the *how that will be achieved*. If this separation clearly has some benefits, such as allowing the

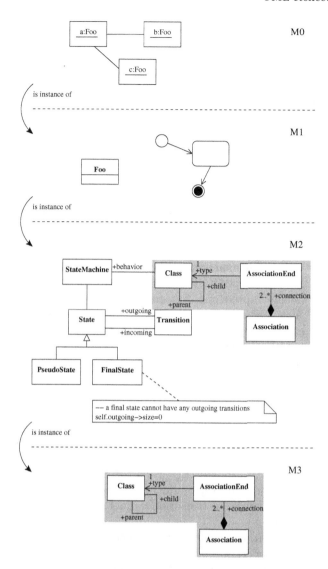

Fig. 2. UML layers (partial and simplified)

designer to focus on system requirements without spreading itself too thin with implementation details, or allowing the reuse of the same analysis model for different implementations, it also has numerous drawbacks. The main one is that this distinction is a hard job in practice, not to say impossible: the boundaries are vague; there is no criteria for deciding what is analysis, and what is not. Rejecting some aspects from analysis makes it incomplete and imprecise; trying to complete it often force to mix some *how* issues for describing the most complex behaviour.

Therefore, three reasons essentially drive the inclusion of an Action Semantics into UML:

1. First and fundamental, the incompleteness in models due to the inability to state often crucial points about the behaviour of model elements becomes a major shortcoming in many contexts.
2. Second, a consequence of the first, the inability to check models early in the software development process, something common now in some critical-software industries using the SDL and related tools, is hampering the acceptance of UML outside the traditional circles of business-management applications.
3. Third, as mentioned earlier, the UML pushes towards a shift of software development efforts from programming to modeling, and a crucial technology to enable this shift is code generation directly from models, which again needs a complete specification of behaviour into models.

UML is quite crude at expressing behaviour. To date, no really defined element in the UML could specifically provide means for such expression. UML allows user to include expressions, but only in the form of so-called "uninterpreted" strings, for which no semantics is given. Interpretation is left to the user. This is true for example in state diagrams, where the specification of a guard on a transition is conceptually realized by a boolean expression, but nothing within UML metamodel allows the designer to express such a condition on the guard and check for at least this basic semantic constraint. This lack of more formal foundations for important behavioural aspects of models is experienced by more and more users.

Also annoying is the fact that models are neither executable nor checkable, simply because they are incompletely specified in the UML. This makes it impossible to verify and test early in the development process, something common now in some critical-software industries using the SDL and related tools. Model checking techniques, for example, would be inapplicable to UML models if elements as crucial as guards on transition cannot be expressed with a precise semantics.

Finally, code generation from models is a feature of many commercial tools today. Although the generation of code templates to be filled by programmers already boosts productivity, few projects never come back to models during the implementation. When they do, keeping models and source code in synchronization is more and more a burden. Therefore, the ideal would be to work out the application by modeling from end to end. That is, the model should be defined with enough precision, including behaviour, to enable the generation of the entire application source code, therefore collapsing all problems due to the dual evolution of models and source code. Maybe less important, but increasingly present in tools, the ability to simulate, that is to execute, the model prior programming also requires completely specified models.

Faced with these shortcomings, tool providers came with several ad hoc solutions, such as adopting a particular programming language to write behavioural expressions in otherwise "uninterpreted" strings (e.g., Java or C++). This kind of ad hoc solutions merely and inevitably trade incompleteness for inconsistencies in UML models when different languages are adopted in different models. Indeed, the interpretation is delegated to the modeling tool, therefore breaking the interoperability of models, a hardly gained property through years of long and painful unification and standardization processes.

The Action Semantics proposal aims at providing modelers with a complete, software-independent specification for actions in their models. The goal is to be able to use UML as an executable modeling language [13], i.e. to allow designers to test and verify early and to generate 100% of the code if desired. It builds on the foundations of existing industrial practices such as SDL, Kennedy Carter's [16] or BridgePoint [24] action languages[1]. But contrary to its predecessors, which all were proprietary, the Action Semantics aims at becoming an OMG standard, a common base and formalism for all the existing and future action languages (mappings for existing languages to Action Semantics are proposed).

3.2   A Quick Reference to the AS

The Action Semantics proposal is based upon three abstractions:

- A metamodel: it extends the actual UML1.4 metamodel, augmenting the uninterpreted items with a precise syntax of actions (see Fig 3). New subclasses of metaclass *Action* are introduced to cope with the usual programming constructs : primitives action such as the creation, deletion or modification of objects, creation or deletion of links between objects, control structures or the sending of a message are defined. Mechanisms for grouping actions (into procedures, for instance) while specifying their partial order of execution are provided. The Action Semantics proposal for the UML does not enforce any notation (i.e. surface language) for the specification of actions. This is intentional, as the Action Semantics goal is certainly not to define a new notation, or to force the use of a particular existing one. But the Action Semantics was conceived to allow an easy mapping of classical languages such as Java, C++ or SDL[2]. Thus, designers can keep with their favorite language, without any learning overhead for a new one.
- A model of execution: it is the UML model of a virtual machine for executing UML specifications. It defines abstractions for modeling the evolutions of the objects in a system at runtime. The life of an object is modeled by its *history*, i.e. a sequence of *snapshots*. Each snapshot shows the value of attributes and links to other objects, and is immutable. Each change to an object, either to one of its attribute values or links, yields a new snapshot in the history.
- A semantics of actions: the execution of an action is precisely defined with a *life-cycle* which unambiguously states the effect of executing the action on an instance of the execution model. Every life-cycle is made of basic steps of execution called *productions*. A production has a precondition and a postcondition. The precondition is evaluated with respect to the current

---

[1] all the major vendors providing an action language are in the list of submitters.
[2] Some of these mappings are illustrated in the AS specification document [10].

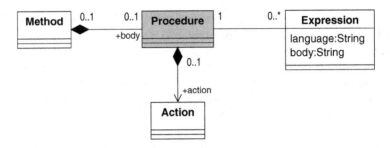

Fig. 3. Action Semantics immersion into the UML

snapshot. When it is true, execution proceeds to the next step in the life-cycle and a new snapshot validating the properties stated in the postcondition is computed.

3.3   Making the AS Reflective

The AS was originally conceived for precisely specifying the behaviour of models. We advocate the extension of its scope beyond this basic role. An UML execution engine, i.e. an implementation of the AS model of execution is originally dedicated to the manipulation of M_0 instances of UML models. Such manipulations are specified at the M_1 level, as part of the whole model of the application. But since both (1) the UML meta-model and (2) the UML execution model for the AS are themselves UML models, we can use the AS to specify the evolution of these models:

- In the first case, thanks to the four-level architecture of the UML, an AS specification would manipulate instances of M_2 level, i.e. UML models. Then, an AS specification describes a *model transformation* (meta-programming).
- In the second case, an AS specification would manipulate instances of the execution model, i.e. the objects at runtime (a representation of M_0 level called a snapshot). Then, the AS specification describes the transformation from one snapshot to the resulting one, that is the *semantics of the AS itself* (reflexivity applied to the execution engine specification).

We propose to combine these two approaches into reflexive meta-modeling tools: the same execution engine would then apply to both the execution of metamodel transformations and the execution of models.

Before detailling the use of the AS for metamodel transformations in the next section, let us now explore the interests of a reflexive definition for the AS. First it would help to structure the current AS definition document (more than 250 pages long) around a kernel of reflexively defined primitive actions and thus minimize the amount of work needed for implementations. These primitive actions fall in the following categories:

- reading and writing of attributes
- creation and deletion of objects
- creation, reading and deletion of links between objects
- communication among objects (call action, signal, exceptions)

These primitive actions are defined with production rules specifying the transition between two snapshots, which are themselves M_0 level UML models, hence the meta-circular definition. Other AS actions could then be defined operationaly based on this kernel of primitive actions. For instance, *SynchronousInvocation-*

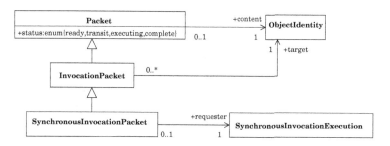

Fig. 4. SynchronousInvocationAction model of execution

Action is defined as an action that sends a message to a target object and blocks until it receives an answer. The semantics of execution for this action is (partially) described in Fig. 4 and completed with the following production extracted from the specification:

```
Production 1 : synchronous invocation action generates a synchronous
invocation packet and blocks itself.
precondition: self.status = #ready
postcondition: self.status@post = #executing -- put call in executing
-- state while subordinate execution proceeds.
packet:SynchronousInvocationPacket.isNew and -- create a call packet
packet.requester@post=self and
packet.status@post= #ready and
packet.target@post=self.input_target() and
packet.content@post=self.input_argument
```

It is obvious to deduce a sequence of AS primitive actions which creates and initializes a *packet* conforming to this postcondition.

```
packet := new SynchronousInvocationPacket -- a CreateObjectAction
packet.requester := self -- a CreateLinkAction
packet.status := #ready -- a WriteAttributeAction
packet.target := self.target -- a ReadLinkAction then a CreateLinkAction
packet.content := self.argument -- n ReadLinkActions, n CreateLinkActions
```

Until now, this has been left out of the OMG specification, where productions focus on giving a precise meaning to the execution of actions, putting aside the building of compliant and efficient execution engines. Productions do not explicitly state *how* to compute the next snapshot in an object history and thus are an inappropriate formalism for tools implementors. This idea could also be used to let the user define new actions based on primitive ones, thus extending the AS.

Finally, we propose to give the programmer the full power of UML reflexivity by providing M_0 level entities with a link to the M_1 level, and M_1 level entities a link to M_2 level in such a way that she can freely navigate between the various levels of modelisations, both at runtime and at design time.

4   Leveraging the UML Reflexivity

In this section, we discuss why and show how to use the behavioural reflection introduced by the Action Semantics to implement model transformations. We present three different uses for this approach: implementing refactorings, applying design patterns and weaving design aspects.

4.1   Separating Concerns: Codesign

Using the UML meta-modeling architecture and the Action Semantics for specifying transformations is appealing: the development of meta-tools capitalizes on experience designers have gained when modeling UML applications. Some recurrent problems suddenly vanish: portability of transformations is ensured for all UML-compliant tools with access to the metamodel, there is no learning-curve for the writing of new meta-tools, as it is pure UML and any development process supporting the UML applies to the building and reuse of transformations [18]. This paves the way to off-the-shelf transformation components.

We strongly believe that this use of the Action Semantics will change the traditional software development process. More concretely, the Action Semantics is an important step towards the use of UML in an effective development environment, since it offers the possibility of enacting early design models and to evolve or refine it until its implementation. The development approach we propose here starts with an early design model, created by the designers from an analysis model. This model is completely independent of the implementation environment, it assumes an "ideal world", where the processing power and the memory are infinite, there is no system crash, no transmission error, no database conflicts, etc. Since this model encloses Action Semantics statements, it can be enacted by the Action Semantics machine and validated. Once the validation is finished, the designer can add some environment-specific aspects to the design model (database access, distribution), apply design patterns and restructure the model using design refactorings.

As already outlined, transformations rank in two categories: the ones related to the application domain and those involved in generating efficient implementations for the target platform. The following example illustrates the difference: if the designer knows a collection of objects has to be notified when another object changes, then she annotates the corresponding classes as collaborating into an Observer pattern [12]. A generic transformation supporting this pattern adds an **update** method to every observer. Specific transformations for implementing the pattern offer designers choices that fit implementation trade-offs: execution speed vs. memory footprint, point-to-point notification vs. broadcasting, depending on requirements on the underlying hardware. This last transformation is not at all related to the application, and must not distract the designer from its application refinement.

The two categories are not exclusive : some transformations bridge the application domain and the implementation domain, thus falling into both categories. These transformations perform the "weaving" of the two aspects into a single implementation model.

4.2   Design Refactorings

Refactorings [23] are behaviour-preserving transformations, used to improve the design of object-oriented programs. We believe that refactorings are an important artifact to software development, and we are interested in bringing them to the design level by means of a UML tool. The implementation of refactorings in UML is an interesting task, since *design* refactorings – as opposed to *code* refactorings – should work with several modelling elements shared among several views of a model. This is also a challenge, since some refactorings (namely moving features) are difficult to implement since we must take into account different UML elements, such as OCL constraints and state charts.

The Action Semantics represents a real gain for refactoring implementation, not merely because it directly manipulates UML elements, but also because of the possibility of combining it with OCL rules to write pre and post-conditions. More precisely, as refactorings must preserve the behaviour of the modified application, they cannot be widely applied. Thus, every refactoring ought to verify a set of conditions before the transformation is carried out.

Below we present an example of a simple refactoring, the generalization of equivalent Attributes. In the UML metamodel, an Attribute belongs to a Class, its *Owner*. It may have *Sisters*, the children of its owner. In addition to the equivalence, which must be satisfied for exactly one Attribute of each sister, two other preconditions should be satisfied. First, private Attributes can not be moved, since they are not visible outside the scope of the owner and are not inherited. Second, the owner must have exactly one parent. These conditions and the transformation itself are defined in OCL and in Action Semantics as follows[3]:

---

[3] Since the Action Semantics does not have an official surface language, we adopt an "OCL-based" version in our examples.

Attribute :: generalize

pre:
>   self . visibility $<>$ private **and**
>   self .owner.parent.**size** $= 1$ **and**
>   self .owner.parent.child→**forAll**(aClass:Class|
>   aClass. feature→**select**(anAttr|
>   anAttr.**oclIsKindOf**(Attribute))→**exists**(a|
>   a.isBasicEquivalentTo(self)))

actions:
>   **let** newAttribute := self.copy()
>   self .owner.parent.addFeature(newAttribute)
>   self .owner.parent.child→**forAll**(aClass:Class|
>   aClass. feature→**select**(anAttr|
>   anAttr.**oclIsKindOf**(Attribute) **and**
>   anAtrr.isBasicEquivalentTo(self))→**forAll**(each | each→delete()

post:
>   self **@pre**.owner.parent.features→**exists**(a:Attribute|
>   a.isBasicEquivalentTo(self))) **and**
>   **not** self **@pre**.owner.parent.child→**forAll**(aClass:Class|
>   aClass. feature→**select**(anAttr:Attribute|
>   anAttr.**oclIsKindOf**(Attribute))→**exists**(a:Attribute|
>   a.isBasicEquivalentTo(self)))

An OCL expert might rightfully notice that the operation *child* is not defined neither in the OCL documentation nor as an additional operation in the UML metamodel. We have defined it symmetrically to the *parent* operation, defined for Classes.

4.3 Design Patterns

Another interesting use for Action Semantics is the application of Design Patterns, i.e. the specification of the proposed terminology and structure of a pattern in a particular context (called instance or occurrence of a pattern). In other words, we envisage the application of a pattern as a sequence of transformations that are applied to an initial situation in order to reach a final situation, an explicit occurrence of a pattern.

This approach is not, and does not intend to be, universal since only a few patterns mention an existing situation to which they could be applied (see [7] for further discussion on this topic). In fact, our intent is to provide designers with metaprogramming facilities, so they are able to define (and apply) their own variants of known patterns. The limits of this approach, such as pattern and trade-offs representation in UML, are discussed in [26].

As an example of design pattern application, we present below a transformation operation that applies the Proxy pattern. The main goal of this pattern is to provide a placeholder for another object, called *Real Subject*, to control access to it. It is used, for instance, to defer the cost of creation of an expensive object until it is actually needed:

Class :: addProxy

pre:
    let classnames = self.package.allClasses→**collect**(each : Class | each.**name**) in
    (classnames→**excludes**(self.**name**+'Proxy') **and**
    classnames→**excludes**('Real'+self.**name**))

actions:
    let name := self.**name**
    let self.name := name.**concat**('Proxy')
    let super :=
        self.package.addClass(**name**,self.allSuperTypes(),{}→**including**(self))
    let real :=
        self.package.addClass('Real'.**concat**(name),{}→**including**(super),{})
    let ass := self.addAssociationTo('realSubject',real)
    self.**operations**→**forAll**(op : Operation | op.moveTo(real))

This operation uses three others (actually, refactorings), that will not be precisely described here. They are however somewhat similar to the *remove-Class()* operation presented above. The first operation, *addClass()*, adds a new class to a package, and inserts it between a set of super-classes and a set of subclasses. The second, *addAssociationTo()*, creates an association between two classes. The third, *moveTo()*, moves a method to another class and creates a "forwarder" method in the original class.

This transformation should be applied to a class that is to play the *role* of real subject [4]. Its application proceeds as follows:

1. Add the 'Proxy' suffix to the class name;
2. Insert a super-class between the class and its super-classes;
3. Create the *real subject* class;
4. Add an association between the *real subject* and the *proxy*
5. Move every method owned by the *proxy* class to the *real subject* and create a forwarder method to it (move methods).

As we have explained before, this is only one of the many implementation variants of the Proxy pattern. This implementation is not complete, since it does not create the *load()* method, which should create the *real subject* when it is requested. However, it can help designers to avoid some implementation burden, particularly when creating forwarder methods.

4.4   Aspect Weaving

Finally, we would like to show how Action Semantics can support the task of developing applications that contain multiple aspects. Aspects (or concerns) [17,28] refer to non-functional requirements that have a global impact on the implementation. The approach used in dealing with this is to separate these aspects from

---

[4] Patterns are defined in terms of roles, which are played by one or more classes in its occurrences

the conceptual design, and to introduce them into the system only during the final coding phase. Ultimately, the merging of aspects should be handled by an automated tool. In our example, we attempt to show how aspects can be weaved as early as the design level through model transformation [14], using the Action Semantics to write the transformation rules.

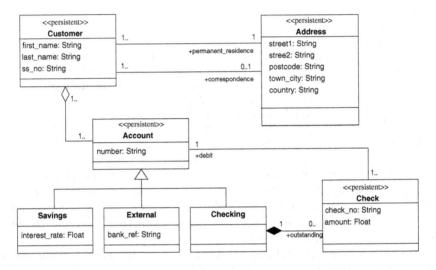

Fig. 5. Information Management System for Personal Finance

The class diagram in Fig. 5 illustrates a model of a bank's personal-finances information-management system. In the original system, the accounting information was stored in a relational database and each class marked with the "persistent" stereotype can be related to a given table in the database. The aim of this re-engineering project is to develop a distributed object-oriented version of the user front-end to support new online access for its customers. One of the non-functional requirements is to map these "persistent" objects to the instance data stored in the relational database. The task involves writing a set of proxy classes that hide the database dependency, as well as the database query commands. An example of the required transformation is illustrated by the model in Fig. 6. In this reference template, the instance variable access methods are generated automatically and database specific instructions are embedded to perform the necessary data access.

Since the re-engineering is carried out in an incremental manner, there is a problem with concurrent access to the database during write-back commits. The new application must cooperate with older software to ensure data coherence. A provisional solution is to implement a single-ended data coherence check on the new software. This uses a timestamp to test if data has been modified by other external programs. If data has been modified since the last access, all commit operations will be rolled back, thus preserving data coherence without having

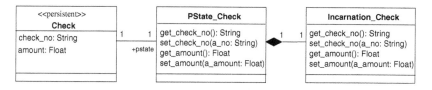

Fig. 6. Persistence proxies and access methods

to modify old software not involved in this incremental rewrite. Fig. 7 shows the template transformation required. It adds a flag to cache the timestamp and access methods will be wrapped by timestamp-checking code.

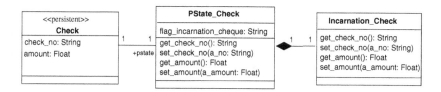

Fig. 7. Timestamp cache flag for concurrent data coherence

The metaprogram needed to generate the proxy classes of figures 6 and 7 is composed of several operations. The first one is defined in the context of a Namespace (i.e. the container of UML modeling elements). It selects all classes that are stereotyped 'persistent' and sends them the *implementPersistent()* message:

Namespace:: implementPersistentClasses
actions:

    self . allClasses →**select**(each : Class| each.stereotype→**notEmpty**)→
        select(each : Class | each.stereotype→**first**.name = 'persistent')→
            forAll(each : Class | each.implementPersistent)

The *implementPersistent()* operation is defined in the context of a Class. This operation will first create two classes, *state* and *incarnation*, and then creates, in these classes, the access methods to its own stereotyped attributes. This operation is defined as follows:

Class :: implementPersistent
actions:

    let pstate :=
        self .package.addClass('PState_'.concat(pclass.name),{},{})
    pstate.addOperation('Load'); pstate.addOperation('Save')
    self .addAssociationTo(pstate, 1, 1)
    let incarnation :=
        self .package.addClass('Incarnation_'.concat(pclass.**name**),{},{})

pstate.addCompositeAssociationTo(incarnation, 1, 1)
let attrs := self . allAttributes →
    select(a : Attribute| a.stereotype→**notEmpty**)
attrs→**select**(a : Attribute | a.stereotype→**first**.**name** = 'getset')→
    forAll(a : Attribute |
            pstate.createSetterTo(a); pstate.createGetterTo(a)
            incarnation.createSetterTo(a); incarnation.createGetterTo(a))
attrs→**select**(a : Attribute | a.stereotype→**first**.**name** = 'get')→
    forAll(a : Attribute |
            incarnation.createGetterTo(a); pstate.createGetterTo(a))
attrs→**select**(a : Attribute | a.stereotype→**first**.**name** = 'set')→
    forAll(a : Attribute |
            pstate.createSetterTo(a); incarnation.createSetterTo(a))

The creation of the access methods is implemented by the *createSetterTo()* and *createGetterTo()* operations. They are both defined in the Class context and implement a similar operation. They take an Attribute as parameter and create a Method for setting or getting its value. These operations use two other operations, *createMethod()* and *createParameter()*, which are explained above:

Class :: createSetterTo(att : Attribute)
actions:
    let newMethod := self.createMethod('set_'.**concat**(att.**name**))
    newMethod.createParameter('a_'.**concat**(attrib_name), att.type, 'in')

Class :: createGetterTo(att : Attribute)
actions:
    let newMethod := self.createMethod('get_'.**concat**(att.**name**))
    newMethod.createParameter('a_'.**concat**(attrib_name), att.type, 'out')

The *createMethod()* operation is also defined in the Class context. Its role is to create a new Method from a string and to add it to the Class:

Class :: createMethod(**name** : **String**)
actions:
    let newMethod := Method.new
    let newMethod.**name** := **name**
    self .addMethod(newMethod)
    let result := newMethod

Finally, the *createParameter()* operation creates a new parameter and adds it to a Method, which is the context of this operation:

Method::createParameter(**name** : **String**, type : Class, direction : **String**)
actions:
    let newParameter := Parameter.new
    let newParameter.**name** := **name**
    newParameter.setType(type)
    newParameter.setDirection(direction)
    self .addParameter(newParameter)
    let result := newParameter

The attractiveness of this approach is not immediately evident. Let us consider a different implementation for the persistent proxy of Fig. 6. In the case where there are composite persistent objects, it is possible to use a single persistent state proxy for a composite object and all its components (see Fig. 8). Through the use of metaprogramming, it is now possible to consider these different implementation aspects independently from the implementation of concurrency. It enables the designer to conceptualize the modifications in a manageable manner. Making changes to a model by hand as a result of a change in an implementation decision is not a viable alternative as it is laborious and error-prone.

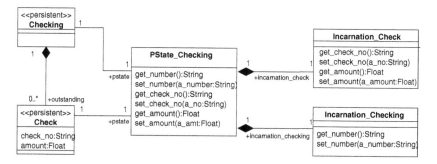

Fig. 8. Implementation template for shared proxy

Metaprogramming using the Action Semantics facilitates the revision of implementation decisions by representing them at a higher level of abstraction. It also leverages the execution machine for the Action Semantics by using it to perform the model transformation.

5   Related Work

Because the complete UML specification of a model relies on the use of uninterpreted entities (strings), with no well-defined and accepted common formalism and semantics, commercial UML tools often use metaprogramming languages to manipulate models. This is the case, for instance, of Softeam's Objecteering that uses J (a "Java-like" language [25]), and of Rational Rose or Ilogix' Rhapsody which both use Visual Basic.

In the worst cases – that is for most of the modeling tools – these statements are simply inserted at the right place into the code skeleton. The semantics of execution is then given by the specification of the programming language. Unfortunately, this often implies an over-specification of the problem (for example, in Java, a sequential execution of the statements of a method is imposed). Verification and testing are feasible only when the source code is available, far too late in the development process. Moreover, the designer must have some knowledge of the way the code is generated for the whole model to have a good understanding of the implications of her inserted code (for instance, if you are using Rhapsody and its C++ code generation tools, a knowledge of the way the tool generate code for associations is required for using them in your own code).

At best, the modeling tool has its own action language, and then the model may be executed and simulated in the early development phases, but with the drawbacks of no standardization, no interoperability, and two formalisms for the modeler to learn (the UML and the action language). The purpose of these languages is similar to the one we look for when using the Action Semantics as a metaprogramming language. There are, however, several advantages in favor of a standard Action Semantics. Users of these tools have toneed not learn yet a new language. Thanks to a tight integration into UML, the Action Semantics leverages other UML facilities, such as OCL, and in particular its navigation facilities.

As reflection is concerned, we have already pointed out in Section 2 the similarities and differences between the structural reflection aspects of UML and those of reflective object-oriented languages. On the behavioural reflection side, most of the existing models are based on an interpretive or compilative pattern. In the first case, reflection is introduced in the language by reifying a metacircular interpreter (consider 3-Lisp and other reflective functional languages), while in the second it is introduced by reifying compilation strategies in the compiler either statically (consider OpenC++) or dynamically (consider Smalltalk and OpenJIT). Elements of the run-time systems are also reified into the language.

Our approach to behavioural reflection in UML is rather based on an execution model close to operational semantics where computations are seen as sequences of states and computation steps transform an initial state into a following state in an history. Thanks to the integration with UML, reflection is achieved by having states represented as models and the Action Semantics enabled to manipulate these models. Hence, reflection in the UML with the AS appears closer to the work on rewriting systems [19,8] and rewriting logics [20] than the more traditional interpretive or compilative approaches.

6   Conclusion

With the standardization of the Action Semantics by the OMG, the metalevel architecture of the UML is now supported by a language allowing the specification of actions in a portable way. In this paper, we have shown how the Action Semantics brings a behavioural reflection dimension to the UML. We have shown that it is not only possible but quite effective to use the AS for manipulating UML models, including the AS metamodel. Behavioural reflection has been brought to the fore by a metacircular definition of the Action Semantics. To enable reflective metamodeling in the AS, we have reified in UML a meta-of link that allows actions defined in a model to act upon model elements through their description at the metamodel level, much in the same way code in a reflective object-oriented language can access class properties through metaclasses.

Applications of reflective modeling with the AS leverages on the UML met-alevel architecture to provide the benefits of a reflective approach, in terms of separation of concerns, within a mainstream industrial context. A complete model can now be built as an ideal model representing the core concepts in the application, to which non-functional requirements are integrated as fully trace-able transformations over this ideal model. For example, we have illustrated how this approach paves the way for powerful UML-defined semantics-based model transformations such as refactoring, aspect weaving, and application of design patterns.

An implementation conforming to the current version of the Action Semantics specification is in development in UMLAUT [5], a freely available UML modeling tool. The complete integration between the Action Semantics and the UML in Umlaut provides an excellent research platform for the implementation of design patterns, refactorings and aspects.

References

1. J. Bézivin and R. Lemesle.   Reflective modelling scheme.   In *Electronic Proceedings of the OOPSLA'99 Workshop on Object-Oriented Reflection and Software Engineering, OORaSE'99*, pages 107–122, 1999.   web site: http://www.disi.unige.it/person/CazzolaW/OORaSE99.html.

2. G. Blair, G. Coulson, F. Costa, and H. Duran. On the design of reflective middleware platforms. In *Proceedings of the Reflective Middleware Workshop, RM 2000*, 2000.

3. D. Bobrow and M. Stefik. *The Loops Manual*. Xerox PARC, Palo Alto CA, USA, December 1983.

4. J.-P. Briot and P. Cointe. The OBJVLISP Model: Definition of a Uniform, Reflexive and Extensible Object Oriented Language. In *Proceedings of ECAI'86*, pages 225–232, 1986.

5. J.-P. Briot and P. Cointe. A Uniform Model for Object-Oriented Languages Using the Class Abstraction. In *Proceedings of IJCAI'87*, pages 40–43, 1987.

6. CCITT. *Red Book, SDL, Recommendation Z.100 to Z.104*, 1984.

7. M. Cinnéide and P. Nixon. A methodology for the automated introduction of design patterns. In *International Conference on Software Maintenance*, Oxford, 1999.

8. M. Clavel and J. Meseguer. Axiomatizing Reflective Logics and Languages. In *Proceedings of the First International Conference on Reflection, Reflection'96*, pages 263–288, 1996.

9. P. Cointe. Metaclasses are first class: the objvlisp model. In *Proceedings of OOPSLA'87*, pages 156–167. ACM, 1987.

10. T. A. S. Consortium. Updated joint initial submission against the action semantics for uml rfp, 2000.

11. J. Floch. Supporting Evolution and Maintenance by using a Flexible Automatic Code Generator. In *Proceedings of the 17th International Conference on Software Engineering*, pages 211–219, Apr. 1995.

---

[5] http://www.irisa.fr/UMLAUT/

12. E. Gamma, R. Helm, R. Johnson, and J. Vlissides. *Design Patterns: Elements of Reusable Object-Oriented Software.* Addison Wesley, 1995.
13. O. M. Group. Action semantics for the uml rfp, ad/98-11-01, 1998.
14. W. Ho, F. Pennaneac'h, and N. Plouzeau. Umlaut: A framework for weaving uml-based aspect-oriented designs. In *Technology of object-oriented languages and systems (TOOLS Europe)*, volume 33, pages 324–334. IEEE Computer Society, June 2000.
15. R. Keller and R. Schauer. Design components: Towards software composition at the design level. In *Proceedings of the 20th International Conference on Software Engineering*, pages 302–311. IEEE Computer Society Press, Apr. 1998.
16. Kennedy-Carter. Executable UML (xuml), http://www.kc.com/html/xuml.html.
17. G. Kiczales, J. Lamping, A. Menhdhekar, C. Maeda, C. Lopes, J.-M. Loingtier, and J. Irwin. Aspect-oriented programming. In M. Akşit and S. Matsuoka, editors, *ECOOP '97 — Object-Oriented Programming 11th European Conference, Jyväskylä, Finland*, volume 1241 of *Lecture Notes in Computer Science*, pages 220–242. Springer-Verlag, New York, N.Y., June 1997.
18. P. Kruchten. *Rational Unified Process: an Introduction.* Addison-Wesley, Reading/MA, 1998.
19. M. Kurihara and A. Ohuchi. An Algebraic Specification and an Object-Oriented Implementation of a Reflective Language. In *Proceedings of the International Workshop on New Models for Software Architecture '92, Reflection and Meta-Level Architectures*, pages 137–142, November 1992.
20. J. Malenfant, C. Dony, and P. Cointe. A Semantics of Introspection in a Reflective Prototype-Based Language. *Lisp and Symbolic Computation, Kluwer*, 9(2/3):153–179, May/June 1996.
21. J. McAffer. Meta-level programming with coda. In *Proceedings of ECOOP'95*, number 952 in Lecture Notes in Computer Science, pages 190–214. AITO, Springer-Verlag, 1995.
22. H. Okamura, Y. Ishikawa, and M. Tokoro. Al-1/d: A distributed programming system with multi-model reflection framework. In A. Yonezawa and B. Smith, editors, *Proceedings of the International Workshop on New Models for Software Architectures, Reflection and Metalevel Architectures*, pages 36–47. RISE (Japan), ACM Sigplan, JSSST, IPSJ, November 1992.
23. W. F. Opdyke. *Refactoring Object-Oriented Frameworks.* PhD thesis, University of Illinois, Urbana-Champaign, 1992. Tech. Report UIUCDCS-R-92-1759.
24. Projtech-Technology. Executable UML, http://www.projtech.com/pubs/xuml.html.
25. Softeam. UML Profiles and the J language: Totally control your application development using UML. In *http://www.softeam.fr/us/pdf/uml_profiles.pdf*, 1999.
26. G. Sunyé, A. Le Guennec, and J.-M. Jézéquel. Design pattern application in UML. In E. Bertino, editor, *ECOOP'2000 proceedings*, number 1850, pages 44–62. Lecture Notes in Computer Science, Springer Verlag, June 2000.
27. S. Tan, D. Raila, and R. Campbell. An Object-Oriented Nano-Kernel for Operating System Hardware Support. In *Proceedings of the International Workshop on Object-Orientation in Operating Systems, IWOOOS'95*. IEEE, Coputer Society Press, 1995.
28. P. Tarr, H. Ossher, and W. Harrison. N degrees of separation: Multi-dimensional separation of concerns. In *ICSE'99 Los Angeles CA*, 1999.

A Hybrid Approach to Separation of Concerns: The Story of SADES

Awais Rashid

Computing Department, Lancaster University, Lancaster LA1 4YR, UK
marash@comp.lancs.ac.uk

Abstract. A number of approaches have been proposed to achieve separation of concerns. Although all these approaches form suitable candidates for separating cross-cutting concerns in a system, one approach can be more suitable for implementing certain types of concerns as compared to the others. This paper proposes a hybrid approach to separation of concerns. The approach is based on using the most suitable approach for implementing each cross-cutting concern in a system. The discussion is based on using three different approaches: composition filters, adaptive programming and aspect-oriented programming to implement cross-cutting concerns in SADES, a customisable and extensible object database evolution system.

1. Introduction

The *separation of concerns* principle proposes encapsulating cross-cutting features [15] into separate entities in order to localise changes to these cross-cutting features and deal with one important issue at a time. A number of approaches have been proposed to achieve separation of concerns. Some of the more prominent of these are meta-object protocols [14], composition filters [1, 3], aspect-oriented programming [15, 30], adaptive programming [17, 19], subject-oriented programming [10] and hyperspaces [11]. All these approaches form suitable candidates for implementing separation of concerns in a system. For example, cross-cutting concerns in collaboration-based designs have been implemented using both adaptive programming [19] and aspect-oriented programming [21]. However, in some scenarios one approach can be more suitable as compared to the others. For example, consider the following three approaches for separation of concerns:

Composition filters [1, 3]

    In this approach separation of concerns is achieved by extending an object with input and output filters. Filters can be of various types e.g. dispatch filters (for delegating messages), wait filters (for buffering messages), error filters (for throwing exceptions), etc.

Adaptive programming [17, 19]

    In this approach the behaviour code is written against a partial specification of a class diagram instead of the complete class diagram itself. The partial specification is referred to as a *traversal strategy* and only specifies the parts of the class diagram essential for a computation.

A. Yonezawa and S. Matsuoka (Eds.): REFLECTION 2001, LNCS 2192, pp. 231–249, 2001.
© Springer-Verlag Berlin Heidelberg 2001

Aspect-oriented programming [15, 30]

> In this approach special program abstractions known as *aspects* are employed to separate any cross-cutting concerns. The links between aspects and program modules (e.g. classes) cross-cut by them are represented using special reference points known as *join points*. An aspect weaver tool is used to merge the aspects and the program modules (e.g. classes) with respect to the join points at compile-time or run-time.

Composition filters are very effective in implementing concerns involving message interception and execution of actions before and after executing a method [8]. Adaptive programming, on the other hand, is more suitable for separating behaviour from object structure [8]. In contrast to these two approaches based on composition mechanisms, aspect languages and weaving tools (in aspect-oriented programming) are more effective when concerns need to be explicitly represented using linguistic constructs [8]. As a result some concerns in a system can be more suitably implemented using one approach while the others can be more effectively addressed using other approaches. This can be perceived as a "meta separation of concerns": employing the most suitable approach for implementing a concern or set of concerns.

This paper discusses the use of multiple separation of concerns techniques during the implementation of the SADES object database evolution system [23, 24, 25, 26]. SADES employs a class versioning approach to evolve the schema of the object database. In class versioning a new version of a class is created each time it is modified. Applications and objects are bound to individual class versions. Objects can, however, be converted across class versions or made to simulate a conversion. This is termed *instance adaptation*. A detailed description of class versioning is beyond the scope of this paper. Interested readers can refer to [20, 24, 26, 29].

One of the key motivations behind SADES was the development of an extensible and customisable object database evolution system which could be customised to the specific needs of an organisation or application[1]. Another motivation was to localise the impact of changes during schema evolution. Separation of cross-cutting concerns in SADES was, therefore, essential in order to localise the impact of changes during customisation and schema evolution. For each concern the most suitable technique was employed to separate it from the rest of the system. As a result three different techniques were used namely composition filters, adaptive programming and aspect-oriented programming. However, specific implementation tools for these three approaches e.g. Sina (for composition filters) [3], Demeter (for adaptive programming) [17] and AspectJ (for aspect-oriented programming) [30] were not used. This was due to the fact that SADES has been implemented on top of the commercially available object database management system Jasmine [12] and makes extensive use of the proprietary language ODQL (Object Data Query Language) and its associated interpreter in order to gain access to some low-level Jasmine features. In addition, most of the concerns cut across persistent entities (entities that live beyond program execution) and, hence, are persistent by nature. To the best of the author's knowledge existing tools for these three techniques do not take into account persistent nature of concerns. Therefore, only general concepts and not specific tools (such as Sina, Demeter and AspectJ) from the three separation of concerns approaches have been

---

[1] Database evolution case studies at an adult education organisation, where day-to-day activities revolve around the database, showed that evolution requirements can vary considerably across organisations and applications [26].

employed. Specific tools to implement these techniques (e.g. aspect language and weaver for aspect-oriented programming), wherever required, have been developed within the constraints imposed by the SADES requirements and the features of the underlying Jasmine object database management system. From this point onwards, unless otherwise stated, the terms composition filters, adaptive programming and aspect-oriented programming refer to the general concepts proposed by these approaches and not any specific tools.

The next section in this paper describes the SADES architecture. Section 3 discusses the hybrid approach to separation of concerns and the various concerns implemented in SADES using the three separation of concerns techniques mentioned above. Section 4 discusses some related work while section 5 concludes the paper and identifies directions for future work.

2. Overview of SADES Architecture

The separation of concerns principle has been employed during all the stages of development of SADES. Therefore, it also forms the basis of the system architecture. As show in fig. 1 the architecture is based on dividing the database system into a set of *spaces* each hosting entities of a particular type. Three basic types of entities and their encapsulating spaces are shown:

Objects: reside in the *object space* and are instances of classes.

Meta-objects: Classes, class properties, class methods, etc. form the *meta-object space*.

Meta-classes: constitute the *meta-class space* and are used to instantiate meta-objects.

Note that fig. 1 shows only three basic types of entities residing in an object database. Later, while discussing the instance adaptation approach in SADES, it will be demonstrated how the above architecture makes it possible to extend the database with new types of entities (and their encapsulating spaces) with minimal effort.

The links between entities residing in different spaces are maintained through *inter-space relationships*. Fig. 1 shows the bi-directional instantiation inter-space relationships between meta-classes and meta-objects, and meta-objects and objects. *Intra-space* relationships can exist among entities residing within the same space. In the meta-object space, for example, these can be the *derives-from/inherited-by* inheritance relationships among class meta-objects or the *defines/defined-in* aggregation relationships among class meta-objects and attribute and method definition meta-objects. In the object space these can be association and aggregation relationships among the various objects residing in that space.

As shown in fig. 1 the notion of spaces and inter-space and intra-space relationships has been derived directly from the viewpoints of the various developer/user roles in the database environment:

The DBMS designer is interested in providing a suitable set of meta-classes that can be instantiated by the database designer/maintainer to create the database schema. S/he is also interested in providing means for introducing new meta-classes so that the system can be extended with new types of entities if required. The new meta-classes might bear some relationships with existing meta-classes. The meta-class space and the notion of intra-space relationships in the meta-class space have been derived from these DBMS designer viewpoints.

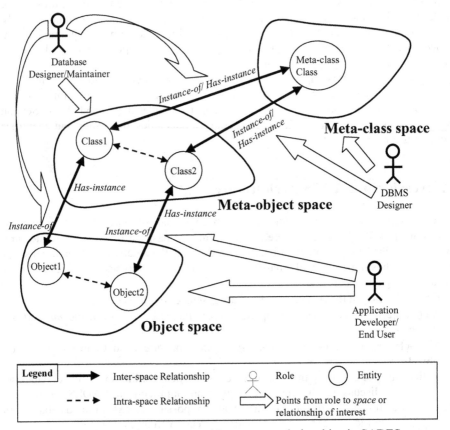

Fig. 1. Spaces, inter-space and intra-space relationships in SADES

The inter-space relationships between the meta-class space and the meta-object space have been derived from two overlapping viewpoints: that of the DBMS designer and that of the database designer/maintainer. The DBMS designer is interested in providing effective instantiation mechanisms for the meta-classes while the database designer/maintainer is interested in using these mechanisms to create the meta-objects forming the database schema.

The database designer/maintainer is also interested in creating appropriate meta-objects forming the database schema which can then be instantiated by the application developer/end user to store application data in the database. S/he is also interested in modifying the relationships among meta-objects (e.g. *derives-from/inherited-by* relationships among class meta-objects or *defines/defined-in* relationships among class meta-objects and attribute and method definition meta-objects), introducing new relationships among meta-objects or removing existing ones in order to evolve the schema of the database in line with changes in application requirements. The meta-object space and the notion of intra-space relationships in this space have been derived from these database designer/maintainer viewpoints.

The overlapping viewpoints of the database designer/maintainer and the application developer/end user roles form the basis of the inter-space relationships between the meta-object space and the object space. The database designer/maintainer is interested in exposing appropriate instantiation mechanisms for the meta-objects while the application developer/end user is interested in using these mechanisms to instantiate the meta-objects and populate the database.

The application developer/end user is also interested in manipulating the objects in the database and any association or aggregation links among them. These viewpoints have been used to derive the notion of an object space and its intra-space relationships.

The viewpoint based division of the database into spaces and identification of the various inter-space and intra-space relationships makes it possible to address the requirements of the various roles in an incremental fashion. In SADES this has provided a clearer mapping from the extensibility and customisability requirements of the various roles to the system architecture making it possible to extend the system with new types of entities (introduction of new meta-classes), spaces, inter-space and intra-space relationships and customising existing spaces by manipulating their inter-space and intra-space relationships with minimal knock-on effect on entities already residing in the existing spaces.

3. Hybrid Separation of Concerns in SADES

The hybrid approach is based on the observation that one separation of concerns technique can be more suitable for implementing certain types of concerns in comparison with other techniques. Consequently multiple techniques can be employed to implement different types of concerns in a system. Fig. 2 shows how this can be achieved in three different fashions:

Use one particular approach to implement a set of interrelated and overlapping concerns (cf. fig. 2(a)).

> This approach is suitable when all concerns in the set of interrelated and overlapping concerns can be suitably implemented using the particular approach.

Use multiple approaches to implement different concerns in a set of interrelated and overlapping concerns (cf. fig. 2(b)).

> This approach is suitable when different concerns in the set of overlapping and interrelated concerns can be better implemented using different techniques.

Implement concerns in different system layers using the same or different sets of approaches (cf. fig. 2(c)).

> Separation of concerns in the higher layer builds upon the separation of concerns based implementation in the lower layer (cf. fig. 2(c)). Approaches in fig. 2(a) and 2(b) can be used to implement different sets of concerns in each system layer.

The following sections describe how the above hybrid approach has been employed to implement SADES. Section 3.1 discusses the implementation of three interrelated and overlapping concerns:

links among entities within a space or different spaces

propagation of changes to the links

maintenance of referential integrity

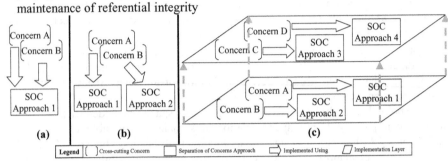

Fig. 2. Hybrid approach to separation of concerns

Using two different approaches: composition filters and adaptive programming. Section 3.2 describes the implementation of versioning in SADES using adaptive programming. This versioning implementation is built on top of the system layer implementing links, change propagation and referential integrity. Section 3.3 discusses the use of aspect-oriented programming and composition filters to implement a customisable instance adaptation approach in SADES. This system layer exploits both the versioning implementation and implementation of links, change propagation and referential integrity.

3.1 Implementation of Links among Entities

In the SADES architecture (cf. fig. 1) the links among entities, whether they reside in the same space or different spaces, are represented by relationships. Relationships are semantic constructs which are natural to manipulate for maintainers and developers of object-oriented system. Therefore, relationships in the SADES architecture have been directly mapped onto implementation. The links among entities are implemented as relationship constructs which are first class objects and encapsulate information about connections among the entities. This results in connection information being separated from the entities localising changes to these connections. This is in direct contrast with existing object database evolution systems, e.g. ORION [2], ENCORE [29], CLOSQL [20], which embed connection information within the entities (cf. fig. 3 (a)) hence spreading the relationships across them. Fig. 3 (b) shows an example schema evolution scenario for a system embedding inheritance links within class meta-objects. In this scenario a meta-object for the class *Staff* forming a non-leaf node in the class hierarchy graph is introduced into the system. All the references to subclass meta-objects will have to be removed from the *Person* meta-object and all the subclass meta-objects will have to be updated to remove the reference to *Person* in their respective collections of superclass references. A reference to the *Person* meta-object will have to be added to the superclasses collection and references to older subclasses of *Person* will have to be added to the subclasses collection in the *Staff* meta-object. A reference to the *Staff* meta-object will have to be added to the subclasses collection (not shown in fig. 3 (b)) in *Person* and to the superclasses collection in each of its subclasses. The number of entities affected upon modification of a connection is m+n where m and n represent the number of participating entities at each edge of the relationship (in this case super-classes edge and sub-classes edge).

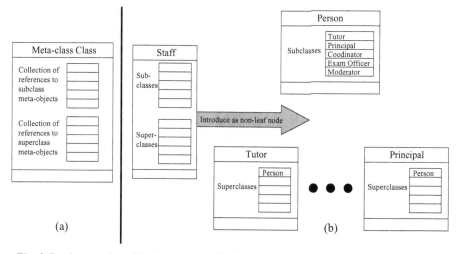

Fig. 3. Implementation of links among entities in existing object database evolution systems

The above example demonstrates that information about connections among entities cuts across them. In SADES this information is separated and encapsulated in the relationship objects. A composition filters mechanism is employed to ensure that any messages manipulating links among entities are received by the relationship objects and not by the entities connected by them. As mentioned earlier composition filters are ideal candidates for situations requiring message interception. In SADES they are implemented as first class objects hence not requiring any extensions to the basic system architecture shown in fig. 1. The method invocation mechanism in SADES has been adapted to keep track of entities with attached filters. It ensures that all messages to and from an entity get routed through its attached input and output filters respectively. As shown in fig. 4 a dispatch filter intercepts all incoming relationship manipulation messages and delegates them to the relationship objects. Since the relationship information is no longer embedded within the participating entities it can be modified in an independent fashion. It is also possible to introduce new relationships or remove existing ones with localised changes. This results in cost-effective schema modifications (changes to intra-space relationships in the meta-object space). It also improves the extensibility of the system as introduction of new meta-classes only requires introduction of new relationship objects. A detailed description of the structure and semantics of the relationship objects and their effectiveness during schema evolution can be found in [23].

Closely related and overlapping with the notion of links or relationships among entities are the concepts of change propagation and referential integrity. Referential integrity means that all entities must always refer to other existing entities. This implies that relationship objects in SADES must always connect entities that exist in the system. If an entity is removed (e.g. a class meta-object during schema evolution) the relationship object should be made aware of this change and must not refer to that entity as a participant in the relationship. Similarly, if an entity no longer participates in a relationship its associated dispatch filter must not attempt to delegate messages to the relationship object.

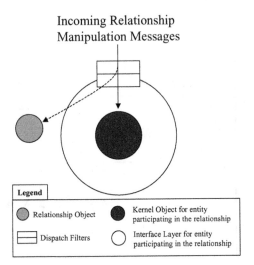

Fig. 4. Implementation of links among entities in SADES using relationship objects and composition filters

Change propagation means that any changes to a particular type of relationship or its participating entities should be propagated to the other parts of the system (e.g. other participating entities) in line with the propagation semantics defined for that type of relationship. A number of different types of relationships with different propagation semantics exist in SADES. Inheritance relationships, for example, require that changes to the structure of a class be propagated to its sub-classes. Similarly, aggregation relationship require that operations be propagated from aggregate to part, with deletion of the aggregate resulting in deletion of the parts, but not vice versa. Note that these propagation semantics cannot be fixed as some applications might require changes to them. [31], for example, identifies a number of different propagation semantics for aggregation relationships. Hence, it must be possible to modify change propagation behaviour with localised changes.

The change propagation and referential integrity behaviour refers to both relationship objects and entities connected by them. It, however, requires very little information about the structure of individual relationship objects or entities. Instead, it requires more generic information such as the type of relationship or the type of evolution operation performed on an entity. Earlier on it was pointed out that adaptive programming is highly suitable for separating behaviour from structure. As shown in fig. 5(a), it has, therefore, been employed to implement change propagation and referential integrity in SADES. A traversal strategy specifies the various operations on relationships and entities requiring referential integrity enforcement. The referential integrity behaviour is described on the basis of this traversal strategy. Similarly, a set of traversal strategies specifies different propagation semantics for different types of relationships in the system. The change propagation behaviour is specified on the basis of these traversal strategies. In SADES traversal strategies are implemented as directed graphs with each node in the graph representing a traversal node in the traversal strategy. Similar to the composition filters implementation this does not require any extensions to the basic system architecture shown in fig. 1. Fig. 6(a) shows a traversal strategy (in pseudo code) for operation propagation in aggregation relationships in

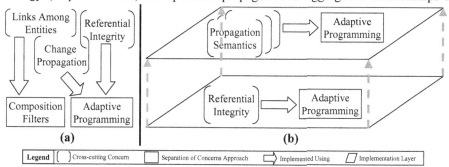

(a)   **(b)**

Fig. 5. Implementation of change propagation and referential integrity using adaptive programming

SADES. It represents the propagation of operations from aggregate to parts as mentioned earlier. Fig. 6(b) shows the traversal graph dynamically generated when an operation needs to be propagated. The black node represents the aggregate where an operation is initially performed while the first-level gray nodes represent parts of the aggregate to which the operation is propagated. Note that the propagation strategy in fig. 6(a) defines recursive propagation. Therefore (as shown in fig. 6(b)), the operation is propagated to the nodes to which the first-level nodes are an aggregate.

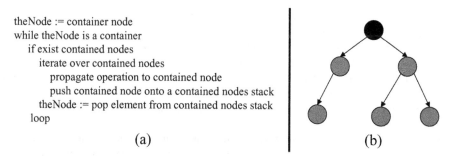

```
theNode := container node
while theNode is a container
    if exist contained nodes
        iterate over contained nodes
            propagate operation to contained node
            push contained node onto a contained nodes stack
        theNode := pop element from contained nodes stack
    loop
```

(a)   **(b)**

Fig. 6. (a) Traversal strategy for operation (change) propagation in aggregation relationships **(b)** Run-time traversal graph for the traversal strategy in (a)

Fig. 5(b) shows that the change propagation behaviour is built on top of the system layer implementing referential integrity. This is because change propagation often triggers the need to ensure referential integrity e.g. dropping of a class meta-object forming a non-leaf node in the database schema requires that this change be propagated to the sub-classes in line with the propagation semantics for inheritance relationships. However, this also requires that the relationship object for the inheritance relationship no longer refers to the removed meta-object as a participant.

3.2 Versioning

As mentioned earlier SADES employs class versioning to evolve the object database schema. In addition to this support for class versioning SADES also provides support for keeping track of changes to the objects in the object space through object versioning. In object versioning a new version of an object is created each time its state needs preservation. This functionality is essential for supporting applications such as computer-aided design (CAD) and computer-aided software engineering (CASE) where there is a need to keep track of changes to design, documentation and code artefacts. In SADES versioning support for entities is customisable. This is because versioning requirements can vary from one application (or organisation) to another. Mostly the workgroup support features (e.g. checking data in and out of the shared database to private or group workspaces) [13] are strongly dependent on the individual work practices of each organisation. Some applications might want to bind objects into *configurations* [13] and use these configurations as units of versioning. Some applications might also want to take class versioning to a higher granularity i.e. version schemas instead of classes [16, 22]. Some applications might only require support for *linear versioning* [18] (where a version is derived from only one existing version) while others might require support for *branch versioning* [18] (where a version may be derived from multiple existing versions). Therefore, it is essential to separate versioning behaviour from the versioned entities in order to localise changes during customisation of the versioning approach.

As mentioned earlier adaptive programming is highly effective in separating behaviour from structure and hence, has been employed to separate versioning behaviour from the versioned entities. As shown in fig. 7 traversal strategies for this separation are specified as version derivation graphs [18]. A general versioning graph exists for any versioned entity. Each node in the general versioning graph has the structure shown in fig. 8(a). Special refinements of the general versioning graph can be defined for specific types of entities (e.g. for classes and objects as shown in fig. 7). The structures of nodes in class version derivation graphs and object version derivation graphs are shown in fig. 8(b) and 8(c) respectively. The versioning behaviour involving any workgroup support features, special semantics for versions, support for linear or branch versioning, etc. is written against the general structure of the various version derivation graphs.

Fig. 9 shows that the versioning functionality has been implemented in a system layer which exploits the separation of concerns in the system layer implementing links among entities, change propagation and referential integrity. The *predecessor/successor* links among the nodes of version derivation graphs are implemented using relationship objects. New propagation semantics are defined for the *predecessor/successor* relationships to ensure change propagation and referential integrity when these relationships are modified by introduction of new versions or removal of existing ones. Further details of versioning in SADES can be found in [26].

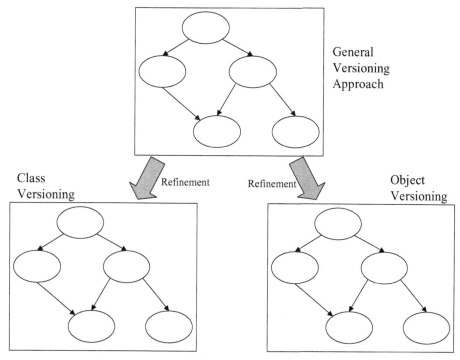

Fig. 7. Traversal strategies based on version derivation graphs

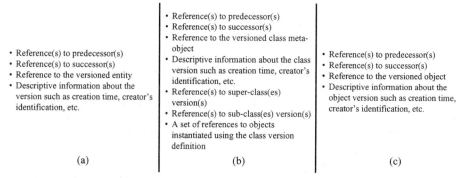

- Reference(s) to predecessor(s)
- Reference(s) to successor(s)
- Reference to the versioned entity
- Descriptive information about the version such as creation time, creator's identification, etc.

- Reference(s) to predecessor(s)
- Reference(s) to successor(s)
- Reference to the versioned class meta-object
- Descriptive information about the class version such as creation time, creator's identification, etc.
- Reference(s) to super-class(es) version(s)
- Reference(s) to sub-class(es) version(s)
- A set of references to objects instantiated using the class version definition

- Reference(s) to predecessor(s)
- Reference(s) to successor(s)
- Reference to the versioned object
- Descriptive information about the object version such as creation time, creator's identification, etc.

(a)   (b)   (c)

Fig. 8. Structure of: **(a)** general version derivation graph nodes **(b)** version derivation graph nodes refined for class versioning **(c)** version derivation graph nodes refined for object versioning

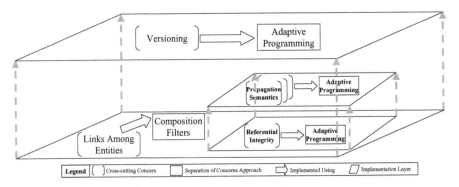

Fig. 9. Implementation of the versioning layer using separation of concerns in the layer implementing links, change propagation and referential integrity

3.3 Instance Adaptation

As mentioned earlier SADES provides support for customising the instance adaptation approach to the specific needs of an organisation or application. For the customisation to be cost effective it is essential to localise the impact of changes. Before discussing the cross-cutting nature of instance adaptation code it is essential to distinguish the *instance adaptation approach* from *instance adaptation routines*. An instance adaptation routine is the code specific to a class version or a set of class versions. This code handles the interface mismatch between a class version and the accessed object. It might be an error handler [29], an update method [20] or a transformation function [9]. The instance adaptation approach is the code which is part of the schema manager and, upon detection of an interface mismatch, invokes the appropriate instance adaptation routine with the correct set of parameters.

Customisation of instance adaptation in existing object database evolution systems is expensive because they introduce the instance adaptation routines directly into the class versions upon evolution. Often the same adaptation routines are introduced into a number of class versions. Consequently, if the behaviour of a routine needs to be changed maintenance has to be performed on all the class versions in which it was introduced. Consider the example of ENCORE [29] which employs error handlers to trap interface mismatches and simulate the presence of missing attributes or methods for an object. As shown in fig. 10 error handlers for missing information are introduced into all the former versions of a class upon each additive change: change which modifies the version set interface defined as a union of all the properties and methods of all the versions of a class. If the behaviour of the *address* handler in fig. 10 (c) needs to be customised maintenance has to be carried out on all the former class versions.

The instance adaptation approach in existing systems is "fixed" as code describing its behaviour is spread across the schema manager. Customisation of the instance adaptation approach or adoption of a new approach is very expensive as it has a large ripple effect on the schema manager and might trigger the need for changes to all, or a large number of existing classes or class versions [24].

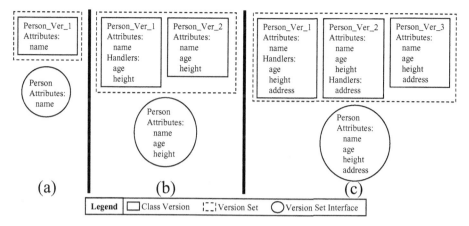

Fig. 10. Instance adaptation routines in ENCORE **(a)** before evolution **(b)** upon an additive change **(c)** upon another additive change

The biggest deciding factor in the choice of an appropriate separation of concerns approach for separating the instance adaptation approach from the schema manager and the instance adaptation routines from the class versions was the need to specify them (and any customisations to them) at the application programming level. This would make it possible for the application programmer to customise the instance adaptation mechanism to the specific needs of an organisation or application with minimal effort. This dictated the need to specify these concerns in a declarative fashion. As pointed out earlier, aspect-oriented programming is an effective mechanism to represent concerns in a linguistic fashion. It was, therefore, chosen as a basis for implementing instance adaptation.

The choice of aspect-oriented programming required support for new persistent abstractions, the aspects, in SADES. The extensible architecture of SADES described in section 2 made it possible to extend the system with the notion of an *aspect space* in a seamless fashion. As shown in fig. 11 aspects reside in the aspect space and are instances of the meta-class *Aspect*. For simplicity only one aspect has been shown. Also note that the concept of inter-space and intra-space relationships (and their implementation through relationship objects and composition filters) seamlessly extends to the aspect space. Aspects in the aspect space bear a*spect-of/has-aspect* relationships with entities residing in other virtual spaces. Although not shown in fig. 11, intra-space relationships can exist within an aspect space.

Using the aspect-oriented extension as a basis the instance adaptation approach is separated from the schema manager and encapsulated in an aspect (cf. fig. 12(a)). As shown by the shaded boxes in fig. 12(a) the instance adaptation approach can then be customised or completely exchanged with changes localised to the aspect. The customisation or exchange may be carried out statically or dynamically as the instance adaptation aspect can be woven (or rewoven) into the schema manager at both compile-time and run-time (as shown by the dotted arrow).

In a similar fashion the instance adaptation routines are separated from the class versions using aspects (cf. fig. 12(b)). It should be noted that although fig. 12(b) shows one instance adaptation aspect per class version, one such aspect can serve a number of class versions. Similarly, a particular class version can have more than one instance adaptation aspect. Fig. 12(c) depicts the case when an application attempts to access an object associated with version 1 of *class A* using the interface offered by version 2 of the same class. The aspect containing the instance adaptation routines is dynamically woven into the particular class version. This code is then invoked to return the results to the application.

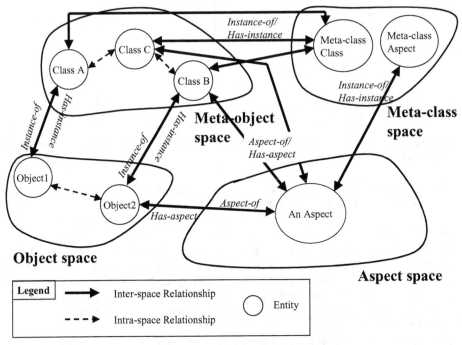

Fig. 11. Extension of SADES with an aspect space

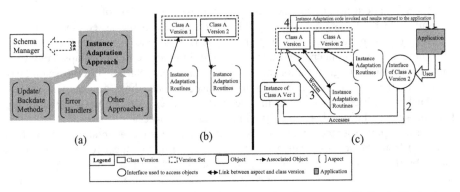

Fig. 12. (a) Customising the instance adaptation approach using aspects **(b)** Separating instance adaptation routines from class versions using aspects **(c)** Invocation process for instance adaptation routines

The instance adaptation aspects in fig. 12 are specified using a declarative aspect language modelled on AspectJ [30]. It provides three simple constructs facilitating:

identification of join points between the aspects and class versions

introduction of new methods into the class versions

redefinition of existing methods in the class versions

The aspect specification provided by the aspect language is parsed to generate the persistent aspects and associate these with the class versions using relationship objects. When an interface mismatch is detected between an object and the class definition used to access it, the weaver dynamically weaves (or reweaves) the required aspect based on a timestamp check. A detailed description of the weaver design and implementation will form the subject of a forthcoming paper.

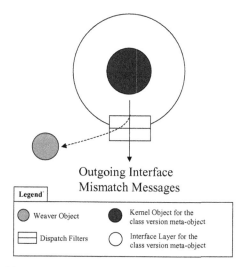

Outgoing Interface
Mismatch Messages

Legend		
⬤ Weaver Object	⬤	Kernel Object for the class version meta-object
▭ Dispatch Filters	○	Interface Layer for the class version meta-object

Fig. 13. Interception of interface mismatch messages and their delegation to the weaver using composition filters

In order to trap interface mismatch messages and delegate them to the weaver to weave (or reweave), composition filters are employed (cf. fig 13). Composition filters are very effective in message interception and hence are an ideal choice for this purpose. An output dispatch filter intercepts any interface mismatch messages and delegates them to the weaver which then weaves (or reweaves) the appropriate instance adaptation routines which are in turn invoked to return results to the application.

The aspect-oriented approach makes it possible to modify the behaviour of the instance adaptation routines within the aspects instead of modifying them within each class version. If a different instance adaptation approach needs to be employed it can be woven into the schema manager with the ripple effect limited to the aspects encapsulating the instance adaptation routines. This avoids the problem of updating the various class versions. These are automatically updated to use the new strategy (and the new adaptation routines) when the aspects are rewoven. As mentioned earlier the need to reweave is identified by a simple run-time check based on timestamps. [24] demonstrates the use of two different instance adaptation mechanisms: error handlers (which simulate object conversion across class versions) [29] and update/backdate methods (which physically convert objects across class versions) [20] in SADES. [26] demonstrates the effectiveness of the aspect-oriented approach in achieving cost-effective customisation in contrast with existing systems.

Fig. 14 shows that the instance adaptation layer in SADES exploits the functionality exposed by the versioning layer and the layer implementing links, referential integrity and change propagation. The links among class versions and aspects are implemented using relationship objects. The instance adaptation mechanism also makes frequent calls to the class versioning mechanism during simulated or physical conversion across class versions (multiple class versions need to be referred to hence requiring traversal through the version derivation graphs with the aid of the versioning mechanism).

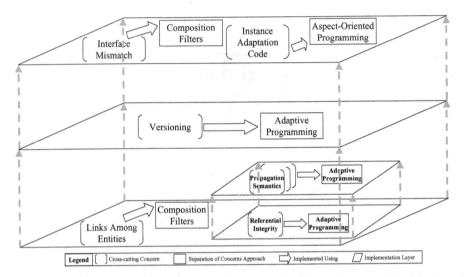

Fig. 14. Implementation of the instance adaptation layer on top of the versioning layer and layer implementing links, change propagation and referential integrity

4. Related Work

The hybrid approach proposed in this paper bears a close relationship with multi-paradigm approaches [5, 6]: using the most suitable mechanism to implement a particular feature or concern. The integration and interaction of features implemented using different separation of concerns techniques poses challenges similar to integration and interaction of features implemented using multiple paradigms. Language cross-binding issues similar to multi-paradigm implementations arise when integrating an aspect language based mechanism with separation of concerns mechanisms realised using an object-oriented language.

The proposed approach can also serve as an implementation mechanism for multi-dimensional separation of concerns [11] as the concerns encountered in SADES are mostly interconnected, overlapping and reside in different system layers. The SADES architecture also bears a close relationship with the meta-object facility for distributed systems described in [7]. However, in [7] the spaces are layered on top of each other and extensions tend to be linear. This is in contrast with both linear and non-linear extensions possible in SADES. Other related work includes meta-space architectures in reflection e.g. [4]. In [4] a space encapsulates a number of closely related but distinct meta-models (e.g. encapsulation, composition, environment, resource, etc.)

while in SADES a space encapsulates a particular type of entities (objects, meta-objects, aspects, etc.). The work presented in this paper is also closely related to the author's earlier work on exploring cross-cutting concerns in persistent environments [27] and developing persistence mechanisms for such concerns (which live beyond program execution) [28].

5. Conclusions and Future Work

This paper has proposed a hybrid approach to achieve separation of concerns in a system. The approach is based on the observation that although different techniques can form suitable candidates for implementing a set of cross-cutting concerns, some of them can be more suitable for the purpose as compared to the others. The hybrid approach has been used to achieve separation of concerns in the customisable and extensible object database evolution system, SADES. Three different separation of concerns techniques: composition filters, adaptive programming and aspect-oriented programming have been employed. The discussion has demonstrated that multiple separation of concerns approaches can co-exist, interact and effectively implement concerns most suitably addressed by them. While some of the approaches can use existing programming constructs in a system (e.g. objects, meta-objects, etc.), others might require specific extensions (e.g. aspects). A system, therefore, should have an extensible architecture in order to effectively exploit the hybrid approach.

The experiences with SADES make it possible to abstract general guidelines for employing a hybrid approach for separation of cross-cutting concerns in a system. These guidelines relate to the suitability of the three techniques (employed in SADES) to express different types of concerns and integration of concerns implemented using these different techniques. The guidelines are as follows:

Adaptive programming is highly suitable for expressing concerns which involve separation of behaviour from object structure. It is very effective in situations where the behaviour may be written against a partial specification of a class diagram or a generic specification of the structure of objects (not relating to information specific to individual instances). Examples of such generic specifications were seen during the implementation of traversal strategies for change propagation and referential integrity. These strategies needed to know the types of relationships or evolution operations but did not need to be aware of the information specific to individual relationship instances.

Composition filters are very effective in implementing concerns involving message interception and execution of actions before and after executing a method. Their key characteristic is the ability to operate at instance granularity and attachment on a per-instance basis. Examples of these characteristics were observed during implementation of relationships among entities. A dispatch filter for handling a relationship was attached with an instance when the relationship was established. If message interception were not required on a per-instance basis then mechanisms similar to *advices* in aspect languages (e.g. AspectJ [30]), which operate on a per-class basis, would have been more suitable than composition filters.

Aspect languages and weavers are most suitable in implementing concerns that need to be explicitly represented using linguistic constructs. Expression of such concerns can be simplified if the aspect language is declarative in nature. An example of such a declarative aspect language was seen in the specification of instance adaptation behaviour in SADES.

The choice of a technique to implement a certain concern may not only be dictated by the chosen design but also by the system requirements. For example, in SADES, the design decision to separate information about links among entities into relationship objects dictated that these relationship objects be attached to their participating entities on a per-instance basis and, hence, led to the choice of composition filters. On the other hand, the system requirement that instance adaptation behaviour be declaratively specified by the maintainer made an aspect language and a weaver the most suitable choice.

The integration of concerns implemented using different techniques can be simplified by identifying concerns that build upon the functionality offered by other concerns. The latter can then be implemented in lower system layers exposing their functionality to the former which reside in higher system layers.

One separation of concerns mechanism can be employed to integrate another into the system. For instance, composition filters were employed to integrate the declarative aspect language and its associated weaver into SADES.

The future direction for this work will be the development of tool support for hybrid separation of concerns. Another area of interest is the development of visualisation mechanisms for observing interactions among concerns implemented using different techniques especially those residing in different system layers.

References

[1] Aksit, M., Tekinerdogan, B., **"Aspect-Oriented Programming using Composition Filters"**, *Proceedings of the AOP Workshop at ECOOP '98, 1998*

[2] Banerjee, J. *et al.*, **"Data Model Issues for Object-Oriented Applications"**, *ACM Transactions on Office Information Systems, Vol. 5, No. 1, Jan. 1987, pp. 3-26*

[3] Bergmans, L., **"Composing Concurrent Objects – Applying Composition Filters for the Development and Reuse of Concurrent Object-Oriented Programs"**, *PhD Thesis, Department of Computer Science, University of Twente, The Netherlands, 1994*

[4] Blair, G., Coulson, G., Andersen, A., Blair, L., Clarke, M., Costa, F., Duran, H., Parlavantzas, N., Saikoski, K., **"A Principled Approach to Supporting Adaptation in Distributed Mobile Environments"**, *Proceedings of the 5th International Symposium on Software Engineering for Parallel and Distributed Systems, IEEE Computer Society Press, 2000, pp. 3-12*

[5] Budd, T. A., **"Multiparadigm Programming in Leda"**, *Addison-Wesley, 1995*

[6] Coplien, J. O., **"Multi-Paradigm Design for C++"**, *Addison-Wesley, 1998*

[7] Crawley, S., Davis, S., Indulska, J., McBride, S., Raymond, K., **"Meta-Meta is Better-Better!"**, *Workshop on Distributed Applications and Interoperable Systems (DAIS) Cottbus, Germany, 1997*

[8] Czarnecki, K., Eisenecker, U., **"Generative Programming: Methods, Tools and Applications"**, *Addison-Wesley 2000, ISBN 0-201-30977-7*

[9] Ferrandina, F., Meyer, T., Zicari, R., Ferran, G., "Schema and Database Evolution in the O2 Object Database System", *Proceedings of the 21st Conference on Very Large Databases, Morgan Kaufmann 1995, pp. 170-181*

[10] Harrison, W., Ossher, H., **"Subject-Oriented Programming (A Critique of Pure Objects)"**, *Proceedings of OOPSLA 1993, ACM SIGPLAN Notices, Vol. 28, No. 10, Oct. 1993, pp. 411-428*

[11] IBM, USA, **"Multi-dimensional Separation of Concerns using Hyperspaces"**, *http://www.research.ibm.com/hyperspace/*

[12] **"The Jasmine Documentation"**, Computer Associates International, Inc., Fujitsu *Limited, c1996-98*

[13] Katz, R. H., **"Toward a Unified Framework for Version Modeling in Engineering Databases"**, *ACM Computing Surveys, Vol. 22, No. 4, Dec. 1990, pp. 375-408*

[14] Kiczales, G., *et al.* **"The Art of the Metaobject Protocol"**, *MIT Press 1991*

[15] Kiczales, G., Lamping, J., Mendhekar, A., Maeda, C., Lopes, C., Loingtier, J., Irwin, J., **"Aspect-Oriented Programming"**, *Proceedings of ECOOP '97, LNCS 1241, pp. 220-242*

[16] Kim, W., Chou, H.-T., **"Versions of Schema for Object-Oriented Databases"**, *Proceedings of 14ᵗʰ International Conference on Very Large Databases, Morgan Kaufmann 1988, pp. 148-159*

[17] Lieberherr, K. J., **"Demeter"**, *http://www.ccs.neu.edu/research/demeter/index.html*

[18] Loomis, M. E. S., **"Object Versioning"**, *Journal of Object Oriented Programming, Jan. 1992, pp. 40-43*

[19] Mezini, M., Lieberherr, K. J., **"Adaptive Plug-and-Play Components for Evolutionary Software Development"**, *Proceedings of OOPSLA 1998, ACM SIGPLAN Notices, Vol. 33, No. 10, Oct. 1998, pp. 97-116*

[20] Monk, S., Sommerville, I., **"Schema Evolution in OODBs Using Class Versioning"**, *SIGMOD Record, Vol. 22, No. 3, Sept. 1993, pp. 16-22*

[21] Pulvermueller, E., Speck, A., Rashid, A., **"Implementing Collaboration-based Designs using Aspect-Oriented Programming"**, *Proc. TOOLS USA 2000, IEEE Computer Society Press, pp. 95-104*

[22] Ra., Y.-G., Rundensteiner, E. A., **"A Transparent Schema-Evolution System Based on Object-Oriented View Technology"**, *IEEE Transactions on Knowledge and Data Engineering, Vol. 9, No. 4, July/Aug. 1997, pp. 600-624*

[23] Rashid, A., Sawyer, P., **"Dynamic Relationships in Object Oriented Databases: a Uniform Approach"**, *Proc. of DEXA '99, Springer-Verlag LNCS 1677, pp. 26-35*

[24] Rashid, A., Sawyer, P., Pulvermueller, E., **"A Flexible Approach for Instance Adaptation during Class Versioning"**, *Proc. of ECOOP 2000 Symposium on Objects and Databases, Springer-Verlag LNCS 1944, pp. 101-113*

[25] Rashid, A., Sawyer, P., **"Object Database Evolution using Separation of Concerns"**, *ACM SIGMOD Record, Vol. 29, No. 4, December 2000, pp. 26-33*

[26] Rashid, A., **"A Database Evolution Approach for Object-Oriented Databases"**, *PhD Thesis, Computing Department, Lancaster University, UK, 2000*

[27] Rashid, A., Pulvermueller, E., **"From Object-Oriented to Aspect-Oriented Databases"**, *Proceedings of the 11ᵗʰ International Conference on Database and Expert Systems Applications DEXA 2000, Lecture Notes in Computer Science 1873, pp. 125-134*

[28] Rashid, A., **"On to Aspect Persistence"**, *Proceedings of 2ⁿᵈ International Symposium on Generative and Component-based Software Engineering (GCSE 2000 part of proceedings of NetObjectDays 2000), pp. 453-463*

[29] Skarra, A. H. & Zdonik, S. B., **"The Management of Changing Types in an Object-Oriented Database"**, *Proceedings of the 1ˢᵗ OOPSLA Conference, Sept. 1986, pp. 483-495*

[30] Xerox PARC, USA, **"AspectJ Home Page"**, *http://aspectj.org/*

[31] Zhang, N., Haerder, T., Thomas, J., **"Enriching Object-Relational Databases with Relationship Semantics"**, *Proc. of the 3ʳᵈ Int. Workshop on Next Generation Information Technologies and Systems (NGITS), Israel, 1997*

Coping with Crosscutting Software Changes Using Information Transparency[*]

William G. Griswold

Department of Computer Science and Engineering
University of California, San Diego
La Jolla, CA 92093-0114
wgg@cs.ucsd.edu

Abstract. Designers are often unsuccessful in designing for change using tra-ditional modularity techniques. A complementary modularity technique called *information transparency* can improve a designer's ability to simplify changes by exposing the interdependence of dispersed program elements that must be changed together for correctness. Information transparency represents modules via *similar-ity* and *architecture*, rather than locality and abstraction. With these, a programmer can create locality with a software tool, easing change in much the same way as traditional modularity. When combined with information hiding, then, more com-plex module structures can be represented. Information transparency techniques include naming conventions, formatting style, and ordering of code in a file. Trans-parency can be increased by better matching tool capabilities and programming style. We discuss applications of information transparency and introduce design principles for software designers and tool designers.

Keywords: Modularity, design, software maintenance, software evolution, pro-gramming methodology, implementation techniques.

1 Introduction

Designing for change—a major tenet of software design—has been cast as a problem of designing software so that it can be extended, replaced in small pieces, or locally changed rather than globally changed [Par72,PHW76]. Locality of change through the application of information hiding is pursued because global changes are hard to reason about and can require the coordination of all the developers who have expertise with the software involved.

1.1 The Problem

Traditional modularity mechanisms are often inadequate for factoring a software sys-tem's changeable design decisions into separate modules [KLL+97,PCW84]. For ex-ample, programming languages generally do not allow grouping changeable *aspects* of

---

[*] This research is supported in part by NSF grants CCR-9508745 and CCR-9970985, and Cali-fornia MICRO proposal 97-061 with Raytheon Systems Company.

A. Yonezawa and S. Matsuoka (Eds.): REFLECTION 2001, LNCS 2192, pp. 250–265, 2001.

a system that are not describable in units of behavior such as sets of procedure (e.g., a class) [KLM+97]. Such crosscutting aspects include performance, error handling, and synchronization constraints.

Consequently, the concept and application of modularity has undergone considerable revision since Parnas first described his information-hiding principles for modular design. As a simple example, an innovation of object-oriented languages is the mechanism for sharing design decisions between a class and its subclasses, as well as incrementally adding new subclasses. Parnas described the application of hierarchical modularity techniques as a principled way to compromise modularity in complex systems [PCW84]. Guidelines for open implementation have been described to help programmers balance the needs of modularity and performance [KLL+97]. More recently, novel applications of subclassing and templates were introduced to better separate design concerns design [VN96]. Programming languages continue to lead the way in managing crosscutting concerns, notably HyperJ and AspectJ [OT00,KHH+01].

Such extensions can be only partially successful. Jackson observes that pure modularity is untenable because the drive for economical implementation requires one component to serve many functions, each with design constraints that may change independently [JJ96]. Parnas observed that his hierarchical modularity techniques failed in the redesign of the A-7 flight program software because of a peculiar hardware architecture and stringent performance requirements [Par96]. Moreover, languages provide less help when the designer has not anticipated the change. This is likely, as it is difficult to anticipate new technological advances, industry standards, and competitor innovations. Finally, many existing systems are not implemented in the newest languages, and so cannot benefit from their features.

1.2   Modularity through Information Transparency

We have directly experienced the breakdown of modular design in the construction of several programming tools, despite the use of modern techniques (Section 2). We also discovered that these breakdowns, although theoretically troubling, were not of practical concern. Our success was largely due to the textual or syntactic similarity of the pieces of code that had to be modified. This similarity permitted the programmer to use software tools to identify the dispersed elements and bring them together into a single view for planning and carrying out the global change. The localized view is like a module in that it permitted the programmer to compare elements without the added difficulty of looking at each element in isolation and attempting to recall other elements' relation to it.

These successes suggest a complement to information-hiding modularity called *information transparency*. When the code relating to a particular change is not localized to a module, an information-transparent module design allows a programmer to use available software tools to economically identify the related code, easing the change. That is, the "signature" of the changing design decision can be used to create locality out of similarity, providing a module view of the code that crosscuts its explicit textual, procedural, module, and file structures. This signature is one or more shared characteristics of the code to be changed, such as the use of particular variables, data structures, language features, or system resources.

Since the intrinsic characteristics of a design decision can be incidentally shared by unrelated code, it is helpful if the programmer has adopted distinguishing conventions such as stylized naming of identifiers. In a few cases we have also used architectural characteristics of the software to order the presentation of related code so that the most closely related pieces of code can be viewed in immediate succession, not just in the same general view. The design of the tools used can also ease the application of information transparency.

Given the ability to create locality out of similarity with available tools, a software designer can describe non-hierarchical, interwoven, crosscutting module structures. When combined with information-hiding modularity, then, a designer can effectively represent more complex modular designs and manage a greater number of design decisions, thereby increasing the maintainability of the software.

In our experience, information transparency has an advantage over a pure languages solution in that it simplifies not only anticipated changes by intentionally encoding similarity into related code, but also *unanticipated* changes by exploiting an underlying similarity discovered after the fact. It has also helped maintenance programmers who were unfamiliar with the system they were evolving. In such cases the use of fast, flexible tools was vital to bootstrapping the change process.

1.3   Related Ideas

Similarity, in the guise of *consistency*, is an important concept in software design. The *consistency principle* advocates "Things that look similar should *be* similar; things that *are* different should look different" [Mac87, p. 323]. Cognitive issues are emphasized, such as reducing the effort to recognize that two system elements are definitely related. Brooks goes a step further with the *conceptual integrity principle*, saying that, "every part must reflect the same design philosophies and the same balancing of desiderata. Every part must even use the same techniques in syntax and analogous notions in semantics" in order to simplify the use and modification of a software system [Bro75, p. 44].

Aiding comprehension with naming conventions is one use of consistency. *Code Complete*, a codification of the experiences of many Microsoft projects, dedicates a chapter to "The Power of Data Names" [McC93, Ch. 9]. One reason cited for using naming conventions is that "they emphasize the relationships amongst related items.... You make up for the weakness of the language by creating pseudostructured data" [p. 197]. No mention is made of exploiting naming conventions with tools.

Information transparency adds value in two ways. First, it conceptualizes a set of similar elements as sharing in a design decision (the "cause" of the similarity) that could change in the future. Second, it advocates the use of tools to bring the similar elements together into a single view, thus achieving some benefits of traditional module structures.

A central idea in managing crosscutting within software is the notion of tracking a set of related yet dispersed crosscutting *points* in the program. These sets of related points can be defined in a wide variety of ways. Information transparency tracks sets of points based on similarity criteria of the program text (appearance, syntax, type, etc.), which are described with patterns. The IronMan configuration management system keeps track of the code implementing a feature via explicit relations that map features to code (e.g., files, functions, components) [Tur99]. HyperJ assembles hyperslices into programs according to the names of classes and methods, either using simple identity or explicit relations [OT00]. AspectJ uses a runtime notion of point: a *pointcut* defines a set of points in a program's execution at which a special kind of method called an *advice* will execute [KHH+01]. DJ uses a regular-expression-like notation to reflectively capture crosscutting traversals through object structures [OL01].

1.4   Scope of the Paper

Many experienced programmers already enhance modularity with consistency. The purpose of this paper is to capture the rationale of these experts, and to provide guidance to software designers and tool designers for increasing the benefits of information transparency.

Several questions arise when considering the application of information-transparent modular design. Which design decisions should be represented with information transparency? How can programmers encode similarity into their code so that tools can more effectively create locality out of it on demand? How should programming tools be designed so they can better recognize this similarity? How can information transparency scale to large systems?

To answer these questions we first describe several experiences with information transparency, culminating in several insights. We then discuss principles of information transparency, including the role of tools and how they can be designed to better meet programmers' needs.

2   Examples

2.1   Retargeting a Programming Tool

A formative experience was the retarget of a classically designed programming environment tool—our 37,000 line star diagram planning tool *CStar* [GCBM96]—from C to Ada [Gra97]. We anticipated restructuring the tool's code to hide design decisions relating to differences between Ada and C, facilitating reuse between the two versions. Although this occurred to some extent in the abstract syntax tree (AST) classes—to accommodate the differences between C and Ada variable initializers, for example—we found that it was best to apply many changes globally rather than restructure. Otherwise, we would have had to abandon the time-tested compiler architecture of components consisting of a lexical analyzer, parser with actions, AST, symbol table, and code generator (in our case code display and visualization). Moreover, we would have lost both the use of such powerful tools as `lex` and `yacc`, and the benefit of downloading free, working, lexical and grammatical descriptions of the new target language.

The programmer took a syntax-directed, architecture-directed approach to the retarget. First the C lexer and parser descriptions were replaced with Ada ones acquired from the web. Then each Ada grammar rule was considered in turn. An analogous construct was identified in the C grammar and its action copied into the Ada grammar, then changed to reflect Ada's semantics and syntax. Then those changes were propagated to the other parts of the system. It was expected that these changes in turn could require changes (including restructuring) in other parts of the system.

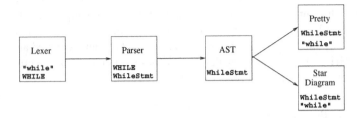

Fig. 1. Naming conventions involving the definition and use of syntactic elements reveal all related elements. The dataflow architecture of the star diagram tools, which is encoded in the source code filenames, allows the programmer to view the elements in an order that consecutively displays the most closely related elements.

For instance, in retargeting the C `while` statement to the Ada `loop while` statement, changes were required in all the major components. However, the changes were straightforward. It was possible to walk through the existing code for the C version of the tool using similarity and the architecture as leverage for making the global change correctly and completely (Figure 1). Starting in the C tool's lexical description `scan.l`, an editor search for `"while"` revealed that this category of syntax corresponded to the `WHILE` terminal. Moving to the C parser description, `gram.y`, the editor was used to search for references to the `WHILE` terminal. The actions corresponding to the `WHILE` statement rule were copied over to the Ada parser's rules for `WHILE` (again, identified by an editor search) and then modified to reflect Ada's syntax and semantics. These actions included an invocation of the AST constructor operation `WhileStmt`. Using the Unix lexical searching tool `grep`, the programmer located the definition and uses of class `WhileStmt`, identifying six files, including the grammar file. Judging from the names of these files, the programmer determined that their roles concerned abstract syntax and display. Since display was judged to be a "downstream" use of the abstract syntax, the programmer first entered the abstract syntax files, and made the necessary changes to the `WhileStmt` definition, as dictated by the changes already made in the parser description and the special characteristics of Ada. Next the programmer moved downstream to the display components, accommodating the changes to the AST code as well as making changes to reflect the differences in Ada's concrete syntax.

The complete pass over the architecture for a single category of language syntax gave the programmer confidence that all relevant code had been changed for that syntactic category. By considering just one category of syntax at a time the overall change was incrementalized as well. By going through the changes "in order", the programmer ensured that all the design information needed in changing a component had already been gathered while working on the previous elements. The process was simplified by the "pipeline" nature of the architecture, as well as by the fact that the programmer of the C tool had consistently named variables and other constructs `WHILE`, `"while"`, `WhileStmt`, etc., when working with the `while` C language construct.

2.2 Replacing a Library

The GNU C++ libraries, once widely used, have completely supplanted by the Standard Template Library (STL) [Vil94]. We failed to defensively design for this change [Gra97], in part because we believed the GNU libraries were becoming a *de facto* standard.

Feeling that the GNU library interfaces were well-designed, we first attempted to use a traditional modularization to localize the port to STL by "wrapping" STL with thin GNU library interfaces. We failed because GNU's iterators are generic pointers, whereas STL's are typed object values. GNU operation signatures that specify the production of iterator pointers do not allow correct memory management of STL iterator objects. Consequently, we used a hybrid porting process, first substituting thin GNU-like wrappers that localized implementation changes unrelated to iterators, then making changes to the declarations of iterators throughout the system. The global changes to iterator references were simplified because their stylized declarations and use were easily recognized with `grep`. For example, iterators of all kinds of objects are declared of type `Pix`, and are initialized and advanced with the `first` and `next` methods. The changes were slightly complicated, however, because the program's `Pix` variables are not consistently named (e.g., `i`, `j`, `h`) and dereferenced via an overloaded, generically named, function call operator. Fortunately, virtually all `Pix` objects were used only in the scope where declared.

To cope with the problem that not every design decision can be hidden in a small module, Parnas introduced the concept of designing with nested modules that are documented by a tree-structured module guide that can direct programmers to the proper scope of a change [PCW84]. The GNU libraries proved to be unstable interfaces whose uses perhaps should be kept low in the module hierarchy or even "restricted" (in Parnas's terminology) to mitigate the possible costs of their instability. However, our system's dependence on the GNU library interfaces did not constitute a tree (except by placing it high in the hierarchy, defeating localization) and similarly could not be restricted without considerable inconvenience (e.g., redundant implementation of the library). Information transparency can be viewed as a descendent of module guides: the documentation to guide programmers to change points is embedded in the program source via similarity rather than indexed in a separate guide. This embedding facilitates extraction by tools and need not be tree-structured.

2.3 The Design of a Hybrid Modular–Layered System

We faced the problem of accommodating changes to both modules (i.e., abstract data types) and global system properties (e.g., integrated, consistent views of related abstract data types) in the design of a meaning-preserving restructuring tool [GN93,GN95]. This system's design consists of three major modules: language syntax, language semantics, and their integration (e.g., when and how to generate a control flow graph from the abstract tree). However, these components are too large and multi-faceted to represent so simply. Also, the low-level functionality of each module could be reusable in building other software tools. To accommodate incremental construction and reuse, the system is also divided into layers (Figure 2). Each layer adds functionality and guarantees some system-wide property. The lowest layer provides unrelated program representations; at

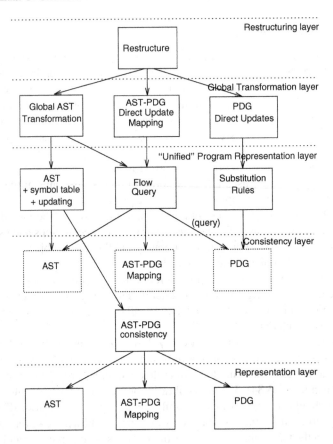

Fig. 2. The modular, layered design of our meaning-preserving restructuring tool. Dotted horizontal lines are layer boundaries, solid boxes are submodules, dotted boxes are submodules reexported from a lower layer, and arrows are calls or event announcements. Columns represent modules.

the next layer the representations are linked and guaranteed to be consistent with each other. The next layer provides an integrated view of the program syntax and semantics. The uppermost layer provides operations on the program representations that are guaranteed to be behavior-preserving. These layered structures are crosscutting to the modules: each module has a portion of its implementation in each layer.

Instead of implementing a "feature guide", we factored the system such that each file constitutes *one* layer's contribution to *one* module. Using a Hungarian-like notational technique (See Section 4), each (Common Lisp) file is named by both the module and layer to which it belongs (e.g., *module-layer*.cl). Consequently, if a module's design decision is changed, all the files to be changed are denoted by the regular expression *module-* *.cl (and conversely for layers). Thus, despite the crosscutting nature of modules and layers, encoding both structures into the file names facilitates changes to either.

The conventions were extended to naming of classes and methods, allowing us to use tools to immediately discern inter-module and inter-layer relationships according to name and the context of use. Using these conventions and other facts conveyed by the designer, RMTool, a reflexion modeling tool, analyzed the dependence structure of this 40,000 line system [MNS95] (See Section 4). Layering and module violations were identified, assisting maintenance of the system's design.

2.4   Microsoft Unicode Port

Microsoft's software continually evolves to meet various needs. One example is evolving their software to handle the Unicode character standard, which permits handling richer alphabets by using two bytes to represent each character.[1] The modification of Microsoft's software to handle Unicode is complicated by the fact that the code uses C language characters (declared `char`) for both characters and other kinds of byte quantities. That is, (at least) two different conceptual types are represented by the same language type. Their Unicode ports must distinguish those `char` and `char[]` (e.g., string) variables that are actually used as language symbols, otherwise some variables will be incorrectly converted. A subtlety is that some clients of character strings require the number of bytes in the object whereas others require the number of characters (i.e., abstractly, byte is a supertype of character). With ASCII strings, these two counts are the same value, but in the ported code the number of characters in a buffer is half the number of *bytes* in the buffer due to the wide character format. Consequently, computations of byte counts and character counts must be selectively converted.

Microsoft Research developed a tool called *Unicorn* to help perform such conversions by identifying required change points. Unicorn uses a combination of syntax tree matching technology [Cre97] and matching on Hungarian notation to distinguish the different uses and interpretations of buffer sizes, i.e., when the size of a buffer in bytes is required, and when the size in characters is required. Unicorn reads in the program source a file at a time, constructing an AST for each function. The AST provides basic syntactic and type information, permitting easy identification of all character literals and identifiers. However, this information is inadequate to distinguish character counts from byte counts. Consequently, Unicorn exploits Microsoft programmers' consistent use of Hungarian notation to distinguish the two. For example, integral variables representing character counts include the tag `cch` (count of characters) in their names, whereas integral variables representing byte counts carry the tag `cb` (for *count of bytes*).

Unicorn in essence creates information transparency with respect to language character and byte quantities, suitably distinguishing the similar representations and their uses into two distinct but related information-transparent modules. Unlike the previous examples, both syntactic information and lexical conventions were required to infer the modules.

3   Observations

From these experiences we can make several observations about applying information transparency to software design.

---

[1] The material in this subsection is based on discussions with Daniel Weise of Microsoft Research.

Some design decisions are either difficult to hide or best not hidden in information-hiding modules. We showed that it is hard to hide issues hinging on language syntax in a programming environment. We also saw that although module interfaces might be intended to be stable, the fact is that they often do (or should) change in response to evolutionary changes to the software. Even when design decisions are not hidden, programmers would like them to be just as easy to change as hidden decisions.

Information transparency depends on some underlying, readily recognizable similarity of related components. Without a concise, automatable description of the underlying commonality (or some other way to identify the code), the programmer is condemned to examine the entire system for the code to be changed. In the retarget of CStar, the consistent use of some form of the substring "while" in the program text was vital to identifying all code to be changed. In performing searches the programmer had to extend his queries to filter out actual while loops in the program implementation, suggesting that it is also important that unrelated pieces of code look different than the code to be changed.

Matching programming conventions to available tools (or vice versa) is critical. Stated another way, the quality of a program design is dependent on the tools provided in the environment. As demonstrated by Microsoft's Unicorn, information transparency is increased by using more powerful syntactic and semantic tools to expose relationships not otherwise visible.

Information transparency is a complement to information hiding, not a replacement for it. Information transparency is useful in describing "secondary" module structures that are contrary to the primary module structure of the system. In retargeting CStar to Ada, for example, the primary module structure was largely dictated by generator tools and a familiar architecture; information transparency helped capture the orthogonal "syntax" dimension of the system. Moreover, information transparency does not provide readily reusable abstractions. On the other hand, by capturing some hard-to-hide design decisions, information transparency may permit designing reusable abstractions around the remaining design decisions of import. Also, information transparency might point to opportunities to refactor to create new modules.

Information-hiding modularity can increase the information transparency of a design. The GNU abstractions provided the necessary similarity and difference to simplify the change to STL. A programmer could of course choose to not use such abstractions, thus obscuring the underlying similarity. However, rich functionality is costly to reimplement, which will usually drive a programmer to use existing abstractions. Also, there are a small number of reasonable implementation choices to be made in a low-level reimplementation (e.g., a programmer might use a C language array to reimplement an existing array abstraction), which a diligent maintenance programmer can use to identify related code.

Software architecture can enhance the information transparency of a design. In retargeting CStar to Ada, searching for variants of "while" was sufficient to identify all the code, but in order to avoid jumping around in the source code, knowledge of the architecture was used to view and change "upstream" code before considering "downstream" code. Again, this software architecture is in large part captured by the primary module (file) structure of the design. Architecture may itself be encoded using information transparency. For instance, knowing that `lex` and `yacc` were used to generate the lexer and parser, the programmer knew to look for files with `.l` and `.y` suffixes to begin the architecture-driven examination.

4   Principles and Techniques

Based on the preceding experiences and observations, we can now state some basic principles of information transparency for both program design and the design of tools intended to enhance information transparency.

4.1   Similarity and Difference

The desire to quickly and accurately identify the code related to a global change leads to the first principle of information transparency:

> *Code elements likely to be changed together as part of a complete, consistent change should look similar, and code elements unlikely to be changed together should look different.*

The effect is that widely dispersed program elements can be easily recognized by a tool as related and quickly brought together into a single view, in effect achieving a module-like view of the related elements. For example, lexical similarity introduced through naming conventions can be recognized by a tool like Unix `grep`, which will collect the matching elements into a compact view.

Achieving similarity can be counterintuitive or awkward. The designers of CStar chose names across components that reflected the concrete syntax associated with the conceptual object being manipulated. For purposes of language neutrality, the conceptual interface of the abstract syntax tree (AST) could have been much more generic (e.g., using `control_statement` or `loop` rather than `while`). Another example of similarity is the consistent formatting of interacting groups of statements—for example, the statements satisfying a messaging protocol. Many programmers tag related elements with comments containing identifying markers.

Achieving differentiation is harder than it sounds. In object-oriented systems it is common to reuse method names across classes even when the classes are not related by type. Pervasive use of overloading can also obscure the fact that a single name refers to distinct functions.

The Hungarian naming convention—used in several of the preceding examples—was designed to inform a programmer of how a variable, procedure, or type is to be used [McC93, Ch. 9.5]. For example, the name `ASTpVHSet` encodes the structure of the object: a set implemented as an open hash table of pointers to AST class objects. If a global change revolves around these particulars, then the naming convention can be of use in information transparency. If the representation used is not important (e.g., it is hidden in a module), but the object's role in the system is prone to change, the programmer can use a tag to denote the variable's role instead (e.g., `ASTpSetDeleting`). Adapting this concept for information transparency leads to the principle of encoding exposed design decisions into a variable, method, type, or file name by including tags in the name that denote the design decisions. To state this as a direct complement to Parnas's information-hiding criterion:

> *The unmodularized code elements relating to a changeable design decision should contain recognizable tags uniquely identifying the design decision.*

This is essentially the principle used in implementing our hybrid module-layered architecture for program restructuring (Section 2.3).

4.2   Use and Design of Tools for Information Transparency

Use of Tools. How such code can be economically identified with similarity and difference depends on the tools available to the programmer, and is a matter of degree, not absolutes. Most environments contain a mix of *lexical* and parsing-based *syntactic* tools. The added accuracy of syntactic tools can be used to infer type relationships, eliminating the need for Hungarian notation to determine explicit type relationships. Both kinds of tools are often a bit more powerful than their pattern recognition components because they are attached to a more general programming language. *Semantic* tools employ techniques such as dataflow analysis or logical inference. For example, a semantic tool could be used to compute component dependences for the programmer, obviating the use of information transparent architectural information for viewing code in an appropriate order. Because of the machine resources required to use these tools and their narrow functionality, semantic tools generally must be reserved for critical applications.

As demonstrated in Section 2.1, in performing a change a programmer might have to discover the coding conventions or other design information that a tool can use to accurately aggregate the related elements. One approach is to start with a conservative query, whose false matches reveal the nature of the underlying similarity and hence suggest refinements to the pattern. Repeated applications narrow the result to just the required elements. Even if the basis for information transparency is known, a programmer will often perform additional overly conservative queries ensure that no case has been overlooked due to inconsistencies in the encoding of the design into the software.

Based on these observations, we can state two additional principles of information transparency:

> – *Programmers should choose conventions that are visible to the tools in their environment.*
>
> – *Conservative program queries should be performed to check the correctness of inferences.*

Design of Tools. There are two challenges for a tool in recognizing a system's crosscutting design information. First, most large systems are implemented in multiple languages.

Historically, this has led programmers to use lexical tools, which are largely insensitive to syntactic details at the expense of matching power. Second, because the design information is implicitly encoded with conventions chosen by the programmer, tools have no *a priori* way to reliably extract the information. This often leads programmers to choose highly customizable tools, which are not always easy to use. The tools described below—most not designed explicitly for information transparency—present a spectrum of design choices with respect to these tradeoffs. Special attention to information transparency issues in tool design can help resolve these tradeoffs.

Inference tools. Inference tools seek out relationships amongst program components because they are no longer readily visible in the code. This work implicitly depends on information transparency. The Desire system, for example, provides a number of inferential techniques so that code related to a change can be better identified [BMW93]. Schwanke uses clustering techniques based on references to data types [Sch91].

RMTool is unique in that it permits a programmer to suggest an architecture and how it is mapped to the source. RMTool takes a programmer's proposed mapping of a program's low-level constructs to a higher level conceptual architecture, and provides a qualitative, graphical report of the congruence between the suggested architecture and the one mapped to the source code [MNS95]. Consequently, if an RMTool user has a sense of the program's information transparency coding conventions, convergence to a useful architecture and its mapping to source code can be accelerated, reducing the need for bottom-up inference. Identifying abstract components in a concrete implementation with these tools can be eased by exploiting information transparency.

Searching tools. Searching tools accept a pattern describing what the programmer wants to find, typically gathering all matching code into a condensed view. The programmer can then use an editor to navigate to the matches in context to investigate further and make changes.

Consider grep, a popular Unix programming tool not designed specifically for programming. Programmers often need to search for the reference of one identifier near another identifier (e.g., in the same statement), but the two could well be on adjacent lines. Unfortunately, grep matches strictly a line at a time. Another common task is specifying a pattern within a word, but grep's definition of a word is fixed and not appropriate for popular scripting languages such as Tcl. Finally, grep has a fixed definition of a successful match. It would be useful if grep let programmers know that there were some *near* matches that could be of interest. In fact, agrep [WM91] partially addresses the first and last concerns by allowing for spelling errors. However, programmers really abbreviate, which is only obliquely captured by the error concept.

The tool lsme (lightweight source model extractor) addresses many information transparency concerns. It uses regular expression pattern matching in a program source's token stream to extract "models" of the source [MN95]. By providing matching at the token level rather than the character level and allowing patterns to be conditionally enabled, lsme supports simple specification of complicated patterns, giving some of the benefits of parsing without being language-dependent *per se*. Moreover, its matching is not limited to a single line, like grep, but rather uses bounded lookahead in the token

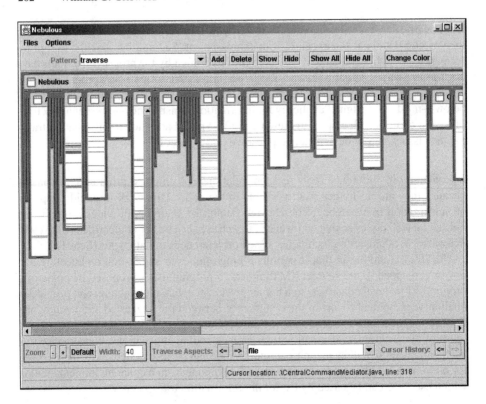

Fig. 3. A screen shot of Aspect Browser. Two crosscutting issues, `traversal` and `forward` are being traversed. Files not involved with these have been "folded under". A round "you are here" cursor near the bottom of the long file strip shows where the programmer is currently located in the traversal (and also what is being shown in the program editor).

stream. It also permits customization of how the input stream is broken into words (tokens).

Some of these features, however, do not permit `lsme` to recognize lower-level encodings of design information. For instance, `lsme` has limited ability to work with white space (e.g., indentation), a common programmer technique for increasing the recognizability of code. Specifying the internal structure of tokens requires some programming at each occurrence in the pattern. The handling of nested structures is likewise difficult; writing a pattern to recognize all the function calls (including nested ones) proved elusive in our experiments. (`awk` in contrast allows taking control of the matching mechanism, although it can be difficult to use.) Finally, `lsme`'s bounded lookahead (controllable by the programmer) is an unpredictable mechanism for matching all (and only) the items of interest.

Visualization tools. Some tools provide graphical views of software that can help reason about unmodularized design decisions. Seesoft, for example, visualizes each file in a system as a linear strip, with each row of pixels denoting a line of code in the file [ESEES92]. By associating a program property with a color, and highlighting lines of code that have that property with its color, it is possible to, say, estimate the cost of a change by seeing how the property crosscuts the primary module structure. Aspect Browser adapts the Seesoft concept to support software evolution [GYK01]. It conceptualizes software evolution as a way-finding activity, and hence provides features comprising a *map metaphor* (Figure 3). Both tools embody the concept that, by leveraging the human visual system, identifiable *symbols* are a viable alternative to *locality* as a way of managing changes to software.

Summary. The above can be summarized in part as a principle of tool design for information transparency:

> *Tool designers should design their tools to be customizable with respect to information transparency programming conventions, regardless of the analytical power of their tools.*

In particular, tools should provide access to token-level or textual information, regardless of their computational power.

5   Conclusion

Designing for change is difficult. Programming languages can help, but human innovation ensures that novel designs will continue to emerge that are hard to express in the design primitives provided. Moreover, languages do not address changes unanticipated by the designer. As a consequence, a critical design element can end up crosscutting the modular structure of the system.

Information transparency complements other modular design techniques, helping designers to describe a larger set of design structures than might otherwise be practical. It uses the signature of a changing design decision to denote the code elements that must change together. A programmer can then use tools to recognize this signature and gather the related elements into a single view for inspection and change. Because of tool limitations, the signature of a design decision may not be unique. Consequently, information transparency is improved by the use of coding conventions like naming of objects and consistent code formatting. Locality can be further increased by using the software architecture to order elements according to the dependences encoded by the architecture.

Information transparency depends on both program designers and tool designers. Coding conventions must be chosen that are visible to the tools available, and tools must allow programmers to easily encode information transparency into their code. Many tools impede the exploitation of information transparency because they cannot access needed information. If we were to pick out one of these insights as a single information-transparency principle, it would be our complement to Parnas's information-hiding criterion:

> *The unmodularized code elements relating to a changeable design decision should contain recognizable tags uniquely identifying the design decision.*

We have described several cases in which information transparency was exploited by coding it into the system or leveraging coding conventions that incidentally allowed tools to exploit similarity. As conveyed in the Microsoft Unicode port, scaling these techniques, like any software engineering technique, benefits from management and automation to ensure consistency across the system.

Acknowledgements. Thanks to Andy Gray, Darren Atkinson, Jim Hayes, and Walter Korman for our early discussions on this topic. I am very grateful to Walter and Jim for participating in a key reengineering case study. I am grateful to Daniel Weise for his discussions on Unicorn. I thank Gregor Kiczales, Gail Murphy, and David Notkin for their insightful discussions, and Mike Ernst for his in-depth comments on an earlier draft.

References

BMW93.   T. J. Biggerstaff, B. G. Mitbander, and D. Webster. The concept assignment problem in program understanding. In *Proceedings of Working Conference on Reverse Engineering*, pp 27–43, May 1993.

Bro75.   F. P. Brooks. *The Mythical Man Month: Essays on Software Engineering*. Addison-Wesley, Reading, MA, 1975.

Cre97.   R. E. Crew. ASTLOG: A language for examining abstract syntax trees. In *Proceedings of the USENIX Conference on Domain-Specific Languages*, pp 229–42, October 1997.

ESEES92.   S. G. Eick, J. L. Steffen, and J. E. E. Sumner. Seesoft – a tool for visualizing line-oriented software statistics. *IEEE Transactions on Software Engineering*, 18(11):957–968, November 1992.

GCBM96.   W. G. Griswold, M. I. Chen, R. W. Bowdidge, and J. D. Morgenthaler. Tool support for planning the restructuring of data abstractions in large systems. In *ACM SIGSOFT '96 Symposium on the Foundations of Software Engineering*, pp 33–45, October 1996.

GN93.   W. G. Griswold and D. Notkin. Automated assistance for program restructuring. *ACM Transactions on Software Engineering and Methodology*, 2(3):228–269, July 1993.

GN95.   W. G. Griswold and D. Notkin. Architectural tradeoffs for a meaning-preserving program restructuring tool. *IEEE Transactions on Software Engineering*, 21(4):275–287, April 1995.

Gra97.   A. J. Gray. Development of an unanticipated member of a program family. Masters Thesis, University of California, San Diego, Department of Computer Science and Engineering, October 1997. Technical Report CS97-560.

GYK01.   W. G. Griswold, J. J. Yuan, and Y. Kato. Exploiting the map metaphor in a tool for software evolution. In *Proceedings of the 2001 International Conference on Software Engineering*, pp 265–274, May 2001.

JJ96.   D. Jackson and M. Jackson. Problem decomposition for reuse. *Software Engineering Journal*, 11(1):19–30, January 1996.

KHH+01.   G. Kiczales, E. Hilsdale, J. Hugunin, M. Kersten, J. Palm, and W. G. Griswold. An overview of AspectJ. In *15th European Conference on Object-Oriented Programming (ECOOP 2001)*, pp 327–353, June 2001.

KLL+97.   G. Kiczales, J. Lamping, C. V. Lopes, C. Maeda, A. Mendhekar, and G. Murphy. Open implementation guidelines. In *Proceedings of the 19th International Conference on Software Engineering*, pp 481–490, May 1997.

KLM+97.   G. Kiczales, J. Lamping, A. Mendhekar, C. Maeda, C. Lopes, J. M. Loingtier, and J. Irwin. Aspect-oriented programming. In *11th European Conference on Object-Oriented Programming*, pp 220–242. Springer-Verlag, June 1997.

Mac87.   B. J. MacLennan. *Principles of Programming Languages: Design, Evaluation, and Implementation*. Holt, Rinehart, and Winston, New York, 2nd edition, 1987.

McC93.   S. McConnell. *Code Complete: A Practical Guide of Software Construction*. Microsoft Press, Redmond, Washington, 1993.

MN95.   G. C. Murphy and D. Notkin. Lightweight source model extraction. In *ACM SIGSOFT '95 Symposium on the Foundations of Software Engineering*, pp 116–127, October 1995.

MNS95.   G. C. Murphy, D. Notkin, and K. Sullivan. Software reflexion models: bridging the gap between source and high-level models. In *ACM SIGSOFT '95 Symposium on the Foundations of Software Engineering*, pp 18–28, October 1995.

OL01.   D. Orleans and K. Lieberherr. DJ: Dynamic adaptive programming in Java. In *Reflection 2001: Third International Conference on Metalevel Architectures and Separation of Crosscutting Concerns*, September 2001.

OT00.   H. Ossher and P. Tarr. Multi-dimensional separation of concerns and the hyperspace approach. In *Proceedings of the Symposium on Software Architectures and Component Technology: The State of the Art in Software Development*. Kluwer, 2000.

Par72.   D. L. Parnas. On the criteria to be used in decomposing systems into modules. *Communications of the ACM*, 15(12):1053–1058, December 1972.

Par96.   D. L. Parnas. Why software jewels are rare. *IEEE Computer*, 29(2):57–60, February 1996.

PCW84.   D. L. Parnas, P. C. Clements, and D. M. Weiss. The modular structure of complex systems. In *Proceedings of the 7th International Conference on Software Engineering*, pp 408–417, March 1984.

PHW76.   D. L. Parnas, G. Handzel, and H. Wurges. Design and specification of the minimal subset of an operating system family. *IEEE Transactions on Software Engineering*, 2(4):301–307, December 1976.

Sch91.   R. W. Schwanke. An intelligent tool for re-engineering software modularity. In *Proceedings of the 13th International Conference on Software Engineering*, pp 83–92, May 1991.

Tur99.   C. R. Turner. *Feature Engineering of Software Systems*. PhD thesis, University of Colorado, Department of Computer Science, May 1999.

Vil94.   M. J. Vilot. An introduction to the Standard Template Library. *C++ Report*, 6(8):22–29, 35, October 1994.

VN96.   M. VanHilst and D. Notkin. Decoupling change from design. In *ACM SIGSOFT '96 Symposium on the Foundations of Software Engineering*, pp 58–69, October 1996.

WM91.   S. Wu and U. Manber. agrep – a fast approximate pattern-matching tool. In *Proceedings of the Winter 1992 USENIX Conference*, pp 153–162, 1991.

Template Metaprogramming an Object Interface to Relational Tables

Giuseppe Attardi and Antonio Cisternino

Dipartimento di Informatica, corso Italia 40, I-56125 Pisa, Italy
{attardi,cisterni}@di.unipi.it

Abstract. We present a general technique to support reflection in C++, exploiting template metaprogramming techniques. The technique is used for building an object interface to relational database tables. By just annotating a class definition with meta information, such as storage attributes or index properties of fields, a programmer can define objects that can be stored, fetched or searched in a database table. A high-performance, full text search engine has been built with this technique.

Introduction[1]

An object oriented interface library to a relational database table must be capable of storing objects of any class into its rows. The library must therefore know the structure of the objects in order to perform serialization. However table schema definition and table usage are independent operations, of which the compiler is unaware. Hence data operations require detailed instructions for reconstructing objects fetched form a table or supplying detailed information about their class. This can be avoided if the library can exploit introspection [1] for determining the attributes of a class and their types, and use intercession [1] to modify the objects. Such solution is more efficient and convenient than traditional embedded database languages and relieves programmers from much burden. A full object-oriented database can be built with limited effort on top of this interface and in fact we used it for implementing IXE, a fully featured, high performance class library for creating customized, full-text search engines.

The needed reflection facilities have been achieved in C++ by exploiting template metaprogramming techniques, without extending the language or the compiler, as in other proposals [3].

We provide both *static reflection*, where metaclass information is only used at compile time to produce class specific code; and *dynamic reflection*, where metaclass objects exist at runtime. Static reflection involves no runtime computations, while dynamic reflection allows defining classes dynamically from a metaclass assembled from field descriptions and other information. Dynamic reflection is necessary for instance in an interactive SQL interpreter.

---

[1] This research has been supported in part by a grant from Ideare SpA.

A. Yonezawa and S. Matsuoka (Eds.): REFLECTION 2001, LNCS 2192, pp. 266–267, 2001.

The Object Interface to Relational Tables

Relational DBMS use tables for storing relations, expressed in SQL-like statements like this:

```
create table Documents (
    name            varchar(2048),
    body            varchar(65536),
    size            INT,
    PRIMARY KEY(name), FULLTEXT(body)
)
```

We represent such table by a C++ class, supplying meta-information, in particular storage attributes or index properties, about each attribute as follows:

```
class Document {
  public:
    char*        name;
    Text<65536>  body;
    int          size;
  META(Document,
    (VARKEY(name, 2048, Field::unique),
     KEY(body, Field::fulltext),
     FIELD(size))
    );
};
```

META, KEY, VARKEY and VARFIELD are macros that exploits template metaprogramming for creating a metaclass for the class. The template class Table implements a relational table for storing objects of a specified class. Here is how to create such table and insert into it an object doc of class Document:

```
Table<DocInfo> table("db/table");
table.insert(doc);
```

The table can be queried obtaining a cursor for accessing the results of the query, similarly to GigaBase [2]. For example:

```
Query query("size < " + size + " and text matches 'PDF'");
QueryCursor<DocInfo> cursor(collection, query);
while (cursor.hasNext())
    dt = cursor.get()->title;
```

Method get() returns a genuine object, whose methods can be invoked directly.

References

K. Czarnecki, U.W. Eisenacker, *Generative Programming – Methods, Tools, and Applications*. Addison Wesley, Reading, MA, 2000.

K.A. Knizhnik, *The GigaBASE Object-Relational database system*, http://www.ispras.ru/~knizhnik.

S. Chiba. *A metaobject protocol for C++*. Conference Proceedings of Object-Oriented Programming Systems, Languages and Applications, pp. 285-299, ACM Press, 1995.

Performance and Integrity
in the OpenORB Reflective Middleware

Gordon S. Blair[1,2], Geoff Coulson[2], Michael Clarke[2], and Nikos Parlavantzas[2]

[1]Dept. of Computer Science, University of Tromsø, N-9037 Tromsø, Norway.
[2]Distributed Multimedia Research Group, Dept. of Computing, Lancaster University,
LA1 4YR, U.K.
gordon@cs.uit.no, {geoff, mwc, parlavan}@comp.lancs.ac.uk

Middleware is playing an increasingly central role in the design of modern computer systems and will, we believe, continue to enjoy this prominence in the future. There is, however, a demonstrable need for more *openness* and *flexibility* in middleware [1]. We believe strongly that *reflective middleware* is the right technology to meet these demands. Indeed, there is strong evidence that such platforms are not only significantly more configurable and reconfigurable than conventional platforms, but that they offer better support for software evolution generally [2]. The main goals of OpenORB v2, the system discussed in this extended abstract, are to address what we perceive as the most pressing shortcomings of current reflective middleware platforms. First, *performance*: in the worst case, this needs to be on a par with that of conventional platforms, and in the best case (e.g. in cut-down configurations) it should be significantly *better*. Second, *integrity*: while permitting maximal reconfigurability, it should be possible to control and constrain reconfigurations so that damaging changes are discouraged and/ or disallowed.

The OpenORB v2 architecture is built in terms of a reflective component model. More specifically, we deploy this component model [3] not just at the application level, but also *for the construction of the middleware platform itself*. The component model is language independent, lightweight and efficient, and forms the basis of our goal of high performance. In addition, to address the issue of integrity, we rely heavily on the concept of *component frameworks* (see below). Thus, an instance of OpenORB v2 is some particular configuration of component frameworks/ components; these are selectable at build-time and reconfigurable at run-time (via reflection).

Our component model, called OpenCOM [2], is based on the core of Microsoft's COM (it avoids dependencies on non-core features of COM such as distribution, persistence, security and transactions), but it enhances COM with richer reflective facilities. Most fundamentally, OpenCOM offers a mechanism for run-time *dependency tracking* between components. To this end, we introduce the notion of 'required' interfaces to express the dependency of a component on an external interface, and then define *receptacles* as first class run-time entities that maintain pointer and type information to represent an explicit *connection* between a component and a 'required' interface. We also deploy a standard *run-time,* available in every OpenCOM address space, that maintains a *system graph* of current connections in the address space.

In addition, OpenCOM offers support for introspection and adaptation of component internals through a number of low-level meta-interfaces supported by each component:

A. Yonezawa and S. Matsuoka (Eds.): REFLECTION 2001, LNCS 2192, pp. 268–269, 2001.
© Springer-Verlag Berlin Heidelberg 2001

1. The *IMetaArchitecture* interface provides access to the component's structure in terms of its internally nested components and their connections (assuming the target component is not primitive);
2. The *IMetaInterface* interface provides meta-information relating to the interface and receptacle types of the component (this can also be used to support dynamic invocation; cf. Java core reflection);
3. The *IMetaInterception* interface enables the dynamic attachment or detachment of interceptors.

The second key technology underpinning OpenORB is an instantiation of the concept of *component frameworks* (CFs) [3]. Each CF focuses on a particular area of functionality; e.g., there are CFs for protocol composition, CFs for thread schedulers and for binding types, and takes responsibility for the maintenance of the *integrity* of that area of the system. CFs exploit domain-specific knowledge and built-in constraints to enforce a desired level of integrity across reconfiguration operations (in terms of both functional and non-functional concerns), and also perform domain specific trade-offs between flexibility and consistency. In OpenORB, CFs are not merely a design concept; rather, they are reified as run-time software entities (packages of components) that support and police components 'plugged into' the CF to ensure that they conform to CF-specific rules and contracts.

In our implementation work, we have confirmed that OpenCOM-plus-CFs supports the construction of ORB functionality that is at least as efficient as conventional object-based ORBs. For example, [2] shows that an OpenORB v2 configuration featuring a CORBA based binding type implementation performs on a par with the popular Orbacus ORB. Furthermore, we have confirmed that the component model scales well in terms of its explicit enumeration of per-component dependencies. This is primarily due to the use of CFs that reduce dependencies by forbidding connections between plug-in components and components outside the CF. In our current implementation, the maximum number of dependencies in any single component is just seven and the average figure is just four. This leaves considerable scope for further reducing the granularity of componentisation that, if carried out with care, should correspondingly increase the ORB's potential for reconfigurability.

In conclusion, we believe that the combination of a reflective component model and the CF-based structuring principle represents a highly promising basis for the construction of configurable and reconfigurable ORBs. While a reflective component model provides a powerful basis for maximal flexibility and reconfigurability, its unconstrained use can easily lead to chaos. The presence of CF-based structuring tempers this expressiveness by imposing domain specific constraints on the reconfiguration process.

References

1. Roman, M., Kon, F., Campbell, R.H., "Reflective Middleware: From the Desk to your Hand", *To appear in* IEEE DS Online, Special Issue on Reflective Middleware, 2001.
2. Blair, G.S., Coulson, G., Andersen, A., Blair, L., Clarke, M., Costa, F., Duran-Limon, H., Fitzpatrick, T., Johnston, L., Moreira, R., Parlavantzas, N., Saikoski, K., "The Design and Implementation of OpenORB v2", *To appear in* IEEE DS Online, Special Issue on Reflective Middleware, 2001.
3. Szyperski, C., "Component Software: Beyond Object-Oriented Programming", Addison-Wesley, 1998.

Data Abstraction in AspectJ

Stephan Gudmundson[1] and Gregor Kiczales[2]

Department of Computer Science, University of British Columbia,
201-2366 Main Mall, Vancouver, B.C., Canada
{stephang,gregor}@cs.ubc.ca

Extended Abstract

The AspectJ project[1] is exploring language support to enable programmers to implement crosscutting concerns in a modular fashion. Previous work in this area has primarily examined the expressiveness of AspectJ, to further aspect-oriented programming language research. In our work we focus on critical software engineering issues related to system modularity. In particular, we want to understand how use of AspectJ interacts with the well-known data abstraction principle[2].

In this abstract, we describe some of our work in identifying the explicit and implicit ways that modules can become dependent upon design decisions of another module in AspectJ. We hope that this information will provide a useful perspective to aspect-oriented programming language designers and will help users of AspectJ make informed design decisions. Given the space constraints, we must assume that the reader is familiar with the AspectJ language[1].

First, consider the following pointcut, which identifies all method calls that move points.

```
pointcut moves():
    calls(Point.setX(int)) || calls(Point.setY(int));
```

The `moves` pointcut clearly depends on the public interface to the `Point` class, which means that the developer responsible for defining `moves` correctly must understand the external interface to `Point`.

Suppose that `moves` crosscut several classes. This increases coupling in two ways. Clearly, the definition of `moves` now relies on the public interface of more classes, depending upon each class in the same way that the previous version depended on `Point`. A subtle additional form of coupling derives from the higher-level knowledge of which classes have contributions for the pointcut. For `moves`, this is fairly clear: only classes that represent geometric objects could be capable of movement. However, there are scenarios where the target classes would not be obvious.

Next, suppose that the definition of `moves` referred to members that would otherwise be hidden by encapsulation. In this case, the level of coupling to the

---

[1] Supported by a grant from the Natural Sciences and Engineering Research Council of Canada.
[2] This work was partially supported by grants from the Natural Sciences and Engineering Research Council of Canada, Xerox Corporation of Canada, and Sierra Systems PLC.

A. Yonezawa and S. Matsuoka (Eds.): REFLECTION 2001, LNCS 2192, pp. 270–271, 2001.

particular class increases from relying solely on the external interface which is visible to all classes already to relying on some feature of the implementation. Modules with such knowledge are usually considered tightly coupled.

Referring to otherwise-encapsulated members of a class in a pointcut definition may also introduce the opposite dependence, in which the class becomes dependent on the pointcut. For instance, imagine that the semantics of moves is clarified so that only join points that change the coordinates of the point are captured. To correctly identify the join points for the new semantics of moves, the Point class is refactored slightly: the setX and setY methods test if the coordinate differs from the current value, and if it does they invoke _setX and _setY (respectively), two private helper methods that actually set the values of the X and Y coordinates. The moves pointcut then targets _setX and _setY instead of setX and setY.

The dependence here is subtle but significant: moves has precipitated a change to the implementation of Point, and so Point now depends on moves. This kind of dependence is also present in Java: when a method is present in an external interface of a class, the overall implementation must be structured as to allow a suitable implementation for that method. The reason that this is not a major issue for Java is that the implementation of a class is considered closely coupled to its interface. The equivalent philosophy in AspectJ would be to consider pointcuts as an external interface to a class, and therefore render the coupling acceptable (as it is in the Java case). Naturally, pointcuts that crosscut classes would be an issue.

Finally, suppose that moves was defined using calls (void Point.set*(..)), which captures calls to any Point methods whose names begin with "set". The dependency in this case is the assumption that the set* naming convention is used for any methods that move points.

There are many other issues at the detailed level, such as pointcut parameterization, property-based crosscutting, other kinds of aspect instantiation, division of work between aspects and classes, and class and aspect inheritance. There are several applications of our findings: to postulate design principles, to suggest language changes, and to comment on open problems in the field of aspect-oriented programming/advanced separation of concerns. In the coming months we expect to present results in these areas.

References

1. Kiczales, G., Hilsdale, E., Hugunin, J., Kersten, M., Palm, J., Griswold, W.: An Overview of AspectJ. In Proceedings of the 2001 European Conference on Object-Oriented Programming (ECOOP). Lecture Notes in Computer Science, Vol. 2072. Springer-Verlag, Berlin Heidelberg New York (2001) 327-353
2. Parnas, D.: On the Criteria To Be Used in Decomposing Systems into Modules. Communications of the ACM, 15(12). ACM Press (1972) 1053-1058

Towards Coping with *Role-Binding Anomaly*

Joon-Sang Lee[1], Doo-Hwan Bae[1], and Ikju Han[2]

[1] Department of Electrical Engineering and Computer Science
Korea Advanced Institute of Science and Technology
{joon, bae}@se.kaist.ac.kr
[2] Department of Computer Engineering Korea Polytechnic University
ijhan@kpu.ac.kr

1 Role-Binding Anomaly

Every role is designed for a specific collaboration, so it can work rightly in the expected context. For example, according to the two role models presented in (a) of Fig. 1, the role *Employer* is modeled to associate with the role *Employee* by *one-or-more* multiplicity, so all of its instances must not be permitted to be handled without an associated instance of the role *Employee*.

Unfortunately, the previous work do not address this issue in depth, so always they have the possibility of allocating roles partially or incorrectly, and missing some preparatory processing before working the roles. Thus, they can allow to manipulate a role or role model in violation of its integrity. We identify this problematic property of roles as *role-binding anomaly*. In this sense, *role-binding anomaly* can be defined as "An problematic phenomenon results in that the structural and behavioral constraints defined in a role model can be violated due to the carelessness of users during role-binding phase, applicable to any mechanism of designing and implementing roles or role models.".

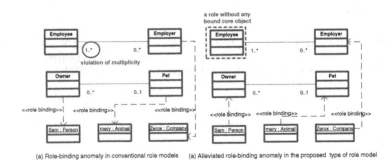

(a) Role-binding anomaly in conventional role models   (a) Alleviated role-binding anomaly in the proposed type of role model

Fig. 1. Coping with role-binding anomaly.

A. Yonezawa and S. Matsuoka (Eds.): REFLECTION 2001, LNCS 2192, pp. 272–273, 2001.

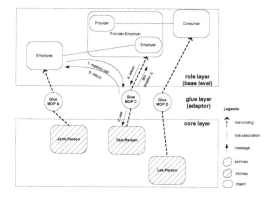

Fig. 2. The enhanced type of role model: overall structure and protocol.

2   Our Proposal

To address this anomaly, we propose an enhanced type of role model, where the system consists of three layers: role layer, glue layer, and core layer as shown in Fig 2. Each layer provides an independent development environment. All classes in the core layer and role layer can be developed without any strong dependency on other layers, and at last glue classes are developed based on MOP, depending on classes in other two layers. The dependency in conventional roles migrates to the glue classes largely. Therefore, the proposed type of role model supports *role encapsulation* in the sense that a core class model and a role model can be developed and tested separately, and also they allow a late binding of each other, acting as software architecture in component-based software developments. We've developed Java *role* package for the proposed type of role model in Javassist 0.8.

Note that the additional properties of roles (*Isolation of core classes, Independence of roles, Role encapsulation, Separation of concerns between Inter-protocol and Intra-protocol, Binding of core objects to role instances*, and *Roles as the first-class entity*) defined in our work help alleviate *role-binding anomaly* more than the conventional role model. *Inter-protocol* describes the interaction way among roles, on the other hand, *Intra-protocol* plays a role of the adaptor between role objects and core objects as a glue object. For illustration, an enhanced role model depicted in (b) of Fig. 1 gives a role-binding mechanism to alleviate *role-binding anomaly* largely, providing *role encapsulation*. Even in case that every roles in a role model has no bound core object, the collaborative protocols defined by the role model can be realized by themselves. This benefit results from dealing with roles according to the inherent properties of role and core objects that the core object describes only intra-object behaviors, on the other hand, the role object inter-object behaviors. Allowing roles to form a basic system network, rather than core objects to do so, helps preserve the integrity of system better.

Removing Reflection from Java Programs Using Partial Evaluation
(Extended Abstract)

Jung Gyu Park[1] and Arthur H. Lee[2]

[1] Department of Computer Science and Engineering, Korea University,
Anam-dong, Sungbuk-ku, Seoul, 136-701 Korea
jpark@korea.ac.kr
[2] School of Computing, University of Utah, 50 S. Central Campus Drive, Rm 3190
Salt Lake City, Utah 84112, USA
alee@cs.utah.edu

Abstract. The reflection in Java provides generality to Java code at the cost of severe overhead at run-time. Partial evaluation have been used to remove reflection from the runtime code, but the feasibility of it for Java programs in general is still an open research issue. We present a partial evaluation technique that can remove reflection in Java programs using type information. We also present a mechanism to deal with exceptions in partial evaluation of Java programs that enables the partial evaluation process fully automatic.

1 Introduction

Reflection enables Java code to discover information about the fields, methods, and constructors of loaded classes. It provides generality to the Java code such as Java object serialization because there is no need for services of the code to be statically bound to some classes. But it introduces interpretation at runtime that causes considerable runtime overheads.

Partial evaluation (PE) that specializes programs using static information has been successfully used to eliminate the reflection layers of the ABCL/R3. The PE can eliminate reflection layers from runtime code if the method call to a metaobject can be computed with static information. There have been some existing attempts on Java PE, but they don't quite address the kinds of problems that we are concerned about. Jspec, existing partial evaluator for Java, performs PE on the base level objects using the statically determined values of variables. Braux and Noyé suggested a PE technique to eliminate reflections in Java, however, the feasibility of it is not clear. And these works do not provide any solutions to deal with exceptions in Java PE, so they need to handle it manually.

In this paper we address these problem by developing a partial evaluator that can eliminate reflections in Java programs fully automatically [1, 2]. Our partial evaluator specializes Java programs using not only the values but also the types of variables. The inputs to the partial evaluator are source code and a descriptor that indicates which variables or arguments are statically bound to values or types.

A. Yonezawa and S. Matsuoka (Eds.): REFLECTION 2001, LNCS 2192, pp. 274–275, 2001.

Our PE is composed of binding-time analysis and specialization. A method call to metaobject (reflection API) can be statically computed and eliminated from the residual code if 1) the type it represents is statically bound by the descriptor and 2) the argument of it is determined at compile-time. To do this, our BTA performs an analysis to figure out the dependency between types and metaobjects. BTA also performs data dependency analysis as existing value based PE. To deal with exceptions during PE of Java programs, BTA performs additional analysis that associates expressions that may cause exceptions with their exception handler.

Specialization is composed of two subphases: specializer derivation and specializer execution. Based on the result of BTA, specializer that evaluates static expressions in source code and generates specialized code is derivated. The handlers that are associated with static expressions are also added in the specializer. Because the types of exceptions that might be thrown during PE process might be different in each PE, specializer that have appropriate exception handler must be generated in each PE. In the following code, let us assume that expr1 (static) may throw exc1 and expr2 (dynamic) may throw exc2. Then the specializer would looks like the right code.

```
try {                              try {
  expr1;                             expr1;
  expr2;                             gen ("try{ expr2;
} catch (exc1 e1) {…}               }catch (exc2 e2) {…}");
  catch (exc2 e2) {…}             } catch (exc1 e1) {…}

       <SOURCE>                          <SPECIALIZER>
```

By compiling and then executing specializer, specialized code is generated. Finally, postprocess is performed to remove remaining reflection APIs by syntax directed transformation.

2   Conclusion

We presented a partial evaluation technique that can remove reflection APIs in Java programs. The measurements we obtained show an average of 34% performance improvement on the serialization code and up to a factor of 61 on some small example codes [2]. Our approach is general and thus applicable in other aspects of Java applications.

References

1. Park, J. G., Lee, A. H.: Specializing the Java Object Serialization using Partial Evaluation for a Faster RMI. Proceedings of International Conference on Parallel and Distributed Systems (ICPADS '01) (2001) 451-458
2. Park, J. G., Lee, A. H.: Removing Reflection from Java Programs Using Partial Evaluation. Technical Report (2001)

Open Implementation of UML Meta-model(s)
Making Meta-modeling and Meta-programming Meet

Pascal Rapicault[1,2] and Jean-Paul Rigault[1,3]

[1] I3S Laboratory, University of Nice Sophia Antipolis and CNRS (UMR 6070)
F-06902 Sophia Antipolis Cedex, France
[2] Object Technology International, Inc. (OTI)
[3] ORION Project, INRIA Sophia Antipolis, France

1 Introduction

From the origin the UML meta-model has been a valuable mechanism to describe the semantics of UML models as well as to extend UML itself. However the approach is purely declarative. In particular the meta-model does not define any behavior nor operation. Thus the implementation of UML CASE tools cannot directly benefit from it, nor can the realization of UML extensions.

This contribution proposes a first attempt toward an "open implementation" of UML meta-models operationalizing behavioral semantics. This makes it possible to implement semantically sound extensions.

2 A MOP for UML

Since the current UML meta-model [3] is too big to be really tractable and understandable, we based our implementation on the MML (Meta-Modeling Language defined by the pUML group) [1]. It defines meta-operations and meta-methods to manipulate the modeling elements and to operationalize the meta-model constraints. Due to the fact that the UML meta-model is itself expressed in UML and that MML offers reflective capabilities, this implementation is naturally reflective and thus constitutes a sort of Meta-Object Protocol (a MOP) [2].

We illustrate the use of our MOP with three examples. Each example corresponds to a particular way of extending UML.

- Semantic improvement by addition of behavior (factorizing attributes into a new superclass);
- Profile definition (defining a sketch of a Java profile); this is an example of a *lightweight* extension (definition of stereotypes);
- Introducing new independent metaclasses (version and author information handling); this is an example of a *heavyweight* extension;.

3 Discussion

Since we operationalize the behavior of the UML meta-model, we naturally face programming problems, or more precisely *meta*-programming problems, such as composition of meta-protocols or dynamic modification of instance type.

A. Yonezawa and S. Matsuoka (Eds.): REFLECTION 2001, LNCS 2192, pp. 276–277, 2001.

For instance, the second problem occurs when applying a newly defined stereotype to an existing class. The first problem arises when several stereotypes need to be applied to the same modeling element.

Another problem is the choice of the implementation language for the MOP. In this first implementation, we chose Java, a language offering no support for intercession. Then implementing the UML meta-model, or even a subset of it, is not an easy operation. Indeed it is possible, but high reflection capabilities facilitate the implementation.

The definition of the MOP itself is not an easy task, either. According to the big number of classes and constraints contained in the original UML meta-model, a fully consistent open implementation appears as an overwhelming task. Fortunately, MML is available and allows a simple and minimal definition of the meta-model.

4   Conclusion

There is no ideal and Almighty MOP. At best one must strive to facilitate the most frequently encountered manipulations. This is even more difficult as the meta-model claims to be open or extensible, as it is precisely the case for UML.

However, hand-crafted implementations are bad, since a major change in the meta-model may induce extensive recrafting of the code. And if meta-models are defined, there are to be implemented. And to be used. And tools should rely on them. And extensions should be defined within them and implemented through them.

Although further work is obviously needed to obtain a complete environment, the simple experiment which has been exposed in this paper is a step toward the operational-ization of meta-modeling as a basis for an automatic and semantically sound extension facility and tool specification.

References

1. The precise UML group. http://www.cs.york.ac.uk/puml/.
2. Gregor Kiczales, Jim des Rivières, and Daniel G. Bobrow. *The Art of the Metaobject Protocol.* MIT Press, 1991.
3. OMG. OMG Unified Modeling Language Specification, Version 1.3. Technical report, OMG, March 2000.

JavaCloak: Reflecting on Java Typing for Class Reuse Using Proxies

Karen Renaud[1] and Huw Evans[2]

[1] University of South Africa renaukv@unisa.ac.za
[2] University of Glasgow huw@dcs.gla.ac.uk

We discuss problems caused by the limitations of Java's reflection mechanism in supporting the specialisation of run-time program behaviour in Java-Cloak. JavaCloak allows programmers to specialise the run-time behaviour of externally-developed code by using pre-generated source-level proxy objects. These proxy objects are of the same type as the original objects that they wrap. The runtime specialisation is achieved in two phases. Firstly, the programmer generates the proxies and tailors them to their local needs. The programmer then generates a JAR file of these proxy classes which is placed at the very start of the application's CLASSPATH variable. The virtual machine is thus diverted into loading the proxy classes instead of the original classes. At runtime the Java-Cloak runtime system accesses the wrapped classes and mediates object creation and method calls across the proxy/original boundary.

When code in the application requests a wrapped type, e.g., package1.T, the Java VM will load this from the JAR file. To gain access to the implementation in the original class, a specialised JavaCloak classloader, accessible from the proxy, loads the wrapped class from a location specified when the virtual machine is started. When a method is invoked on the proxy, the Java reflection mechanism is used to forward this call onto the wrapped class and to handle the return of any result or exception objects.

However, a number of implementation problems arise. For example, if the programmer is using a specialised classloader, they can bypass the JavaCloak facilities, and load the wrapped class from a different location than the JAR file. Java does not provide any support in its reflection mechanism to divert *all* classloader requests via a central point, which would be possible if Java supported a meta-object protocol. Without this separation of concerns between the base and meta levels, it is not possible for the JavaCloak mechanism to integrate with other code in the general case.

The second problem occurs because the proxy defines a number of extra methods, over and above those defined by the original class. If the original application reflects over what it thinks is the original class and retrieves the signatures of all its methods, the list of methods that is passed back will be a superset of those expected. This may cause the application to fail. It is not possible to solve this problem inside JavaCloak as there is no way to programmatically control the information returned by the reflection mechanism.

Thirdly, if the original class defines a public, non-static field, then this field should be directly reachable from the proxy. However, the field is actually defined on the real class and not on the proxy. Unfortunately, Java does not model field

A. Yonezawa and S. Matsuoka (Eds.): REFLECTION 2001, LNCS 2192, pp. 278–279, 2001.

access as method invocation, so there is no opportunity to redirect all accesses to the public field via the proxy. This forces JavaCloak to assume a clean object-oriented programming model where the programmer only accesses class fields via method invocations, which reduces its flexibility.

By working at the Java-level, JavaCloak is forced to implement the proxy class and the wrapped class separately. This leads to two problems, the well known **self** problem and the encapsulation problem. The meaning of self (or **this** in Java programs) is different in the proxy and the real instance. Therefore, JavaCloak must adopt a forwarding model, whereas a delegation model would be preferable so that calls originating in the original object would be delegated to the proxy object. In terms of the encapsulation problem, the wrapping is only logical and this can therefore be broken. For example, the real object may pass back a direct reference to itself as part of the state of another object. A method can then be invoked on this object to obtain this direct reference, thus bypassing the proxy. This occurs because JavaCloak cannot reinterpret the meaning of **this** in the original object. Therefore, in the general case, the two instances must be treated differently.

Another problem is the forwarding of method calls from the proxy to the real object. In JavaCloak, all invocations on the public methods of an object are forwarded, including **hashCode** and **equals**. This means it is not possible to call these methods on the proxies themselves. Therefore, at the JavaCloak implementation level, these methods cannot be used to manage the proxy. This has required additional objects to be registered with the JavaCloak mechanism to operate as tokens for the proxy when calling across the proxy/wrapped boundary. In certain circumstances, the **hashCode** and **equals** could be applied to the proxy as the source code could be edited. However, this is not a solution in the general case as this cannot be guaranteed.

In conclusion, the problems identified above highlight the inflexibility of Java's reflection mechanism. Java's reflection mechanism is really an introspection mechanism, allowing the programmer to gain access to certain information about objects and classes. However, it does not allow the programmer to associate new behaviour with the basic building blocks of the language, such as method dispatch or redefining the meaning of **this**. The above mentioned problems, when programming at the Java source-level, are insurmountable given the current definition of Java and current virtual machine implementations. It is not possible to provide a system to specialise the run-time behaviour of programs using source-code level proxy objects. Therefore, the programmer is forced to operate at the bytecode level. However, even operating at this level does not solve all problems as some policies are hard-wired into the virtual machine itself, e.g., bytecode verification policy.

Therefore, to be truly flexible, and to facilitate runtime specialisation at the Java-level, Java needs to define a behavioural reflection mechanism and future Java virtual machines need to give the programmer access, via this reflection mechanism, to the internal policy decisions. The conclusion of this work is that providing this kind of facility at the Java level does not work in the general case and that the only solution currently available is to work at the bytecode level.

Aspects of Exceptions at the Meta-level

(Extended Abstract)

Ian Welch, Robert J. Stroud, and Alexander Romanovsky

Department of Computer Science, University of Newcastle upon Type,
Newcastle upon Tyne, United Kingdom
{i.s.welch, r.j.stroud, alexander.romanovsky}@ncl.ac.uk
http://www.cs.ncl.ac.uk/research/dependability/reflection/

1 Introduction

In this paper we describe our motivation for explicitly considering exceptions at the meta-level and outline an extension of the *Kava* [4] metaobject protocol that brings exception raising under the control of the meta-level.

2 Motivation

Most metaobject protocols (MOPs) provide a way of intercepting method execution but these protocols are usually discussed solely in terms of arguments and results. The exceptions that may be raised during method execution and returned to the caller are usually ignored. However, in order to successfully implement non-functional requirements using metaobject protocols it is important they are handled at the meta-level. For example, imagine implementing object distribution using a meta-level. This requires that not only are method invocations turned into remote method invocations but also local exceptions are turned into remote exceptions. More generally, we can imagine the following mappings at the meta-level: from one exception to another; from one exception to a value; or from a value to an exception. For example, assertion checking [2] requires that a value is mapped to an exception. Here, a value of a member variable or a value of a method parameter causes an exception to be raised. The exception could be raised at the meta-level but this would reveal the existence of the meta-level to clients of the class. Therefore the MOP should allow the exception to be reflected back to the base level and raised there.

3 Overview of Kava Extension

Kava is a portable reflective Java implementation [4]. It uses byte code transformations to add hooks into the binary structure of a class that switch control at runtime from the base level to the meta-level. The meta-level is composed of metaobjects that are written in the same way as any other Java class.

When a meta-level programmer builds a new metaobject class, the programmer must extend the default metaobject class and override those methods that

A. Yonezawa and S. Matsuoka (Eds.): REFLECTION 2001, LNCS 2192, pp. 280–281, 2001.

control the behaviours the programmer wishes to redefine. In *Kava* we define *around* style meta methods, so for each behaviour there is a *before* and *after* method. So for method execution there is a meta-level *before* method that is called before the method is executed, and a meta-level *after* method that is called after the method has executed.

A context object is passed as an argument to each of the meta-level methods. The context object represents the context of the meta-interception, for example the parameters of the method being executed or the result of its execution.

In order to explicitly consider exceptions at the meta-level *Kava* has been changed in four ways. First, when an exception is raised during method execution the meta-level method *after* method execution is called. Second, any exceptions that are raised during the execution of a method are reified and included as part of the meta-interception context. Third, exceptions can be created or modified at the meta-level and reflected back to the base level. Fourth, an exception raised at the base level can be masked causing a *normal* return to take place with a default return value.

The closest work to ours is that of Garcia et al. [1] who propose a unified meta-level software architecture for sequential and concurrent exception handling and who have implemented their system using Guaraná [3]. Our system could be seen as one implementation of aspects of the patterns that they describe. However, unlike our implementation their implementation depends on the use of a modified Java virtual machine.

We believe that the extensions to the *Kava* metaobject protocol can be used to successfully implement non-functional requirements. The extensions can also support a number of useful Java language extensions. We are currently exploring extensions such as multi-level handlers for exceptions (statement, block, method, class and exception level), design by contract, and n-version programming.

Acknowledgements

We would like to acknowledge the financial support of the ESPRIT projects: MAFTIA project (IST-1999-11583), and DSOS project (IST-1999-11585).

References

1. Alessandro F. Garcia, Delano M. Beder, and Cecilia M. F. Rubira. Unified Meta-Level Software Architecture for Sequential and Concurrent Exception Handling. *The Computer Journal (Special Issue on High Assurance Systems Engineering)*, 2001. to appear.
2. B. Meyer. Design by Contract. In D. Mandrioli and B. Meyer, editors, *Advances in Object-Oriented Software Engineering*, pages 1–50. Prentice-Hall, 1991.
3. Alexandre Oliva and L. E. Buzato. The Design and Implementation of Guaraná. In *Usexnix COOTS*, pages 203–216, San Deigo, California, USA, 1999. Usenix.
4. Ian Welch and Robert Stroud. Kava – Using Byte-Code Rewriting to Add Behavioral Reflection to Java. In *6th USENIX Conference on Object-Oriented Technologies and Systems (COOTS 2001)*, pages 119–130, San Antonio, Texas, 2001.

Author Index

Lecture Notes in Computer Science

For information about Vols. 1–2104
please contact your bookseller or Springer-Verlag